LIBRARY OF HEBREW BIBLE/
OLD TESTAMENT STUDIES

634

Formerly Journal for the Study of the Old Testament Supplement Series

Editors
Claudia V. Camp, Texas Christian University
Andrew Mein, Westcott House, Cambridge

Founding Editors
David J. A. Clines, Philip R. Davies and David M. Gunn

Editorial Board
Alan Cooper, Susan Gillingham, John Goldingay, Norman K. Gottwald,
James E. Harding, John Jarick, Carol Meyers,
Daniel L. Smith-Christopher, Francesca Stavrakopoulou,
James W. Watts

RIDDLES AND REVELATIONS

Explorations into the Relationship between Wisdom and Prophecy in the Hebrew Bible

Edited by

Mark J. Boda, Russell L. Meek, and William R. Osborne

LONDON · NEW YORK · OXFORD · NEW DELHI · SYDNEY

T&T CLARK
Bloomsbury Publishing Plc
50 Bedford Square, London, WC1B 3DP, UK
1385 Broadway, New York, NY 10018, USA

BLOOMSBURY, T&T CLARK and the T&T Clark logo
are trademarks of Bloomsbury Publishing Plc

First published in Great Britain 2018
Paperback edition first published 2020

Library of Congress Cataloging-in-Publication Data
Names: Boda, Mark J., editor.
Title: Riddles and revelations : explorations into the relationship between
wisdom and prophecy in the Hebrew Bible / edited by Mark J. Boda, Russell L. Meek,
and William R. Osborne.
Description: 1 [edition]. | New York : Bloomsbury Academic, 2018. | Series:
The library of Hebrew Bible/Old Testament studies ; volume 634 | Includes bibliographical
references and index.
Identifiers: LCCN 2018000624 (print) | LCCN 2018016493 (ebook) |
ISBN 9780567671653 (ePDF) | ISBN 9780567671646 (hardback : alk. paper)
Subjects: LCSH: Bible. Old Testament--Criticism, interpretation, etc. |
Wisdom literature. | Wisdom. | Prophecy.
Classification: LCC BS1171.3 (ebook) | LCC BS1171.3 .R53 2018 (print) | DDC 221.6--dc23
LC record available at https://lccn.loc.gov/2018000624

ISBN: HB: 978-0-5676-7164-6
PB: 978-1-4411-6532-9
ePDF: 978-0-5676-7165-3
eBook: 978-1-4411-2382-4

Series: Library of Hebrew Bible/Old Testament Studies (ISSN 2513-8758), volume 634

Typeset by: Forthcoming Publications (www.forthpub.com)

To find out more about our authors and books visit
www.bloomsbury.com and sign up for our newsletters.

CONTENTS

Part I
METHODOLOGY

Part II
WISDOM AMONG THE PROPHETS

CONTRIBUTORS

Leslie C. Allen, Senior Professor of Old Testament, Fuller Theological Seminary

Mark J. Boda, Professor of Old Testament, McMaster Divinity College

Katharine J. Dell, Reader in Old Testament Literature and Theology, Faculty of Divinity, University of Cambridge and Fellow of St. Catharine's College, Cambridge

John W. Hilber, Professor of Old Testament, Cornerstone University

Timothy Johnson, Senior Pastor, Rock Valley Chapel

Will Kynes, Associate Professor of Theology, Whitworth University

Tremper Longman, III, Distinguished Scholar and Professor Emeritus of Biblical Studies, Westmont College

Russell L. Meek, Assistant Professor of Old Testament and Hebrew, Louisiana College

Ryan O'Dowd, Chesterton House Senior Scholar, Cornell University

Eric Ortlund, Tutor in Hebrew and Old Testament, Oak Hill College

William R. Osborne, Associate Professor of Biblical and Theological Studies, College of the Ozarks

Martin A. Shields, Honorary Associate, Department of Hebrew, University of Sydney

Richard Schultz, Blanchard Professor of Old Testament, Wheaton College

Mark Sneed, Professor of Bible, Lubbock Christian University

Andrew E. Steinmann, Distinguished Professor of Theology and Hebrew, Concordia University Chicago

Daniel C. Timmer, Professor of Old Testament, Puritan Reformed Theological Seminary; Faculté de théologie évangélique (Montreal)

Stuart Weeks, Professor of Old Testament and Hebrew, Durham University

PREFACE

The modern era of biblical scholarship is quite remarkable. Over the past two hundred years numerous theories regarding the Bible have hypnotically captured the minds of scholars, only then to vanish into the archive of novel footnotes within the decade. The speed with which ideas are formulated, celebrated, and then discarded is alarming. However, there are times when an idea slowly is transformed into an assumption and thereby begins to serve as the foundation for further extrapolation. Biblical Studies as a discipline has moved forward largely because of these hardened foundations that have opened the door for greater inquiry and study.

However, there remains a time for reexamination. There is a season for revisiting the assured results that have come to support massive theoretical structures. Can these foundations hold? Can the views regarding wisdom and prophecy that dominated much of the nineteenth and twentieth century continue? Such is the purpose of this volume.

We are deeply honored and grateful to the team of researchers and scholars that have chosen to probe these questions with us. As is often the case with edited collections, not all participating parties agree, but we believe that the collection of informed opinions both reveals former weaknesses and opens the way forward to new avenues of investigation. *Riddles and Revelations* is the published product of the Wisdom and Prophecy in the Hebrew Bible research group of the Institute for Biblical Research (IBR). We appreciate the support of the IBR in facilitating these sessions and hope this project serves to demonstrate the fruitfulness of collegial dialogue in the production of academic resources.

Russell would like to thank Louisiana College and its faculty development committee for supporting this project, and most especially his wife, Brittany, who has demonstrated repeatedly that "He who finds a wife finds a good thing, and has obtained favor from Yahweh" (Prov 18:22).

William is deeply grateful for the academic, financial, and collegial support provided by the College of the Ozarks over the past five years. In particular, the Dean of the College, Eric Bolger, has continually encouraged and supported his professional development over the years, and good friends and colleagues have also proved faithful sounding boards. Nathan Miller kindly agreed to help with the bibliography, and his services are much appreciated. As always, no project of any size that William is a part of would ever see its completion without the unceasing love of his wife Sara and their four children: Sophia, Eleanor, Moses, and Henry.

Mark is thankful for the enduring support of his home institution, McMaster Divinity College, and its commitment to the highest level of academic engagement. He'd also love to honor his beloved wife Beth who truly embodies the picture of Wisdom in Proverbs 1 as she offers a depth of spiritual insight to those (including himself) who have the courage to listen.

We all deeply appreciate the team at Bloomsbury, including the editors of LHBOTS, Claudia Camp and Andrew Mein, as well as the house editorial team, especially Duncan Burns, for embracing this project and providing editorial support throughout the publication process.

Abbreviations

AB	Anchor Bible
ABD	David Noel Freedman (ed.), *The Anchor Bible Dictionary* (6 vols.; New York: Doubleday, 1992)
ABRL	Anchor Bible Reference Library
ACEBT	*Amsterdamse Cahiers voor Exegese en bijbelse Theologie*
AGJU	Arbeiten zur Geschichte des Antiken Judentums und des Urchrisentums
AIL	Ancient Israel and Its Literature
AMD	Ancient Magic and Divination
ANES	*Ancient Near Eastern Studies*
ANET	James B. Pritchard (ed.), *Ancient Near Eastern Texts Relating to the Old Testament* (2 vols.; Princeton: Princeton University Press, 3rd edn, with supplement, 1969)
AOAT	Alter Orient und Altes Testament
ARM	Archives royales de Mari
ATANT	Abhandlungen zur Theologie des Alten und Neuen Testaments
ATD	Das Alte Testament Deutsch
AThR	*Anglican Theological Review*
BBR	*Bulletin for Biblical Research*
BBRSup	Bulletin for Biblical Research, Supplements
BCOTWP	Baker Commentary on the Old Testament Wisdom and Psalms
BETL	Bibliotheca ephemeridum theologicarum lovaniensium
BHS	K. Elliger and W. Rudolph (eds.), *Biblia Hebraica Stuttgartensia Stuttgart* (Stuttgart: Deutsche Bibelgesellschaft, 1983)
Bib	*Biblica*
BibOr	Biblica et Orientalia
BJS	Brown Judaic Studies
BKAT	Biblischer Kommentar: Altes Testament
BZ	*Biblische Zeitschrift*
BZAW	Beihefte zur *ZAW*
CAH	Cambridge Ancient History
CBET	Contributions to Biblical Exegesis and Theology
CBQ	*Catholic Biblical Quarterly*
CBQMS	Catholic Biblical Quarterly Monograph Series
CD	Cairo Genizah copy of the Damascus Document
CHANE	Culture and History of the Ancient Near East
CIPOA	Cahiers de l'Institut du Proche-Orient Ancien du Collège de France

COS	William Hallo and K. Lawson Younger (eds.), *The Context of Scripture* (3 vols.; Leiden: Brill, 1997–2002)
CurBR	*Currents in Biblical Research*
DSD	Dead Sea Discoveries
EBR	Hans-Josef Klauck et al. (eds.), *Encyclopedia of the Bible and Its Reception* (Berlin: de Gruyter, 2009–)
EvQ	*Evangelical Quarterly*
ExAud	*Ex auditu*
ExpTim	*Expository Times*
FAT	Forschungen zum Alten Testament
FOTL	The Forms of the Old Testament Literature
FRLANT	Forschungen zur Religion und Literatur des Alten und Neuen Testaments
HALOT	Ludwig Koehler, Walter Baumgartner, and Johann Stamm, *The Hebrew and Aramaic Lexicon of the Old Testament* (trans. and ed. under supervision of M. E. J. Richardson; 2 vols.; Leiden: Brill, 2001)
HBM	Hebrew Bible Monographs
HBT	*Horizons in Biblical Theology*
HCOT	Historical Commentary on the Old Testament
HS	*Hebrew Studies*
HSM	Harvard Semitic Monographs
HSS	Harvard Semitic Studies
HTS	HTS Teologiese Studies/Theological Studies
HUCA	*Hebrew Union College Annual*
IEJ	*Israel Exploration Journal*
Int	Interpretation
JAOS	*Journal of the American Oriental Society*
JBL	*Journal of Biblical Literature*
JCS	*Journal of Cuneiform Studies*
JEA	*Journal of Egyptian Archaeology*
JEOL	*Jaarbericht…ex oriente lux*
JESOT	*Journal for the Evangelical Study of the Old Testament*
JETS	*Journal of the Evangelical Theological Society*
JNES	*Journal of Near Eastern Studies*
JQR	*Jewish Quarterly Review*
JSJSup	*Journal for the Study of Judaism*, Supplement Series
JSNT	*Journal for the Study of the New Testament*
JSOT	*Journal for the Study of the Old Testament*
JSOTSup	*Journal for the Study of the Old Testament*, Supplement Series
JSPSup	*Journal for the Study of the Pseudepigrapha*, Supplement Series
JTI	*Journal of Theological Interpretation*
LAI	Library of Ancient Israel
LBS	Library of Biblical Studies
LHBOTS	Library of Hebrew Bible/Old Testament Studies
LXX	Septuagint
MT	Masoretic Text

NAC	New American Commentary
NICOT	New International Commentary on the Old Testament
NIVAC	NIV Application Commentary
NSBT	New Studies in Biblical Theology
OIS	Oriental Institute Seminars
OTE	*Old Testament Essays*
OTL	Old Testament Library
OTS	Old Testament Studies
RB	*Revue biblique*
RQ	*Restoration Quarterly*
SAA	State Archives of Assyria
SAAS	State Archives of Assyria Studies
SAOC	Studies in Ancient Oriental Civilization
SBLDS	SBL Dissertation Series
SBLSymS	SBL Symposium Series
SBT	Studies in Biblical Theology
SemeiaSt	Semeia Studies
SJOT	*Scandinavian Journal of Theology*
SJT	*Scottish Journal of Theology*
SOTSMS	Society for Old Testament Monograph Series
StPohl	Studia Pohl
SymS	Symposium Series
TLZ	*Theologische Literaturzeitung*
TynBul	*Tyndale Bulletin*
VT	*Vetus Testamentum*
VTSup	*Vetus Testamentum*, Supplement Series
WAW	Writings from the Ancient World
WBC	Word Biblical Commentary
WMANT	Wissenschaftliche Monographien zum Alten und Neuen Testament
WTJ	*Westminster Theological Journal*
YOS	Yale Oriental Series, Texts
ZAW	*Zeitschrift für die altentestamentliche Wissenschaft*
ZTK	*Zeitschrift für Theologie und Kirche*

Part I

METHODOLOGY

Prophet and Sage in Dialogue: History and Methodology

Russell L. Meek

"Is the theme 'prophecy and wisdom' played out?
Is there really no more to be said about it?"[1]

Introduction

The question of the influence of the wisdom tradition upon the prophetic tradition[2] has enjoyed only a relatively brief period of popularity in biblical studies, beginning in the mid-twentieth century with the publication of Johannes Fichtner's 1949 article "Jesaja unter den Weisen."[3] Fichtner's article was a form-critical study that pointed to generic similarities, overlapping vocabulary, and method of presentation to argue that Isaiah was once a member of "the wise," which explained the apparent wisdom influence upon his work. After Fichtner's article broached the relationship between these two types of literature, studies abounded that sought wisdom influence in various prophetic books. As is often the case, the influx of research resulted in significant methodological inconsistency across the board.

The goal of the present work is to survey the literature and propose a more refined methodology for determining literary influence between prophet and sage. The first task is to chronicle the quest for wisdom

1. R. N. Whybray, "Prophecy and Wisdom," in *Israel's Prophetic Tradition: Essays in Honour of Peter R. Ackroyd* (ed. Richard Coggins, Anthony Phillips, and Michael Knibb; Cambridge: Cambridge University Press, 1982), 196.

2. I am using "tradition" to refer to the entire complex that gave rise to particular bodies of literature.

3. Johannes Fichtner, "Jesaja unter den Weisen," *TLZ* 74 (1949): 75–80.

influence in prophetic literature.[4] Form criticism has dominated this endeavor, so in the final section of the essay we hope to forge a way toward developing a methodology that utilizes previous work but moves beyond solely form-critical considerations. As Christopher Hays has pointed out in his study of ancient Near Eastern echoes in the Hebrew Bible, intertextual methods will prove vital to this endeavor.[5] But before outlining a methodology, we will define "wisdom" because this definition will necessarily determine where and in what way any potential influence is discernible. Since considerably less disagreement exists over what constitutes prophecy in the Hebrew Bible, we will not define it.

Historical Overview of Methodologies

Johannes Fichtner was the first to popularize the notion that the wisdom tradition exerted influence over prophetic writings in the Hebrew Bible, though he notes that the prophetic tradition prior to Isaiah betrayed no such influence. Anticipating the criticism that James Crenshaw would level at attempts to determine wisdom influence in other biblical genres, Fichtner asserts that the commonalities between these two genres result from shared culture, not literary borrowing.[6] However, he argued that Isaiah displayed significant influence from the wisdom tradition in its use of wisdom terminology, generic wisdom forms, and its presentation of the material itself.

Writing a few years after Fichtner, Johannes Lindblom builds upon Fichtner's form-critical observations to develop his own methodology.[7] Lindblom first establishes the presence of a particular class of people, "the wise," of whom the prophets were aware.[8] He then argues for wisdom influence upon the prophets "when, in the sayings of the prophets, we meet with words and thoughts which are alien to the prophetic thought-world

4. The literature review focuses on the search for wisdom influence in prophetic literature because there is a dearth of research on the influence of the prophetic tradition upon wisdom literature, as we will see below.

5. Christopher B. Hays, "Echoes of the Ancient Near East? Intertextuality and the Comparative Study of the Old Testament," in *The Word Leaps the Gap: Essays on Scripture and Theology in Honor of Richard B. Hays* (ed. J. Ross Wagner, C. Kevin Rowe, and A. Katherine Grieb; Grand Rapids: Eerdmans, 2008), 20–43.

6. Fichtner, "Jesaja," 76.

7. Johannes Lindblom, "Wisdom in the Old Testament Prophets," in *Wisdom in Israel and in the Ancient Near East* (ed. Martin Noth and D. Winton Thomas; VTSup 3; Leiden: Brill, 1955), 192–204.

8. Ibid., 193–96.

in general, but characteristic of the doctrines of Wisdom."[9] Lindblom points to such things as wisdom vocabulary (e.g., מוסר, חכמה, דעת, עצה), forms (e.g., parables, allegories, proverbs), literary techniques (repetition), and themes (e.g., creation). In Lindblom's view, the confluence of these factors demonstrates that the prophets knew of wisdom from abroad, knew of a class of "the wise" in Israel, appreciated wisdom, adopted some wisdom features, were influenced stylistically by wisdom, and finally that "several late additions in the prophetic books originated in the Wisdom circles."[10]

Samuel Terrien examined the role of wisdom in Amos in 1962,[11] and though some scholars have discounted his methodology, it deserves mention.[12] Terrien argues that wisdom influence can be detected by examining language, style, and ideas similar to those found in wisdom literature, such as numerical pairs, Yahweh's activity in Sheol, and the repetition of words such as סוֹד and נִבְחָה. However, Terrien's methodology is problematic because it relies heavily on shared vocabulary, which can easily be attributed to wisdom as a shared reality unless an intentional textual relationship can be established.

James Crenshaw's 1967 and 1969 works have been pivotal in developing a methodology for determining wisdom influence upon other genres in the Hebrew Bible.[13] In his 1967 article, Crenshaw argued that flawed methodologies often led scholars to conclude that wisdom directly influenced Amos when in fact the wisdom influence detected in Amos actually results mostly from a shared approach to reality. Since wisdom literature is based on experience, "a degree of similarity of style, vocabulary and theology between wisdom and the prophetic and priestly traditions is unavoidable,

9. Ibid., 197.

10. Ibid., 204.

11. Samuel Terrien, "Amos and Wisdom," in *Israel's Prophetic Heritage: Essays in Honor of James Muilenburg* (ed. Bernard W. Anderson and Walter J. Harrelson; London: Harper), 108–15; repr. in *Studies in Ancient Israelite Wisdom* (ed. James L. Crenshaw; Library of Biblical Studies; New York: Ktav, 1976), 448–55.

12. E.g. Whybray, "Prophecy and Wisdom"; J. A. Soggin, "Amos and Wisdom," in *Wisdom in Ancient Israel: Essays in Honour of J. A. Emerton* (ed. John Day, Robert P. Gordon, and H. G. M. Williamson; Cambridge: Cambridge University Press, 1995), 119–23. However, note Fey's study of Isaiah and Amos, which indicates that Terrien's conclusions are valid (Reinhard Fey, *Amos und Jesaja: Abhängigkeit und Eigenständigkeit des Jesaja* [WMANT 12; Neukirchen-Vluyn: Neukirchener Verlag, 1963]).

13. James Crenshaw, "The Influence of the Wise Upon Amos: The 'Doxologies of Amos' and Job 5:9–16; 9:5–10," *ZAW* 79 (1967): 42–52; idem, "Method in Determining Wisdom Influence upon the Wise," *JBL* 88 (1969): 129–42.

for the wise did not have a monopoly on experience."[14] Furthermore, Crenshaw points out the importance of establishing the uniqueness of thematic elements used to determine wisdom influence. Crenshaw also argues that shared vocabulary and similar theology between Amos and Job indicate wisdom influence.

The methodology for determining wisdom influence in historical books that Crenshaw developed in his 1969 article applies equally to prophetic literature. First, scholars must define wisdom broadly enough to capture wisdom sufficiently but not so broadly that its definition becomes useless.[15] Second, scholars must isolate literary forms and ideologies that occur primarily in wisdom literature.[16] Third, one must explain differences in nuance between genres.[17] That is, does a prophetic text employ a wisdom theme/form for a different purpose than the wisdom literature? If so, why? If the purpose is different, then this could indicate shared experience rather than dependence.[18] Fourth, one must remember that those outside the wisdom tradition—such as prophets—often viewed wisdom with suspicion, making wisdom influence less likely.[19] And finally, one

14. Crenshaw, "The Influence of the Wise," 44.

15. Crenshaw, "Method in Determining Wisdom Influence," 130–32.

16. Ibid., 133–34.

17. Note that Michael Fishbane makes a similar observation when he argues that sometimes the use of legal texts in prophetic genres "transforms the prophetic oracle into a legal indictment," in which case the prophetic material is using legal material for a related, but different purpose than it was used in its original context ("Revelation and Tradition: Aspects of Inner-Biblical Exegesis," *JBL* 99 [1980]: 351).

18. Ibid., 134. However, note Cynthia Edenburg, who argues that "[t]ransformation and reactualization of a common element" actually indicates intentional allusion ("How [Not] to Murder a King: Variations on a Theme in 1 Sam 24; 26," *SJOT* 12 [1998]: 72). Likewise, Benjamin Sommer points out that the use of common language for a different purpose (what he terms a "reversal allusion") could indicate influence ("Allusions and Illusions: The Unity of the Book of Isaiah in Light of Deutero-Isaiah's Use of Prophetic Tradition," in *New Visions of Isaiah* [ed. Roy Melugin and Marvin Sweeney; Sheffield: Sheffield Academic Press, 1996], 158).

19. Crenshaw, "Method in Determining Wisdom Influence," 134. However, Mark Sneed has recently argued that such conflict is somewhat manufactured: "The same authors who composed the wisdom literature are also responsible for the composition and preservation of other types of literature. These literary sages, who were not primarily courtiers, represent Israelite scholarship, and, as such, they were concerned with all the differing traditions and lore of Israelite culture and were involved also in its production. This means that these scholars were not particularistic. As teachers, they studied and taught all the traditions, types of literature, and genres to their students. The wisdom literature, then, needs to be viewed as complementary, not

must consider the history and development of wisdom as one attempts to determine wisdom's influence.[20]

J. William Whedbee's 1971 monograph, *Isaiah and Wisdom*, argues for the interrelationship between the traditional law, prophecy, and wisdom, concluding that the three genres are much more dependent on each other than earlier research would suggest.[21] Whedbee begins his treatment of Isaiah and wisdom where Fichtner's study left off. Whedbee's methodology consists of examining "distinctive content" found within prophetic texts that occur primarily within wisdom, including משל forms, vocabulary, and other thematic elements, such as "gnomic truths from the realm of common experience…expressed in wisdom terms."[22] Whedbee's insistence on finding multiple points of overlap between wisdom and prophecy to determine influence is an important methodological development for it recognizes the cumulative weight of evidence over against isolated indicators of influence.

In 1978 George Landes set out to examine the literary genre of Jonah to determine whether it could have been a משל that originated in Israel's wisdom tradition.[23] After examining the features of the משל form,[24] Landes concludes that Jonah likely is a משל whose origins lie outside the wisdom tradition. Importantly, Landes argues that the משל is not a literary form in itself but rather is a literary technique "in which a variety of forms could be shaped to serve a special didactic purpose or function."[25] Landes's contention that the משל is a literary technique used in multiple genres and not a literary form unique to wisdom is borne out by his investigation of משלים in relevant biblical texts. Though in the end Landes concludes that Jonah likely originated within the prophetic tradition, his

---

inimical, to the other types of literature found in the Hebrew Bible." In Sneed's view, the wisdom "tradition" is not, in fact, a tradition opposed to the prophetic tradition, but wisdom teachers themselves were responsible for the final editing and content of the entire Hebrew Bible, including the prophetic books. Mark Sneed, "Is the 'Wisdom Tradition' a Tradition?" *CBQ* 73 (2011): 50–71, here 54.

20. Ibid., 135.

21. J. William Whedbee, *Isaiah and Wisdom* (Nashville: Abingdon, 1971).

22. Ibid., 24.

23. George M. Landes, "Jonah: A *MĀŠĀL*?" in *Israelite Wisdom: Theological and Literary Essays in Honor of Samuel Terrien* (ed. John G. Gammie, Walter Brueggemann, W. Lee Humphreys, and James M. Ward; Missoula: Scholars Press, 1978), 137–58.

24. I.e., Landes believes that משלים are characterized by their content (comparison/analogy) and their didactic function.

25. Ibid., 148–49.

methodological treatment of the מָשָׁל demonstrates the value of isolating
a particular literary feature to explore its occurrence in a cross section of
texts. Furthermore, he demonstrates that one must look for a confluence
of elements to determine influence rather than rely solely on a singular
literary feature or thematic element.

C. L. Seow has examined the book of Hosea with attention to the
"foolish people" motif, common to wisdom literature, which he found
running throughout chs. 4–14.[26] Seow attempts to demonstrate wisdom's
influence throughout Hosea because scholars have associated 14:10
with the wisdom tradition and therefore assigned it to a later redactor.[27]
To counter their argument, Seow investigates this particular sapiential
motif but also explains that scholars have found many parallels between
Hosea and the wisdom tradition in terms of various "forms and styles."[28]
He demonstrates his case by highlighting the use of parallel word pairs
and a similar discussion of "fools" in Hosea and wisdom literature. The
thematic and linguistic overlap that Seow finds leads him to conclude that
the wisdom tradition influenced Hos 4–14, if not the entire book.

Norman Whybray's 1982 article surveys the then-present state
of research on the question of the relationship between wisdom and
prophecy, including the difficulty caused by defining wisdom.[29] Whybray
spends much of his article pointing out the methodological flaws in the
approaches of Fichtner, Lindblom, Terrien, Wolff, and Whedbee. His
primary criticism is that one cannot rely on a single feature, which leads
him to view Whedbee's "cumulative method" more favorably because
it shows "how each passage contains vocabulary, motifs and themes,
that can all be paralleled in the specifically wisdom books of the Old
Testament or of other ancient Near Eastern literatures."[30] Whybray also
points out that wisdom and prophecy studies do not often approach the
subject from the perspective of prophecy's influence on wisdom "due to
the paucity of the evidence available."[31]

Raymond Van Leeuwen made the same observation regarding the
influence of prophecy on wisdom books in his 1990 article that surveys the
role of wisdom in Jeremiah, Ezekiel, and Obadiah, stating that a detailed
study of "the parallels among the prophetic literature and secondary

26. C. L. Seow, "Hosea 14:10 and the Foolish People Motif," *CBQ* 44 (1982):
212–24.
27. Ibid., 212.
28. Ibid., 214.
29. Whybray, "Prophecy and Wisdom."
30. Ibid., 191.
31. Ibid., 196.

wisdom literature (Job, Qoheleth) is yet to be undertaken."[32] For Van Leeuwen, methodology is the critical issue in determining the relationship between wisdom and prophecy—studies approach the relationship either using canonical criticism or form criticism, which seeks "the original life and literary settings of the various poems and oracles that betray the stamp of wisdom or reveal the presence of a stage."[33] He argues that both approaches are problematic, concluding that the way forward is to better define "wisdom."

Andrew Macintosh's 1995 essay reexamined the relationship between wisdom and prophecy in the book of Hosea.[34] He argues that Hosea "contains both the vocabulary and the antithetic structure which typifies the wisdom tradition," thus relying on multiple evidences for wisdom influence, and argues that Hosea demonstrates significant interaction with the wisdom genre.[35] That is, Hosea "was greatly interested in the connection between thought and action, and, above all, was convinced that wrong perceptions of reality, of the way things were, would lead inevitably to the demise and ruin of his people and nation."[36] However, Macintosh contends that Hosea used this interest as a *prophet*.[37] To demonstrate his thesis, Macintosh examines Hosea's use of several technical vocabulary terms, concluding that Hosea's use of wisdom forms an important part of the prophet's message, but it is just that—a part— which he "modified and transformed" for his own use.[38]

In the same volume as Macintosh's essay, J. A. Soggin examined Samuel Terrien's thesis regarding Amos's use of wisdom.[39] Soggin rejects Terrien's conclusions, arguing instead that Amos, as "[a] biblical author…writes in his own style, and uses particular devices for expressing himself."[40] This perhaps includes wisdom, but the *use* of wisdom does not

32. Raymond C. Van Leeuwen, "The Sage in the Prophetic Literature," in *The Sage in Israel and the Ancient Near East* (ed. John G. Gammie and Leo. G. Perdue; Winona Lake: Eisenbrauns, 1990), 295–306.

33. Ibid., 296.

34. Andrew A. Macintosh, "Hosea and the Wisdom Tradition: Dependence and Independence," in Day, Gordon, and Williamson, eds., *Wisdom in Ancient Israel*, 124–33.

35. Ibid., 124.

36. Ibid., 125.

37. As above, the reformulation of particular themes or motifs for a different purpose is an important indicator of allusion.

38. Ibid., 132.

39. J. A. Soggin, "Amos and Wisdom," in Day, Gordon, and Williamson, eds., *Wisdom in Ancient Israel*, 119–23.

40. Ibid., 120.

entail *dependence* upon it. Soggin concludes that there are four options for the relationship between wisdom and prophecy but does not offer a way to discern which of the options is preferable: (1) wisdom influence derives from an early tradition of which "little or nothing is known," (2) prophets and wisdom share common ideas, vocabulary, and writing styles, (3) wisdom directly influences prophecy, or (4) wisdom influence in later books results from redaction.[41] Soggin rightly notes that these options are not necessarily mutually exclusive so that at the end of the day we are left with the same question: Is wisdom's influence discernible or not?

Other scholars have also addressed the relationship between wisdom and prophecy,[42] but the preceding discussion fleshes out the primary methodological avenues that have been taken. Some scholars have focused on determining wisdom influence by looking at vocabulary alone, others have tried to determine influence through borrowed concepts and theological motifs, and still others have combined multiple pieces of evidence to argue for influence. Our task remains to determine what is an appropriate methodology for determining the relationship between wisdom and prophecy, that is, how—and if—each influenced the other, but first we must attend to definitions.

41. Ibid., 123.

42. E.g., Keun-Jo Ahn, "The Trace of Wisdom in the Book of Jeremiah," in *Mapping and Engaging the Bible in Asian Cultures: Congress of the Society of Asian Biblical Studies 2008 Seoul Conference* (ed. Yeong Mee Lee and Yoon Jong Yoo; Korea: Christian Literature Society of Korea, 2009), 177–93; Joseph Blenkinsopp, *Sage, Priest, Prophet: Religious and Intellectual Leadership in Ancient Israel* (LAI; Louisville: Westminster John Knox, 1995); D. Gowan, "Habakkuk and Wisdom," *Perspective* 9 (1968): 157–66; Lester L. Grabbe, *Priests, Prophets, Diviners, Sages: A Socio-Historical Study of Religious Specialists in Ancient Israel* (Valley Forge: Trinity, 1995); H.-J. Hermisson, *Studien zur isralitischen Spruchweisheit* (WMANT 28; Neukirchen-Vluyn: Neukirchener Verlag, 1968); Joseph Jensen, *The Use of Tôrâ by Isaiah: His Debate with the Wisdom Tradition* (CBQMS 3; Washington, DC: Catholic Biblical Association of America, 1973); Morgan F. Donn, "Wisdom and the Prophets," in *Studia Biblica 1978*. Vol. 1, *Papers on Old Testament and Related Themes* (ed. E. A. Livingstone; Sheffield: JSOT Press, 1978), 209–44; Martin A. Shields, "Prophecy and Wisdom," in *Dictionary of the Old Testament: Prophets* (ed. Mark J. Boda and Gordon McConville; Downers Grove: InterVarsity, 2012), 642–50; Hans Wildberger, *Jahwewort und prophetische Rede bei Jeremia* (Zürich: Zwingli-Verlag, 1942), esp. 120–25; Walther Zimmerli, "The Place and Limit of Wisdom in the Framework of the Old Testament Theology," *SJT* 17 (1964): 146–58.

It Depends on What You Mean by "Wisdom"

R. N. Whybray has argued that the primary methodological problem in determining the relationship between wisdom and prophecy is that scholars have been unable to settle upon a definition of "wisdom."[43] This lack of agreement has inevitably led to no small amount of confusion. As a potential way forward in defining wisdom literature, James Crenshaw proposed that scholars should use different vocabulary to discuss three separate areas of wisdom: wisdom literature, *paideia*, and *hokmah*.[44] In Crenshaw's view, "wisdom literature" should be used exclusively to refer to the actual wisdom books: Job, Proverbs, Ecclesiastes, Sirach, Wisdom of Solomon, and Wisdom Psalms. *Paideia* should be used to refer to "the wisdom movement itself, its educational curriculum and pedagogy."[45] Finally, *hokmah* should be used to refer to a particular approach to reality. I have adopted Crenshaw's three categories here because they take into account the various manifestations of wisdom in Israel and provide the necessary vocabulary to differentiate between them.

Wisdom Literature: Wisdom as a Type of Literature
Though starting with wisdom as a type of literature seems to beg the question, the widely agreed-upon corpus of wisdom literature offers a safe entry point into the discussion. By limiting the scope of inquiry when establishing the baseline for determining wisdom influence in other portions of the Hebrew Bible, we are able to proceed into further discussion regarding the other two manifestations of wisdom: *paideia* and *hokmah*

Paideia: Wisdom as a Tradition or Movement
Crenshaw notes that *paideia* should be used to describe "the wisdom movement itself, its educational curriculum, and pedagogy."[46] *Paideia* is characterized by the unique thematic elements, vocabulary, and methods of instruction—such as the use of proverbs—that were employed by those who composed the wisdom literature. Early studies on the relationship between wisdom and prophecy focused on this aspect of wisdom because it allowed them to employ form criticism to isolate wisdom's unique elements then search for them within other types of literature.

---

43. Whybray, "Prophecy and Wisdom."
44. Crenshaw, "Method in Determining Wisdom Influence," 130 n. 4.
45. Ibid.
46. Crenshaw, "Method in Determining Wisdom Influence," 130 n. 4.

Ḥokmah: Wisdom as a Way of Viewing the World or Approach to Reality
Roland Murphy has argued that the relationship between wisdom and
prophecy "[i]s not a question of the direct influence of the sages or of the
wisdom literature, but rather of an approach to reality which was shared by
all Israelites in varying degrees... [A sapiential understanding of reality]
was not a mode of thinking cultivated exclusively by one class; it was
shared at all levels of society that interpreted daily experience."[47] Murphy
goes on to note that this interpretation of reality was "crystallized" in
the wisdom tradition.[48] For Murphy, determining wisdom influence is a
non-issue because we should *expect* various "wisdom influences" to show
up because wisdom pervaded every aspect of Israelite society. Thus, we
should not read too much into the traces of wisdom that we might detect
in other genres.

If Murphy has defined wisdom correctly, then the whole endeavor of
determining any sort of influence either upon the sage or the prophet is
destined to be fruitless. In response to Murphy's optimism about his own
definition of wisdom (that it would "open up the research of wisdom
influence upon various parts of the OT without the false problems
raised" by genre, motif, and vocabulary[49]), Whybray states that Murphy's
definition of wisdom may in fact prove to do the exact opposite. Murphy's
definition of "shared approach to reality" is so broad as to run the risk of
reducing the concept of Israelite wisdom, outside the "wisdom books"
proper, to no more than native common sense such as is to be found
generally in human nature. All literature would then be "wisdom literature" insofar as it had any kind of intellectual content, and to say of any
author's work that it showed traces of "wisdom thought" would be to say
no more than that he was not a fool.[50]

Whybray is correct to point out the inherent danger of overgeneralization. In response, we would argue along with Mark Sneed that
the wisdom genre suffers from the same sort of elusiveness as the
pornography genre, and just as we know intuitively that some things
are pornography while others are not, we know that the wisdom genre
exists, even if a precise definition eludes us.[51] However, while Murphy is
correct that wisdom is a particular approach to reality, it is also more than

47. Roland Murphy, "Wisdom—Theses and Hypotheses," in Gammie et al., eds.,
Israelite Wisdom, 39–40.
    48. Ibid.
    49. Murphy, "Wisdom—Theses and Hypotheses," 40.
    50. Whybray, "Prophecy and Wisdom," 186.
    51. Mark Sneed, "'Grasping After Wind': The Elusive Attempt to Define Wisdom"
(paper presented at the annual meeting of the SBL, Chicago, IL, 18 November 2012).

that. A particular approach to reality was necessary to cultivate wisdom (*ḥokmah*), but that wisdom was then formalized through the wisdom tradition, or *paideia*.

In Fichtner's view, the Hebrew Bible's wisdom tradition became distinct from other traditions or streams of thought in ancient Israel. Certainly this assessment is true to some extent: there are particular books in the Hebrew Bible that display certain characteristics that typify it as a genre. Furthermore, we can compare these writings with other ancient Near Eastern literature to demonstrate that the genre existed in the cultures surrounding Israel. However, as Sneed has shown, we must be careful not to artificially create some sort of ultimate fighting match between Israel's sages and prophets.[52]

A Proposed Methodology

Previous examinations of the relationship between wisdom and prophecy relied on form criticism to demonstrate that the two genres have unique features that can be discerned in each other. By isolating the unique elements of the wisdom tradition—*paidea*—scholars have pointed to multiple instances in which wisdom influence could be detected in the prophetic books. Form-critical studies have laid a solid foundation that, when combined with inner-biblical exegesis and inner-biblical allusion, form a robust methodology with which to investigate the literary relationship between wisdom and prophecy in the Hebrew Bible.

Form Criticism
In our methodological survey we presented the form-critical ways in which scholars have examined wisdom influence in prophetic literature. While cognizant of the criticism of circular reasoning, the clearest starting point seems to be a thorough investigation of the widely agreed-upon literature of the prophetic and wisdom genres. Previous work in this area has focused primarily on the prophetic and wisdom literature within the Hebrew Bible, but to move forward in the conversation it will be important to investigate the distinct features of wisdom and prophetic literature within the ancient Near East as a whole. The form-critical task will be to isolate thematic and linguistic elements unique to each of the genres. Once this has been accomplished, we may seek to determine whether these unique features appear in other genres, as many previous studies have done. Such investigation occurs at the genre level, where

---

52. See Sneed, "Is the 'Wisdom Tradition' Really a Tradition?"

it may be argued that the wisdom or prophetic tradition as a whole has exerted some sort of influence on the other tradition.

Inner-Biblical Allusion

In moving closer to the idea that influence has occurred in either prophetic or wisdom literature, we may look for instances of inner-biblical allusion. If allusion can be sufficiently demonstrated, then we may argue that one tradition—or at least its adherents—have exerted influence on another. In order to accomplish this task, we must demonstrate that intentional allusion has occurred, along with the directionality of that influence. Several principles may be outlined for each of these aspects of allusion.

Authorial Intent. Several textual features may indicate whether allusion has occurred. The confluence of multiple features will strengthen the case that an intentional relationship exists between texts.[53] We may examine "shared lexical features" between texts as a first step in discerning a relationship.[54] This includes the presence of the same words or phrases in each of the texts; however, caution must be used here because the shared words may be commonly used in the Hebrew Bible or may result from a shared worldview.[55] Jeffrey Leonard has outlined the following eight principles for determining the value of linguistic similarities between texts:

1. Linguistic similarity is all-important for determining textual relationships;
2. Linguistic similarity is more important than linguistic diversity;
3. Uncommon language is more valuable for determining textual relationships than common language;
4. Phrases are better evidence than single words;
5. Multiple instances of linguistic overlap are better evidence than single instances;

---

53. See Richard Hays, *Echoes of Scripture in the Letters of Paul* (New Haven: Yale University Press, 1989), 29–32; Russell L. Meek, "Intertextuality, Inner-Biblical Exegesis, and Inner-Biblical Allusion: The Ethics of a Methodology," *Bib* 95 (2014): 280–91.

54. Geoffrey Miller, "Intertextuality in Old Testament Research," *CurBR* 9 (2011): 295. See also Mark J. Boda, *Praying the Tradition: The Origin and Use of Tradition in Nehemiah 9* (BZAW 277; Berlin/New York: de Gruyter, 1999), 3; Jeffrey M. Leonard, "Identifying Inner-Biblical Allusions: Psalm 78 as a Test Case," *JBL* 127(2008): 246–51.

55. Miller, "Intertextuality," 295.

6. Linguistic overlap in similar contexts is a stronger indicator of borrowing than overlap in different contexts;
7. Ideological similarity is not necessary for demonstrating textual relationships;
8. Formal similarity is not necessary for determining textual relationships.[56]

Additionally, Michael Lyons has demonstrated that the "inversion of [lexical] elements" and the "splitting and redistribution of [lexical] elements" indicates intentional allusion.[57] A final important clue for determining the importance of shared vocabulary is what Edenburg calls "ungrammaticality," which "arises in a narrative due to expressions formulated or used without regard for language norms, or dysfunctional motifs."[58] Thus, when a word or phrase appears to be used incorrectly in a text, it may be an effort on the author's part to cause the reader "to seek another text in which the marker is well integrated, and to create a link between the two (or more) texts."[59]

Other than shared lexical features, we may also point to shared content as a means for determining allusion.[60] This can occur in the form of thematic similarities, such as when Qoheleth refers to the garden of Eden through his *carpe diem* passages. In each context, the focus is on the quality of life experienced in relationship with God.[61] Additionally, later authors may pattern either the plot or characters of their narrative off of previous texts.[62] However, with each of these three criteria caution must be exercised because, as Paul Noble has pointed out, such resemblances may be the result of the authors' use of " 'type narratives' which manipulate a set of shared motifs in such a way as to provide meaningful

---

56. Leonard, "Identifying Inner-Biblical Allusions," 246–57.

57. Michael A. Lyons, "Marking Innerbiblical Allusion in the Book of Ezekiel," *Bib* 88 (2007): 245–50. See also Sommer, "Allusions and Illusions," 159.

58. Edenburg, "How (Not) to Murder a King," 72–73.

59. Ibid., 68. Note also the discussion of Zechariah's use of sustained allusion in Michael R. Stead, *The Intertextuality of Zechariah 1–8* (LHBOTS 506; New York: T&T Clark International, 2009), 74–132. Thanks to Mark J. Boda for this reference.

60. See Miller, "Intertextuality," 296–97.

61. See Craig Bartholomew, *Ecclesiastes* (BCOTWP; Grand Rapids: Baker Academic, 2009), 150–53; Russell L. Meek, "The Meaning of הבל in Qohelet: An Intertextual Suggestion," in *The Words of the Wise Are Like Goads: Engaging Qohelet in the 21st Century* (ed. Mark J. Boda, Tremper Longman III, and Cristian G. Rata; Winona Lake: Eisenbrauns, 2013), 250–52.

62. Miller, "Intertextuality," 296.

variations on essentially the same underlying plot."[63] Therefore, we must remember that "the weight of cumulative evidence will strengthen the claim of interrelatedness" between texts.[64]

Directionality of Influence. In order for inner-biblical allusion to be useful in examining the relationship between wisdom and prophetic texts that appear to have influenced each other, directionality of influence must be determined.[65] Cynthia Edenburg points out that directionality may be determined where "an element in one text motivates the shape, formulation or topic of the other text" and where "the comprehension of one text is dependent upon knowledge of the other text."[66] If either of these two things can be demonstrated for a particular text, then directionality of influence may be argued.

Inner-Biblical Exegesis

Inner-biblical exegesis brings us into the deepest level of influence that we may posit between two texts. With inner-biblical allusion we are able to posit likely instances in which a source text exerted influence by means of a receptor text alluding back to it. Inner-biblical exegesis, on the other hand, argues for direct influence in the sense that the receptor text modifies the source text in some way. As with inner-biblical allusion, inner-biblical exegesis must demonstrate authorial intention as well as directionality of influence. It does this through the same basic principles of discerning thematic and linguistic correspondence between two texts. However, since inner-biblical exegesis moves beyond inner-biblical allusion in arguing for reactualization, reapplication, or some other modification, it must also demonstrate a change in form, content, or purpose of the source text.

---

63. Paul R. Noble, "Esau, Tamar, and Joseph: Criteria for Identifying Inner-Biblical Allusions," *VT* 52 (2002): 233.

64. Edenburg, "How (Not) to Murder a King," 72.

65. Of course, directionality of influence is not always easy to determine, but it is an important factor in the methodology of inner-biblical allusion as opposed to intertextuality. See further the criteria outlined by Michael A. Lyons, "Transformation of Law: Ezekiel's Use of the Holiness Code (Leviticus 17–26)," in *Transforming Visions: Transformations of Text, Tradition, and Theology in Ezekiel* (ed. William A. Tooman and Michael A. Lyons; Princeton Theological Monographs 127; Eugene: Wipf & Stock, 2010), 1–32. Thanks to William R. Osborne for pointing out this essay to me.

66. Edenburg, "How (Not) to Murder a King," 73–74.

After having determined that some sort of allusion is operative within a text, we may then utilize inner-biblical exegesis to determine whether or not the receptor text has modified the source text. Thus, for example, Jer 17:21–22 makes reference to the Sabbath law found in Exod 20:18–20 and Deut 5:12–14, yet expands it to prohibit the "bearing of burdens from one's house to the gates of Jerusalem for storage or sale; and [to prohibit] the transfer of burdens from the private to the public domain."[67] Jeremiah's repetition of vocabulary indicates that he is referring to the previous Sabbath laws, but his expansion of the laws indicates that he is modifying the text to make it applicable to the present situation. A receptor text may also modify the source text through what Fishbane calls "homiletical elaboration," such as when Ezek 22:5–8 expands the prophecy of Zeph 3:3–4.[68] Finally, we may discern inner-biblical exegesis in cases where a previous text has been reformulated such that it takes on an entirely different meaning, as in the case of Job's (7:7–18) use of Ps 8:5–7: "Whereas the psalmist exalts the human species to near-divine status, and regards this exaltation as a sign of divine favor, Job inverts the liturgical teaching and mocks it, for he implies that God's providence is less than beneficial for humankind."[69] Thus, if having determined that allusion is present on some level, we find clues that the receptor text has in some way modified the previous text for the purpose of explicating or changing its meaning, then we may be fairly certain that a strong level of influence is at work in the receptor text.

Conclusion

"Is the theme 'prophecy and wisdom' played out? Is there really no more to be said about it?"[70] Not at all. Form criticism has enabled scholars to cover much ground in determining the relationship between wisdom and prophecy. The excesses of the earliest attempts to find wisdom influence in prophetic literature have been corrected, most especially by the likes of James Crenshaw and Norman Whybray. Studies in the relationship between wisdom and prophecy have focused heavily on investigating wisdom's influence on the prophetic tradition; therefore, studies that

67. Michael Fishbane, "Inner-Biblical Exegesis: Types and Strategies of Interpretation in Ancient Israel," in *Midrash and Literature* (ed. Geoffrey H. Hartman and Sanford Budick; New Haven: Yale University Press, 1986), 27.

68. Fishbane, *Biblical Interpretation*, 462.

69. Ibid., 285.

70. Whybray, "Prophecy and Wisdom," 196.

focus on wisdom's influence upon prophecy are as needed as when Van Leeuwen mentioned the lacuna a few decades ago.

The methodology presented here seeks to combine the most methodologically sound principles of form criticism with the principles of inner-biblical allusion and inner-biblical exegesis. Form criticism allows us to examine wisdom and prophetic influence on a generic level in an effort to determine the relationship between the traditions as a whole. Inner-biblical allusion and inner-biblical exegesis give us the tools necessary to investigate the relationship between wisdom and prophecy on a textual level. Both of these methods require us to demonstrate both authorial intention and textual provenance in arguing for intentional influence. Finally, inner-biblical exegesis brings us to the most central portion of textual influence. We must demonstrate that an author has intended to refer to an earlier text and that the author has in some way modified that text for the author's own purposes. By examining the textual relationships between prophetic texts and wisdom texts at these four levels, we will be much closer to determining if and when each tradition influenced the other.

"Wisdom" as Mask and Mirror: Methodological Questions for "Wisdom's" Dialogue with the Canon*

Will Kynes

Given recent questions raised about the "wisdom" genre and its associated "tradition," the effort in this volume to seek out and carefully evaluate connections between prophecy and "wisdom literature" is timely.[1] Like Mark Sneed, who has led the way in raising these questions,[2] and Russell Meek (in this volume), I share the growing concerns about the way wisdom has been cordoned off from the rest of the Old Testament and about any "sort of ultimate fighting match," as Meek puts it, that results between wisdom and not only prophecy but also the rest of the Old Testament. The "marginalization of wisdom" has indeed created a "need for integration with the rest of the Old Testament."[3]

---

* The substance of this essay was originally presented as "'Wisdom' as Mask and Mirror: Response to Russell L. Meek, 'Prophet and Sage in Dialogue: History and Methodology'" (Wisdom and Prophecy in the Hebrew Bible; Institute for Biblical Research Annual Meeting, Baltimore, 22 November 2013).

1. As others have begun to do, I use scare quotes around the term "wisdom" when it is used to describe a distinct genre of biblical literature and the "movement" or "tradition" associated with it in order to reflect that it is a scholarly construct. However, for ease of reading I will henceforth dispense with them. See Mark Sneed, "Is the 'Wisdom Tradition' a Tradition?" *CBQ* 73 (2011): 50–71; Katharine J. Dell, "Deciding the Boundaries of 'Wisdom': Applying the Concept of Family Resemblance," in *Was There a Wisdom Tradition? New Prospects in Israelite Wisdom Studies* (ed. Mark Sneed; AIL; Atlanta: SBL, 2015), 145–60; Stuart Weeks, "Is 'Wisdom Literature' a Useful Category?" in *Tracing Sapiential Traditions in Ancient Judaism* (ed. Hindy Najman and Jean-Sébastien Rey; JSJSup 174; Leiden: Brill, 2016), 3–23.

2. Sneed, "Wisdom Tradition"; Mark Sneed, ed., *Was There a Wisdom Tradition? New Prospects in Israelite Wisdom Studies* (AIL; Atlanta: SBL, 2015).

3. Katharine J. Dell, *The Book of Proverbs in Social and Theological Context* (Cambridge: Cambridge University Press, 2006), 188.

However, the methods employed to reintegrate wisdom with the broader canon present their own problems. This reintegration has been attempted in various ways since the mid-twentieth century. In that time a tendency has developed to reconcile the two on wisdom's terms, finding wisdom influence across the Hebrew Bible. As Katharine Dell observes, "It is odd that wisdom might have had influence outside, but never itself been influenced from outside."[4] Over time, this unidirectional approach to the relationships between wisdom texts and the rest of the canon has consistently expanded wisdom's reach to the point that pan-sapientialism threatens.[5] This has occurred despite the fact that many of the "wisdom" books are widely considered later works than the texts their views are said to influence.[6]

In his contribution to this volume, Meek proposes a "more refined" methodology for determining influence between wisdom and prophecy. He begins by surveying previous work on this question, which, true to form, focuses primarily on wisdom's influence on prophecy, or lack thereof. Meek then attempts to define "wisdom," following James Crenshaw's distinction between wisdom as a type of literature ("wisdom literature"), a tradition or movement (*paideia*), and an approach to reality (*ḥokmah*).[7] This distinction is reasonable and would be helpful if it were not completely impractical. Though Meek suggests we "start" with the wisdom literature in order to define the wisdom tradition and wisdom approach to reality, this raises the question of why certain texts are chosen to be grouped as a separate type of literature associated with wisdom in the first place. In other words, does the word "wisdom" in the title "wisdom literature" for a type of literature refer to "wisdom" as a tradition or "wisdom" as an approach to reality or both? Reflecting the widespread confusion, when Meek seeks to define the wisdom approach to reality, he ends up making an argument for wisdom as a genre. This conflation of terms continues when Meek turns to his proposed methodology for examining the influence between wisdom and prophecy. He begins with form criticism, which, he writes, has been used in the past "to demonstrate that the two *genres* have unique features" (p. 13, emphasis mine). In the

4. Dell, *Proverbs*, 14.

5. See Will Kynes, "The Modern Scholarly Wisdom Tradition and the Threat of Pan-Sapientialism: A Case Report," in Sneed, ed., *Was There a Wisdom Tradition?*, 11–38.

6. Stuart Weeks, *An Introduction to the Study of Wisdom Literature* (New York: T&T Clark International, 2010), 136.

7. James L. Crenshaw, "Method in Determining Wisdom Influence Upon 'Historical' Literature," *JBL* 88 (1969): 130 n. 4.

next sentence, though, he writes, "By isolating the unique elements of the wisdom *tradition—paidea*—scholars have pointed to multiple instances in which wisdom influence could be detected in the prophetic books" (p. 13, emphasis mine).[8] Next, in order to evaluate the degree of influence more deeply, his methodology seeks inner-biblical allusions and inner-biblical exegesis between particular texts within the two traditions.

Meek's work does provide some valuable refinements on previous approaches, particularly in his addition of insights from recent intertextual study. However, it also perpetuates many of the unquestioned presuppositions of previous approaches and thus provides an opportunity to examine these broader trends in biblical scholarship. The present essay, then, is motivated by my appreciation for both the project the editors of this volume have initiated and Meek's admirable efforts to provide it with greater methodological clarity. To that end, I offer here two related questions intended to refine further the methodologies undertaken to reevaluate the relationship of wisdom to the rest of the canon, including prophecy. These questions have been widely overlooked, but, I believe, like the elephant in the room, are also too large to be avoided as these efforts progress. Like that elephant, these questions are, in fact, so large that they are likely to place significant pressure on methodologies like the one Meek presents as this task moves forward.

Question 1: Is the Term "Wisdom" More of a Hindrance Than a Help?

This first question, in fact, goes right to the heart of any attempt to evaluate the relationship of the wisdom literature corpus with other texts in the Hebrew Bible. As Meek acknowledges, "[the] definition [of wisdom] will necessarily determine where and in what way any potential influence is discernible" (p. 4). However, Meek recognizes a potential weakness in his attempt to answer this crucial question. He writes, "Though starting with wisdom as a type of literature seems to beg the question, the widely agreed-upon corpus of wisdom literature offers a safe entry point into the discussion" (p. 11). But is this scholarly consensus actually "safe"? It

---

8. This seamless move from genre to tradition, which broadly characterizes form-critical study, appears again in the following paragraph: "The form-critical task will be to isolate thematic and linguistic elements that are unique to each of the *genres*. Once this has been accomplished, we may seek to determine whether these unique features appear in other *genres*, as many previous studies have done. Such investigation occurs at the *genre* level, where it may be argued that the wisdom or prophetic *tradition* as a whole has exerted some sort of influence on the other *tradition*" (emphasis mine).

is "widely agreed-upon," at least as long as one does not ask how many psalms or texts from the ancient Near East or Qumran are included[9] and as long as one does not question whether works that show significant "wisdom influence" should actually be considered wisdom texts as well, which would invite into the discussion texts such as the primeval history (Gen 1–11), the Joseph story (Gen 37–50), Deuteronomy, the Succession Narrative (2 Samuel and 1 Kgs 1–2), Isaiah, Amos, or Esther, to name a few which have been suggested.[10] Where wisdom "influence" ends and wisdom membership begins is a question yet to be satisfactorily answered.[11]

But, as far as Proverbs, Ecclesiastes, and Job go, this widely agreed-upon consensus does provide a certain safety in numbers. Few would disagree that these are wisdom literature's core. Repeatedly, when pressed on the definition of wisdom (as genre or tradition), scholars fall back on this consensus.[12] As Crenshaw says, "[T]he wisdom corpus alone (itself the result of a subjective decision on the part of each interpreter) defines what is in the last resort 'wisdom.'"[13]

9. For debate on "wisdom" psalms, see, most recently, Simon Chi-Chung Cheung, *Wisdom Intoned: A Reappraisal of the Genre "Wisdom Psalms"* (LHBOTS 613; London: Bloomsbury T&T Clark, 2015). The application of the wisdom category from biblical studies to ancient Near Eastern texts has long been disputed by specialists in the latter field (R. N. Whybray, "Slippery Words. IV. Wisdom," in *Wisdom: The Collected Articles of Norman Whybray* [ed. Katherine J. Dell and Margaret Barker; SOTSMS; Aldershot: Ashgate, 2005], 7). As Paul-Alain Beaulieu observes, "In ancient Mesopotamia, there was no such concept or category as wisdom literature" (Paul-Alain Beaulieu, "The Social and Intellectual Setting of Babylonian Wisdom Literature," in *Wisdom Literature in Mesopotamia and Israel* [ed. Richard J. Clifford; Atlanta: SBL, 2007], 3). For discussion of potential Qumran wisdom texts, see Matthew Goff, "Qumran Wisdom Literature and the Problem of Genre," *DSD* 17 (2010): 315–35; Benjamin G. Wright, "Joining the Club: A Suggestion About Genre in Early Jewish Texts," *DSD* 17 (2010): 289–314.

10. Weeks, *Introduction*, 135.

11. See ibid., 85.

12. See, e.g., Katharine J. Dell, "Wisdom in Israel," in *Text in Context: Essays by Members of the Society for Old Testament Study* (ed. A. D. H. Mayes; Oxford: Oxford University Press, 2000), 353; Goff, "Qumran Wisdom Literature," 319; Wright, "Joining the Club," 298.

13. James L. Crenshaw, "Prolegomenon," in *Studies in Ancient Israelite Wisdom* (ed. James L. Crenshaw; LBS; New York: Ktav, 1976), 9. When it comes to his own study of wisdom based on the limited grouping of Proverbs, Job, Ecclesiastes, Sirach, Wisdom of Solomon, and a few Psalms, Crenshaw admits the "subjective nature" of his "assumption" (5).

However, if we are relying on consensus, the numbers are not actually on the side of the modern conception of wisdom literature. The first time we get a clear delineation of wisdom literature consisting of Proverbs, Ecclesiastes, and Job (and in this case Ben Sira and Wisdom of Solomon as well) is in 1851 in the work of Johann Friedrich Bruch.[14] The category does not become part of the common parlance of Old Testament scholarship until the early twentieth century, which means this definition of the wisdom genre is clinging to merely the latest sliver of the history of biblical interpretation. Given that no consensus exists on the characteristics that define this purported genre,[15] this does not appear to be one of the places in which modern scholars can be confident in their consensus over the views of centuries worth of "pre-critical" biblical interpreters, who grouped the books differently. In fact, texts were grouped in a number of ways by early Jewish and Christian interpreters, as is attested by the differing structures of Hebrew and Greek canons, the Solomonic attribution (which includes Song of Songs but excludes Job), and the title "wisdom," which is applied to Wisdom of Solomon and potentially Ben Sira (51:30) but none of the biblical texts associated with wisdom.[16] None of these groupings equates with the modern wisdom category either quantitatively, in content, or qualitatively, in uniting features, and it is unclear whether any would have been considered literary genres in the way genres are currently understood.

But Meek suggests, following Sneed,[17] that wisdom is like pornography, at least in the sense that "just as we know intuitively that some things are pornography while others are not, we know that the wisdom genre exists, even if a precise definition eludes us" (p. 12). As Supreme Court Justice Potter Stewart famously said of pornography, "I know it when I see it." But the important word there is "I." This is a subjective judgment. Presumably, some would disagree with Justice Stewart, otherwise his

---

14. Johann Friedrich Bruch, *Weisheits-Lehre der Hebräer: Ein Beitrag zur Geschichte der Philosophie* (Strasbourg: Treuttel & Würtz, 1851). For the origins of the category traced back to Bruch's work, see Will Kynes, "The Nineteenth-Century Beginnings of 'Wisdom Literature,' and Its Twenty-First-century End?" in *Perspectives on Israelite Wisdom: Proceedings of the Oxford Old Testament Seminar* (ed. John Jarick; LHBOTS 618; London: Bloomsbury T&T Clark, 2015), 83–108.

15. John J. Collins, "Epilogue: Genre Analysis and the Dead Sea Scrolls," *DSD* 17 (2010): 429; Weeks, *Introduction*, 85.

16. See n. 18 below.

17. Mark Sneed, "'Grasping After the Wind': The Elusive Attempt to Define and Delimit Wisdom," in Sneed, ed., *Was There a Wisdom Tradition?*, 39.

judgment would not have been necessary. This subjectivity is all the more problematic when modern judgments are applied to the products of a culture from more than two millennia before. Sure, *modern Western scholars* agree on what *they* believe to be wisdom, but, unless the current lack of ancient evidence for the category is addressed,[18] this subjective agreement is irrelevant to the question of which genres influenced the ancient Israelite prophets. It is like developing a methodology for determining the influence of pornographic literature on the prophets and starting with modern Western intuitive ideas of what might make up the pornographic literature in the Old Testament.[19]

And just as some cultures would consider uncovered ankles pornographic while they rarely raise an eyebrow in the modern West,[20] it seems unlikely that the Israelites would have grouped texts together because they demonstrated individualism, humanism, empiricism, rationalism, universalism, or secularism.[21] That list sounds a lot more like a conception of wisdom from the modern age, more specifically the nineteenth century, which, suspiciously enough, is when the definition of the current wisdom literature genre first appears. One could argue that Proverbs, Ecclesiastes, and Job are distinctive in the Old Testament in those regards, but would the Israelites even have thought in such categories, which are much more congenial to the modern mind?[22] In fact, Bruch, who was the first to systematically address wisdom literature, defines his project as an attempt to defend the philosophy of the Hebrews to the philosophers of his day, and his subtitle, *Ein Beitrag zur Geschichte der Philosophie*, makes his

18. See Goff, "Qumran Wisdom Literature," 333–35; Weeks, *Introduction*, 144. Goff notes the absence of "wisdom" as a categorical indicator in "wisdom texts" in early Judaism. The designation is not used by Josephus or Ben Sira. Even the concluding phrase, "the wisdom of Ben Sira" (51:30), in the latter is likely a later addition, and the title of the Wisdom of Solomon may not denote the genre of the text, which is, after all, a non-traditional wisdom work.

19. See, e.g., Athalya Brenner, "Pornoprophetics Revisited: Some Additional Reflections," *JSOT* 70 (1996): 63–86.

20. Caroline West, "Pornography and Censorship," in *The Stanford Encyclopedia of Philosophy* (ed. Edward N. Zalta; Stanford: Metaphysics Research Lab, Stanford University, Fall 2013). Available online: http://plato.stanford.edu/archives/fall2013/entries/pornography-censorship (accessed 8 December 2015).

21. Crenshaw criticizes several of these characterizations of wisdom as "too narrow and false," and yet they perpetuate in scholarship, and even Crenshaw's comments tend only to modify them rather than reject them. See Crenshaw, "Method in Determining Wisdom Influence," 131–32.

22. Weeks, *Introduction*, 115–16, 119.

interests clear.[23] Wisdom literature, as Crenshaw has observed, often does indeed stand "as a mirror image of the scholar painting her portrait."[24]

If a precise definition eludes us, do we in fact *know* that the wisdom genre exists, as Meek claims and Sneed implies? Perhaps we *believe* it does, but couldn't we be wrong? This may be why wisdom scholarship has had a constant tendency toward the dangerous overgeneralization we see in Roland Murphy's conception of wisdom as a "shared approach to reality."[25] We have had a consensus handed down to us from the nineteenth century that the wisdom literature consists of Proverbs, Ecclesiastes, and Job, and we have attempted *ex post facto* to find justification for this article of our critical faith.[26] The actual wisdom tradition is a scholarly tradition. Thus, opening discussions of the difficulty of defining the genre have become *de rigueur* in introductions to wisdom literature, which consistently begin by assuming the consensus on the genre's contents and then look for arguments to support it. But the contents of this supposed genre do not fit together comfortably in that genre container, so scholars have to keep developing bigger ones, more abstract definitions of wisdom, until they can finally cram them all in.[27] Soon they have a container so big—one like Murphy's—that hardly a book in the Old Testament does not fit. Pan-sapientialism threatens, and an appeal back to the consensus that created the problem in the first place is not going to thwart it, even

23. Bruch, *Weisheits-Lehre der Hebräer*, ix, xv–xvi.

24. Crenshaw, "Prolegomenon," 3. For the widespread tendency of critics to read earlier texts through the genre categories of their own time as if those genres were static and universally applicable, see Alastair Fowler, *Kinds of Literature: An Introduction to the Theory of Genres and Modes* (Oxford: Clarendon, 1982), 51.

25. Roland E. Murphy, "Wisdom—Theses and Hypothesis," in *Israelite Wisdom: Theological and Literary Essays in Honor of Samuel Terrien* (ed. John G. Gammie, Walter Brueggemann, W. Lee Humphreys, and James M. Ward; Missoula: Scholars Press, 1978), 47–48; cf. R. N. Whybray, "Prophecy and Wisdom," in *Israel's Prophetic Heritage: Essays in Honour of Peter R. Ackroyd* (ed. R. Coggins, A. Phillips, and M. Knibb; Cambridge: Cambridge University Press, 1982), 186.

26. For an example of this type of *ex post facto* justification, see Wright, "Joining the Club," 297–98. Beginning with the scholarly consensus on the contents of the genre, he looks for a means of explaining it, finding one in prototype genre theory.

27. Weeks, *Introduction*, 108, cf. 6. For example, Alistair Hunter acknowledges that Job cannot be identified as wisdom literature on the basis of "formal linguistic features," so, to justify the "effective unanimity" of "the intuitive urge to include Job," he claims an examination of "the underlying perspectives which emerge from a consideration in broader terms of what these books are concerned with" is necessary (Alastair Hunter, *Wisdom Literature* [London: SCM, 2006], 23).

though that is the recourse scholars since Crenshaw have consistently taken. If a definition of wisdom based on the scholarly consensus either turns back on itself or expands indefinitely, then perhaps that consensus is itself the problem.[28]

Questioning this scholarly consensus may not be particularly safe, but not doing so may be even more dangerous. Too many educated edifices have been built on this flimsy foundation, and I would like to encourage those who attempt to relate wisdom to prophecy to test carefully how much more weight this scholarly superstructure can bear before they add another floor. It was nearly half a century ago, in 1970, that Gerhard von Rad observed that "wisdom…is by no means directly rooted in the sources," having instead "first emerged in the scholarly world," and so "[t]he question is therefore justified whether the attractive codename 'wisdom' is nowadays not more of a hindrance than a help, in so far as it disguises what stands behind it rather than depicts it properly."[29] But others are raising serious questions about the nature of the genre once again,[30] with one scholar even wondering if "in the next generation of scholarship the term 'wisdom' might seem like a rather antiquated scholarly term, such as the amphictyony, the putative tribal federation of ancient Israel, or the Elohist source."[31]

Question 2: Is Form Criticism the Best Starting Place?

Given the problems with the wisdom category, form criticism does not in fact appear to have "laid a solid foundation," as Meek says. The method itself has faced increasing criticism recently. It is unclear how its interest in identifying shared features among groups of texts is distinguishable from genre criticism. This leads Weeks to wonder why biblical scholars add the name form criticism to their practice of genre theory, unless perhaps it is to "avoid playing rough games with the other children."[32]

---

28. See Kynes, "Modern Scholarly Wisdom Tradition."

29. Gerhard von Rad, *Wisdom in Israel* (trans. James D. Martin; Harrisburg: Trinity, 1993), 7–8; trans. of *Weisheit in Israel* (Neukirchen-Vluyn: Neukirchener, 1970).

30. See nn. 1 and 2 above.

31. Goff, "Qumran Wisdom Literature," 325.

32. Stuart Weeks, "The Limits of Form Criticism in the Study of Literature, with Reflections on Psalm 34," in *Biblical Interpretation and Method: Essays in Honour of John Barton* (ed. Katharine J. Dell and Paul M. Joyce; Oxford: Oxford University Press, 2013), 19.

Further, Weeks demonstrates that the attempts to link "forms" of literature to specific historical settings, which he compares to the etymological fallacy, have the potential to distort interpretation.[33] Erhard Blum similarly finds the addition of the designation "form criticism" to genre theory "unnecessary" and "linked to portentous shortcomings," particularly as the term "form," which should describe the structure of an individual text, is confused with "genre."[34] If this distinction were maintained, there might be individual forms used in texts currently associated with wisdom, such as the proverbial sentence, or instruction, debate, and intellectual reflection,[35] but no singular wisdom form, which could be equated to a genre, though the latter is precisely what Meek's use of form criticism is intended to provide.

Meek's use of form criticism to identify genres is understandable given how often this is done in biblical scholarship. What is more concerning (though unfortunately just as common) is his suggestion that the comparison of wisdom to prophecy begin with this step. Further, he uses the identification of a wisdom genre as a means of "isolating the unique elements of the wisdom tradition—*paideia*." If at least one of your genres is poorly defined, is it methodologically responsible to begin your comparison with genre criticism and then extrapolate an ancient tradition from it? Norman Whybray argued thirty years ago that the lack of a clear definition of wisdom has hindered discussion of its relationship to prophecy,[36] and, as I have argued above, that problem persists today. Instead of simply building on the widespread and yet questionable presupposition of a separate wisdom literature genre, an investigation of the relationships between texts traditionally grouped together as wisdom and others grouped as prophecy could be an excellent way to test some of the common assumptions about the nature of the purported wisdom genre and its relationship with the rest of the Hebrew Bible. But this testing will be most effective if it does not presuppose its conclusion but instead treats the so-called wisdom books as individual texts *before* it groups

33. Weeks, "Form Criticism," 18.

34. Erhard Blum, "Formgeschichte—a Misleading Category? Some Critical Remarks," in *The Changing Face of Form Criticism for the Twenty-First Century* (ed. Marvin A. Sweeney and Ehud Ben Zvi; Grand Rapids: Eerdmans, 2003), 45, 33; cf., in the same volume, Anthony F. Campbell, "Form Criticism's Future," 24–25.

35. James L. Crenshaw, *Old Testament Wisdom: An Introduction* (Louisville: Westminster John Knox, 1998), 11.

36. Whybray, "Prophecy and Wisdom," 181.

them as wisdom literature, if it does so at all.[37] Thus, I would suggest reversing the methodology Meek has proposed and considering questions of type of literature last, *after* individual connections have been identified and analyzed, rather than first. Identifying types of literature is the most subjective of the steps he has proposed. As Meek says, form criticism allows an examination of "the traditions as a whole," while inner-biblical allusion and inner-biblical exegesis investigate the relationship between them "on a textual level." Given its distance from the text, form or genre criticism should have the most data available to inform its conclusions. This would help the methodology avoid the criticism of circular reasoning.

In effect, I am suggesting that this method's foundation be more intertextual than form critical, by which I mean that it make explicit what form criticism was content to assume, that meaning is produced through the interaction of texts. Textual comprehension is "an act of intertextuality," in which we "[c]onsciously or unconsciously…locate this text in relation to others with which we are already familiar."[38] Genres themselves are just the formalization of these intertextual comparisons. But genres are not neutral. Classification is interpretation. Genres serve as echo chambers, magnifying similarities between the texts within them and muffling connections with texts outside. This has particularly been the case with wisdom literature, which depends on the echo chamber to legitimate the unity of its diverse contents. For example, the extent of Job's connections to psalmic laments has often been overlooked due to its wisdom classification, which has drowned its existential message under a torrent of philosophical interpretations.[39] Noting this danger in biblical scholarship, George Nickelsburg writes,

---

37. For this approach to the question, see Katharine J. Dell and Will Kynes, eds., *Reading Job Intertextually* (LHBOTS 574; New York: Bloomsbury T&T Clark, 2013); Katharine J. Dell and Will Kynes, eds., *Reading Ecclesiastes Intertextually* (LHBOTS 587; New York: Bloomsbury T&T Clark, 2014); Katharine J. Dell and Will Kynes, eds., *Reading Proverbs Intertextually* (LHBOTS 629; New York: Bloomsbury T&T Clark, forthcoming).

38. Carol A. Newsom, "Pairing Research Questions and Theories of Genre: A Case Study of the Hodayot," *DSD* 17 (2010): 273.

39. Claus Westermann, *The Structure of the Book of Job: A Form-Critical Analysis* (trans. Charles A. Muenchow; Philadelphia: Fortress, 1981), 1. For Westermann, a "form-critical analysis" actually encourages new intertextual connections to be pursued, but only because he is willing to set aside the dominant form-critical view that Job is wisdom literature.

> The history of scholarship also attests the ways in which our categories have become hermetically sealed compartments that give the impression that each refers to, or contains something totally different from the other. Thus "wisdom" or "sapiential" is distinct from "apocalyptic." By focusing intently on one or the other, as the thing itself, we fail to see that in the world from which they have come to us, they were related parts of an organic whole, each with some of the same genes as the other.[40]

Therefore, a more consciously intertextual approach would be concerned not to let a genre categorization, particularly an ill-defined, circularly justified, modernly developed, and extrinsically imposed one like wisdom literature, restrict the potential interpretive significance of links between Proverbs, Ecclesiastes, and Job and other texts across the canon. By comparing the contents of wisdom literature with a number of prophetic texts, this project has the potential to break through those genre walls, but by beginning with form criticism it might instead perpetuate those boundaries by exchanging the comparison of individual texts for the comparison of two genres abstracted from the texts, and, even worse, the "movements" or "traditions" then abstracted from those genres.

An intertextual approach to genre, which seeks to appreciate the myriad ways each text interacts with those around it, is among the current challengers to the classic list-of-features approach to genre, which sought to draw bold taxonomic lines and declare texts either in or out.[41] This binary approach was vital to form criticism since firmly delineated genres and forms could facilitate historical conjecture. But its abstractions from the text created space for modern scholars to import their own under-standings of wisdom, treating the genre as a mirror. In so doing they have masked the unique ways each of these texts, wisdom and prophecy alike, interact with other texts to devise its own distinctive message. A better understanding of the intertextual network in which these texts participate will enable a more accurate depiction of these messages, which have for too long been disguised.

---

40. George W. E. Nickelsburg, "Wisdom and Apocalypticism in Early Judaism: Some Points for Discussion," in *Conflicted Boundaries in Wisdom and Apocalypticism* (ed. B. G. Wright and L. Wills; SBLSymS; Atlanta: SBL, 2005), 36.

41. Other challengers include Sneed's general dismissal of "generic realism" in favor of "generic nominalism" and more specific approaches such as, family resemblance, speech-act, or prototype theories. See, respectively, Sneed, "Wisdom Tradition," 66–67; Dell, "Deciding the Boundaries," 155–56; Cheung, *Wisdom Intoned*, 16–19, 38–48; Wright, "Joining the Club," 302–3.

METHODS, MUDDLES, AND MODES OF LITERATURE: THE QUESTION OF INFLUENCE BETWEEN WISDOM AND PROPHECY

Mark Sneed

Introduction

This essay will question the notion of influence between the so-called wisdom and the prophetic traditions. This question of influence assumes that these two traditions arose and were transmitted as separate phenomena by distinct groups that only later came into contact with each other. This notion would be comical if it were not still the consensus among biblical scholars. It rests on the following faulty assumptions: (1) genres are not systemic; (2) the social matrix of genres in some way determines them, and vestiges of this matrix continue in their later usages; (3) genres are always the domain of certain groups who control them; (4) there were separate "schools" of sages and prophets in ancient Israel; (5) the epistemologies of the prophets and sages were different, and this is reflected in their respective literatures. In the following, these assumptions will be shown to be faulty.

Genres Are Systemic

Both types—I prefer modes[1]—of literature, prophetic and wisdom, operate in differing fields of thought, with little overlap. The respective modes should not be viewed as antagonistic to each other or as influencing

---

1. On mode of literature, see John Frow, *Genre* (The New Critical Idiom; London: Routledge, 2006), 63–67; Alastair Fowler, *Kinds of Literature: An Introduction to the Theory of Genres and Modes* (Cambridge, MA: Harvard University Press, 1982), 106–11.

one another. Rather, they are simply treating differing domains and should be viewed, thus, as complementing each other, though the various works (e.g., Proverbs) participating in a particular mode (e.g., wisdom literature) contain differing, even contradictory, theologies between themselves (e.g., Proverbs vs. Ecclesiastes) and works participating in other modes (e.g., Isaiah). Each mode of literature has a job to do, and thus both are necessary for the Israelite culture as a whole.

Genres have a tendency to be systemic, i.e., the niche or domain in reality that a particular genre treats will not be treated by the other genres in the larger economy of genres. In other words, genres do not do double duty.[2] They only treat the slice of reality they are supposed to treat and nothing more. Another way of putting this is that what constitutes a genre is not only the positive features that characterize it (e.g., wisdom literature is universalistic in perspective) but also what it lacks (e.g., wisdom literature contains few historical references). What makes a genre is as much what it does not do as what it does do. For example, what makes a movie a comedy is that it has a tendency to make us laugh. But being a comedy means that it simultaneously does not make us cry, at least not primarily, as in a melodrama. Tears of laughter do not count. It also does not scare us as a horror movie does. Thus, cinematic and literary genres form economies or systems that avoid redundancy. And like chess pieces, each genre serves a particular function within that economy, which is defined in relation to all the other genres.

All of this may seem elementary and banal, but I feel compelled to spell it out because biblical scholars who speak of influence between two literary "traditions" are assuming that genres are not systemic. Instead, they assume that the prophetic literature reflects the distinctive worldview of the prophets over against that of the sages. However, when you examine the prophetic literature, it is self-evident that it represents divinatory literature in the sense that it contains inspired revelation to the nation that reveals the will of the deity, whereas the wisdom literature does not represent itself as divinatory literature that predicts the future. It represents practical instruction on the question of the summum bonum and focuses largely on advice for the individual and not the nation. Its

2. Frow, *Genre*, 125; as Martin Buss puts it, *"The Hebrew Bible is largely arranged according to what appear to be culturally significant genres, which each represent a dimension of life and which engage metaphorically in a dialogue with each other"* (emphasis original) ("Dialogue In and Among Genres," in *Bakhtin and Genre Theory in Biblical Studies* [ed. Roland Boer; Semeia Studies 63; Atlanta: SBL, 2007], 13).

sphere of operation is that of ethics and dealing with the problem of evil, again, as it relates to individuals. Prophetic literature focuses more on the sphere of politics and also on the problem of evil, but as it applies to the nation.

The Social Matrix of a Genre (or Mode) Does Not Dictate Its Later Instantiations

When biblical scholars view genres as functioning systemically, this avoids the erroneous assumption that the social matrix of a genre determines its later instantiations. An example of the faultiness of this thinking is the genre of blues guitar music.[3] The social matrix of the blues has little if any relation to its modern implementation. Originally, this style of music arose in the Reconstructionist period after the Civil War among African Americans. It expressed the negative emotions about the impoverished and dire circumstances of their lives in the South, even though they were technically free. The music conveyed the period's harshness and brutality and yet their attempt to deal with it as best they could. Today, the blues is a multimillion dollar industry that has been coopted by whites such as Eric Clapton and the Rolling Stones, whose life experiences are nothing like that of the original producers of this genre. Thus, fans of Eric Clapton would be wrong to think he embodies the experience of Reconstructionist-era African Americans. Another example is Amy Winehouse, the famous Jewish blues artist, whose style of singing is known as "blue-eyed soul" because she was not African American. Instead of dying of hardship and poverty, she died of a drug overdose and the effects of a hyper-privileged lifestyle. Yet the genres she engaged—blues, jazz, and soul—all originated among the former slaves in America. Winehouse's songs express her romantic conflicts and struggles with drug addiction rather than the hardships of the Reconstructionist period. So, the form or genre is the same even if the content is different. Conflating her genre with the experiences of Reconstructionist African Americans is wrongheaded because of the vast differences between their respective social contexts.

As for the biblical wisdom literature, the various sapiential genres that are found within it may go back originally to folk genres, like folk proverbs, taught by parents and grandparents to young children in the Israelite village and also most likely cited in rhetorical situations such as

---

3. See Adam Roberts, *Fredric Jameson* (Routledge Critical Thinkers: Essential Guides for Literary Studies; London: Routledge, 2000), 89.

at the city gate in court cases. Gunkel, in fact, speculated that the original sayings were coined by old men or elders, who sat at the city gate or open squares, sharing them, while the young listened.[4] However, this does not mean that the proverbs we find now in the wisdom literature contain vestiges of their original social matrix or function in the same way. In fact, the proverbs we find in the book of Proverbs, specifically the sentences (the short bicolon sayings found chiefly in Prov 10:1–22:16; chs. 25–29), are not folk proverbs. They are more like epigrams coined by famous persons because the superscriptions in the book, even if unreliable, indicate that these sayings were composed by notable people, like Solomon (1:1; 10:1). Folk proverbs are anonymous. They are the product of the people, passed down from generation to generation. Though the American proverb, "A stitch in time saves nine," is actually a proverb that came from Ben Franklin's *Poor Richard's Almanac*,[5] which he took from a collection of British proverbs, most Americans are unaware of this. As far as they are concerned, it is a typical folk proverb, as it functions like one, being unassociated with Franklin.

Other evidence that the sentences in Proverbs are not anonymous folk proverbs comes from the phenomenon known as "twice-told proverbs," involving 223 verses or 24 percent of its total verses.[6] These are cola or sometimes bicola that are repeated or reused in other sentences. Here is an example of a bicolon repeated almost verbatim in another place (italics indicate the differing word choice):

A false witness will not be found blameless,
And he who utters lies will not *escape*. (19:5)[7]

A false witness will not be found blameless,
And he who utters lies will *perish*. (19:9)

4. Hermann Gunkel, "The Literature of Ancient Israel," trans. Armin Siedlecki, in *Relating to the Text: Interdisciplinary and Form-Critical Insights on the Bible* (ed. Timothy Sandoval, Carleen Mandolfo, and Martin J. Buss; JSOTSup 384; London: T&T Clark International, 2003), 69–70.

5. See James N. Green and Peter Stallybrass, "Benjamin Franklin: Writer and Printer: Inventing Poor Richard," The Library Company of Philadelphia. Available online: http://www.librarycompany.org/bfwriter/poor.htm (accessed 9 December 2015).

6. See Knut Martin Heim, *Poetic Imagination in Proverbs: Variant Repetitions and the Nature of Poetry* (BBRSup 4; Winona Lake: Eisenbrauns, 2013), 3.

7. All Hebrew translations are the author's.

Here is an example of a colon from one aphorism repeated in another (italics indicate repetition):

> Blessings are upon the head of the righteous,
> *But the mouth of the wicked conceals violence.* (10:6)

> A living fountain is the mouth of the righteous,
> *But the mouth of the wicked conceals violence.* (10:11)

Both of these examples indicate that many of these aphorisms have been created from the parts of other aphorisms. This kind of creation of new proverbs from the parts of other ones points to a scribal phenomenon whereby scribes who had access to scrolls could easily create new maxims from old ones. It is highly doubtful that any of these proverbs would have been recited much among the common Israelites. These "proverbs" then are more accurately described as epigrams by famous people and not folk proverbs. And if recited orally, they would have been largely confined to coteries of scribes and not disseminated outside such circles.[8]

The content of most of these epigrams indicates this as well. They are very self-evident and banal: be wise, avoid folly, honor your parents. However, their aesthetics and the use of punning and other literary devices makes them aesthetically very sophisticated. In fact, their structure is such that Robert Alter has described the book of Proverbs as the "poetry of wit."[9] Thus, the pretty package these epigrams come in more than compensates for any banality. Their form would have piqued the interest of young scribes who would rather have been doing other things than studying. This points then to an academic, not colloquial, setting for their intended usage.

The same can be said for Sumerian "proverb" collections. They were recited or copied as scribal exercises to teach both the rudimental elements of Sumerian and also for enculturating apprentice scribes, especially regarding morality and cultural mores. Round tablets have been found by archaeologists with lexical lists on one side and matching

---

8. Cf. Gunkel, "Literature of Ancient Israel," 70; David M. Carr believes this phenomenon points to the scribal use of memory ("Orality, Textuality, *and* Memory: The State of Biblical Studies," in *Contextualizing Israel's Sacred Writings: Ancient Literacy, Orality, and Literary Production* [ed. Brian B. Schmidt; AIL 22; Atlanta: SBL Press, 2015], 166). But this still demonstrates that these proverbs are a scribal product.

9. Robert Alter, *The Art of Biblical Poetry* (New York: Basic, 1985), 163.

proverbs on the other.[10] The collections also functioned as a source for rhetorical phrases used in debates.[11] Bendt Alster maintains that these "proverbs" had folk origins, though he notes that they are politically conservative and do not represent the perspective of the poor.[12] However, Niek Veldhuis, who reviews Alster's work, believes one should stick with the evidence and prefers to avoid trying to speculate on the social matrices of these "proverbs" and focuses instead on how they were used in schools to educate scribal apprentices.[13] Veldhuis points out that in the Old Babylonian period young scribes at Nippur were trained in two phases.[14] In the first phase students copied lexical texts; this activity imparted the writing system and introduced Sumerian vocabulary. At the end of the first phase, tablets with "proverbs" were used, and their contents prepared students for studying Sumerian in the second phase, which involved the actual reading of literature.

Even if we could trace the origins of the epigrams in Proverbs to a folk setting, that would not change the fact that as they stand they represent the product of an elite group of sages or scribes, and thus are a literary product used for pedagogical purposes. And even if the sentences in Proverbs should have originally a folk setting, that does not mean they still carry any traces of it with them.

It is likewise with prophetic literature. It is important to make a distinction between prophets and what could be called prophetic scribes or scribes who might have specialized in composing prophetic literature. Also, it is important to distinguish between the original oracles of prophets and those people who wrote them down, putting them in good literary form, no doubt. As Claus Westermann points out, the speeches of the writing prophets *"are completely literary formations."*[15] So who created the phenomenon of literary prophecy? Not likely the prophets. We can only speculate, but these had to be persons who had received advanced scribal training, like Baruch, who records Jeremiah's prophecies (Jer 36:10). He also has access to the royal scribal chamber, which

10. Bendt Alster, *Proverbs of Ancient Sumer: The World's Earliest Proverb Collection* (2 vols.; Bethesda: CDL Press, 1997), 1:xviii.

11. Ibid., 1:xix.

12. Ibid., 1:xiii, xxiii.

13. Niek Veldhuis, "Sumerian Proverbs in Their Curricular Context," *JAOS* 120 (2000): 383.

14. Ibid., 383–87.

15. Claus Westermann, *The Basic Forms of Prophetic Speech* (trans. Hugh Clayton White; Louisville: Westminster John Knox, 1991), 172.

means he was known by fellow scribes. Did Baruch simply transcribes these oracles, or did he place them in good literary form, with parallelism, the main feature of Israelite poetry? Or did Jeremiah originally proclaim his oracles in poetry? I would suggest the former, though again, we have no evidence. At any rate, what is important to point out here is that with literary prophecy we not only have a new *Sitz im Leben*, we also have a *Sitz im Literatur*, both distinct from the oral prophecies!

Thus, whether we are speaking of the wisdom or prophetic traditions, it is important to distinguish between oral and literary forms and, likewise, the oral and literary *Sitze im Leben*. There is no necessary or even direct correlation between the early and/or oral forms of wisdom or prophecy and the later literary versions of them. They are certainly related but represent different products and reflect different social settings that need to be clearly distinguished.

Genres Are Rarely the Controlled Domain of Certain Groups

It is true that certain genres are utilized only within a strict domain, such as the deposition used during the discovery process of legal cases. This genre is a truly professional one that can only be actuated authentically by a lawyer and by none other. But even if one would never do a deposition in formal settings, one might do something similar outside a legal setting. While the rest of us are not lawyers, we know about this particular genre because of personal experience or due to cable shows that might portray lawyers. Thus, though the deposition is technically a private and professional genre, it has disseminated to the wider public and can even be imitated by non-lawyers, like actors, for entertainment. Basically, once a genre is created and diffuses throughout a culture, anyone who has the capability can choose to employ it for various purposes, i.e., it takes on a life of its own. This tendency of diffusion is also demonstrated by the example of blues guitar music mentioned earlier.

In the same way, there is no evidence for groups of prophets who controlled the production of prophetic literature or groups of sages who controlled the production of wisdom literature. Rather, both of these kinds of literature were "controlled" by high-ranking scribes. Basically, anyone with enough scribal training could theoretically compose in any respective genre or mode of literature. The ancient Near Eastern archaeological evidence from Mesopotamia, Anatolia, Syria, and Egypt demonstrates that scribes read the same kinds of literature in their training: legal, mythological, historical, liturgical, divinatory and prophetic, erotic, wisdom literature, as well as non-literature such as models for writing letters and contracts.[16] They also studied mathematics, metrology and surveying, and often music. Thus, from a scribal standpoint, wisdom literature is but one of many modes of literature and academic disciplines that young scribes needed to learn in order to function in various roles as administrators, officials, and business persons. The same would be true for divinatory or prophetic literature.

But the reality is that unlike in our own modern world, only a few people in ancient Israel could actually read or compose this kind of sophisticated literature.[17] In the ancient Near East, scribes were essentially the only persons who could both read and write in the native tongue of their people. They were also often bi- or tri-literate, due to assuming the role of messengers or ambassadors. Other literati, such as some priests, could read Hebrew literature as well, but they would have had to receive scribal training to do this. It is possible that some high-ranking soldiers could read and write letters, as may be indicated in the Lachish Letter #3, but this is to be distinguished from high literacy that involves the composition and reading of actual literature. And all who received scribal training, either to serve later as scribes or in other high-level positions, received the same elementary training. One could specialize in the later stages of the training, say, in Mesopotamia, in divination/exorcism or medicine. Thus, all the literati, which consisted mainly of scribes, could read and perhaps write in all the major literary genres represented by their respective cultures.

While prophetic literature is found among Mesopotamian cuneiform tablets, the bulk of its divinatory literature was omen texts. It should be

16. On Israelite scribes within the ancient Near Eastern context, see the essays in Brian B. Schmidt, ed., *Contextualizng Israel's Sacred Writings: Ancient Literacy, Orality, and Literary Production* (AIL 22; Atlanta: SBL, 2015); Philip R. Davies and Thomas Römer, eds., *Writing the Bible: Scribes, Scribalism and Script* (Bible World; London: Routledge, 2013); Mark Sneed, *The Social World of the Sages: An Introduction to Israelite and Jewish Wisdom Literature* (Minneapolis: Augsburg Fortress, 2015); cf. also David Carr, *Writing on the Tablet of the Heart: Origins of Scripture and Literature* (Oxford: Oxford University Press, 2005); Karel van der Toorn, *Scribal Culture and the Making of the Hebrew Bible* (Cambridge, MA: Harvard University Press, 2007); William M. Schniedewind, *How the Bible Became a Book: The Textualization of Ancient Israel* (Cambridge: Cambridge University Press, 2010); cf. the LBA Syrian scribes: Yoram Cohen, *The Scribes and Scholars of the City of Emar in the Late Bronze Age* (HSS 59; Winona Lake: Eisenbrauns, 2009); cf. also idem, *Wisdom from the Late Bronze Age* (WAW 29; Atlanta: SBL, 2013).

17. See Christopher A. Rollston, *Writing and Literacy in the World of Ancient Israel: Epigraphic Evidence from the Iron Age* (ABS 11; Atlanta: SBL, 2010).

pointed out that prophecy is technically a form of inspired divination
versus deductive divination, where scribes learned to interpret various
types of omens for predicting the future and discerning the will of the
gods. The Mesopotamians believed the gods placed signs within the
cosmos, which wise diviners could discern and interpret. The role of
Israelite prophets was the same, except that God did not primarily reveal
his will through signs but more directly in visions during a dream or when
the prophet was awake during the day, though the Hebrew God frequently
revealed his will through dreams that needed interpreting (e.g., Joseph
[Gen 40] and Daniel [Dan 1–6]), a form of deductive divination called
oneiromancy.

It is interesting that Westermann has demonstrated that the oracles
recorded in the Deuteronomistic History and the prophetic books reflect
the genres used by the world of communication, the messengers who
repeated the words of those who sent them.[18] The messenger formula,
"Thus, says the Lord," is their trademark. The prophets or their scribes
also drew on the world of forensics, with the "covenant lawsuit" as a
classic example.[19] And Ezekiel employs "sapiential" genres like parables
(משלים; chs. 17, 19). If the prophets and their scribes have coopted genres
from various spheres of life, can one really speak of pure "prophetic"
genres at all?

Prophetic literature was apparently important to ancient Near Eastern
royalty, including Israel. During the eighteenth century BCE, prophetic
letters were preserved at Mari which record both accounts of the oracular
proclamation and the oracles themselves. In one, the prophet requests a
scribe to come and record his oracle so that it may be read to the king.[20]
Some of these oracles criticize the king, though most are oracles of salvation.[21] So, why would the Israelite kings and his scribes of, say, the eighth
century, not have been interested in the prophetic literature composed
during this time, even if critical of the king?[22] Even if objectionable,
recorded prophecy provided keys to discerning the will of the deity.

18. Westermann, *Prophetic Speech*, 98–128.

19. See Herbert B. Huffmon, "The Covenant Lawsuit in the Prophets," *JBL* 78
(1959): 285–95.

20. See Herbert B. Huffmon, "Prophecy in the Mari Archives," in *Prophecy and
Prophets: The Diversity of Contemporary Issues in Scholarship* (ed. Yehoshua Gitay;
SemeiaSt; Atlanta: Scholars Press, 1997), 11.

21. Ibid., 18; cf. Westermann, *Prophetic Speech*, 127.

22. Contra Annette Schellenberg, who argues that the prophetic literature is
not likely to have been written by royal scribes because they would have been too
loyal to the king ("A 'Lying Pen of the Scribes' [Jer 8:8]? Orality and Writing in

The persons who put the prophetic oracles in their literary form do not themselves claim revelatory authority; the oracles themselves make this claim. These authors—they are more than redactors—are the ones who refer to the prophet in the third person and have collected his oracles to pass on to future generations. This is an important distinction. Baruch never claims to be a prophet, though he is rightly a prophetic scribe who preserved the words of his guru. Similarly, David Petersen refers to the anonymous composers of prophetic accounts in the Deuteronomistic History as "prophetic historians."[23]

Thus, it makes sense that Israelite scribes, even royal ones, would have been interested in prophecy, just as Mesopotamian scribes were keen on omens. When Ben Sira speaks of the love scribes had for studying simultaneously prophetic literature and wisdom literature, this was no new scribal interest:

> The wisdom of the scribe depends on the opportunity of leisure; only the one who has little business can become wise... He seeks out the wisdom of all the ancients, and is concerned with prophecies; he preserves the sayings of the famous and penetrates the subtleties of parables; he seeks out the hidden meaning of proverbs and is at home with the obscurities of parables. (38:24; 39:1–3; NRSV)

This reflects the typical ancient Near Eastern interest that all scribes had in divination and prophecy.

And who composed the wisdom literature? Again we need to distinguish between the typical political sage and those who composed wisdom literature. Jeremiah 18:18 refers to sages (חכם) whose trademark is the "counsel" (עצה). These sages are either royal elders or courtiers who advised the king about political matters. The "sages" who composed the wisdom literature were sophisticated authors who assume or are given the name "sage" (e.g., Prov 22:17; Eccl 12:9) because they compose literature devoted to wisdom (משלים). This title lends a certain degree of authority to their writings that they might not otherwise have, in contrast to proverbs by Solomon (Prov 1:1; 10:1) or other famous people (Prov 30:1; 31:1). While a courtier could be both wise in the political realm and a composer of sapiential literature (e.g., Ahikar is at least portrayed as

the Formation of the Prophetic Books," in *The Interface of Orality and Writing: Speaking, Seeing, Writing in the Shaping of New* Genres (ed. Annette Weissenrieder and Robert B. Coote; Tübingen: Mohr Siebeck, 2010), 285–309.

23. David Petersen, "Rethinking the Nature of Prophetic Literature," in Gitay, ed., *Prophecy and Prophets*, 29.

assuming both roles), this would be unusual. In fact, courtiers were often illiterate. Ahithophel, who served David as a courtier, is contrasted with Jonathan, David's uncle, who was both a scribe and counselor (1 Chr 27:32–33). The "sages" or scribes who composed the wisdom literature were no doubt conversant in many modes of literature and genres and could have certainly composed "prophetic" oracles.

There Is No Evidence for Separate Academic Schools for Priests, Prophets, and Sages

Of course, there are references to prophetic "schools" or, literally, the "sons of the prophets" (e.g., 2 Kgs 6:1). What these "schools" are meant to describe is open to debate. The Reformers saw them as guilds or fraternities of prophets and their followers.[24] Another suggestion is that they were loyal adherents to a spiritual father.[25] But the evidence is not clear on what these "schools" consisted of. Whatever the nature of the "schools," none of the prophetic roles involved would have necessarily required literacy. It appears that Elijah and Elisha were illiterate prophets who worked often among the common people. Thomas Overholt has compared this style of prophecy with shamanism because these prophets were primarily miracle workers and healers who served the needs of the masses.[26] Shamanism obviously does not require literacy. But even the so-called writing prophets were not necessarily literate, at least not to the extent of composing high literature: Jeremiah seems very dependent on his scribe, Baruch.

Some biblical scholars have proposed the existence of three distinct scribal schools, one each for priests, prophets, and sages.[27] The inference is that each studied literature appropriate for each group. Again, Jer 18:18 is usually cited in support of this supposition: "And they said, 'Come and let us scheme concerning Jeremiah plans, for instruction will not perish from the priest, nor counsel from the wise, nor the word from the prophet.'" The usual explanation is that priests would study the instruction or "Torah," i.e., the legal material, though much of this is

24. See Jack P. Lewis, "A Prophet's Son (Amos 7:14) Reconsidered," *RQ* 49, no. 4 (2007): 237–38.

25. James G. Williams, "The Prophetic 'Father': A Brief Explanation of the Term 'Sons of the Prophets,'" *JBL* 98 (1979): 344–48.

26. Thomas Overholt, *Cultural Anthropology and the Old Testament* (Guides to Biblical Scholarship; Minneapolis: Fortress, 1996).

27. E.g., Michael Fishbane, *Biblical Interpretation in Ancient Israel* (rev. ed.; Oxford: Clarendon, 1988), 78–79.

not specifically "priestly" in nature. Prophets would study the "word" of the Lord, and sages would study "counsel," or wisdom literature. Robert Gordis has even suggested that there were two distinct wisdom schools, one for conservative sages as represented by traditional wisdom, like in Proverbs, and the other was more radical, with one of its teachers the venerable Qohelet himself![28]

The use of Jer 18:18 to suggest three different professional groups who studied distinctive curricula and employed distinctive genres is dubious because this verse does not necessarily refer to the authors of the respective types of literature.[29] But it also represents an anachronistic view of how different professional groups might disagree with each other. It projects a Greco-Roman pattern of factional political parties (e.g., Pharisees, Sadducees, Essenes, and Zealots) onto an ancient Near Eastern context. Or it may involve a similar projection of the differing Greek philosophical schools, like the Hedonists or Epicureans.[30] However, this is not the world of ancient Near Eastern scribalism, where the only literate persons were essentially scribes or those with scribal training. If the empires of Egypt and those in Mesopotamia did not have splintered or segregated scribal schools until the more developed stages, why would such a tiny state such as Israel have three? It does not make good economic or practical sense to have so many distinctive scribal schools when it could have been done by one prototype found in a few locations. And it should be pointed out here that, like prophets, many priests would have had no need for scribal schooling because their roles did not call for literacy. Many of the Levites, who did the menial tasks, like cleaning up after a sacrifice, would not have needed to be literate, and this was true probably for most of the Zadokites. One learns ritual primarily through practice, though there had to be some literate priests who composed the book of Leviticus.

The Sapiential and Prophetic Epistemologies Were Not So Different

It is a misnomer to claim that because the wisdom writers rarely appeal to revelation in their teaching—and one must limit this to the Jewish canonical wisdom books—then that means they rejected revelation as a

---

28. Robert Gordis, *Koheleth—The Man and His World: A Study of Ecclesiastes* (New York: Schocken, 1968), 28, 77.

29. See Mark Sneed, "Is the 'Wisdom Tradition' a Tradition?" *CBQ* 73 (2011): 60–61.

30. Per a private conversation with Michael V. Fox.

means of knowledge. The reality is that the sages accepted all forms of knowledge as valid because they believed that all wisdom and knowledge ultimately came from God (Prov 2:6). The sages who composed Proverbs did not find revelation "unnecessary," as Michael Fox has claimed.[31] Neither is Fox's claim that Qohelet was an empiricist tenable,[32] which James Crenshaw has effectively demonstrated.[33] However, Crenshaw is wrong when he claims that the Israelite sages were non-Yahwistic and their tradition essentially non-revelatory.[34] It is very clear that Crenshaw considers the few instances of revelation found in the Jewish wisdom literature anomalies. He believes that the silence of this literature about the main tenets of the Jewish faith until the days of Ben Sira shows that the sages were not interested in these matters.[35]

However, not only does this invoke the shaky argument from silence, it is not true. The composer of Prov 1–9 imitated the language of Deuteronomy long before the days of Ben Sira (cf. Prov 3:3; 7:3; 6:20–23 with Deut 6:6–9). And we can mention several allusions to revelation in the Jewish canonical wisdom literature apart from these chapters. There are two sapiential oracles in Prov 30 and 31, one from Agur and the other from king Lemuel's mother. The word משא in each case should not be translated as "Massa," an Arab territory, but as an "oracle," from נשא, "to lift up" (a request for a divine response).[36] Apparently the last testimony of someone about to die, here Agur, was viewed as oracular.[37] Also, Job receives a frightening vision during the night (ch. 4). The divine speeches in the book of Job are certainly by definition revelation. In fact, this is what troubled Crenshaw concerning the identification of Job as wisdom

31. Michael V. Fox, "The Epistemology of the Book of Proverbs," *JBL* 126 (2007): 682.

32. Michael V. Fox, "The Innerstructure of Qoheleth's Thought," in *Qohelet in the Context of Wisdom* (ed. A. Schoors; BETL 136; Leuven: Leuven University Press and Uitgeveru Peeters, 1998), 225–38.

33. James L. Crenshaw, "Qoheleth's Understanding of Intellectual Inquiry," in Schoors, ed., *Qohelet in the Context of Wisdom*, 205–24.

34. James L. Crenshaw, *Old Testament Wisdom: An Introduction* (3rd ed.; Louisville: Westminster John Knox, 2010), 243–47.

35. Ibid., 216–17, 225.

36. See Mark Sneed, "Inspired Sages: *Massa'* and the Confluence of Wisdom and Prophecy," in *Schreiber als Weisheitslehrer und Propheten: Prophetische une weisheitliche Traditionen in dem Wiesheitsschriften une im Zwölfprophetenbuch* (BZAW 496; Berlin: de Gruyter, forthcoming).

37. Duane F. Watson, "The Second Letter of Peter: Introduction, Commentary, and Reflections," in *Hebrews; James; 1 & 2 Peter; 1, 2, & 3 John; Jude; Revelation*, in *New Interpreter's Bible* (ed. Leander Keck; Nashville: Abingdon, 2001), 12:327.

literature.[38] And Qohelet alludes to Deut 23:21–22 as authoritative in 5:4–5 (Eng.), concerning the making and keeping of vows. Though Qohelet does not advocate zealous keeping of the Torah, he certainly does not advise ignoring it.

The reality is that all the Israelites, including wisdom writers and the composers of the prophetic literature and including royal courtiers and prophets, shared the same supernatural worldview and epistemology. This worldview might have differed slightly according to social class, but it was still largely the same. The wisdom writers were open to supernatural revelation through prophecy; they just did not usually claim oracular charisma themselves. They did, however, believe that their sapiential literature was just as authoritative as the prophetic literature, and just as inspired, though in a different way.[39] Different factions of political alliances between scribes, priests, prophets, kings, and other leaders may have differed in terms of theology and praxis, but not worldview.[40]

Conclusion

What appears to be "influences" between two distinct corpora of wisdom and prophetic literature is in reality merely the mixing of genres or modes of literature by the scribes who studied and composed both types of literature. In other words, what appears to be influence between these two distinct types of literature is merely the synaptic reflexes of scribes whose patterning of prophetic and wisdom genres/modes existed in separate sections of their brains, not in separate social traditions. Thus, the prophetic and wisdom traditions are nothing more than literary traditions, which do not require separate groups of specialists to compose in them.[41]

---

38. James L. Crenshaw, "Prolegomenon," in *Studies in Ancient Israelite Wisdom* (ed. James L. Crenshaw; Library of Biblical Studies; New York: Ktav, 1976), 5; Similarly, Katharine J. Dell also rejects the book as wisdom literature, not because it contains prophetic elements, but because the book is parasitical regarding genres (*The Book of Job as Sceptical Literature* [BZAW 197; Berlin: de Gruyter, 1991], 147).

39. See Brian Kovacs, "Is There a Class-Ethic in Proverbs?" in *Essays in Old Testament Ethics* (ed. James L. Crenshaw and John T. Wills; New York: Ktav, 1974), 184–85.

40. Patricia Dutcher-Walls, "The Social Location of the Deuteronomists: A Sociological Study of Factional Politics in the Late Pre-exilic Judah," *JSOT* 52 (1991): 77–94.

41. On the question of whether the wisdom tradition was really a "tradition" see the essays in Mark Sneed, ed., *Was There a Wisdom Tradition? New Prospects in Israelite Wisdom Studies* (AIL 23; Atlanta: SBL, 2015).

Those trained in the art and lore of scribalism would have been more than competent to engage in the production of both types of literature. The question of influence between prophetic and wisdom texts is therefore banal and moot, and other more significant and pressing questions, such as how the differing conventional worlds of each type of literature rhetorically functioned to persuade scribes and others to accept various theological and ideological positions, need to be addressed.

Of course, these two "traditions" may have arisen in separate social contexts, wisdom as one kind of epistemological tradition, which included both non-revelatory and revelatory elements, though primarily the former, and prophecy as another, with also both revelatory and non-revelatory elements, though primarily the former. But there was much overlap and mainly difference in emphasis. From this standpoint, these traditions no doubt could be referred to as "influencing" each other, perhaps. But from the above literary standpoint, there is no actual influence, only the engagement of particular modes of literature by the minds and hands of scribes.

OVERLAP? INFLUENCE? ALLUSION? THE IMPORTANCE OF ASKING THE RIGHT QUESTIONS*

Stuart Weeks

In *The Hitchhiker's Guide to the Galaxy* by Douglas Adams (which is a book better known, perhaps, to British than to American readers),[1] a race of hyper-intelligent, pan-dimensional beings build a computer to calculate the answer to the Ultimate Question of Life, the Universe, and Everything. This answer turns out, after several million years of processing, to be "42," an anti-climax which requires those same beings to construct a new, more powerful computer that can meet the challenge of formulating a proper question. I find myself reminded of this story every time the issue of "wisdom influence" is raised because that issue seems so often to present answers that are looking for a good question—a problem that is encapsulated by the very expression "wisdom influence." In Adams's book, the new, more powerful computer is destroyed prematurely, just before generating the question, and two of the aliens responsible for supervising it are forced to invent one that might sound plausible. "That's excellent!" says one of them, about his companion's suggestion, "Sounds very significant without actually tying you down to meaning anything at all." In an area where the most famous study of methodology dwells at length on the definition of "wisdom" but does not once ask what we might mean by "influence," there is surely a danger that the whole idea of "wisdom influence" might likewise sound very significant without actually tying us down to meaning anything at all.[2]

---

* This paper originated in a response to Russell L. Meek, "Prophet and Sage in Dialogue: History and Methodology" (Wisdom and Prophecy in the Hebrew Bible; Institute for Biblical Research Annual Meeting, Baltimore, 22 November 2013).

1. It was first published as a novel by Pan Books in London in 1979, but this novel was based on a radio series broadcast the previous year by the BBC.

2. James Crenshaw, "Method in Determining Wisdom Influence Upon 'Historical Literature,'" *JBL* 88 (1969): 129–42.

In his study, James Crenshaw sought to bring a degree of rigor and consistency at a time when the quest for "wisdom influence" had led to a plethora of different proposals, and when the whole biblical corpus seemed likely to be implicated. Particular texts were linked to wisdom not just on formal grounds, such as the use of aphorisms or of particular terms, and not just on ideological grounds, such as an interest in providence or creation, but for reasons that ranged from some circumstantial connection with governance or with particular places, through to a perception that they were in some sense didactic. If much of this reflected the common characterization of wisdom literature as the product of scribal schools, much also reflected an assumption that wisdom extended into areas such as folk wisdom or manticism while remaining a meaningfully coherent tradition. The quest brought together, therefore, not only different sorts of connection but also different sorts of wisdom.[3] What made such connections worthy of notice at the time, and more apparently remarkable than, say, the influence of Deuteronomy on Jeremiah, was the widespread understanding that wisdom literature was supposed to have emerged from circles that were distinct from, and perhaps even antagonistic toward, those circles that produced the prophetic or narrative texts and that were now taken to show "wisdom influence."[4] Correspondingly, the quest for such influence was inextricably linked to the increasing isolation of wisdom literature within the canon during the last century, which problematized any connections between that and other literature—this may explain why scholars chose to focus so much on the fact of "influence" and so little on the implications of the term.

Some decades later, there is less scholarly emphasis on the historical distinctiveness of wisdom literature and a greater inclination to think in terms of a broader literate class responsible for all our literature rather than an assortment of different, rival groups and circles. The very notion of wisdom, moreover, has increasingly been subject to much greater scrutiny, and although it is possible still to encounter confident depictions of a coherent tradition with its own specific ideas and interests, recent work has tended to advocate a much more cautious approach than was typical in the past. I have recently argued myself that we should, at least, try to avoid talking about connections with "wisdom" when what we are actually referring to are connections with specific books or phenomena:

3. Most of the main proposals up to that point are conveniently surveyed in Donn F. Morgan, *Wisdom in the Old Testament Traditions* (Atlanta: John Knox; Oxford: Blackwell, 1981).
4. Perhaps the clearest statement of this position is in William McKane, *Prophets and Wise Men* (London: SCM, 1965).

it is generally unhelpful to evoke some broad concept of wisdom in order to suggest, say, that something resembling material in Proverbs must therefore be related to Job, or to forge some link between the wisdom books and apocalypticism via notions of mantic wisdom. Whatever one's position on such issues, however, it is undeniably true that the term "wisdom" has to be used with much greater care now, and that this change in itself should discourage casual references to "wisdom influence."[5]

Arguably, indeed, that expression "wisdom influence" is itself a product of the same earlier attitudes, and the use of it should be deprecated altogether. On the one hand, its very vagueness about the nature of the relationship between wisdom and other materials allows it to aggregate a wide range of studies that have made various, distinct suggestions and thereby to imply that they share more in common than was ever actually the case. On the other, it embodies a very specific idea about the direction of travel in that relationship, which excludes other studies that propose, say, the dependence on psalmic traditions of certain materials in Job or the use of Deuteronomy by Prov 1–9.[6] If we use such terminology, or imply through its use that "wisdom influence" is a distinct phenomenon, then we run the risk not only of prejudging the character and causes of resemblances between wisdom and other texts but also of isolating those resemblances from more general questions about links between any or all biblical texts. The concept of "wisdom influence" succeeds, therefore, in affirming particular views about the otherness of wisdom and the corresponding specialness of links with wisdom, but at the same time as it promotes their distinctiveness, it also blurs the distinctions between them and ultimately tells us nothing useful.

If we let go of the old assumptions and vocabulary, then we need a different way to talk about our perceptions of common ground between different materials. Even the use of a more general terminology, however, can hide traps for the unwary. In particular, the growing scholarly inclination to think in terms more of a literary culture in early Judaism than of competing schools of thought has brought with it a renewed emphasis on the idea of "allusion," and this idea has been prominent in discussions of intertextuality by biblical scholars. Allusion, however, is a phenomenon or device that can have many different implications. I doubt, for instance,

---

5. The present state of the question is reflected well in Mark R. Sneed, ed., *Was There a Wisdom Tradition? New Prospects in Israelite Wisdom Studies* (AIL 23; Atlanta: SBL, 2015).

6. Such as Katharine J. Dell, *The Book of Job as Sceptical Literature* (BZAW 197; Berlin: de Gruyter, 1991); A. Robert, "Les Attaches Littéraires Bibliques de Prov. I–IX," *RB* 43 (1934): 42–68, 172–204, 374–84; *RB* 44 (1935): 344–65, 502–25.

that we can begin to understand the key themes of Prov 1–9 without recognizing its deliberate use of Deuteronomic and Deuteronomistic motifs, and feel confident that the author of that work anticipated such recognition on the part of his readers.[7] In such cases allusion may create an important bridge between two works. On the other hand, I could make no less deliberate an allusion by saying, for example, that the 1960s were the best of times and the worst of times for biblical scholarship. You would be unwise to assume if I did so, however, either that my views had been shaped extensively by Charles Dickens or that I wished to understand biblical scholarship in terms of *A Tale of Two Cities*—a book that I must confess to never having read. An allusion may act as a bridge, but it may also reflect nothing more than the broader influence of a text on its culture or even the general adoption of a pretty phrase: we all know that "procrastination is the thief of time," but how many of us know the rest of Young's "Night-Thoughts"? It is not always easy to establish the presence of an allusion, and when we do, it can be very difficult to determine which text is citing the other, or whether both depend on some other source. Even if we manage all that, however, the fact of an allusion does not in itself establish the significance of that allusion, and is at best a datum for which we need to account in our reading alongside other data.[8]

7. See Stuart Weeks, *Instruction and Imagery in Proverbs 1–9* (Oxford: Oxford University Press, 2007).

8. "Allusion" has, naturally, attracted the interest of literary critics and theorists in other disciplines. Amongst the studies that seek to examine the phenomenon in general, James H. Coombs, "Allusion Defined and Explained," *Poetics* 13 (1984): 475–88, attempts an all-embracing definition that emphasizes the importance of "implication" alongside "reference" but leaves open the nature of the implication. Michael Leddy, "Limits of Allusion," *British Journal of Aesthetics* 32 (1992): 110–22, in contrast, sees considerable diversity and examines the difficulty of the terminology through attempts to apply it to music and art. After surveying a wide range of opinions, William Irwin, "What Is an Allusion?," *The Journal of Aesthetics and Art Criticism* 59 (2001): 287–97, focuses upon the issue of authorial intent as a necessary component of allusion but examines also the phenomenon of accidental associations in which readers find allusions that were not intended. Although put in rather different terms and subsumed within an attempt to establish a typology, this is a central interest also in Carmela Perri, "On Alluding," *Poetics* 7 (1978): 289–307. Perri understands allusion as a performance that requires certain conditions to be met if it is to work, and the first of these is that "the alluding author and his audience share the same language and cultural tradition" (p. 300)—a pre-condition, of course, that suggests modern readers will never be able to read biblical allusions in the way that they were intended to be read even if they are capable of distinguishing genuine allusions from accidental associations.

There is a broader issue here, tied up with concepts like the dialogism of Bakhtin or the intertextuality of Kristeva: in a literate culture, no text is an island, and the reading and composition of texts is necessarily shaped by experience of other texts. Since it is commonly believed, furthermore, that ancient scribes memorized texts in order that they could enrich their own language and demonstrate their own education, just as much later generations of writers would pepper their discourse with allusions to classical literature (or to Dickens), it is important that we do not understand even apparently specific references always to represent the conscious evocation of another text: as with broader resemblances, they may reflect no more than a cultural heritage shared across the literate élite. To take some examples from within the wisdom literature, it has been observed widely that Ecclesiastes seems to draw on Deuteronomy, and perhaps on *Gilgamesh* also, although it shows no interest in the broader themes or ideas of either work.[9] Commentators less frequently note its use of expressions that are more closely associated with Song of Songs and Lamentations, but these likewise seem to reflect no broader dependence: they are most plausibly explained rather as an evocation of style or genre, poetically aligning the exploited with those dispossessed by war and, perhaps humorously, describing Qohelet's intellectual quest in terms of a lover's desperate search.[10] Such markers can operate at a level that is more linguistic than consciously ideological, but even when authors deploy genre more deliberately and conspicuously, it may be in

---

9. Amongst more recent studies, see Bernard M. Levinson, *A More Perfect Torah: At the Intersection of Philology and Hermeneutics in Deuteronomy and the Temple scroll* (Critical Studies in the Hebrew Bible 1; Winona Lake: Eisenbrauns, 2013); Nili Samet, "The Gilgamesh Epic and the Book of Qohelet: A New Look," *Bib* 96 (2015): 375–90.

10. Although other links with Lamentations have sometimes been suggested, the clearest verbal resemblances are between Eccl 4:1 and Lam 1:2, 9, 16, 17, 21. Similar language and motifs are to be found also in Isa 22:1 (cf. 54:11) and Ps 69:21. Of the verbal links link between 7:28 and Song 3:1–4, Seow suggests, rightly I think, that "the motif of seeking and not finding belongs to the language of a lover's pursuit"; see Choon Leong Seow, *Ecclesiastes: A New Translation with Introduction and Commentary* (AB 18C; New York: Doubleday, 1997), 264. More generally, see Brittany Melton, "Solomon, Wisdom, and Love: Intertextual Resonance Between Ecclesiastes and Song of Songs," in *Reading Ecclesiastes Intertextually* (ed. Katharine J. Dell and Will Kynes; LHBOTS 587; London: Bloomsbury T&T Clark, 2014), 130–41. In neither case does it seem likely that we are dealing with a specific reference to the other book, and it is more probable that Qohelet is simply using language that would have been more familiar in other literary or musical contexts in order to evoke those contexts.

order only to evoke particular associations or to set a particular tone. We see something of this, perhaps, when psalmists borrow the style of instructions or of sentence literature, probably in order to borrow the authority or perspective associated with those styles[11]—although there may be a more parodic or satirical edge when Jonah or Job conversely borrows the language and style of psalms.[12]

The idea of a common literary culture does not imply the existence of a common outlook: people who share such a culture do not all have to agree with each other about everything, and marks of style and genre can be deployed without writers thereby asserting any particular viewpoint or their affiliation to any particular school of thought. That does not exclude the possibility, however, that those writers may betray such affiliations through their choices or may deliberately use allusion to proclaim them. In some cases, indeed, we may certainly be dealing with the sort of conscious allusion and interpretation that Fishbane has studied in depth.[13] The most significant point, once again, is that the recognition of a link between texts cannot simply by itself tell us the nature of the relationship, but it is also important to recognize that in a literate culture any such relationship may be extremely loose or indirect, even when resemblances seem striking to us. When we encounter such links, they have to be evaluated as part of a much broader consideration of the texts in which we find them and not presumed to be important keys to an understanding of those texts or their background. They are probably not susceptible, moreover, to any particular method of measuring their reality or significance: a slight and subtle evocation of vocabulary may offer as many insights as a direct quotation, if not more, but may fail to clear the bar of any test that we set up. I would be inclined to suggest, for example, that its links with Song of Songs are far more significant for our understanding of Ecclesiastes than its virtual citation of *Gilgamesh*, even if they are far less obvious.

It may be clear from all of this that I see the endless collection of allusions, or attempts to establish a methodology for such collection, as a prime instance of the tail wagging the dog. Rather than keep trying to define what constitutes a "wisdom psalm," for instance, as though this

11. See Stuart Weeks, "The Limits of Form Criticism in the Study of Literature, with Reflections on Psalm 34," in *Biblical Interpretation and Method: Essays in Honour of John Barton* (ed. Katharine J. Dell and Paul Joyce; Oxford: Oxford University Press, 2013), 15–25.

12. See, e.g., Dell, *Job*; John A. Miles Jr., "Laughing at the Bible: Jonah as Parody," *JQR* 65 (1975): 168–81, esp. 173–75.

13. Especially in Michael A. Fishbane, *Biblical Interpretation in Ancient Israel* (Oxford: Clarendon, 1985).

were some single and simple phenomenon that has merely proved difficult to pin down, I think we would do better to ask how styles and expressions associated with wisdom literature function within each individual psalm that employs them—often alongside other interesting links and traits. More broadly, any quest for "wisdom influence," even if it somehow manages to avoid all the other pitfalls outlined above, will always be inclined to separate the fact of allusions out from the purposes of the texts in which they are found. Such suspicions, however, do need to be qualified by a recognition that there is a place for such study, so long as it does not drive all else. One of the most significant obstacles that we face in the exegesis of ancient texts lies in the very area of genre and allusion: we cannot apply to those texts the sort of skills and information that we bring almost unconsciously to the reading of texts from our own time and culture, where choices of style and expression, or sometimes the employment of specific motifs, permit the author to communicate important information about the way in which they intend us to understand what we are reading. Although we shall never be in a position to recognize all such hints, there is potentially much to be learned from sharing and collating the information that we do find in our study of individual texts. I do not doubt, for instance, that the very idea of a "foreign woman" would have had very specific resonances for a Jewish reader, that did not have to be spelled out any more than we have to be told that the black hat in a Western marks a villain.[14] Because it is not spelled out, however, this is a cue that has to be inferred from the portrayal of such women in a variety of texts. It seems likely that, similarly, some of the styles and motifs most commonly associated with the wisdom books would have conveyed other such nuances to readers and that we might begin to identify such nuances were we to go beyond simply identifying them as an alien presence in other works.

Such study can involve a rather microscopic examination of expressions and vocabulary, but it is also important sometimes to think big. Turning finally to the specific issue of links between wisdom and prophetic literature, we find here, in fact, one of the biggest issues of all, even if it has commonly been neglected: the overall presentation of such books. One aspect of this, the emphasis on speech, is shared with a certain amount of other material, both in the Bible and elsewhere in the ancient Near East. A great deal of ancient literature, indeed, is presented in the form of a first-person monologue, contextualized to a greater or

---

14. See Weeks, *Instruction and Imagery*, 129–46; Nancy Nam Hoon Tan, *The "Foreignness" of the Foreign Woman in Proverbs 1–9: A Study of the Origin and Development of a Biblical Motif* (BZAW 381; Berlin: de Gruyter, 2008).

lesser extent by a preface or by narrative elements, and from that point of view there are strong structural similarities between, say, Ecclesiastes and Hosea, in both of which an editorial framework contains a monologue that shifts from first-person memoir through to more miscellaneous units of speech. A more specific issue is associated with this. Since classical times there has been nothing unusual in the fact that books are presented as the work of named authors, and that is why, perhaps, we see nothing odd about the fact that so many biblical books are also described as containing the words of named individuals. In the context of the ancient Near East more generally, however, literature is usually anonymous, and attributions are associated only with specific types of writing—most notably instructions—in which they serve the very particular purpose of contextualizing the content and lending it authority. The biblical wisdom and prophetic books again resemble each other in this respect, however, and in doing so stand out against most other biblical texts.

It is not hard to understand why such compositional elements have received so little attention, especially when scholars have so often been inclined to take them literally and to treat the books as though they were virtual recordings of events. Without going into such vexed questions as, for instance, whether there ever was a teacher called Qohelet or a prophet called Hosea, however, it should at least be acknowledged that the books in which they appear are secondary, literary creations and that they would have been read in terms of existing conventions—as, perhaps, would Deuteronomy, which also adopts the form of a speech by a named speaker.[15]

The question, really, is whether we should apparently complicate matters by approaching them in this way rather than simply accepting the books on their own terms as the preserved words of particular individuals. There are two good reasons, however, to suppose that we should. The first is simply that the study of many other works suggests, in fact, that such a presentation would not most naturally have been understood in such terms: this is not the "natural" reading unless one has been enculturated with the norms of a very different literary tradition, and even then it is not the only reading—*Robinson Crusoe* is just one of many more modern books that present themselves as memoirs written by their protagonists, but nobody is accused of being overly skeptical for reading it as fiction.

---

15. On this issue in prophetic literature, see Stuart Weeks, "Predictive and Prophetic Literature: Can Neferti Help Us Read the Bible?," in *Prophecy and the Prophets in Ancient Israel: Proceedings of the Oxford Old Testament Seminar* (ed. John Day; London: T&T Clark International, 2010), 25–46.

The second arises from some of the books themselves. On the wisdom side, we have good reason to be suspicious of the attribution of work to Solomon in Proverbs, as well as to the mysterious Lemuel and incomprehensible Agur, while we also find attributions to anonymous wise men that suggest the conventional need for an attribution even when no name is available or desired. On the prophetic, Malachi perhaps raises similar issues about anonymous attribution, but it is hardly to be denied, rather differently, that much material is seeking to "borrow" the names of, for instance, Isaiah and Zechariah. More particularly, we find much sophistication and complexity in the use of characters and voices, both in, say, the opacity of the name Qohelet and its relationship with Solomon, and in the mingling of Hosea's voice with that of God—to considerable literary effect.[16]

It is not just the observation of a similarity, therefore, but problems arising from some of the individual texts themselves that might drive us to suppose that we are dealing with literary conventions rather than simple facts here, and the interesting questions around all this lie in the understanding of such conventions by the readers who would initially have received the various books. It is probably true to say, for instance, that in virtually none of the earlier, pre-biblical literature is the character who is represented as the speaker actually the author of the book: most compositions were attributed either pseudonymously to real people or else featured speakers who were fictional from the outset. In post-biblical Jewish literature, of course, we similarly find large numbers of pseudonymous testaments and accounts. Although it is difficult to know whether pseudonymity was always acknowledged, it is at least very probable, in the light of what went before and after, that the original readers of works like Ecclesiastes and Hosea would have anticipated that they were being offered the names not of authors but of protagonists who might be more or less closely modeled on actual, historical individuals. Much more could be said here, but my point is simply that conventions shared by wisdom and prophetic books can potentially, in fact, be very illuminating—so long as we are both willing to recognize them as conventions and to allow that literary techniques and markers of genre may transcend questions of subject matter.

16. See Stuart Weeks, "Whose Words? Qoheleth, Hosea and Attribution in Biblical Literature," in *New Heaven and New Earth: Prophecy and the Millennium: Essays in Honour of Anthony Gelston* (ed. P. J. Harland and C. T. R. Hayward; VTSup 77; Leiden: Brill, 1999), 151–70.

To finish, then, the whole matter of links between wisdom and prophetic books, indeed, the whole issue of links between books more generally, has been complicated in the past by historical assumptions about the relation-ships between authors. More especially, the notion of "wisdom influence" was a very loaded way of trying to address the problem of links that were not supposed to exist. It is possible to go beyond the limitations of that approach, but if we dwell on questions of allusion then we risk simply assembling a collection of decontextualized data, with each apparent allusion potentially representing some quite distinct phenomenon. We need in fact to go also beyond questions about the recognition of links and allusions and to ask what resemblances between our texts might each mean in the context of interpreting those texts. To be sure, this may allow us better in time to understand broader aspects of genre and composition, and perhaps even offer glimpses of historical relationships. If we are looking for real significance, however, we need to start by being clear about what we are looking for and to avoid the pursuit simply of answers in search of questions.

The Relationship of Prophecy and Wisdom in the Ancient Near East

John W. Hilber

Purpose and Definitions

Much has been written on the possible interplay between prophecy and wisdom in the Old Testament, but reflections on the relationship between the two in the broader ancient Near East are difficult to find. This essay is an attempt by one who works primarily with prophecy to cross specialize—always a dangerous undertaking—and to consider examples of literary interplay between the two genres as well as explore the religious thought-world of prophets, diviners, and those who composed or transmitted didactic traditions. For reasons that will become apparent, it is impossible to discuss the relationship between prophecy and wisdom without considering as well the broader revelatory category of technical divination. In special focus, this essay is an attempt to relate both prophecy and wisdom to the broad notion of revelation

The introductory paragraph enters a quagmire of definitional problems. In this essay, "prophecy" is a divine message intuitively received by a human agent with a commission to transmit it to a third party.[1] Although

---

1. Manfred Weippert, "Aspekte Israelitischer Prophetie im Lichte Verwandter Erscheinungen des Alten Orients," in *Ad Bene et Fideliter Seminandum: Festgabe für Karlheinz Deller zum 21. Februar 1987* (ed. Gerlinde Mauer and Ursula Magen; AOAT 220; Kevelaer: Butzon & Bercker, 1988), 289–90; Martti Nissinen, "What Is Prophecy? An Ancient Near Eastern Perspective," in *Inspired Speech: Prophecy in the Ancient Near East (Essays in Honour of Herbert B. Huffmon)* (ed. John Kaltner and Louis Stulman; JSOTSup 378; London: T&T Clark International, 2004), 20. Guinan has proposed: "When a divinity speaks directly by intervening in human cognition and utilizing a selected person as a channel of communication, divination is often associated with revelation or prophecy" (Ann K. Guinan, "A Severed Head Laughed:

prophecy is usually considered a subcategory of divination, the distinction between intuitive and technical revelatory processes is important for the purposes of this study. The boundary between intuitive and technical divination is occasionally thin, as in dream incubation or interpretive discourse associated with binary, oracular inquiry (e.g., extispicy or Egyptian bark movements). But even in these cases one can differentiate the stages between mechanical inducement of the revelatory experience and the intuitive reception of an associated message.[2] The former involves external ritual and objective observation, but the latter involves an internal, subjective experience of receiving a divine message.

While the term "wisdom" enjoys general acceptance as a genre in Old Testament studies and Egyptology, the suitability of this term for Mesopotamian culture and literature has been disputed.[3] Nevertheless, Yoram Cohen's three observations offer reasonable support for identifying what in Old Testament terms is "wisdom" in Mesopotamian tradition.[4] First, scribal exercise tablets and library catalogues group

Stories of Divinatory Interpretation," in *Magic and Divination in the Ancient World* [ed. Leda Ciraolo and Jonathan Seidel; AMD 2; Leiden: Brill, 2002], 18). The helpful emphasis here is on "direct intervention" in human cognition.

2. This distinction has been important in the history of discussion. Recently, Hamori has questioned whether a "sustained category distinction" is possible (Esther J. Hamori, *Women's Divination in Biblical Literature: Prophecy, Necromancy, and Other Arts of Knowledge* [ABRL; New Haven: Yale University Press, 2015], 29–30); however, in my judgment the intuitive/technical distinction remains sound for the reason stated. Further, see Jonathan Stökl, *Prophecy in the Ancient Near East: A Philological and Sociological Comparison* (CHANE 56; Leiden: Brill, 2012), 7–11.

3. Even for Egypt, Schneider argues that "teaching" or "instruction" are better classifications for what is normally construed as "wisdom literature" (Thomas Schneider, "Knowledge and Knowledgeable Persons in Ancient Egypt: Queries and Arguments About an Unsettled Issue," in *Scribes, Sages, and Seers: The Sage in the Eastern Mediterranean World* [ed. Leo G. Perdue; FRLANT 219; Göttingen: Vandenhoeck & Ruprecht, 2008], 45–46). However, the association of some didactic texts with the domain of Maat and magic presses for a broader term, for which "wisdom" still strikes me as serviceable and perhaps more suitable. For a more recent defense of Egyptian wisdom literature (at least "ethical instruction") as a genre, see Michael V. Fox, "Three Theses on Wisdom," in *Was There a Wisdom Tradition? New Prospects in Israelite Wisdom Studies* (ed. Mark R. Sneed; AIL 23; Atlanta: SBL, 2015), 77–88.

4. Yoram Cohen, *Wisdom from the Late Bronze Age* (WAW 29; Atlanta: SBL, 2013), 13–19. See also Paul-Alain Beaulieu, "The Social and Intellectual Setting of Babylonian Wisdom Literature," in *Wisdom Literature in Mesopotamia and Israel* (ed. Richard J. Clifford; SymS 36; Leiden: Brill, 2007), 3. Cohen's observations

together compositions that are comparable to what we could identify as "wisdom" in Old Testament terms. One might call this a genre classification defined by the ancients themselves. Second, key themes found in Old Testament and Egyptian wisdom are present in these texts; both traditional (positive) wisdom on attaining success in life and critical (negative) wisdom that nothing has intrinsic value and therefore one should seize the day. One might add to Cohen's observation here the impressive collection of Akkadian terms offered by Sweet that expresses concepts normally identified with wisdom.[5] Third, at the social-functional level, one might look to the institutional context that produced such literature to find what Cohen calls "common humanistic traditions" of a didactic nature. For this essay, the definition offered by Beaulieu is useable: "The general tenure of wisdom texts is to teach the art of leading a successful life, in harmony with society and the divine will."[6] Although "wisdom in protest" (i.e., negative wisdom) offers a counter voice to positive, didactic texts, it nevertheless tackles the question of skillful living.

The term "divination" denotes acquiring secret knowledge from the divine realm by any means. The product of this acquisition (whether actively sought or passively received or observed) is revelation. What complicates the discussion of the relationship between prophecy and wisdom is that, across the ancient Near East, "wisdom" consists of divinatory skill as well as knowledge of the didactic tradition, and both originate from the divine realm. One primary endeavor of this essay is to examine differences in their ultimate revelatory origins as well as explore some of the complexities of their respective socio-performative functions.

overcome the hesitancy of some to ascribe the term "wisdom" to any corpus of Mesopotamian texts, e.g., W. G. Lambert, *Babylonian Wisdom Literature* (Oxford: Clarendon, 1960), 1–2. Mack-Fischer shares Lambert's doubts in his discussion of Ugaritic literature as well (Loren R. Mack-Fisher, "A Survey and Reading Guide to the Didactic Literature of Ugarit: Prolegomenon to a Study on the Sage," in *The Sage in Israel and the Ancient Near East* [ed. John G. Gammie and Leo G. Perdue; Winona Lake: Eisenbrauns, 1990], 74). See further Cohen, *Wisdom from the Late Bronze Age*, 10–13.

5. Ronald F. G. Sweet, "The Sage in Akkadian Literature," in Gammie and Perdue, eds., *The Sage in Israel*, 45–65.

6. Beaulieu, "The Social and Intellectual Setting of Babylonian Wisdom Literature," 3.

The absence of Hittite literature in this discussion is not for lack of consideration. My personal suspicion is that prophecy existed in this culture, but there is no textual attestation. The "man of god" or "old woman" are possibilities, but what we can determine is that they likely utilized inductive practices rather than spoke from intuitive revelation.[7]

Discernment of prophetic themes in wisdom literature and, correspondingly, identification of wisdom in prophecy, are not easy tasks; nor is there clarity on the nature or means of indirect influence. Old Testament scholarship has wrestled with these challenges for a considerable time, especially the employment of wisdom in prophecy.[8] Methodological agreement and results are quite diverse, and there is no attempt here to settle the question for ancient Near Eastern literature in general. I have worked as best I can with my definitions and with my knowledge of the potentially relevant literature, which is far from comprehensive! My hope is merely to further a conversation on the topic.

Citations, References, or Thematic Links

Wisdom in Prophecy
A Thrice Repeated Proverb (ARM 197, 199, 202). Three Mari letters report prophetic speeches that allude to the same threat facing Zimri-Lim. The three oracles originate from two different prophetic functionaries in three different performance scenarios.[9] Nevertheless, all three utilize the same proverbial expression, "beneath the straw water runs." There is debate as to exactly what this proverb means in the context of the oracles— probably a warning that circumstances are not what they appear on the surface.[10] If this is correct, the citation of the proverb lends authority to the illocutionary force of all three reports that warn the king to be cautious.

---

7. Richard H. Beal, "Hittite Oracles," in Ciraolo and Seidel, eds., *Magic and Divination*, 57–81. This has been confirmed to me in personal communication by Hanna Marcuson, who is currently finishing her dissertation on the Hittite "old woman" at the University of Chicago. For Hittite wisdom, see Gary Beckman, "Proverbs and Proverbial Allusions in Hittite," *JNES* 45 (1986): 19–30.

8. James L. Crenshaw, "Method in Determining Wisdom Influence Upon 'Historical' Literature," *JBL* 88 (1969): 130–35.

9. This is not, as often asserted, a varied repetition of the same oracle. See John W. Hilber, "The Culture of Prophecy and Writing in the Ancient Near East," in *Do Historical Matters Matter to Faith?* (ed. James K. Hoffmeier and Dennis Magary; Wheaton: Crossway, 2012), 225–27.

10. For an alternative interpretation of the proverb, see Jack M. Sasson, "Water Beneath Straw: Adventures of a Prophetic Phrase in the Mari Archives," in *Solving*

Gilgamesh and Adapa in Neo-Assyrian Prophecy (SAA 9.9). The theme of mortality and purposeful living is significant in The Epic of Gilgamesh, and therefore some regard this as an expression of wisdom thought.[11] An allusion to Gilgamesh's search for life appears in prophetic text SAA 9.9 (lines 8–15) in the form of an analogy to the hero, Gilgamesh, in which Ishtar searches the countryside to the point of exhaustion on behalf of Assurbanipal.[12] However, the rhetorical point to which this allusion is employed is limited to a description of physical depletion that highlights her commitment to the king and does not draw on the wisdom motif of elusive immortality that this episode serves in Gilgamesh.[13] Similarly, a possible allusion to the breaking of the South Wind's wing in the story of Adapa (SAA 9.1.1:6; 9.2.3 ii 19)[14] only reinforces the depiction of the forceful nature of the goddess's protection.[15]

Conclusion: In spite of some links between wisdom literature and other genres, such as epics or laments,[16] the integration of wisdom traditions into prophetic material is scarce.

Prophecy in Wisdom
There is little evidence of the incorporation of prophetic messages into wisdom texts. As discussed below, Egyptian wisdom texts contain

Riddles and Untying Knots: Biblical, Epigraphic, and Semitic Studies in Honor of Jonas C. Greenfield (ed. Ziony Zevit, Seymour Gitin, and Michael Sokoloff; Winona Lake: Eisenbrauns, 1995), 606–7. But the commentary by Marzal remains convincing: Angel Marzal, *Gleanings from the Wisdom of Mari* (StPohl 11; Rome: Pontifical Biblical Institute, 1976), 27–31. To insist with Sasson that the straw must be moving with the underlying water is to force the metaphor into reality farther than intended.

11. While not included in his anthology of texts, Lambert discusses the themes of mortality and hedonism from this epic as they correspond to developing wisdom themes in Mesopotamian literature (Lambert, *Babylonian Wisdom Literature*, 11–12).

12. Simo Parpola, *Assyrian Prophecies* (SAA 9; Helsinki: University of Helsinki Press, 1997), 41 n. 8.

13. Another possible allusion to Gilgamesh's wandering is in SAA 9 1.8 (see Martti Nissinen, C. L. Seow, and Robert K. Ritner, *Prophets and Prophecy in the Ancient Near East* [ed. Theodore J. Lewis; WAW 12; Atlanta: SBL, 2003], 109 n. b). For discussion see Charles Halton, "Allusions to the Stream of Tradition in Neo-Assyrian Oracles," *ANES* 46 (2009): 57–58.

14. Parpola, *Assyrian Prophecies*, cv n. 246.

15. Halton, "Allusions," 52–55. Another possible allusion in a Mari prophecy, also discussed by Halton, does not invoke Adapa for any wisdom motif.

16. Cohen, *Wisdom from the Late Bronze Age*, 61–62. Sporadic examples are offered throughout his work.

prognostication but not "prophecy" in the sense of messenger speech. Although one might imagine a situation in which a prophetic word could become applicable to the didactic or speculative concern of wisdom, evidently such interests never materialized.[17]

Mesopotamia.

Ludlul Bēl Nēmeqi. The worshiper in *Ludlul* shows awareness of prophetic performances along with other divinatory prognostics. This is most striking in the version of *Ludlul* found at Ugarit:

> The diviner (*barû*) could not determine the meaning of my oracular prognosis... My brothers (were mournful) like the *maḫḫu* bathed in their own blood.[18]

In other lines the sufferer refers to divine messages through a dream: first a goddess speaks the reassurance formula, "Fear not, she said..." (*Ludlul* iii 29–38) followed by an incantation priest who uses a messenger formula, "Marduk has sent me" (*Ludlul* iii 39–44). He also acknowledges a favorable oracle by divination in the waking world (*Ludlul* iii 45–47).

These examples show an awareness of communication between the divine and human realms through prophecy, dreams, and inductive divination, and such references serve to underscore the desperate plight of the afflicted (similar to Urad Gula's failed attempt to find solace from diviners and prophets[19]).

17. Such examples would be difficult to validate. Isaiah's warning, "There is no peace for the wicked" (Isa 48:22; 57:21; author's translation) has a formulaic introduction as prophecy. Yet, this expression finds use aphoristically in modern times to joke about a person's work never being done. It is impossible to ascertain whether this originated as an aphorism or in prophetic composition.

18. Cited from Nissinen, Seow, and Ritner, *Prophets and Prophecy in the Ancient Near East*, §122, p. 184; other citations are from Lambert, *Babylonian Wisdom Literature*. See *Ludlul* i 51–52 and ii 6–9.

19. For text, see Nissinen, Seow, and Ritner, *Prophets and Prophecy in the Ancient Near East*, 162. Lenzi suggests that the purpose of *Ludlul* was to show the ineffectiveness of scholarly "wisdom" without the cooperation of Marduk (Alan Lenzi, "The Curious Case of Failed Revelation in *Ludlul Bēl Nēmeqi*: A New Suggestion for the Poem's Scholarly Purpose," in *Mediating Between Heaven and Earth: Communicating with the Divine in the Ancient Near East* [ed. C. L. Crouch, Jonathan Stökl, and Anna Elise Zernecke; LHBOTS 566; London: T&T Clark International, 2012], 63).

Babylonian Theodicy. This text sets the sufferer's experience over *against* wisdom that entails conformity to the decrees of the gods in oracles:

> Did it [the onager] pay attention to the giver of assured divine oracles? (line 49)[20]

Since animals find no benefit in following the protocols of piety, why should humans? The author likely has only inductive divination in mind and not prophecy, but it suggests a difference in attitude toward revelation between conventional (positive) wisdom, which is to be mindful of divine messages, and critical (negative) wisdom, which dismisses divine revelation as ultimately unhelpful or useless.

Mantic Historiography. Texts such as the Marduk Prophecy present an interesting point of discussion for the relationship between prophecy and wisdom.[21] They have been classified as "prophecy," "apocalyptic," "autobiographical fiction," "literary predictive texts," and most recently "mantic historiography." As Nissinen observes, although these texts and prophecy both presuppose the disclosure of information from the divine council to the human realm, the manner of transmission is quite different—scholarly meditation on omen series in the first instance and intuitive prophetic speech in the other.[22] Due to the possible role of

---

20. Lambert, *Babylonian Wisdom Literature*, 73.

21. For the five texts in this category and initially proposed genre classifications, see A. K. Grayson and W. G. Lambert, "Akkadian Prophecies," *JCS* 18 (1964): 7–30; William W. Hallo, "Akkadian Apocalypses," *IEJ* 16 (1966): 231–42. For more recent discussion of genre, the following sources are especially significant: Maria de Jong Ellis, "Observations on Mesopotamian Oracles and Prophetic Texts: Literary and Historiographical Considerations," *JCS* 41 (1989): 156–59; Tremper Longman III, *Fictional Akkadian Autobiography: A Generic and Comparative Study* (Winona Lake: Eisenbrauns, 1991); Martti Nissinen, "Neither Prophecies Nor Apocalypses: The Akkadian Literary Predictive Texts," in *Knowing the End from the Beginning: The Prophetic, the Apocalyptic, and Their Relationship* (ed. Lester L. Grabbe and Robert D. Haak; JSPSup 46; London: T&T Clark International, 2003), 134–48; Matthew Neujahr, *Predicting the Past in the Ancient Near East: Mantic Historiography in Ancient Mesopotamia, Judah, and the Mediterranean World* (BJS 354; Providence: Brown University Press, 2012), esp. 8, 110, 114–15.

22. Martti Nissinen, "Prophecy and Omen Divination: Two Sides of the Same Coin," in *Divination and Interpretation of Signs in the Ancient World* (ed. Amar Annus; OIS 6; Chicago: Oriental Institute of the University of Chicago, 2010), 342, 345.

historical reflection in these literary predictive texts, they may even be closer to historiography than to pseudo-prediction, hence the classification "mantic historiography."[23] This is particularly relevant to the interest of this essay, since the functionaries behind the literary-predictive texts hail from a scholarly class whose skills can be traced back to the antediluvian sages; and therefore, these texts offer a glimpse at the contrast in epistemological foundations between sages and prophets. The former relies on technical skill and tradition whereas the latter depends on intuitive perception of a divine message.

Egypt. The inclusion of prognostication in Egyptian wisdom texts has been explored at length.[24] Shupak's observation that these texts lack divine messenger speech is most important for differentiating them from prophecy. In addition, as will be shown, the element of prediction probably stems from the employment of magic as well as reflection on the patterns of the past.

Prophecies of Neferti.[25] This text utilizes prognostication by the sage ("a sage from the east"; *COS* 1.45: 107) to portray a time of chaos that is in the future from the viewpoint of the story. He regards his predictions within the portfolio of the sage:

> The wise man will pour out water for me,
> When he sees that what I have spoken comes to pass. (*COS* 1.45: 110)

23. Neujahr, *Predicting the Past*, 98–101, 245.

24. For summary discussion and bibliography, see John W. Hilber, "Prophetic Speech in the Egyptian Royal Cult," in *On Stone and Scroll: Essays in Honour of Graham Ivor Davies* (ed. James K. Aitken, Katharine J. Dell, and Brian A. Mastin; BZAW 420; Berlin: de Gruyter, 2011), 40–41. Most important is the work Nili Shupak, "Egyptian 'Prophecy' and Biblical Prophecy: Did the Phenomenon of Prophecy, in the Biblical Sense, Exist in Ancient Egypt?," *JEOL* 31 (1989–1990): 5–40; idem, "The Egyptian 'Prophecy': A Reconsideration," in *Von Reichlich Aegyptischem Verstande: Festschrift für Waltraud Guglielmi zum 65. Geburtstag* (ed. Hans-W. Fischer-Elfert and Karol Zibelius-Chen; Wiesbaden: Harrassowitz, 2006), 133–44. For Ptolemaic prophecy, which is outside the scope of this essay, see Hilber, "Prophetic Speech in the Egyptian Royal Cult," 41, 44–45.

25. Of relevance to this essay is the use of a proverb embedded within the predictions: "What will happen is hidden according to the saying, 'When sight and hearing fail, the mute leads'" (*COS* 1.45: 108). This saying supports the prognostication; the future will be a time when employment of human senses is to no avail.

Admonitions of Ipuwer. In lamentation for social chaos, Ipuwer says "What the ancestors foretold has happened" (*COS* 1.42: 94).[26]

Merikare. The father's advice draws upon what was once foretold:

Troops will fight troops
As the ancestors foretold;
Egypt fought in the graveyard,
Destroying tombs in vengeful destruction.
As I did it, so it happened,
As is done to one who strays from the god's path.
Do not deal evilly with the Southland,
You know what the residence foretold about it;
As this happened so that may happen. (*COS* 1.35: 63)

Shupak draws attention to similarities between *Neferti, Ipuwer, Merikare,* and the *Admonitions of Khakheperre-sonb* in the employment of this ancestors motif.[27] The notion of social calamity is a tradition passed down by the sages from days of old. Khakheperre-sonb speaks of things "spoken by the ancestors," "in accord with what I have seen," and notes, "I meditate on what has happened" (*COS* 1.44: 105–6). Shupak argues that prognostication in the wisdom tradition comes by way of reflection on past experience.[28] Nevertheless, these texts regard the ancestors, at least, as capable of foretelling. Perhaps the mechanism is related to that found in The Story of King Kheops and the Magicians.

King Kheops and the Magicians. In this tale of wonders a magician predicts the birth of triplets who will comprise the next dynasty of Egyptian kings. The means of revelation comes through magical arts (*AEL* 1:219).[29] This is consistent with comments in the Egyptian text, *The Immortality of Writers*, where one reads the list of famous sages of

26. See the dependency on past tradition in *The Complaints of Khakheperre-sonb,* noted below in comments by Shupak (*COS* 1.44: 105 n. 10).

27. *COS* 1.42: 94 n. 9; 1.44: 105 n. 10; 1.45: 107 n. 5 and 108 n. 16.

28. *COS* 1.44: 105 n. 10 and Shupak, "Egyptian 'Prophecy' and Biblical Prophecy," 27.

29. Ritner and Lloyd suggest that the boundary between magic and intuitive prophecy might be unclear (Robert K. Ritner, *The Mechanics of Ancient Egyptian Magical Practice* [SAOC 54; Chicago: The Oriental Institute, 1993], 36–38; Alan B. Lloyd, "Heka, Dreams, and Prophecy in Ancient Egyptian Stories," in *Through a Glass Darkly: Magic, Dreams & Prophecy in Ancient Egypt* [ed. Kasia Szpakowska; Swansea: Classical Press of Wales, 2006], 71–94). But the story implies that the mechanism was magic.

the past, concerning whom the comment is made: "Those sages who foretold the future; What came from their mouth occurred"; yet they "hid their magic from the masses" (*AEL* 2:177). On the basis of this text, Fox observes that foretelling was well understood as within the portfolio of Egyptian sages.[30] But the mechanism was not intuitive prophecy.

Tale of the Shipwrecked Sailor. This text is "instructional" and so might be included in the genre "wisdom." The story describes the predictions of a divine serpent and so illustrates the concept of future-telling among the Egyptian literary class, but within the story it is an example of divine disclosure of the future directly revealed to an individual and does not constitute messenger speech.

Conclusion. While foretelling the future is a common enough motif in these Egyptian wisdom texts, the mode of revelation about the future appears not to be intuitive prophecy; rather, it is a tradition told to the ancestors in the remote past or secrets about how to ascertain the future derived from the magical arts.

Revelation and Tradition

Prophecy: Divine Secrets Directly Disclosed

In prophecy a deity intervenes "directly...in human cognition."[31] This does not preclude careful composition, whether oral or in writing (e.g., divine letters); however, in each case the human intermediary *perceives* and conveys intelligible content. This self-awareness is reinforced by the prophets' use of introductory speech formulas and impersonation of the deity.[32] The prophet consciously participates in secret disclosures of the divine council that could not otherwise be known (ARM 26 196, 208; SAA 9 9 [indirectly]; SAA 12 69; FPL 1678).[33]

In performance of prophetic speech, the message has relevance to the immediate situation of the addressee. This does not preclude prophecy being resignified in later contexts. The divine message, immediately relevant to its original audience, enters a stream of tradition in which

---

30. Fox, "Three Theses on Wisdom," 74–75.

31. Guinan, "A Severed Head Laughed: Stories of Divinatory Interpretation," 18.

32. E.g., "Thus says Šamaš" (ARM 26 194, line 3); "Word of Ištar" (SAA 9 3.4, line ii 33). I thank Friedrich-Emanuel Focken for this observation.

33. Robert P. Gordon, "Where Have All the Prophets Gone? The 'Disappearing' Israelite Prophet Against the Background of Ancient Near Eastern Prophecy," *BBR* 5 (1995): 78–79. For the texts cited by Gordon, see Nissinen, Seow, and Ritner, *Prophets and Prophecy in the Ancient Near East.*

the prophetic word can be adapted to new settings. For example, one of the prophetic archival tablets from Esarhaddon's reign features oracles that were originally uttered in the throes of civil war but were adapted a short time later for an enthronement liturgy.[34] An Assyrian letter to Assurbanipal applies to him a prophecy that was originally delivered to his father, Esarhaddon, assuring success in campaigns against Egypt.[35] In each case, the original prophet intended his or her words primarily for an immediate situation but these words were later reapplied with new significance.

Wisdom: Tradition Endowed by Divine Secrets[36]

Wisdom as Divine Secret. Mesopotamian scholars, who were the custodians of wisdom, traced the origins of their knowledge to the gods. The gods disclosed divine secrets to the antediluvian *apkallu*, who were royal sages or sages associated with antediluvian kings.[37] This is illustrated in the legend of Enmeduranki (king of Sippar), which tells how Šamaš and Adad endowed the king with divinatory skills: "they gave him the Tablet of the Gods, the liver, a secret of heaven and nether world…"[38] Further, these traditions were passed down to later kings and their counsellors, ideally from father to son: "the learned savant, who guards the secrets of the great gods, will bind by oath before Šamaš and Adad by tablet and stylus the son whom he loves and will teach him."[39] Once in practice, divination sought verdicts from the assembly of the gods to be written on the animal's liver.[40]

---

34. Assyrian oracle collection 3, see Parpola, *Assyrian Prophecies*, lxviii–lxx.

35. Simo Parpola, *Letters from Assyrian and Babylonian Scholars* (SAA 10; Helsinki: University of Helsinki Press, 1993), §174.

36. The classification of wisdom that follows punctuates differences in relationship to the type of "revelation" involved. Other classifications are possible, as for example Assman's four types of wisdom adapted by Alster for Mesopotamian wisdom (Bendt Alster, *Wisdom of Ancient Sumer* [Bethesda: CDL, 2005], 21). However, his categories overlap and are therefore themselves limited in use (Schneider, "Knowledge and Knowledgeable Persons," 39–40).

37. Beaulieu, "The Social and Intellectual Setting of Babylonian Wisdom Literature," 15–18.

38. W. G. Lambert, "The Qualifications of Babylonian Diviners," in *Festschrift für Rykle Borger zu seinem 65. Geburtstag am 24. Mai 1994* (ed. S. Maul; Groningen: Styx, 1998), 152, line 8.

39. Ibid., lines 19–22.

40. YOS 11 23 (Benjamin R. Foster, *Before the Muses: An Anthology of Akkadian Literature* [Bethesda: CDL, 2005], II.28.b, pp. 212–13).

Numerous texts link kings with divinely revealed wisdom. The most celebrated example is that of Assurbanipal, who claims: "I learned the art of the *apkallu*, Adapa, (so that now) I am familiar with the secret storehouse of all scribal learning... I have studied inscriptions on stone from before the flood."[41] Pongratz-Leisten argues that such self-presentation was necessary to project exclusive control of divine secrets and to assert competence to govern the world.[42] Particularly important was the ability of the king to execute social justice and lead in war. So the wisdom was not simply esoteric knowledge but also practical skill.

This divine origin was believed true for *all* specialized knowledge and crafts, whether art, medicine, or building skills.[43] That such wisdom also extended to the abstract lessons of life is evident from the report of Gilgamesh, who returned from his quest with the "sum of wisdom" that was "secret" from before the flood.[44] The oldest collection of proverbs, The Instructions of Shuruppak, came from "far remote days" when the Sumerian flood hero received this teaching from his father.[45] So, as Glassner states, "Wisdom was the daughter of revelation."[46]

Wisdom as Tradition.[47] Nevertheless, the question of the relationship between revelation and wisdom is more complicated than a simple

41. Sweet, "The Sage in Akkadian Literature," 55. See listing of texts on pp. 51–57.

42. Beate Pongratz-Leisten, *Herrschaftswissen in Mesopotamien: Formen der Kommunikation zwischen Gott und König im 2. und 1. Jahrtausend v. Chr.* (SAAS 10; Helsinki: University of Helsinki Press, 1999), 295–301.

43. Rykle Borger, "The Incantation Series *Bīt Mēseri* and Enoch's Ascension to Heaven," *JNES* 33 (1974): 183–96; Sweet, "The Sage in Akkadian Literature"; Jean-Jacques Glassner, "The Use of Knowledge in Ancient Mesopotamia," in *Civilizations of the Ancient Near East* (ed. Jack M. Sasson; repr. Peabody: Hendrickson, 2000), 2:1815–16; Beaulieu, "The Social and Intellectual Setting of Babylonian Wisdom Literature," 4–8.

44. Epic of Gilgamesh (i 6–8).

45. Beaulieu, "The Social and Intellectual Setting of Babylonian Wisdom Literature," 4–5.

46. Glassner, "The Use of Knowledge in Ancient Mesopotamia," 2:1816. This association became more pronounced in the first millennium than in the second (Beaulieu, "The Social and Intellectual Setting of Babylonian Wisdom Literature," 15–17; Karel van der Toorn, "Why Wisdom Became a Secret: On Wisdom as a Written Genre," in Clifford, ed., *Wisdom Literature in Mesopotamia and Israel*, 21–29).

47. This discussion directly addresses only inductive divination (e.g., extispicy), but the same points apply to the category of observational divination (e.g., astronomy, oil in water).

equation. There remains a dominant element of tradition underlying the revelatory aspect of wisdom. This tradition stems from empirical observation expanded by exegetical reflection on omen texts.

On the one hand, divination as a *skill* originated from revelation, and the interpretation of omens brought new revelation to bear on an immediate situation facing the diviner and his patron.

> You grant wisdom, O Shamash, to humankind…
> You make their omens the right ones for them,
>   you preside over sacrifices.
> You probe their future in every way. (Šamaš Hymn, lines 149, 151–52)[48]

But in practice, the interpretation of omens depended on an ever-growing stream of tradition based upon continual, empirical observation. As Stefen Maul notes, the classification of omens "is based on an epistemological development" that is "initially built on empirical knowledge."[49] As omen series grew, they offered further resources for future interpretation and speculation on omens and their relationship to one another. Ann Guinan writes:

> Most forms of divination produce meaning that is singular and applicable to the situation at hand. However, the recording of omens produces meaning that appears fixed. By transforming singular perception into an intelligible object whose meaning is applicable in other contexts, it suggests a process of abstraction and establishes a system of knowledge. When both signs and their meaning are envisioned in the human mind, divinatory inquiry seems to make an intellectual leap into new epistemological territory.[50]

Offering a different explanation, Van de Mieroop challenges the extent to which omen series actually originated from empirical observation. Some protases are actually impossible (e.g., the sun appearing in the middle of the night), hence a matter of speculative exploration. Babylonian scholars began with the endless possibilities inherent in cuneiform text: e.g., ambiguity of sign values, homonyms, overlapping semantic domains, and similarities between the physical appearance of

48. Foster, *Before the Muses*, 633. Lambert, probably on the basis of "omens" mentioned in the parallel lines, translates the word *uznum* ("ear," in the sense of "wisdom," "understanding") as "revelation" (Lambert, *Babylonian Wisdom Literature*, 135).

49. Stefan M. Maul, "Divination Culture and the Handling of the Future," in *The Babylonian World* (ed. Gwendolyn Leick; London: Routledge, 2007), 361.

50. Guinan, "A Severed Head Laughed," 19.; cf. Ellis, "Observations," 171–72.

signs themselves.[51] Observations of their world drove scholars to their existing texts that had been derived by linguistic deduction, much in the manner a modern scientist turns to mathematics for explanation of natural phenomena. The process was, therefore, more a rational application of hermeneutics than an empirical, inductive process.[52]

The gods had created a sensible world out of chaos, and the universe was the tablet upon which they set order and revealed their judgments. An opening line to a Šamaš Hymn declares: "As if they were cuneiform signs you [Šamaš] explore all lands with your light!" So, by analogy, the cuneiform script was also a text that enabled scholars to make sense of the world they observed.[53] Van de Meiroop writes, "[there was] a new perception about the path to wisdom: it lay in understanding the written word."[54]

The relevance of all this for understanding the relationship between wisdom and revelation is this: whether by empirical observation or by deductive reasoning from texts, wisdom was based in the skills of tradition, not direct revelation.[55] This fundamental role of tradition pertains to Egyptian wisdom as well. Egyptians viewed the secret knowledge of magic as a divine gift from the primordial past, handed down from gods to humanity ("he made for them magic"; Merikare, *AEL* 1:106). Yet, while the *techniques* originated by revelation, the exercise of these skills came by professional training in the tradition.[56]

51. Marc Van de Mieroop, *Philosophy Before the Greeks: The Pursuit of Truth in Ancient Babylonia* (Princeton: Princeton University Press; Oxford: Oxford University Press, 2016), 115–16, 126–27.

52. Ibid., 188–90.

53. Ibid., 185–86. For the translation, Van de Meiroop follows Livingston (*COS* 1.143: 474), who interprets the words *tikip satakki* ("impress of a cuneiform wedge") in line 3 as an expression of the poet and not a scribal notation for a lost line of text (contrast *ANET*, 387 n. 1). Note, however, that the Mesopotamian concept of the heavens as a "tablet" upon which the gods write does not depend on this single text (see Francesca Rochberg, *The Heavenly Writing: Divination, Horoscopy, and Astronomy in Mesopotamian Culture* [Cambridge: Cambridge University Press, 2004], 1–2).

54. Van de Mieroop, *Philosophy Before the Greeks*, 196.

55. One might consider whether this sort of epistemological process contributed not only to omen texts but to some didactic wisdom as well, as, for example, in the "Advice to a Prince," which imitates omen style and phraseology (lines 5 and 6; and "chief officer" [omen vocabulary], lines 14, 45, 55). See Lambert, *Babylonian Wisdom Literature*, 110.

56. J. F. Borghouts, "Divine Intervention in Ancient Egypt and Its Manifestation (*Bꜣw*)," in *Gleanings from Deir El-Medîna* (ed. R. J. Demarée and Jac J. Janssen; Leiden: Nederlands Instituut voor het Nabije Oosten, 1982), 1776, 1784.

Wisdom as Instruction. Wisdom, in the sense of esoteric knowledge and divinatory skills, was exclusively in the hands of kings and the professional elite. But wisdom was also available to the common person. As already mentioned, the skills of a craftsman or builder were viewed as a divine gift. So, Esarhaddon prays that builders of a temple receive wisdom granted by the gods.[57] It is in this indirect sense of acquiring wisdom that we should understand the opening line of The Instructions of Šūpê-amēli [*Šimâ Milka*]), which attributes its maxims to Ea, god of wisdom: "whose ear Enlilbanda opened…to whom Enlilbanda granted wisdom [ear opening]."[58]

Commenting on this text, Horowitz argues that while "special wisdom" is attributed to Ea, it "does not derive from any special divine inspiration or revelation"; rather it flows from "human experience of daily life."[59]

Concerning the dialogue in the Babylonian Theodicy, Lambert notes that an empirical method shows in the argumentation: "I have looked around society, but the evidence is contrary" (Babylonian Theodicy, xxiv 243–244).[60] As noted above, the Šamaš Hymn attributes wisdom to the god (Šamaš Hymn, lines 149, 151), but the final lines of the hymn attribute to the god all "discretion, consultation, discussion, advice" (line 186). This broad range can hardly be construed as "revelatory" in the conscious experience of the royal counsellors who would offer such wisdom.

Lambert suggests that because we have so few Babylonian proverbs that they were beneath the dignity of the scribal class. The scribes simply passed on the repertoire from Sumer.[61] But there was some recognition and preservation of popular sayings derived from common folks.[62] While some scholars propose that Sumerian proverbs were collected from non-literary people, others dispute this. Cohen offers a mediating position that it is likely they originated from diverse sources, including common

---

57. Sweet, "The Sage in Akkadian Literature," 59. Sweet's list also includes soldiers and musicians

58. Cohen, *Wisdom from the Late Bronze Age*, 84–85.

59. Victor Avigdor Hurowitz, "The Wisdom of Šūpê-amēli—a Deathbed Debate Between a Father and Son," in Clifford, ed., *Wisdom Literature in Mesopotamia and Israel*, 44. He maintains a similar "indirect" process for the wisdom attained by Assurbanipal from Marduk (p. 73).

60. Lambert, *Babylonian Wisdom Literature*, 65. See also the relationship between reason and wisdom in lines 212–14. The dispute is over the limitation of human reason set against the ways of the god.

61. Ibid., 275–76.

62. Ibid., 213–21.

people.[63] As noted above, The Instructions of Shuruppak were thought to pass down from the antediluvian period when *apkallu*'s were informed by the gods; yet the proverbs contained in this collection are rather pedestrian, often applicable to the agrarian life but not the settings of elite society.

For Egyptians as well, there was a type of wisdom comprised of carefully guarded knowledge; yet scribes also attributed the origins of even every day wisdom to the gods (Amenemope 20.5–6 [*AEL* 2:158]: "Maat is a great gift of god, He gives it to whom he wishes." While the god receives praise for granting wisdom, the instructions of Amenemope could be reasoned, understood, and appropriated by anyone. This process is evident in other Egyptian wisdom texts. In the Instruction of Any, the son replies to his sagacious father: "Tell the god who gave you wisdom…" (*AEL* 2:144–45); yet this wisdom is a tradition passed on from father to son "in the books." Similarly, in the Wisdom of Ptah-hotep:

> May this servant be ordered to make a staff of old age
> So as to tell him the words of those who heard
> The ways of the ancestors who have listened to the gods…
> instruct him then in the sayings of the past. (*AEL* 1:63)

In this, Ptah-hotep spoke about acquiring wisdom from the gods, but he also speaks of wealth as a divine gift: "which came to you as gift of god" (*AEL* 1:71 [Ptah-Hotep]). Therefore, the revelatory credit given to the gods was likely thought of in terms of providential mediation in the course of life, similar to the acquisition of wealth.

Conclusion

Leaving aside the *emic* theories about revelation held by the ancients, modern *etic* categories might be helpful. One can construe prophecy as "above reason" in the sense that it is information that cannot be known apart from direct divine disclosure. However, didactic wisdom is "according to reason," that is, human reason can discern it empirically or "logically," although once discerned the pious sage credits the process of discovery to the gods.[64] In regard to wisdom as divine gift in Prov 2,

---

63. Cohen, *Wisdom from the Late Bronze Age*, 58.

64. I wish to acknowledge my theology colleague, Jonathan Marko, for these epistemological categories. As an additional note, this essay does not extend to the concept of wisdom espoused in some late Second Temple writings. Texts at Qumran and the Enochian Book of Watchers (ch. 36) attribute wisdom more directly to

Michael Fox uses the helpful phrase: a "synergy of endowment and development."[65] This also expresses well the link between wisdom and divine gift in Mesopotamian and Egyptian texts. Divination, on the other hand, occupies a middle ground between the two. The *skills and method* of divination, including the hermeneutical resources necessary to read the omens, are based upon reason applied to tradition; however, the "answer" written into the liver, or the message "written" on the astronomical phenomena, are placed there directly by the gods and so are "above reason" once the answer is revealed. The following graphic illustrates the relationship of prophecy and wisdom to their respective revelatory status and performance expectations:

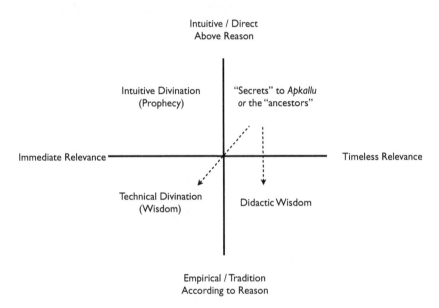

With reference to the collection of essays in this volume and the current discussion regarding the relationship between prophecy and wisdom in the Old Testament, the ancient Near Eastern analogues provide little support

revelation, as a sort of scribal prophecy. See Leo G. Perdue, "Sages, Scribes, and Seers in Israel and the Ancient Near East: An Introduction," in Perdue, ed., *Scribes, Sages, and Seers*, 16; and in the same volume, Armin Lange, "Sages and Scribes in the Qumran Literature," 282, 287, 291.

65. Michael V. Fox, "Joseph and Wisdom," in *The Book of Genesis: Composition, Reception, and Interpretation* (VTSup 152; Leiden: Brill, 2012), 18. Professor Fox was kind enough in our helpful correspondence to direct my attention to his relevant publications.

for attributing biblical wisdom to *direct* revelation. On the contrary, both Mesopotamian and Egyptian sages based the authority of their teaching on tradition, albeit tradition that was "endowed and developed" with divine guidance. Regarding the distinction between revelation in biblical wisdom and revelation in the biblical prophets, Schellenberg aptly notes: "it remains that there are essential epistemological differences between prophetic/apocalyptic and sapiential writings—though not in the question of revelation but, rather, in the question of revelation's exclusivity."[66] Both affirm the role of revelation as an epistemological reality, but they construe the means of acquiring knowledge from God differently. Ascribing the same revelatory status to wisdom by analogy to prophetic revelation confuses the distinctions maintained by the ancients themselves.

66. Annette Schellenberg, "'Wisdom Cries Out in the Street' (Prov 1:20) On the Role of Revelation in Wisdom Literature and the Relatedness and Differences Between Sapiential and Prophetic Epistemologies," in *Scribes as Sages and Prophets* (ed. Jutta Krispenz; Berlin: de Gruyter, forthcoming). I thank Dr. Schellenberg for sharing a pre-publication copy of her article.

Part II

WISDOM AMONG THE PROPHETS

SPIRITUAL BLINDNESS AND WISDOM TRADITIONS IN THE BOOK OF ISAIAH

Eric Ortlund

At a number of junctures in the book of Isaiah, the poet-prophet[1] draws upon traditions known to us only from other parts of the Hebrew Bible or texts from the ancient Near East, such as the reference to that fleeing, twisting serpent which Baal defeated (*KTU* 1.5.I.27–31) or those passages in chs. 40–55 that use the exodus as a framework for describing the return from exile (e.g., Isa 43:16–17). References to specific terms and themes that figure prominently in wisdom literature form another example of the book of Isaiah's complex interaction with other traditions and are the focus of this essay. A number of previous studies have, of course, already explored wisdom in Isaiah, searching the book for possible allusions to wisdom (according to keywords or concepts and forms of speech) and forming hypotheses about the original social locations of wisdom and prophetic speech—especially focusing on forms of prophetic speech that could have originated in a wisdom context.[2] Not a few of these studies

---

1. I use deliberately vague language when speaking of the author/editors of the book of Isaiah because, with all due respect for scholars of previous generations, hypotheses concerning the editorial layers of the Hebrew Bible and individual books that once seemed secure have become increasingly less so. I do not want to commit myself to a particular theory of redaction that may not carry weight much longer. The trajectory of this essay is, in any case, largely unaffected by hypotheses concerning the putatively complicated authorship of the book.

2. Important studies include (in chronological order) Johannes Fichtner, "Isaiah Among the Wise," *TLZ* 74 (1949): cols. 75–80 (reprinted in an English translation in *Studies In Ancient Israelite Wisdom* [ed. James Crenshaw; Library of Biblical Studies; New York: Ktav, 1976], 429–38); Erhard Gerstenberger, "The Woe-Oracles of the Prophets," *JBL* 81 (1962): 249–63; J. William Whedbee, *Isaiah and Wisdom*

use Old Testament texts as a window by which to observe different strata of ancient Israelite society and religious life and trace their relations. Although the present study proceeds within the context of this previous research, it focuses on a simpler question that, if not absent, has not always received sufficient attention: How are wisdom themes deployed in the book of Isaiah? How does the prophet weave them into his own discourse? It is from this perspective that broader reflections on the status of wisdom in the book of Isaiah will be made.

To anticipate our conclusion, wisdom language is often invoked in Isaiah to express Israel's spiritual blindness. Wisdom literature portrays wisdom as at least potentially available to all, if they are receptive and willing to search for it (e.g., Prov 2:1–8)—but in Isaiah Israel has collectively failed in this enterprise. No one is wise. As is typical in the book's hopeful trajectory, however, this does not mean wisdom is "dead," for YHWH will give leaders who are wise (11:2) and whose wisdom will spread beyond their own person (11:9). To this extent, my conclusion overlaps with Fichtner's in his early article, "Isaiah Among the Wise,"[3] although I hope to explore it in more detail, as well as considering passages from Isa 40–55.

(Nashville: Abingdon, 1971); Joseph Jensen, *The Use of* tôrâ *by Isaiah: His Debate with the Wisdom Tradition* (CBQMS 3; Washington, DC: Catholic Biblical Association, 1973); Donald Morgan, *Wisdom in the Old Testament Traditions* (Atlanta: John Knox, 1981), 76–83; R. Norman Whybray, "Prophecy and Wisdom," in *Israel's Prophetic Tradition* (ed. Richard Coggins et al.; Cambridge: Cambridge University Press, 1984), 181–99; Jacques Vermeylen, "Le Proto-Isaïe et La Sagesse d'Israël," in *La Sagesse de l'Ancien Testament* (ed. M. Gilbert; BETL 51; Leuven: Leuven University Press, 1990), 39–58; Hugh Williamson, "Isaiah and the Wise," in *Wisdom in Ancient Israel: Essays in Honour of J. A. Emerton* (ed. John Day et al.; Cambridge: Cambridge University Press, 1995), 133–41; Hans Wildberger, *Isaiah 28–39* (trans. Thomas Trapp; Continental Commentary; Minneapolis: Fortress, 2002), 596–615; Hans-Jürgen Hermisson, "Prophetie und Weisheit," in *Weisheit in Israel* (ed. D. J. A. Clines et al.; Altes Testament und Moderne 12; Münster: Lit-Verlag, 2003), 111–30; Lindsay Wilson, "Wisdom in Isaiah," in *Interpreting Isaiah: Issues and Approaches* (ed. David Firth and H. G. M. Williamson; Downers Grove: IVP Academic, 2009), 145–67; Katherine Hayes, "'A Spirit of Deep Sleep': Divinely Induced Delusion and Wisdom in Isaiah 1–39," *CBQ* 74 (2012): 39–54.

3. Fichtner, "Isaiah Among the Wise." I do not follow Fichtner's opinion that Isaiah was originally a sage; none of the relevant passages necessitate such a conclusion.

Methodological Considerations and False Leads
in the Search for Wisdom in Isaiah

Given the focus and aims of other studies on wisdom in Isaiah, it should be stated early that no assumptions are being made in this essay about a distinct class of trained sages at work in the palace as the original life-setting of this genre of ancient Israelite literature. The Hebrew Bible certainly does know of professional sages surrounding the throne in other nations (Gen 41:8; Exod 7:11; Esth 1:13), but I can think of no reason to insist on a similar life-setting for the wisdom traditions with which Isaiah interacts—nor does it greatly affect the present argument to do so. I assume only that wisdom existed in ancient Israel as a living tradition, distinguishable if not totally distinct from other movements in Israelite society, from which the prophet occasionally drew in order to speak to his contemporaries.[4] Although the complex nature of wisdom literature makes simple definitions problematic, and although it cannot be defended in depth here, it will also probably be helpful to state that I understand wisdom to be that skill or facility by which one engages with the complexities of YHWH's created order for blessing and *shalom*.[5]

Furthermore, no assumptions are made about the dating and editing of Old Testament wisdom literature relative to the book of Isaiah. Although assumptions of this kind are not implausible,[6] it is not necessary to define precisely the process of editing and date of completion of these texts in order to turn to wisdom literature as "the literary deposit of a specifically

---

4. Scholars working in this area sometimes make a distinct life-setting for wisdom (and sometimes even distinct life-settings for different kinds of wisdom) a *necessary* hypothesis and define Israel's wisdom movement accordingly. However probable such hypotheses might be, I cannot think of any reason why they should be necessary to understand wisdom influence on other forms of Old Testament literature. For examples of this claim, see James Crenshaw, "Method in Determining Wisdom Influence Upon 'Historical' Literature," *JBL* 88 (1969): 130; and Raymond Van Leeuwen, "The Sage in the Prophetic Literature," in *The Sage in Israel and the Ancient Near East* (ed. John Gammie and Leo Perdue; Winona Lake: Eisenbrauns, 1990), 297.

5. This study is thus distinguished from others which understand Israelite wisdom merely as human reflection on life experience and thus distinguishable from prophetic preaching around YHWH's action in history (as John McLaughlin appears to do in "Is Amos (Still) Among the Wise?," *JBL* 133 [2014]: 286).

6. Michael Fox makes a compelling case for an early edition of the book of Proverbs under Solomon's rule that was subsequently edited in several stages (*Proverbs 10–31* [AB 18B; New Haven: Yale University Press, 2009], 499–509).

defined movement characterized by a particular approach to reality" and explore how the book of Isaiah interacts with it.[7]

Two other methodological issues should briefly be mentioned. First, it is sometimes claimed that establishing a connection between prophetic and wisdom literature involves determining not simply whether similar language and themes are used in both kinds of texts, but whether they are used in the same way.[8] If this principle were consistently followed, however, it would make it difficult or impossible to establish any connection to other traditions whatsoever, for the book of Isaiah often quotes or alludes in ways that are transformative and not merely repetitive.[9] Second, it is insufficient to show that words and themes appear in wisdom literature to establish a connection with wisdom; one must show that they are specific to wisdom literature, rather than spread throughout the Old Testament.[10]

This second consideration will explain why certain passages are left untreated that other studies of wisdom in Isaiah discuss at length. For instance, Joseph Jepsen understands (in addition to other factors) the use of תּוֹרָה in Isa 1:10; 2:3 to signal a wisdom background in those passages (such as when the father calls for attention to his torah from the son).[11] William Whedbee makes a similar claim for עֵצָה in passages like 9:6 or 30:1, writing that the majority of occurrences for this word show that "it was the wise man who dispensed counsel."[12] Although the arguments of both are involved and although these terms do sometimes occur in significant ways in wisdom contexts (see the below discussion of Deut 32:28 and Isa 11:2), the words themselves are scattered widely throughout the Old Testament and thus do not always signal a wisdom context.[13]

7. Crenshaw, "Method in Determining Wisdom Influence," 130.

8. See ibid., 133; Gary Tuttle, "Wisdom and Habakkuk," *Studia Biblica et Theologica* 3 (1973): 7; McLaughlin, "Is Amos (Still) Among the Wise?" 283.

9. Meir Sternberg writes that "to quote is to mediate and to mediate is to interfere" ("Proteus in Quotation-Land: Mimesis and the Forms of Reported Discourse," *Poetics Today* 3 (1982): 108. I am thankful to Dr. Samuel Hildebrandt for this reference. See also Richard Schultz, *The Search for Quotation: Verbal Parallels in the Prophets* (JSOTSup 180; Sheffield: Sheffield Academic Press, 1999), 186–87.

10. Whybray appropriately (if trenchantly) exposes this mistake in "Prophecy and Wisdom," 189–91. Whybray's entire article is a very helpful discussion of these methodological issues.

11. Jensen, *The Use of* tôrâ *by Isaiah*, 70–71, 73–74, 81.

12. Whedbee, *Isaiah and Wisdom*, 116, as part of his chapter on this word (111–48).

13. Vermeylen, "Le Proto-Isaïe et La Sagesse d'Israël," 43, and Wildberger, *Isaiah 28–39*, 610, agree with Whedbee, but less than half of the eighty or so

The same could be said for Fichtner's argument that the use of בִּין and ידע in 6:9 specifically indicate a failure in wisdom in Israel's hard-hearted response to Isaiah's preaching.[14] The present essay will argue for a wisdom background for these same verbs in 1:4 and for a connection between the Isaianic theme of spiritual blindness and the people's failure to be wise. In 6:9, however, these verbs seem more closely paired with the verbs immediately preceding them than with each other (thus, שמע with בִּין and ראה with ידע). But searching for those combinations of verbs shows no obvious wisdom influence.[15] As a result, the text does not seem to identify the people's hard-hearted response to Isaiah's preaching specifically as a failure to be wise—even though that implication will be made elsewhere. The same holds for the similarly worded 28:9.

Proverb-like sayings in Isaiah have also been suggested as a possible point of contact with wisdom traditions, such as 2:22; 3:10; 10:15; and 29:15–16.[16] While the formal similarities between these verses and biblical proverbs are obvious, positing a wisdom background does not seem to affect the interpretation of these verses in Isaiah. For instance, Whedbee and John Oswalt interpret Isa 10:15 in much the same way, even though Whedbee does so from a wisdom perspective and Oswalt does not.[17] Similar comments could be made about Gerstenberger's hypothesis concerning the wisdom setting of prophetic woe oracles.[18]

---

occurrences of עֵצָה (the root may express more than one homonym [see *HALOT* 866–67], so it is difficult to give a precise number) occur in wisdom texts or obvious wisdom contexts outside wisdom texts: in addition to twenty occurrences in Proverbs and Job, see Deut 32:38; 1 Sam 15:31; Isa 11:2; 19:11; 40:13; Jer 18:18; Pss 1:1; 73:24. But this is not enough in itself to assign it as a wisdom term. On the other hand, it is plausibly used that way in passages like Isa 11:2 and 19:11–12 (to be discussed below).

14. Fichtner, "Isaiah Among the Wise," 436.

15. שמע is found with בִּין elsewhere in Isa 52:15; Job 13:1; and Dan 12:8, while ראה is paired with ידע fifteen other times, and only rarely in wisdom texts (Lev 5:1; Deut 4:35; 1 Sam 16:18; 18:28; 23:23; 26:12; Pss 31:8; 138:6; Eccl 6:5; Isa 29:15; 41:20; 44:9; 58:3; Jer 2:23; 5:1).

16. Fichtner, "Isaiah Among the Wise," 434; Whedbee, *Isaiah and Wisdom*, 68–75.

17. See Whedbee *Isaiah and Wisdom*, 72, and John Oswalt, *The Book of Isaiah: Chapters 1–39* (NICOT; Grand Rapids: Eerdmans, 1986), 267.

18. Erhard Gerstenberger, "The Woe-Oracles of the Prophets," *JBL* 81 (1962): 249–63. Gerstenberger's hypothesis has received criticism from J. A. Soggin, "Amos and Wisdom," in Day, ed., *Wisdom in Ancient Israel*, 120; Vermeylen, "Le Proto-Isaïe et La Sagesse d'Israël," 41–42; McLaughlin, "Is Amos (Still) Among the Wise?" 288–91.

We are on stronger ground in 3:3 and 5:21. The former verse refers to those skillful in charms (חֲכַם חֲרָשִׁים) while the latter describes merely human wisdom which is blind to YHWH's plan with a phrase that occurs only elsewhere in Proverbs (being "wise in their own eyes"; see Prov 3:7; 26:5; 26:12; 28:11).[19] But these verses do not tell us much about Isaiah's view of wisdom per se.[20] The same could be said for 29:14.

Sons Who Neither Know Nor Understand (Isaiah 1:2–3)

Isaiah's first interaction with wisdom traditions occurs in the book's earliest verses.[21]

Sons I have raised and brought up, but they have rebelled against me.	בָּנִים גִּדַּלְתִּי וְרוֹמַמְתִּי וְהֵם פָּשְׁעוּ בִי
An ox knows its owner, and a donkey the crib of its master;	יָדַע שׁוֹר קֹנֵהוּ וַחֲמוֹר אֵבוּס בְּעָלָיו
but Israel does not know, my people do not understand.	יִשְׂרָאֵל לֹא יָדַע עַמִּי לֹא הִתְבּוֹנָן

The strongest allusion in this passage is, of course, to the Song of Moses (Deut 32:1). In fact, Ronald Bergey has shown that the whole of the first chapter of Isaiah alludes to Deut 32, such that Deut 32 provides a decisive cast for Isa 1.[22] Although Bergey does not quite state matters this way, it appears that the poet-prophet is activating Deut 32 for his own time: Israel has betrayed their covenant Lord and is suffering the consequences laid out in that earlier passage; YHWH will, however, intervene to deliver, as promised in Deut 32.

19. Gerstenberger, "Woe-Oracles," 605; Hayes, "'A Spirit of Deep Sleep,'" 43 n. 19.

20. In disagreement with Vermeylen, "Le Proto-Isaïe et La Sagesse d'Israël," 41; see further Johannes Lindblom, "Wisdom in the Old Testament Prophets," *Wisdom in Israel and the Ancient Near East* (ed. M. Noth and D. Winton Thomas; VTSup 3; Leiden: Brill, 1955), 194.

21. Although the connection is made in different ways, an allusion to wisdom is found in this passage by Whedbee, *Isaiah and Wisdom*, 26–43; Hermisson, "Prophetie und Weisheit," 117–18; Morgan, *Wisdom in the Old Testament Traditions*, 77; Vermeylen, "Le Proto-Isaïe et La Sagesse d'Israël," 49. What import this allusion has in context in Isaiah is, however, given less attention in these studies.

22. Ronald Bergey, "The Song of Moses (Deuteronomy 32:1–43) and Isaianic Prophecies: A Case of Early Intertextuality?" *JSOT* 28 (2003): 39–40.

Within this larger framework of allusions to the Song of Moses, it is revealing that the verbs that describe Israel's incomprehension before YHWH (ידע and בין), although common in themselves, occur together most frequently in wisdom contexts (Job 14:21; 15:9; 23:5; Prov 1:2; 24:12; 29:7; Pss 92:7; 139:2; Dan 1:4; Jer 4:22) and only rarely elsewhere (Ps 82:5; Neh 10:29; and Mic 4:12, as well as three other occurrences in Isaiah to be discussed below [43:10; 44:18; 56:11]). It appears that, within the larger evocation of the framework and expectations of the Song of Moses, Isaiah is also pointing to a failure in wisdom's basic requirements.

It is worth noting that Deut 32 has an interlude that uses wisdom terminology but which finds no allusion in Isa 1. In Deut 32:28–29 we read of the perishing of עֵצָה, "counsel," and תְּבוּנָה, "insight," from Israel, a people who are not wise (חכם) to understand (שׂכל Hiphil and בין) their latter end. Even though Isaiah could have both implied a failure of wisdom and continued his interaction with Deut 32 by alluding to these verses, he does not do so. The allusions move in more than one direction in Isa 1:2–3.

A second and somewhat weaker gesture to wisdom literature may exist in Isa 1:2–3 in the reference to Israel as sons. Although the corrupt sons of Deut 32:5 stand as a closer source for this metaphor,[23] the constant address of the father to the son in Proverbs to pay attention (1:10, 10:1, etc.) is easily recalled. If vv. 2–4 gesture both to the Song of Moses and that kind of insight known from wisdom traditions, then these rebellious sons may also be meant to be understood in two frames of reference.

The implication of this wisdom echo in this passage will become clearer if we recall the "democratic" nature of wisdom in the Hebrew Bible: however much some people may be constitutionally unable to receive wisdom, wisdom itself is, in principle, available to all. Lady Wisdom calls out in public places to anyone willing to listen (1:20–22). Similarly, the only conditions in the father's call to the son are a willingness to listen (2:1–2) and that the son do some searching himself (vv. 3–4). If those conditions are met, the son will become wise (v. 5) and will enjoy the blessed life in the land that is promised to those following wisdom (vv. 20–21). The availability of wisdom in Job and Ecclesiastes is somewhat more complicated: the book of Job overturns the superficially

---

23. The nation is not often described metaphorically as a son in the Hebrew Bible. Bergey lists Deut 32:19; Isa 30:1, 9 (negative) and Exod 4:22; Hos 2:1; 11:1; Jer 31:9; and Ps 73:15 (positive) as other examples ("Song of Moses," 39). Deuteronomy 14:1 can be added to this list (*HALOT*, 138).

plausible "wisdom" of the friends and surprisingly affirms Job (42:7), while Qohelet will claim that wisdom is simply beyond him (7:23–24). However, even in these books the wisdom whose place no one knows in Job 28 is identified with the fear of YHWH and turning from evil (v. 28), qualities that can potentially characterize any human being. For his part, Qohelet balances his skeptical claims with assurances that he did gain wisdom (2:8, 15).[24]

All of this is to say that wisdom is not, in the OT's major wisdom texts, restricted to an elite few. If someone fails to become wise, it is not because wisdom is too difficult or inaccessible. But the poet-prophet opens the book of Isaiah by implying that Israel has failed even these basic requirements. The common trope in wisdom literature of using animal imagery to teach (e.g., Prov 6:6–11; Job 8:14) is reversed: Israel cannot understand what even an ox grasps.[25]

But failed how, exactly? Hermisson understands the comparison with animals in Isa 1:3 to activate the larger theme of creation order in wisdom: Israel does not understand her place in the ordering of the world.[26] Order in creation is a prominent wisdom theme, but this may be an overly fine interpretation, for the verse simply says that Israel does not know what oxen and donkeys know: their owner (קנה, cf. Deut 32:6) and master (בעל). Israel's foolishness—their failure in wisdom—is an incomprehension before YHWH and part of their betrayal of him. Since wisdom itself is fundamentally oriented toward YHWH (Prov 1:7; Job 28:28), this does not lessen the allusion to wisdom; but it does show that Israel's failure in wisdom is raised in the larger context of their failure in the covenant relationship.

This is the first significant gesture toward wisdom in the book of Isaiah. Apparently Israel's covenant failure is caused by their misunderstanding of YHWH—since they do not understand him, since Israel is unwise with regard to the covenant Lord, they have failed in their covenant relationship.

---

24. See further Michael Fox, *A Time to Tear Down and a Time to Build Up: A Rereading of Ecclesiastes* (Grand Rapids: Eerdmans, 1999), 263–65, on Eccl 7:23–24. Qohelet is claiming in 7:23–24 that he has not grasped "what has happened": "an understanding of events, including anomalous and unjust occurrences" (265).

25. Whedbee, *Isaiah and Wisdom*, 40–41.

26. Hermisson, "Prophetie und Weisheit," 118.

Wise and Unwise Kings (Isaiah 10:13; 11:1–9; 19:11–12)

When Isaiah turns from pronouncing woe over Israel's sin (5:8–24; 10:1–4) and the terrifying advance of the Assyrian juggernaut (5:25–30) to Assyria's judgment for pride (10:5–19), he puts two speeches in the mouth of the Assyrian king that form the basis for judgment (vv. 8–11, 13–14). In the latter, the Assyrian king refers to both his strength (כֹחַ) and wisdom (חָכְמָה and בִין Niphal, v. 13). This is wisdom as "effective ability," the same wisdom that stood by Qohelet in his royal accomplishments (Eccl 2:9), but which can be distinguished from wisdom in its more spiritual dimensions (Eccl 2:13–14). This passage does not deny that the Assyrian ruler is mighty and can accomplish what he plans, but it does condemn the pride with which he does so (10:12), to the exclusion of YHWH's appointment of him as an instrument of judgment (10:5–6).

Although there are no obvious echoes between the two passages, it is difficult not to see a contrast between the brutal military "know-how" of the Assyrian king in ch. 10 and the better kind of wisdom of the coming Davidic king in 11:1–5.[27] Among other endowments, this king clearly displays all the virtues called for in wisdom literature: the spirit of wisdom and insight (חָכְמָה וּבִינָה), counsel and might (עֵצָה וּגְבוּרָה), and knowledge and the fear of YHWH (דַּעַת וְיִרְאַת יְהוָה). These qualities allow this king to give just judgment for the poor (vv. 3–4). And it is under the wise reign of this king that creation itself is transformed (vv. 6–9). Although the connection between vv. 1–5 and 6–9 is not obvious to modern readers, Isaiah (and ancient Near Eastern thought generally) did not neatly separate the moral and natural order: breakdown or renewal in the former inevitably affected the latter (cf. Isa 32:14–20). The reference to the דֵּעָה אֶת־יְהוָה that spreads from the cosmic center in v. 9 helps to bind vv. 1–4 and 6:9 while simultaneously prolonging the wisdom elements of the passage because it echoes the knowledge of the divine king in v. 2. But the knowledge of YHWH fills the earth in v. 9, not the king's knowledge. Apparently this Davidic king acts as a mediator and conduit for the knowledge of YHWH: under this rule, his subjects come to know YHWH as he does. The wise king mediates wisdom to his people, to blessed cosmic effect.

---

27. Fichtner also sees a contrast here, noting that the king of Assyria relies on his own wisdom while the Davidic king relies on divine wisdom ("Isaiah Among the Wise," 436).

This passage shows a number of themes that are not common in wisdom literature (e.g., the reign of the king from the cosmic center). But this does not mean they are evacuated of their wisdom content. As Wildberger notes, there is a fusion of royal ideology and wisdom in this passage that causes no dissonance for either domain of discourse.[28] The book of Proverbs explicitly connects the successful rule of any king to wisdom (8:15) and insists on the necessity of just rule (16:12; 20:8), even if it does not ascribe cosmic effect to that kind of rule. In a parallel fashion, this passage in Isaiah shows wisdom playing a crucial role in the rule of this king: just as Israel's foolish incomprehension before their covenant Lord (1:2–3) leads to rampant injustice (1:15–17), so they are given a ruler full of wisdom from YHWH himself (11:2) who establishes justice (v. 5). Wisdom is, if not the main engine of Israel's restoration, a central part of it. There is no hesitance or reservation about the kind of wisdom presented in Proverbs.

The next passage where wisdom language is found takes us out of Isa 1–12 and into the oracles against the nations, but it intersects so neatly with Isa 10:13 and 11:2 that it should be noted here. As YHWH rides on a swift cloud to judge Egypt (19:1–4), the Egyptian economy (vv. 5–10) and royal counsel (vv. 11–15) collapse. Because the Egyptian sages cannot predict or know YHWH's plan for Egypt (v. 12), their wisdom is "foolish counsel" (עֵצָה נִבְעָרָה) and their claim to be among the wise invalidated (v. 11). Together with the arrogant wisdom of the Assyrian king in 10:13 and the Davidic king's wise justice in 11:2, a pattern is beginning to emerge: however much practical skill foreign kings might have in war (10:13), YHWH's plan (עֵצָה) of judgment and restoration for Egypt (19:12) and the whole earth (14:26–27) renders any competing wisdom or counsel utter foolishness (19:11). On the other hand, Israel's failure in wisdom (1:2–3) is redressed with the gift of a wise king (11:1–9)—a king whose rule the nations will benefit from as well (11:10).

Spiritual Blindness and Wisdom in Isaiah 28–35

Isaiah 1–35 can be organized in an A-B-A' pattern, with Israel's judgment under Assyria and restoration under David in Zion in chs. 1–12 and 28–35

---

28. Wildberger, *Isaiah 28–39*, 609–10. As Vermeylen notes, the establishment of the royal throne in righteousness belongs not so much to the world of wisdom as much as it is a reflection of a common ideology ("Le Proto-Isaïe et La Sagesse d'Israël," 48).

surrounding YHWH's judgment of the nations in chs. 13–27. When the book returns to the judgment of Israel in chs. 28–35, however, we find a deeper reflection on the theological significance of the coming Assyrian invasion and the meaning of the promises of deliverance. At several points in these chapters, it is implied that the same action of YHWH will count as a judgment on Israel and an act of salvation: in 29:1–8, for instance, YHWH both reduces his people to a ghost-like state (v. 4) and routs the enemy so completely that they seem no more real than a dream (vv. 7–8). The ambiguity of פקד in v. 6, which could be translated in context as either "punish" or "visit" (to intervene), is probably intentional—indeed, the message of the passage is contained within that ambiguity. This is YHWH's "strange work" of salvation in judgment (28:21). These chapters are not hopeful, however, about a receptive response to the proclamation of this message. It is within these contexts that wisdom allusions are found.

The first passage that undeniably shows a wisdom stamp is 28:23–29. Instead of declaring a word from YHWH (as in 28:14; 30:1, 12), vv. 23–29 begin with a call to listen similar to those made by the father to the son in Proverbs (4:1; 7:24).[29] It also contains a didactic comparison with the natural order (in this case, agriculture) that would fit easily in a wisdom book and ends by highlighting the ever-increasing תּוּשִׁיָּה of YHWH, a word almost exclusively restricted to wisdom literature.[30] But the wisdom lesson itself seems to stand in some tension with its context. These verses speak of the natural sequence and technique for sowing (vv. 24–26) and harvesting (vv. 27–28) as wisdom from YHWH—and "miraculous" or "wonderful" wisdom (הִפְלִיא, v. 29) at that. But how does the apparently simple matter of the sequence of the agricultural year count as miraculous wisdom, and how does it relate to YHWH's strange work of salvation/judgment elsewhere in the chapter?

The repetition of the root פלא in 28:29 and 29:14 helps answer these questions. Although this root is not used in 28:21, both 28:21 and 29:14 refer to the strange work of Jerusalem's simultaneous judgment and salvation in the coming Assyrian invasion. The reference to miraculous counsel in 28:29 thus prompts us to read these agricultural practices as an allegory for YHWH's action both against and in favor of his people: no matter how terrifying the invading army might be, it is only one stage

---

29. Vermeylen, "Le Proto-Isaïe et La Sagesse d'Israël," 54.

30. The noun is found in Mic 6:9 and otherwise only in Proverbs (2:7; 3:21; 8:14; 18:1) and Job (5:12; 6:13; 11:6; 12:16; 26:3). See the further echoes to wisdom listed by Wildberger (*Isaiah 28–35*, 51).

in a natural sequence that ends in a rich harvest (vv. 24–25).[31] No matter how hard-pressed Jerusalem might be, they will not be utterly crushed (v. 28). This passage clearly shows that understanding of YHWH's intervention through Assyria requires the kind of insight called for in wisdom literature.[32]

Since we have already referenced 29:14, it is just as well to note here the reference to wisdom in 29:13–14, where Israel's duplicity (29:13) leads to a deepening of the strangeness or miraculous nature of YHWH's judgment and salvation in the context of the Assyrian invasion (v. 14a). This strangeness explodes human wisdom (the חָכְמַת חֲכָמָיו) and insight (בִּינַת נְבֹנָיו, v. 14b). This is not an attack on the wisdom tradition itself, nor is the prophet here distancing himself from wisdom circles,[33] for wisdom literature agrees with this prophetic claim (e.g., "There is no wisdom or insight or counsel against YHWH" [Prov 21:30]). The point is only that the best human insight into politics and military strategy—the best human ideas about how this aspect of reality works—simply cannot comprehend what YHWH is up to in the coming invasion.[34] Isaiah 31:2 sounds the same note: Egypt will prove no help (v. 1) because of YHWH's unmatched ability to plan and strategize for war. This verse does not refer to the wisdom internal to the divine mind;[35] it only promises that YHWH can out-compete any human strategy for war.

Wisdom allusions are also found in descriptions of restoration in this part of the book. The first such passage is found in 29:24, which contains a number of wisdom terms as it looks forward to the day when those "wandering in spirit" (תֹּעֵי רוּחַ) will (literally) "know insight" (ידע and בִּינָה) and "those complaining will learn instruction" (וְרוֹגְנִים יִלְמְדוּ־לֶקַח). In addition to the close correlation of ידע and בין, רגן and לֶקַח occur predominantly in wisdom texts.[36] The healing of Israel's spiritual

---

31. Brevard Childs, *Isaiah: A Commentary* (OTL; Louisville: Westminster John Knox, 2011), 211. For other interpretations of this passage, see Wildberger, *Isaiah 28–35*, 53–56.

32. See further Hermisson, "Prophetie und Weisheit," 117.

33. As claimed by Fichtner; see further Wildberger, *Isaiah 28–39*, 598–99; Hermisson, "Prophetie und Weisheit," 115–16; Wilson, "Wisdom in Isaiah, 157."

34. Hayes rightly understands vv. 9–14 to describe blindness to YHWH's action in vv. 1–8 ("'A Spirit of Deep Sleep,'" 49).

35. Compare Michael Fox's discussion of this dimension of wisdom in "Ideas of Wisdom in Proverbs 1–9," *JBL* 116 (1997): 627.

36. The former root is found in Deut 1:27; Ps 106:25; Prov 16:28; 18:8; 26:20, 22; the latter in Deut 32:2; Job 11:4; Prov 1:5; 4:2; 7:21; 9:9; 16:21, 23.

blindness (vv. 17–18) is thus joined to a new-found wisdom and spiritual insight (v. 24). The same promise of restoration to wisdom is probably present in 30:20–21, a passage that mirrors the natural and spiritual restoration promised in 29:17–24. The reference to YHWH as teacher (מוֹרֶה, elsewhere in Job 36:22; Prov 5:13; Hab 2:18) and Israel hearing a word (see Prov 1:8; 4:1; 5:7, 13; etc.) that guides them as to their way (הַדֶּרֶךְ, Prov 2:8, 12, 13, 20; 3:6, 17, 23; etc.), whether left or right (Prov 4:26, 27; Eccl 10:2), strongly echoes the language of Proverbs. When YHWH restores his people, they will see their Teacher and receive the wisdom they presently lack. A third reference to wisdom is found in 33:6. Although textually difficult,[37] the treasures of salvation, wisdom, knowledge, and the fear of YHWH that are promised as part of YHWH's rule in Zion constitute a similar promise to those in 29:24 and 30:30–21. That no fools wander on the highway back to Zion in 35:8 should be read in the same way—just as the spiritual sight of those redeemed and returning to Zion (vv. 5, 10) is restored by YHWH's own theophanic approach (v. 4), so their folly is implicitly healed, for fools are excluded from this highway.[38]

A final important reference to wisdom in Isa 28–35 in a passage of restoration is found in 32:3–8, which promises a single royal figure as part of Israel's restoration instead of speaking of the nation in general.[39] According to this passage, when the coming king reigns in righteousness, Israel's blind eyes are opened and their deaf ears sharpened (v. 3). The people's new wisdom runs deep: their hearts understand knowledge (יָבִין לָדַעַת) and their speech responds in kind, changing from clumsy to dazzling (צַח). (Although expressed differently, ch. 11 shows a similar connection between the wise rule of the coming king and its effects on the people.)

---

37. See discussion in Wildberger, *Isaiah 28–35*, 74–75, 268.

38. In the above interpretation, I am reading the MT of the second line of v. 8 essentially as it stands. It is possible to emend so that it would read that fools will not wander on the way as they travel (cf. *BHS* n. 9c), but it is unclear how the redeemed of v. 10 could be called fools. I understand the line to deny fools or anything unclean access to this way, thus securing its holiness (v. 8). See further the discussion of Claire Mathews, *Defending Zion: Eden's Desolation and Jacob's Restoration (Isaiah 34–35) in Context* (BZAW 236; Berlin: de Gruyter, 1995), 122 n. 2.

39. For present purposes, it is not necessary precisely to identify the nature of the expectations surrounding this king, or whether the hope for a future king in this passage is best labeled "Messianic." For a range of opinions, see John Oswalt, *The Book of Isaiah, Chapters 1–39* (NICOT; Grand Rapids: Eerdmans, 1986), 579–80; and Wildberger, *Isaiah 28–35*, 234–36.

The new wisdom of restored Israel is expressed in ways that echo
other passages in chs. 28–35. For instance, when we read of the dazzling
speech of newly wise Israel, it is not difficult to remember the people's
stuttering, sarcastic resistance to the prophetic message in 28:10 (cf. the
dumb tongue singing for joy in 35:6). The first clause of 32:4 shows
similar echoes: even though the root מהר has not been used in chs. 28–31,
one thinks of how the one believing will not be in haste in 28:16 (הַמַּאֲמִין
לֹא יָחִישׁ) and how the people refuse rest (נַחַת) and quietness (הַשְׁקֵט) in
order to ride on horses (30:15–16). The call to the hasty of heart in 35:4
to behold YHWH as he theophanically approaches to bring his people
back from exile should also be mentioned, since it forms with 32:4 the
only other place in Isaiah where לב and מהר are joined. The significance
of these echoes is to show that the wisdom promised to the people in vv.
3–4 means they will never again be blind to YHWH and his judging and
saving work. Wisdom terminology continues in vv. 4–8 in lines that would
hardly be out of place in the book of Proverbs (compare, for example, v.
6a with Prov 12:23b). Their import in context, however, is that fools and
nobles will no longer be confused and the former no longer tragically
given positions of leadership (cf. Isa 3:4–5). In Motyer's apt phrase, this
future king will usher in "a true aristocracy of character."[40]

Wisdom references in Isa 28–35 run along two main lines: Israel's
spiritual blindness to YHWH is sometimes portrayed in terms suggesting
a specific failure in wisdom, and their restoration is similarly sometimes
described as a restoration of that same facility. Just as Israel presently
lacks the facility to comprehend YHWH's strange work in the Assyrian
invasion and so falls under judgment, so there is coming a time when their
new spiritual sight of YHWH will grant them sensitivity to his strange
way of working (e.g., 29:23–24).

Blind Israel and the Suffering Servant (Isaiah 40–55)

The first possibility of wisdom influence in Isa 40–55 is found in
40:12–26. This passage unfolds in two parallel movements in vv. 12–18
and 19–26. The passage's main contention is stated at the end of both of
these movements in vv. 18 and 25: since God is so utterly transcendent,
so utterly unworthy of comparison with anything in creation, it is impossible that he has forgotten or mistreated his people (v. 27). The strongest
possible candidate for wisdom influence is found in v. 14, which exposes

---

40. J. A. Motyer, *The Prophecy of Isaiah: An Introduction and Commentary*
(Downers Grove: InterVarsity, 1993), 258.

the impossibility of YHWH needing counsel (יעץ) so that he might under-stand (בין) and learn (למד) the path of justice (אֹרַח מִשְׁפָּט, a phrase found only elsewhere in Prov 2:8; 17:23), knowledge (דַּעַת), and the path of understanding (דֶּרֶךְ תְּבוּנוֹת). The image of a king receiving counsel from his sages is clearly in the background, the point being that the divine King has no such need. YHWH's speeches in the book of Job most often form the point of comparison. The speech begins with some similar terms, questioning Job's darkening of counsel (עֵצָה) in words without knowledge (דַּעַת, 38:2).[41] YHWH then points to different aspects of creation to challenge Job's claim that YHWH is mishandling his role as sovereign over the universe (e.g., 9:22–24; 12:6). This is the עֵצָה referred to in Job 38.2: YHWH's strategy for governing creation. YHWH appeals to public and verifiable evidence to answer Job's contention (40:2) that YHWH is the cosmic destroyer (e.g., 9:5–7).

The arguments of both passages do, admittedly, move in opposite directions: Isa 40:12–26 shows YHWH distinguishing himself from everything in creation while Job 38 describes different aspects of creation to draw inferences about his manner of governing it. The stance of the human conversation partner is also different: while YHWH confronts the antagonistic Job, he speaks tenderly to his exiled people in Isa 40.[42] But the argument of both passages is the same and is made in the same way. Creation is redescribed in order to change the human audience's view of God (as monstrous and unjust in the case of Job, or neglectful in the case of exilic Israel).

Before moving on to the Servant's wisdom, we can briefly note that, in a manner similar to 29:13 and 31:2, Isa 44:25 and 47:10 promise the frustration of conventional wisdom. Spiritual blindness also recurs as a theme in these chapters. Although certain passages in Isa 1–39 might lead the reader to expect that the restoration from exile would entail the resto-ration of Israel's blindness (e.g., 35:1–10), Israel surprisingly remains uncomprehending to who YHWH really is (42:18–22; 43:8–10) even as he proves his sole deity and humiliates every idol in the return of Israel from

---

41. Wilson, "Wisdom in Isaiah," 160; James Ward, "The Servant's Knowledge in Isaiah 40–55," in *Israelite Wisdom* (ed. John Gammie; Missoula: Scholars Press, 1978), 122–24; and J. Gerald Janzen, *At the Scent of Water: The Ground of Hope in the Book of Job* (Grand Rapids: Eerdmans, 2009), 98–99. Meindert Dijkstra draws a form-critical connection between Isa 40:12–26 and Mesopotamian wisdom texts in his article "Lawsuit, Debate, and Wisdom Discourse in Second Isaiah," in *Studies in the Book of Isaiah* (ed. J. Van Ruiten and M. Vervenne; BETL 132; Leuven: Leuven University Press, 1997), 256–59.

42. Ward, "Servant's Knowledge," 124.

exile (41:4–7, 21–29). Furthermore, just as a few passages in chs. 1–39 imply that the people's blindness counts as a failure in wisdom (29:13–14, 18–24, as discussed above), the same implication is made in two passages in Isa 40–55. In 41:20 YHWH's renewal of the desert—a key dimension of his restorative, saving action in these chapters (compare 43:20–21)—is accomplished so that the nations may know (ידע) and understand (שׂכל Hiphil) that YHWH is the only God. Although the verb שׂכל is found throughout the Hebrew Bible, it features so prominently in Proverbs as a term for wisdom that it appears the author is presenting wise insight into YHWH's sole deity (v. 20) as a result of his action (vv. 17–19). The same verbs are used to describe the blindness of idolatry in 44:18 with the same purpose: idolaters simply do not comprehend the folly of praying to a god one makes for oneself. The essence of wisdom—an insight into who YHWH is (Prov 2:1–8), leading to a blessed and secure life (2:9–22)—is lacking. Tragically, God's people are not much better in Isa 40–55. Isaiah 43:10 laments blind Israel's failure to know (ידע), believe (אמן Hiphil), and understand (בין Hiphil) YHWH as the only God. God's servant fails in its role as witness to the only God who can restore and save.

Wisdom and spiritual sight are intertwined again in 52:13–53:12. Without at all doing justice to the many questions this text raises, two points of contact with the wisdom tradition should be noted: the wise action or success of the servant (הִנֵּה יַשְׂכִּיל עַבְדִּי) in 52:13 and his knowledge (דַּעַת) in 53:11. It is difficult to know how to translate the first clause of 52:13. The verb can either mean to succeed (e.g., Josh 1:7–8) or to show wise insight (Isa 41:20, see *HALOT* 1328–29). Either sense would fit here: either the success of the servant stands in parallel to his exaltation in v. 13b, or his wisdom throughout his horrendous suffering (53:1–9) eventually contributes to his exaltation. Perhaps both senses are intended, so that the servant perseveres in his suffering because of his wisdom, which leads to success in his mission (vv. 10–12).[43]

The articulation of the theme of spiritual blindness within this subsection of the song (52:13–15) is important to appreciate the full significance of the chapter's wisdom allusions. Although the recognition of "the many"[44] dawns only slowly (52:14), they come to see what was

---

43. Jan Koole shows how both ancient and modern interpretations of Isa 53 are split neatly on this question and how reading the word in either way activates a larger field of reference which would be appropriate in context—the Servant's wisdom (compare 50:4) or his royal success (1 Sam 18:5, 14). See *Isaiah III*. Vol. 2, *Isaiah 49–55* (trans. A. P. Runia; HCOT; Kampen: Kok Pharos, 1998), 264–65.

44. D. J. A. Clines discusses the relationship between the otherwise unidentified "we" and the "they" in this passage and how both groups eventually come to have

not told them and understand what they have not heard (וַאֲשֶׁר לֹא־שָׁמְעוּ הִתְבּוֹנָנוּ, v. 15). Since שׁמע and בין are found together only elsewhere in Isa 6:9–10, it seems that the spiritual blindness that has plagued Israel both before and during the exile is finally healed in the ministry of the Suffering Servant.[45] How exactly this happens is perhaps not entirely clear: we are told only that the servant is wise/successful and exalted (52:13) and that the earlier shocked response to him (v. 14) eventually breaks into understanding (v. 15). Is it possible that this change occurs not only because of the Servant's exaltation (13b) but also because of wisdom (13a)? If this is the case, then 52:13–15 shows the same pattern in the presentation of the royal figures in 11:1–20 and 32:1–8. Although an identification of the royal figures promised in the first half of the book and the despised Servant in the second half would of course require a longer argument,[46] the implicit effect of the Servant's wisdom/success on others is the same as those other figures.

Just as the description of the Servant's exaltation in 52:13–15 is paralleled in 53:10–12, so the Servant's דַּעַת in 53:11 parallels his wisdom in 52:13.[47] Koole points out that it probably does not refer to others' knowledge of the Servant since the suffixes on this noun elsewhere in Isa 40–55 refer to the subject's knowledge, not the knowledge others have (44:25; 47:10; 48:4).[48] Ward moves in a different direction by arguing that this verse speaks of the Servant's knowledge of God—everything Isa 40–55 proclaims about YHWH as the only Savior, the Servant

the same relation to the Servant and benefit from his suffering (*I, He, We, and They: A Literary Approach to Isaiah 53* [JSOTSup 1; repr., Sheffield: Sheffield Academic, 1983], 40). Although it is not crucial to the above discussion, I understand the former to represent members of God's people who at first misunderstand the purpose of the Servant's suffering, only slowly realizing that he is bearing "our" sins (53:1–6), while the "they" represents foreign nations (the גּוֹיִם of 52:15).

45. John Goldingay notes this link and a number of other echoes between this verse and other passages in Isa 40–55 (*The Message of Isaiah 40–55: A Literary-Theological Commentary* [New York: T&T Clark International, 2005]), 494.

46. Goldingay traces a number of royal hints and echoes to David in the description of this figure (ibid., 489).

47. Not a few commentators shift the verse divisions in *BHS* and link בְּדַעְתּוֹ with the servant's justification of the many in the next line. I read the word with יִשְׂבָּע because the verb not infrequently takes objects with בְּ (e.g., Pss 65:6; 88:4; 103:5; Isa 58:11; Lam 3:15, 30) and because in vv. 4–6 the Servant does not justify the many specifically on the basis of his knowledge but because of his substitutionary suffering. See further Koole, *Isaiah III*. Vol. 2, *Isaiah 49–55*, 331–32.

48. Ibid., 331.

understands.[49] This would certainly fit with verses like 50:4. In the context of v. 11, however, the Servant's satisfaction probably has to do with the success of his mission—even when his suffering was so profound that others shunned him (53:3) without understanding why he was suffering (v. 4), the Servant's mission is successful (vv. 10–12). He is satisfied in his knowledge of this.[50] If this reading is correct, then דַעַת has a somewhat more restrictive sense than the use of שׂכל in 52:13. This is the case because the former term's association with new-found spiritual sight suggests that the Servant's wisdom is related to the healing of the foolish blindness of "the many." The servant's knowledge, however, seems to be entirely his own. Whether or not this דַעַת counts specifically as *wise* knowledge (as in, e.g., Isa 11:2) or is intended only in a more general sense (as in 5:13) is more difficult to determine; the parallel with 52:13 may tip the scales in favor of the former.

To my knowledge, this is the last plausible candidate for wisdom influence in Isaiah. I find no evidence of wisdom language or themes in Isa 54–55 nor in Isa 56–66. The only exception is 56:11, which condemns shepherds who have no understanding (לֹא יָדְעוּ הָבִין). But this is so similar to other expressions of the failure of wisdom on the part of the people or their leaders that it hardly requires further comment.

Conclusion: The Status of Wisdom in Isaiah

Wisdom plays a role both in the judgment and restoration of Israel in the book of Isaiah. One dimension of Israel's covenant failure and their spiritual blindness to YHWH is a failure in wisdom (1:2–3; 43:20). Everyone fails in this score in the book: Israel's leaders (29:13–14) and foreign nations and their leaders are utterly foolish (10:13; 19:11–12; 44:18; 47:10). But God's action in the tumult of history will expose their folly for what it is (31:2; 44:25). Understanding YHWH's action of simultaneous judgment and salvation requires wisdom (28:23–29), and YHWH's action in history is meant to provoke this kind of insight (41:20). But it is only after YHWH effects a deeper spiritual restoration in his people that they will regain wisdom (29:24; 30:20–21; 33:6; 35:8). Furthermore, the restoration of wisdom is focused more than once in the leaders YHWH gives his people (11:1–5, 10; 32:1–8; 52:13; 53:11). These leaders not only rule wisely but spread wisdom and the knowledge of YHWH among the people they rule over (11:1–10; 32:1–8).

---

49. Ward, "The Servant's Knowledge," 129.

50. This does not imply that the Servant's knowledge is initially imperfect (see further Koole, *Isaiah III*. Vol. 2, *Isaiah 49–55*, 332).

Nowhere in the book is criticism made of wisdom per se; nowhere does the text indicate hesitation about the search for that insight into YHWH and the created order that Proverbs details.[51] At the same time, the book of Isaiah never presents wisdom itself as a catalyst of restoration. This is hardly surprising: wisdom can make its appeal to the simple, but when rejected, wisdom is lost (Prov 1:20–33). Wisdom itself shows no mechanism for recovering those who have turned away. Similarly, in Isaiah it is the direct action of YHWH (29:17–24; 30:18–26) or the leaders YHWH gives (11:1–10; 32:1–8) that effect restoration. One part of this restoration is renewal in wisdom—the renewal in that very lack of insight that led to Israel's judgment. But although wisdom is one necessary dimension of Israel's restoration, it cannot in itself effect that restoration.

The conclusion offered here is somewhat stronger than some other conclusions on the same subject. For instance, Wilson argues that, because wisdom terms in Isaiah are used in connection with covenant judgment and an eschatological future, "wisdom terms have been incorporated into the book for a different purpose," i.e., a purpose different from their use in wisdom literature.[52] According to Wilson, Isaiah's interest is not in wisdom itself; he uses wisdom terms only because they were accepted by his audience and consistent with his prophetic agenda. But they lose their sapiential character in the book of Isaiah.[53] Donald Morgan argues essentially along the same lines.[54] The gestures to wisdom in Isaiah are brief, but the above discussion suggests that wisdom terms and ideas are used as wisdom, not merely because they were an accepted form of discourse that otherwise conveniently fit into the prophetic program.

51. In disagreement with Hayes, "'A Spirit of Deep Sleep,'" 52. Hayes (correctly, in my opinion) understands Isaiah to identify Judeans with the fool in Proverbs because both are shut off to wisdom from the outside, regardless of the consequences. In my opinion, however, she errs in claiming that "Isaiah 1–39 borrows wisdom's own language to expose the deceptive and dangerous aspects of wisdom and its praxis." It is not clear to me what aspects of wisdom and its practice are resisted in the book of Isaiah; the criticisms laid against certain kinds of wisdom in Isaiah are paralleled in Proverbs (recall the discussion above concerning Isa 29:13–14). It would perhaps be better to distinguish not some aspects within wisdom, but true and false wisdom—something both prophetic and wisdom literature does.

52. Wilson, "Wisdom in Isaiah," 161.

53. Ibid., 162.

54. Morgan, *Wisdom in the Old Testament Traditions*, 82.

In Isaiah, every facet of YHWH's covenant with Israel has failed: sacrifice is useless (1:10–19), the priesthood only leads people astray (28:7), and torah has been rejected (5:24). Israel's failure in wisdom's generous conditions is one part of this massive collapse in the people's covenant existence before God. And yet, even while exposing the hopelessness of Israel's condition (1:5–9), YHWH is perfectly and gloriously able to restore. And the wisdom found in what we know as the book of Proverbs is one part of that restoration.

THE STRUCTURAL ROLE OF WISDOM IN JEREMIAH

Leslie C. Allen

Any attempt to study wisdom in the book of Jeremiah is confronted by two separate sets of problems barring the way. First, wisdom is a slippery, complex term beset by uncertainty about its roles in Judean society and its meaning in particular literary contexts. Second, the book of Jeremiah is generally acknowledged to be a multi-layered composition that poses problems of redaction, setting, and purpose. As to the second issue, I have already had to face it in the commentary in the Old Testament Library series and here do not find it necessary to do more than echo its conclusions. My present intention is to conduct a literary study based on the final form of the book, while respecting the likely historical settings of its diverse content. As for the first of the two issues, my conviction is that of Roland Murphy and Raymond Van Leeuwen, namely that in principle R. N. Whybray's thesis was right in understanding Old Testament wisdom in terms of an intellectual tradition but is not to be followed in denying there was a professional class of sages in Israel.[1] Each context deserves separate consideration as to the precise meaning of wisdom, and being prepared to find what Murphy called "an approach to reality which was shared by all the Israelites in varying degrees"[2] and what Van Leeuwen has similarly called "the general wisdom common

---

1. Roland E. Murphy, "Wisdom—Theses and Hypotheses," in *Israelite Wisdom: Theological and Literary Essays in Honor of Samuel Terrien* (ed. J. G. Gammie et al.; Missoula: Scholars Press, 1978), 39; Raymond C. Van Leeuwen, "The Sage in the Prophetic Literature," in *The Sage in Israel and the Ancient Near East* (ed. J. G. Gammie and L. G. Perdue; Winona Lake: Eisenbrauns, 1990), 299–301. Both are referring to R. N. Whybray, *The Intellectual Tradition in the Old Testament* (BZAW 135; Berlin: de Gruyter, 1974).

2. Murphy, "Wisdom," 40.

to cultured Israelites."[3] Perhaps a partial parallel to Israel's intellectual tradition is pop psychology in Western culture, in which such terms as inferiority complex and schizophrenia have been taken over from their precise, professional settings and are widely used in society in more general ways.

The thesis of this essay is that "wisdom" (חָכְמָה) and "wise" (חָכָם) function as keywords in a particular block of Jeremiah, chs. 7–10, and that their presence outside that block has anticipatory and recapitulating functions. Literary blocks in Jeremiah are usually signaled by an initial prophetic word heading, such as appears in 7:1 (at least in the MT edition of the book, though lacking in the earlier edition represented by the LXX) and next in 11:1: "The word that came to Jeremiah from the LORD."[4] This block is an important one. Its opening prose sermon that in 7:1–8:3 summarizes from a Deuteronomistic perspective the content of Jeremiah's prophesying is the first and foremost of a number of others in the book. In my commentary I understood the main thrust of the block to be the certainty of exile as divine retribution for Judah's sins. I entitled the block "the self-paved road to exile."[5] Wisdom appears to play a supporting role as a sub-theme for this general theme, and the nature of that role requires consideration.

Of the seventeen occurrences of "wisdom/wise" in the book, no fewer than ten turn up in this block.[6] This clustering appears structurally important. In studying it I want to steer between too narrow a perspective and one that is too broad. On the one hand, it could be said that the meaning of the instances varies so much that they can hardly be considered as a group. If one has in mind only a particular class that represents wisdom, then the cases in 9:17 (16); 10:9 should be excluded from consideration.[7] On the other hand, there are scholars, especially in older studies of wisdom, who have included many items in their coverage: wisdom vocabulary other than the root חכם, wisdom genres, stylistic elements characteristic of wisdom literature, and wisdom themes. In this study such

---

3. Van Leeuwen, "The Sage in Prophetic Literature," 298.

4. Unless otherwise indicated, biblical quotations are taken from the NRSV.

5. Leslie C. Allen, *Jeremiah: A Commentary* (OTL; Louisville: Westminster John Knox, 2008), 92.

6. Jer 8:8–9 (3×); 9:12 (MT 11), 17 (16; NRSV "skilled"), 23 (22; 2×); 10:7, 9 (NRSV "skilled workers"), 12.

7. Johannes Lindblom, "Wisdom in the Old Testament Prophets," in *Wisdom in Israel and in the Ancient Near East Presented to H. H. Rowley* (ed. M. Noth and D. Winton Thomas; VTSup 3; Leiden: Brill, 1955), 193–94.

material is left out of consideration unless it occurs in a passage alongside the terms "wise" or "wisdom." This approach is adopted for two reasons: the study has in view these rhetorical keywords as structural indicators and it is doubtful whether such other wisdom criteria have exclusive wisdom associations.[8]

As to the wisdom orientation of this particular block, Walter Brueggemann, in his 1978 study of Jer 9:23–24 (22–23), found here "the general movement of 8:4–10:25."[9] He included the motif of knowledge in his survey of wisdom features, along with analogy, rhetorical questions, and admonition. However, Lindblom two decades earlier had observed that knowing Yahweh "is of course genuinely prophetic and has nothing to do with the doctrines of the Wisdom teachers,"[10] while others have drawn attention to the usage of the concept in both Hosea and Jeremiah that distinguishes them from the wisdom tradition. As Crenshaw has written in more general terms, "the mere use of wisdom phraseology by a prophet does not make him a sage, for his meaning may be completely alien to wisdom thinking."[11] Timothy Polk likewise singled out 8:4–10:25 as a special locus for wisdom concerns, but he too included the prophetic term "know" and also the overall emphasis on right speech and the bird references in 8:7 as wisdom characteristics.[12] Douglas Jones observed the use of wisdom categories in the structuring of chs. 8–10.[13] He included in his purview rhetorical questions, proverbs, and vocabulary such as "know" and "understand." Gerlinde Baumann gave a good, brief overview of wisdom in chs. 8–10 in the course of an article on 9:23–24 (22–23)

8. See, e.g., with regard to forms, James L. Crenshaw, "The Influence of the Wise Upon Amos," *ZAW* 79 (1967): 46–49, and with regard to vocabulary, Whybray, *Intellectual Tradition*, 121–43.

9. Walter A. Brueggemann, "The Epistomological Crisis of Israel's Two Histories (Jer 9:22–23)," in Gammie et al., eds., *Israelite Wisdom*, 89.

10. Lindblom, "Wisdom in the Old Testament Prophets," 199.

11. James L. Crenshaw, "Method in Determining Wisdom Influence Upon 'Historical' Literature," in *Urgent Advice and Probing Questions: Collected Writings on Old Testament Wisdom* (Macon: Mercer University Press, 1995), 317.

12. Timothy Polk, *The Prophetic Persona: Jeremiah and the Language of Self* (JSOTSup 32; Sheffield: JSOT Press, 1984), 102–4, 120–24.

13. Douglas R. Jones, *Jeremiah* (NCB; Grand Rapids: Eerdmans, 1992), 158–77. Most of the article by Hermisson has a similarly wide agenda. Hans-Jürgens Hermisson. "Weisheit im Jeremiabuch," in *Schriftauslegung in der Schrift: Festschrift für Odil Hannes Steck zu seinem 65. Geburtstag* (ed. K. Schmidt et al.; BZAW 300; Berlin: de Gruyter, 2000), 75–91.

but did not relate it to the main theme of exile.[14] From a quite different perspective, William McKane's essay, broadly entitled "Jeremiah and the Wise," identified "the wise" with statesmen and traced their attitudes to the prophet in chs. 26 and 36.[15] There is room for a fresh, more rigorous contextual examination of wisdom in Jer 8–10.

Jeremiah 8:8–9

The theme of wisdom is given a rousing send-off in 8:8–9, which refers to it no less than three times. The terms occur in a disputation of a type analyzed by Donald Murray in prophetic texts apart from Jeremiah.[16] The type first presents a thesis (v. 8a), then disputes it (vv. 8b–9b*a*), and finally offers a counter-thesis (v. 9b*b*). The disputation is part of a complex oracle of disaster in vv. 4–13. The drift of the oracle can be discerned in the reasons for judgment in vv. 4–7 and the announcement of judgment in vv. 9a, 10a, and 13. The disputation functions as a bridge between the grounds for judgment and the judgment itself, embracing both components.[17] The confrontational nature of disputation accounts for the temporary switch to direct address in v. 8.[18] The reference to "the law of the LORD" is no longer clear, but what precedes and follows sheds a little light. The ensuing mention of scribal activity suggests that a written form of the torah traditions had in some crucial respects been amended to blunt its force. There is a parallel of sorts in a NT passage: Mark 7:9–13. Nevertheless, in Jeremiah's time the community gullibly accepted the adaptations as true when in fact they no longer represented Yahweh's covenantal "requirements" (מִשְׁפַּט, v. 7 NIV).

---

14. Gerlinde Baumann, "Jeremia, die Weisen und die Weisheit: Eine Untersuchung von Jer. 9,22f.," *ZAW* 114 (2002): 77–78.

15. William McKane, "Jeremiah and the Wise," in *Wisdom in Ancient Israel: Essays in Honour of J. A. Emerton* (ed. J. Day, Robert P. Gordon, and H. G. M. Williamson; Cambridge: Cambridge University Press, 1995), 142–51.

16. Donald F. Murray, "The Rhetoric of Disputation: Reexamination of a Prophetic Genre," *JSOT* 38 (1987): 95–121.

17. The passage is complicated by the inclusion of a separate oracle of judgment in the MT edition of the book at vv. 10b–12, repeated from 6:13–15. This extra material is absent from the edition represented in the LXX.

18. Michael Moore has aptly compared Isa 19:11b: "How can you say to Pharaoh, 'I am one of the sages?'" Michael S. Moore, "Jeremiah's Progressive Paradox," *RB* 93 (1986): 396–97. Both a rhetorical question of the same type and a switch to direct address occur there.

Whybray has rightly observed that the community is addressed in v. 8 as claiming to be wise.[19] Then there is coherence with the references to "this people" and "my people" in vv. 4 and 7. The claim amounts to confident self-approval as following the right course. This claim is reminiscent of the sapiential charge of being wise in one's own eyes (e.g., Prov 3:7),[20] which Isaiah transferred to a wider setting (Isa 5:21). Jeremiah implicitly does the same in denying conventional wisdom, which he does in two respects. The claim runs ominously counter both to the people's abandonment of true torah traditions and to their rejection of Jeremiah's prophesying ("the word of the LORD"). The prophet also condemns both faults in 6:19 while the prose sermon at the head of the block has highlighted them in 7:5–6, 9, 13, 25–26, 28. Now they are linked with the claim of wisdom. Such opposition to that double divine revelation disproves their professed wisdom. It can only lead to military defeat and capture. So it is not wisdom after all, but an attitude that is reprehensibly wrong. From Jeremiah's perspective, true wisdom is grounded in respect for covenantal traditions.

Jeremiah 9:12 (11)

Jeremiah 9:12–16 (11–15) continues the wisdom theme at v. 12 (11). The prose passage appears to be a redactional summary of 8:4–9:11 (10). It ruminates on the ghastly desolation of Judah that left people asking a bewildered "Why?" The two religious authorities representing wisdom and prophecy, committed as they were to a paradigm of communal security, were left without any answer. "The first reference is to the wise man and the second to the prophet."[21] The rift between such spokespersons for God and Jeremiah himself will resurface at 18:18 in a different context. Only a prophet like Jeremiah, who prophesied destruction for the land and exile for the people, realized that their rejection of torah traditions made such a fate inevitable. Not only the conventional wisdom of 8:8–9, but now professional wisdom is portrayed negatively. It lacked understanding concerning an unprecedented national experience of deportation to strange lands, with worse to come (v. 16 [15]).

19. Whybray, *Intellectual Tradition*, 22–23.
20. Cf. Gilbert's comment: "Avoir cette Loi, voilà, aux yeux du peuple sa sagesse." M. Gilbert, "Jérémie en conflit avec les sages?" in *Le livre de Jérémie: le prophète et son milieu, les oracles et leur transmission* (ed. P.-M. Bogaert; 2nd ed.; Leuven: Leuven University Press, 1997), 111.
21. William McKane, *Jeremiah 1–25* (ICC; Edinburgh: T. & T. Clark, 1986), 206.

Jeremiah 9:17 (16)

No wonder the next unit, vv. 17–22 (16–21), calls for lament and so for the guild of (literally) "wise women" to practice their expertise (cf. Amos 5:16). The juxtaposition of this unit with the previous one creates the irony that a quite different kind of wisdom is needed to help in the grief work that invasion culminating in exile will warrant: "We must leave our land because our homes are in ruins" (v. 20 [19] NIV). "The wise men have failed (9:11) and the only wisdom valued is that which knows how to weep," Brueggemann rightly commented.[22]

Jeremiah 9:23–24 (22–23)

Just as three references to wisdom occurred in the first unit at 8:8–9, the next wisdom-related units are grouped together with equal emphasis in a triad that concludes with 9:23–24 (22–23). The historical setting of this unit is uncertain.[23] It features wisdom in an admonition, along with two other values prized in Judean society. The professionally wise— here evidently political counselors—warriors, and the wealthy were classes respectfully set apart from the rest of the community, and so they regarded the three separate things that made them special as intrinsic priorities. However, in their place a set of three covenantal priorities is commended: "steadfast love, justice, and righteousness." A lack of respect for such priorities is implied. The Hebrew verb for "boast," הִתְהַלֵּל, can refer not only to a negative sense of self-centeredness but also to a positive expression of praise, as in Jer 4:2 ("in him they will glory," NIV). Here the verb glides from one sense to the other. Since the latter usage is generally associated with YHWH as the focus of praise, the text does not present a direct balance between the three secular values and their spiritual replacements. Instead, an appreciation of YHWH as one who practices these virtues is commended: "I the LORD act with kindness, justice and equity in the world" (NJPS). In an overall context that has exile in view, the significance of his doing so "in the earth" appears to anticipate the references to the earth in 10:10–13, which refer to YHWH as creator and maintainer of the world. Here God's providential control of the world at large is in view (cf. Ps 33:5).[24] Implicitly, Judean exiles outside their land are encouraged to identify themselves

---

22. Brueggemann, "Epistemological Crisis," 90.

23. Brueggemann (ibid., passim) assumed the saying to be pre-exilic because he found in it a royal perspective.

24. Baumann, "Jeremia," 76.

with such a universal God in their own lifestyle. Appreciation of these divine qualities involves practicing them in turn. Ernst Kutsch observed that knowing God means to know God's will and to follow it, citing 22:16.[25]

The addition in the LXX at 1 Sam 2:10, which reappears in *Odes* 3:10, alludes to Jer 9:23–24 (22–23) in a condensed form. It significantly makes the qualities human: "to understand and know the Lord and to do justice and righteousness in the midst of the earth."[26] Similarly, the allusion in *1 Clem.* 13:1 has "in order to seek him and do justice and righteousness." Moreover, since God's delight is very often associated in the Old Testament with human activities and qualities, such seems to be the case with the spiritual threesome here in Jeremiah.[27] They are not only divine attributes but must become human ones too. One may compare Hos 2:19 (21), where the threesome is included among God's marriage gifts to be given to Israel ("bestowing righteousness and justice, loyalty and love" [REB]) and is linked with knowing YHWH in v. 20 (22).[28] The secular values of Jer 9:23 (22) are to be replaced with the spiritual ones of v. 24 (23) as a consequence of understanding and knowing YHWH.

25. Ernst Kutsch, "Weisheit und Prophetenwort: Zur Traditionsgeschichte des Spruches Jer. 9,22–23," *BZ* 25, no. 2 (1981): 164–5; repr. in *Kleine Schriften zum Alten Testament* (ed. L. Schmidt and K. Eberlein; BZAW 168; Berlin: de Gruyter, 1986), 197–215.

26. Emanuel Tov considers the *Vorlage* of the LXX in 1 Samuel probably original in Jeremiah, since "the clearly defined opposition between the actions and views of humans, as in the addition in Samuel, is more natural than in Jeremiah." Emanuel Tov, "Different Editions of the Song of Hannah and of Its Narrative Framework," in *Tehillah le-Moshe: Biblical and Judaic Studies in Honor of Moshe Greenberg* (ed. M. Cogan et al.; Winona Lake: Eisenbrauns, 1977), 166 n. 59. Cf. Kutsch's view ("Weisheit und Prophetenwort," 170–76) that a proverb appearing in an earlier form in 1 Sam 2:10; *1 Clem.* 13:1 was changed to a prophetic version in Jeremiah.

27. Wanke rendered the close of v. 24 (23) "den an solchen (Menschen) habe ich Gefallen." Gunther Wanke, "Weisheit im Jeremiabuch," in *Weisheit ausserhalb der kanonischen Weisheitschriften* (ed. B. Janowski; Veröffentlichungen der Weisheitschaftlichen Gesellschaft für Theologie; Gutersloh: Chr. Kaiser, 1996), 97. Wanke was implicitly following Kutsch ("Weisheit und Prophetenwort," 175), who interpreted in terms of "those who boast in such knowledge of Yahweh." If a human reference is preferred, a better interpretation would be "those who, like YHWH, practice steadfast love, justice, and righteousness."

28. Baumann ("Jeremia," 77) has drawn attention to Ps 147:10–11, which states the LORD's delight not in military prowess but "in those who fear him, in those who wait for his steadfast love."

The literary context of this unit pushes wisdom to the fore. Over against right priorities, the unit downplays wisdom, in line with the first of the wisdom-related units (v. 12 [11]), and places a renewed emphasis on the covenantal concerns that marked 8:8–9.

Jeremiah 10:7, 9, 12

Jeremiah 10:1–16 contains the last references to wisdom in the literary block. The composition is made up of an admonition in vv. 2–5 and a hymn in vv. 12–16, with an exhortation written in Aramaic in v. 11. The admonition and the hymn appear to have an exilic provenance in contrasting Yahwism and Babylonian religion based on astrology and image worship. Verses 6–10 are also in the style of a hymn, but apart from the first four cola of v. 9 do not appear in the edition represented by the LXX. They make up an extra stanza for the hymn. The hymn represents the glorification of YHWH for which 9:24 (23) called.[29] The type of hymn is one found in prophetic literature rather than in the Psalms and celebrates motifs of idolatry and judgment. Verse 12 praises YHWH as the maker (עֹשֶׂה) of the earth rather than something made (מַעֲשֶׂה; v. 3 "worked with," v. 9 "the work of") like the images of pagan gods. "Power," "wisdom," and "understanding" are the attributes demonstrated by this creator God, a claim that echoes and endorses a sapiential tradition (cf., e.g., Prov 3:19; Job 37:16).[30] The first two attributes remind the reader of the first two of the human priorities decried in 9:23 (22). By contrast, only YHWH has genuine wisdom. Humans are here declared to be "stupid and without knowledge" (10:14).

The statement about wisdom in v. 12 provides a climax within the literary block. The preexilic community proved to be unwise despite their claim of wisdom in 8:8–9. In turn, professional wisdom was unable to explain Judah's disaster in 9:12–16 (13–15). By contrast, in 9:17–22 (16–21) "wise women" ironically shine out as exemplary in their celebration of grief in response to Judah's ruin. The extra material in the MT amplifies

---

29. Polk, *Prophetic Persona*, 123.

30. The difference between an echo and an allusion is that the latter is an intentional, indirect reference to an earlier text that depends on knowledge evidently shared by the authors and their immediate readers, while the former is a less specific reference that uses thematically related language. For these definitions see Stanley E. Porter, "Allusions and Echoes," in *As It Is Written: Studying Paul's Use of Scripture* (ed. S. E. Porter and C. D. Stanley; SBLSymS 50; Atlanta: SBL, 2008), 29–40. Both terms are used to support the authors' own arguments.

the hymn and takes the message about wisdom a little further. The "skilled workers" or wise men in the last colon of v. 9 are Babylonian idol makers, who are thus sarcastically contrasted with YHWH, who is truly wise. It is probable that v. 7 broaches this motif (NRSV "wise ones," NIV "wise leaders").[31] They are essential for the pagan religion of "the nations," but insignificant before the God who is "King of the nations."

Wisdom and Exile

What contribution does wisdom make to the main theme of exile in the literary block of chs. 7–10? The prose sermon in 7:1–8:3 explores the human and divine necessity of exile from the land YHWH had given his people. In 8:8–9 the community's claim of wisdom is shown to be invalid, and captivity is to be their lot (cf. 6:11; NRSV "taken" in both cases). Rejection of covenantal standards and of the prophetic word that exposed such rejection could only have such a result. Jeremiah 9:12–16 (11–15) includes professional sages in the negative assessment. The fate that culminated in exile had been beyond their ken. It is left to the wise women of vv. 17–22 (16–21) to lament deportation from the land. Ironically, they were the only truly wise members of Judah. In 9:23–24 (22–23) covenantal standards are celebrated once more, leaving professional wisdom a poor alternative. Such standards align with YHWH's own attributes in controlling the world. YHWH is not only the God of the land but of the entire world, and those in exile outside the land should base their lifestyle on such a God. In an exilic setting, 10:1–16 celebrates this universal deity as the God of true wisdom, with whom magnificent idols made by "the wise" cannot compare. This God's wisdom and understanding, evident in earth and sky, transcend claims made for the stars, claims made by the nations who inhabit the earth. Yahwism is the true faith, and the exiles should not be cowed into rejecting it by the impressive dominance of pagan religion.[32]

31. William L. Holladay, *Jeremiah 1: A Commentary on the Prophet Jeremiah Chapters 1–25* (Hermeneia; Philadelphia: Fortress, 1986), 332; P.-M. Bogaert, "Les mécanismes en Jér. 10,1–16 (MT) et la significance des supplements," in Bogaert, ed., *Le livre de Jérémie*, 233–34.

32. Pagan religion provides an *inclusio* for the block. It is one of the causes of the land's destruction that was the precursor of exile (7:6, 9, 17–20). In ch. 10 it raises its ugly head again as a threat to be addressed in the exile itself.

In the literary journey that traces exile as both a future prospect and a present experience, wisdom plays a variety of supporting negative and positive roles. The critique of communal wisdom adds weight to Jeremiah's unpopular messages of national destruction and exile as inconsistent with covenantal traditions. Such conventional wisdom was declared to be utterly wrong. The sages and royal counselors on whom the people relied were misguided. Ironically, the only wise group Jeremiah could commend were experts in mourning. Judah's God was behind the exile as part of his wise work of maintaining the created world. The Judean exiles are to maintain their old covenantal values. Yet, despite the choice of Babylon as YHWH's political agent, Babylon's idolatrous worship, the product of technical wisdom, was doomed to be swept away.

Jeremiah 4:22

Apart from the conglomeration of occurrences of "wisdom/wise" in the literary block of chs. 7–10, there is one instance in Jeremiah that anticipates those occurrences and six instances that echo them in recapitulation. They all have a negative view of human wisdom. The pre-exilic community's lack of wisdom in 8:8–9 gets a preliminary mention in 4:22, where an emotionally overwhelming prophetic vision is capped by a divine reason for such a judgment of impending invasion that will devastate the whole of the land. Negative wisdom vocabulary is piled up and combined with ethical flagrancy. God's "people are foolish, they do not know me; they are stupid children, they have no understanding." The term "wise" (NRSV "skilled") is applied sarcastically to "doing evil," while "they do not know how to do good."

Jeremiah 18:18

As for the cases that come after the block, 18:18 reinforces the disparaging references to professional wisdom in 9:12 (11), 23 (22). The verse supplies a prose introduction to a so-called confession of Jeremiah, providing a setting for the poem and explaining it in terms of the perilous verbal attacks of his "adversaries" (v. 19) that so distressed him. They were evidently planning to bring judicial charges against him on the grounds that his prophetic ministry ran radically counter to the line pursued by Judah's entire religious establishment. It contradicted, for example, the "counsel" of "the wise" as well as the instruction of the priests in torah traditions and the oracles of prophets other than Jeremiah. The sandwiching of the wise between priests and prophets imparts to them a religious flavor. The torah reference is also reminiscent of 8:8–9, where the people's perception of it is described as opposed to Jeremiah's own perception and to the basis of his own prophesying. A more obvious link is with the references to professional wisdom in ch. 9. Here the sages are portrayed as giving religious support to the politicians of the day (cf. 2 Sam 16:23).

Jeremiah 49:7; 50:35; 51:57

The remaining cases appear in the oracles against the nations. The most significant one occurs in the second oracle against Babylon, within 51:15–19. The passage is a citation of 10:12–16 that already appears in the earlier edition of the book represented by the LXX. The citation of the basic hymn in this oracle of judgment represents an endorsing application of its claims. The link between the citation and its context is the forthcoming fall of Babylon, described as YHWH's vengeance for the Babylonians' destruction of the temple (51:11; cf. v. 51). That vengeance would be appropriately worked out by destroying the idols (v. 18; cf. v. 52). The retribution would vindicate YHWH as the true God, acting as powerfully and wisely in history as in nature (v. 15). By contrast, the idolatrous Babylonians would be shown to be "stupid and without knowledge" (v. 17).

What was earlier said about Judah's professional class of sages is extended to Babylon's "sages" at 50:35; 51:57. After "officials," one thinks of these sages as royal counselors. However, there is little evidence that they were called wise in Akkadian. More likely, the reference in a Babylonian setting is to diviners, who were so regarded.[33] In that case it is significant that a specific reference to diviners occurs in 50:36 by way of explanation (cf. Isa 44:25). The two remaining examples in the oracles against the nations are in Jer 49:7, in the oracle against Edom. An announcement of judgment is prefaced by a taunt against Edom's traditional wisdom (cf. Obad 8). Edom's defeat was to prove its present lack of wisdom. It would lose out against YHWH's "plan" and "purposes" (Jer 49:20). That superior wisdom is reminiscent of 10:12. As in 51:15, it was to be put into operation against one of Judah's foes.

---

33. Ronald F. G. Sweet, "The Sage in Akkadian Literature: A Philological Study," in Gammie and Perdue, eds., *The Sage in Israel and the Ancient Near East*, 60–63.

Wisdom and Falsehood

Nearly half a century ago, Thomas Overholt designated שֶׁקֶר, "falsehood, deception," as a theologically important term in the book of Jeremiah.[34] It occurs no less than thirty-seven times with a range of meanings that reflect a basic concept, so that Overholt could say, "The message of Jeremiah is dominated by the notion of 'falsehood.'"[35] It is worth asking whether the term intersects at any points with "wisdom/wise." Strikingly, it does so at the beginning and end of the "wisdom/wise" occurrences in the literary block in a framing fashion. In 8:8 the absence of the wisdom the community claimed for itself is traced back to the adoption of torah interpretations that represented a falsification of the original intent, so that covenantal traditions were ignored. The term occurs twice: "the false pen of the scribes has made it into a lie." The term occurs again in v. 10b, in the portion of text in the MT that reuses 6:13–15. In v. 10b both prophets and priests are accused of acting "falsely." The charge reinforces the rejection of the true torah and of true prophecy in vv. 8–9. The threefold occurrence in vv. 8–10 is a rhetorical match for the threefold use of "wisdom/wise" in the disputation of vv. 8–9, so that the amplified passage has a forceful effect that fits its purpose of exposing false wisdom. Scribes, priests, and prophets were misleading the community. Overholt understood שֶׁקֶר in terms of false security,[36] an interpretation that accords both with the promise of "peace" castigated in v. 11 and with the disastrous consequences foreseen in vv. 9–10, 12. The point of adding 6:13–15 to 8:8–10a, despite form-critical awkwardness, is now evident.

The case in 10:14, stating that Babylonian idols are "false," interacts with "wisdom" in v. 12, especially as the wisdom-linked terms "stupid" and "without knowledge" occur in v. 14.[37] This particular contrast makes a major contribution to the claim of YHWH's supremacy in vv. 1–16. Overholt applies the term "false" to the ineffectiveness of the gods who are symbolized by the images.[38] YHWH's "power" and "wisdom" trump their ineffective presence. The repetition of 10:12–16 in 51:15–19 appropriately picks up this semantic interaction in the second of the Babylonian oracles.

34. Thomas W. Overholt, *The Threat of Falsehood: A Study in the Theology of the Book of Jeremiah* (SBT 2/16; Naperville: Allenson, 1970).

35. Ibid., 101.

36. Ibid., 75.

37. For the combination see Ps 73:22; Prov 12:1; 30:2–3.

38. Overholt, *The Threat of Falsehood*, 86–87; cf. his longer treatment in "The Falsehood of Idolatry: An Interpretation of Jer. X.1–16," *JTS* 16 (1965): 9–12.

Paul's Letters to Corinth

The letters appear to reflect an awareness of the structural integrity of Jer 8–10, in that they make no fewer than five references to these chapters. There is a loose but contextually alert quotation of 9:24 (23) at 1 Cor 1:31; 2 Cor 10:17: "Let the one that boasts, boast in the Lord." Boasting in the Lord (understood christologically) has an ironic force, since the Greek verb καυχάομαι, which was used in the LXX of that text, lacks the positive sense of its Hebrew counterpart. Paul reveals his sensitivity to this negative nuance throughout 2 Cor 11:6–12:13, with his recurring talk about being a fool in boasting as he defends his work as an apostle.

Paul was not unaware of the importance of wisdom in the context of 1 Cor 1:31. "The immediate context of the Jeremiah citation resonates not just with 1 Corinthians 1:31 but with the whole foregoing passage."[39] This awareness comes to the fore in v. 24, where Christ is described as "the power of God and the wisdom of God" and in v. 30, where he "became for us wisdom from God." God's power and wisdom, shown in creation in Jer 10:12, are applied to the crucified Christ. But mostly Paul draws an implicit parallel between the prophet's revealed message of destruction and exile and his own, equally unpopular, message of God revealed at work in a new, strangely destructive way. Jeremiah 9:23 (22) is reflected in the references to "wise" and "strong" at 1 Cor 1:26–27. In 1:19 Paul cites Isa 29:14, "I will destroy the wisdom of the wise." The combination of terms suggests an implicit association with the pairing "wisdom/wise" in Jer 8:8–9, especially as his question 'Where is the scribe?" in v. 20 appears to reflect mention of "the scribes" in Jer 8:8. Moreover, the very question at the beginning of 1 Cor 1:20, "Where is the one who is wise?" sounds like an echo of the rhetorical question in Jer 9:12 (11): "Who is wise enough to understand this?"

Paul clearly had in mind the wider stretch of material in the book of Jeremiah, which he reapplies to the Corinthian context in his repudiation of human wisdom that is at odds with God's new revelation. He was walking in Jeremiah's footsteps (cf. the reflection of Jer 1:5, as well as of Isa 49:1, in Gal 1:15), drawing an analogy between the prophetic disclosure of God's will and his own apostolic message. Paul's proclamation of a crucified and risen Christ was a theological parallel to

---

39. Richard B, Hays, *First Corinthians* (Interpretation; Louisville: John Knox, 1997), 34. See the detailed study of H. H. Drake Williams III, *The Wisdom of the Wise: The Presence and Function of Scripture within 1 Cor. 1:18–3:23* (AGJU 49; Leiden: Brill, 2001), 103–10, 124–30.

Jeremiah's own proclamation of Judah's destruction and exile, presented throughout the book as a prelude to the eventual rebuilding of God's people, first in Jer 1:10.

Conclusion

This essay has investigated the major role played by wisdom in the block of Jer 7–10 and its relation to the block's main theme of exile. God's wise purposes behind Judah's experience of exile are contrasted with human beliefs to the contrary, whose wisdom is dismissed as perilously inconsistent with covenantal traditions. Yet, despite using Babylon in these purposes, Judah's God stands over against Babylon where its religion is concerned, as the wise creator God confronting mere idols of human manufacture. The block's concentration on wisdom is anticipated at one earlier place in the book and reinforced by six later cases. These other cases endorse the perspectives expressed in the block. "Falsehood," a versatile keyword for the entire book, is applied as an *inclusio* to the human wisdom exemplified both in Judah's wrong interpretation of the divine will and in Babylon's making and revering images of its own gods. Paul, in his letters to Corinth, found great value in Jer 9:23–24 (22–23) and its wider context of chs. 8–9 and made significant use of this Jeremian subtheme in his dealings with the Corinthian church. Both the book of Jeremiah and these letters of Paul take seriously the question posed in the book of Job: "Where shall wisdom be found?" (Job 28:12).

WISDOM GETS "TYRED" IN THE BOOK OF EZEKIEL

William R. Osborne

In an effort to explore the relationship between wisdom and prophecy, the present chapter asks the question: What is the nature of the relationship between wisdom and prophecy as presented in the book of Ezekiel? Guided by initial impressions, we might be tempted to abandon the project from the beginning. Indeed, several significant studies on wisdom and prophecy in the Hebrew Bible have neglected the book.[1] As Paul Joyce indicates, "One might not expect the wisdom tradition to be of particular importance in Ezekiel, since wisdom is a relatively secular tradition, whereas Ezekiel is a markedly priestly book."[2] However, Joyce notes some points of contact, and this article will explore in more depth these factors, as well as other possible features that relate wisdom to the book of Ezekiel. Therefore, seeking to contribute to the present volume's ongoing exploration into the relationship between wisdom and prophecy

1. Ezekiel and wisdom has received little attention in past studies. For example, the volume *Wisdom in Ancient Israel* includes chapters on Isaiah, Amos, Jeremiah, Daniel, Hosea, and the Psalms (see John Day, Robert P. Gordon, and H. G. M. Williamson, eds., *Wisdom in Ancient Israel: Essays in Honour of J. A. Emerton* [Cambridge: Cambridge University Press, 1995]). However, two noted exceptions are Mark Hamilton, "Riddles and Parables, Traditions and Texts: Ezekielian Perspectives on Israelite Wisdom Traditions," in *Was There a Wisdom Tradition? New Prospects in Israelite Wisdom Studies* (ed. Mark R. Sneed; AIL 23; Atlanta: SBL, 2015), 241–64; Paul Joyce, "'Even if Noah, Daniel, and Job Were in It…' (Ezekiel 14:14): The Case of Job and Ezekiel," in *Reading Job Intertextually* (ed. Katharine J. Dell and Will Kynes; LHBOTS 574; London: Bloomsbury T&T Clark, 2013), 118–28. Both works are helpful in many ways, but the majority of Hamilton's study focuses on Ezek 17 and 19, giving only a little attention to the Tyre passages, which are the focus of this study.

2. Paul Joyce, *Ezekiel: A Commentary* (LHBOTS 482; London: T&T Clark International, 2009), 34.

in the Hebrew Bible, this study examines potential relatedness including aspects of shared literary forms, the possibility of societal influences or connections, and semantic and thematic overlap.

A Prophet of Parables

Interestingly, the noun מָשָׁל ("proverb," "saying," or "parable") occurs eight times in Ezekiel, with another eight occurrences of the verb משל ("to formulate a saying" or "expound a riddle"), occurring in the Qal and Piel stem.[3] Ezekiel records more occurrences of these two words than any other book in the Hebrew canon, including Proverbs, which makes reference to מָשָׁל six times. In Ezekiel, communication via משלים is both divinely critiqued and prescribed. In 12:23 the Lord rebukes a common proverb about the apparent failure of prophetic visions and says, "Therefore, say to them, 'Thus says Lord YHWH, I will put an end to this proverb, and they shall not use it as a proverb again in Israel.'"[4] In 18:1–4 the Lord critiques the use of the sour grapes proverb: "As I live, a declaration of Lord YHWH, this proverb will not be used as a proverb any longer in Israel." Based upon these instances, combined with Ezekiel's evident priestly orientation, it would be easy to assign a negative assessment to proverbial sayings according to the priestly prophet's perspective. Indeed, it is a striking contrast of immediate revelation trumping the validity of interpretations on present events by means of traditional wisdom.

However, in 17:2 the Lord commands Ezekiel to "propound a riddle and to speak a parable to the house of Israel," and in 24:3 the Lord says, "speak a parable to the rebellious house." Ezekiel himself bemoans that the people were saying, "Is he not one who speaks in parables?" While proverbial and parabolic sayings in and of themselves do not equal Israelite wisdom,[5] the above examples reveal that Ezekiel (seemingly both prophet and book) is by no means cut off from the proverbial wisdom circulating among the Judean exiles, as well as those remaining in the land.[6]

---

3. משל is a likely a denominative verb form that designates an action implicit in the noun root. See Bruce K. Waltke and M. O'Connor, *An Introduction to Biblical Hebrew Syntax* (Winona Lake: Eisenbrauns, 1990), 373, 410–12.

4. Unless otherwise noted, all translations are original to the author.

5. See the chapters by Meek, Kynes, Sneed, and Dell in this volume for further discussion on the difficulties of defining wisdom, as well as Sneed, ed., *Was There a Wisdom Tradition?*

6. See Raymond C. Van Leeuwen, "The Sage in the Prophetic Literature," in *The Sage in Israel and the Ancient Near East* (ed. John G. Gammie and Leo G. Purdue; Winona Lake: Eisenbrauns, 1990), 298.

And while it is commonly acknowledged that the book of Ezekiel reflects an editorial perspective in its arrangement and final composition, there is nothing jarring or contextually puzzling about the above references so that one might conclude these forms arise from a later sapiential editorial phase.[7]

A Prophet Among the Wise

Ezekiel's apparent familiarity with such proverbial sayings might also be expected given the prophet's repeated interactions with the elders (זקנים) of Israel. As elders of the people, this group appears to have maintained a significant leadership function and was expected to provide sound counsel and wisdom (cf. Deut 1:15).[8] The elders continued to have an important societal role during the monarchy, so that Josiah summons all of the elders upon discovering the Book of the Law (2 Kgs 23:1). Given the unraveling of the monarchy in Jerusalem and the instability of life in a foreign land, it is not surprising that the elders emerged as important Jewish leaders in the exiled community.

In 27:9 we read it was the elders of Gebal, listed alongside the wise, who guide the great metaphorical Tyrian ship. However, when it comes to the elders of Judah, 7:26 indicates their counsel was perishing. In 8:1 Ezekiel is sitting in his house with the elders of Judah, and in 14:1 certain elders sought him out and sat down in front of him and heard a word from the Lord. In 20:1 the elders came to inquire a word from the Lord from Ezekiel. There is little doubt that it is in these, or similar, contexts that the prophet is made aware of the proverbs mentioned above.[9]

According to the book of Ezekiel, the prophet went into exile in 597 with King Jehoiachin and his courtiers.[10] However, it is difficult

---

7. See Hamilton, "Riddles and Parables, Traditions and Texts," 241–45.

8. Iain M. Duguid, *Ezekiel and the Leaders of Israel* (VTSup 56; Leiden: Brill, 1994), 110–11.

9. There is much sense found in Samuel Terrien's conclusion regarding the prophet Amos: "That various groups, such as priests, prophets, and wisemen existed should not be denied. At the same time, such groups were not alien one from the others, and they lived in a common and mutually interacting environment" (Samuel Terrien, "Amos and Wisdom," in *Israel's Prophetic Heritage: Essays in Honor of James Muilenburg* [ed. B. W. Anderson and W. Harrelson; London: SCM, 1962], 115).

10. See Walther Zimmerli, *Ezekiel 1: A Commentary on the Book of the Prophet Ezekiel, Chapters 1–24* (trans. Ronald E. Clements; Hermeneia; Minneapolis: Fortress, 1979), 10–11.

to ascertain the nature of the exiles' socio-economic status in Babylon. Jonathan Stökl has recently argued that there were three possible socio-economic communities in exile: "1) upper class Judeans at the royal court in Babylon, 2) traders throughout the Babylonian cities, and 3) subsistence farmers in the Nippur region."[11] Stökl goes on to assert boldly that the author of Ezekiel likely went to cuneiform scribal school where he became familiar with the writing and traditions of Babylon, which were then utilized in his own writing.[12] While Stökl honestly addresses several challenges to his own position, the benefit of his study is to point out that there is enough interaction between the book of Ezekiel and Babylonian material to require an explanation. "It appears that some of the texts in the book of Ezekiel show evidence of not only priestly lore of Israel and Judah but also to some of the *niṣirtu*, the secret knowledge, to which only people had access who had undergone a certain amount of training."[13] Whether the book is the product of a cuneiform-trained Judean is hard to prove, but a learned familiarity with the competing stories of the broader ancient Near East emerges from the text. The apparent familiarity becomes a factor in evaluating the oracles against Tyre, where the text takes up mythopoetic language, drawing from Mesopotamian traditions in a powerful critique.[14] Thus, the book of Ezekiel presents a unique familiarity with both the colloquial and proverbial wisdom of the Judeans and the mythical traditions of Babylon. And it is in this intercultural milieu that we find many of the prophet's uses of wisdom language.

A Prophet Against the Wisdom of Tyre

The only explicit references to wisdom in the book of Ezekiel are found in prophetic oracles not directed toward the people of Judah. There are eight instances where the word חָכָם/חָכְמָה is used in Ezekiel, and they all

---

11. Jonathan Stökl, "'A Youth without Blemish, Handsome, Proficient in all Wisdom, Knowledgeable and Intelligent': Ezekiel's Access to Babylonian Culture," in *Exile and Return: The Babylonian Context* (ed. Jonathan Stökl and Caroline Waaerzeggers; BZAW 478; Berlin: de Gruyter, 2015), 227.

12. Stökl is quick to note the possibility that multiple hands were involved with the production of the book, so this claim may or may not apply directly to the historical prophet without detracting from his overall argument.

13. Stökl, "'A Youth without Blemish,'" 251.

14. Marvin A. Sweeney, "Myth and History in Ezekiel's Oracle Concerning Tyre (Ezekiel 26–28)," in *Myth and Scripture: Contemporary Perspectives on Religion, Language, and Imagination* (ed. Dexter Callender, Jr.; Resources for Biblical Study 78; Atlanta: SBL, 2014), 135–41.

occur in the prophet's oracles against the foreign nation of Tyre in chs. 27 and 28. Scholars have long wrestled with the perplexing priority the book devotes to decrying the Phoenician port city. Martin Alonso Corral states: "Tyre is an exceptional case among the foreign nations condemned in these oracles. No obvious reason for rivalry, resentment, or anger is discernible in the Tyrian oracles."[15] However, whether the motivation is political (Tyre's opposition to Babylon)[16] or primarily economic,[17] John Strong's conclusion that the oracles against Tyre are fundamentally theological resonates with the strong theological and theocentric message of the book.[18]

Wisdom Aboard the City-Ship Tyre (Ezekiel 27)

Ezekiel 27 presents a multi-part lament (קִינָה) over the city of Tyre that takes the form of an elaborate metaphor, but the actual lament does not arise until vv. 25–36. While the language of this lament is profoundly metaphorical, many have strained the imagery found here in their pursuit of *Chaoskampf* themes.[19] There is no doubt that Ezekiel takes up ancient Near Eastern imagery in his discussion of YHWH's judgment against

---

15. Martin Alonso Corral, *Ezekiel's Oracles Against Tyre* (BibOr 46; Rome: Pontifico Istituto Biblico, 2002), 3 n. 6.

16. Zimmerli, *Ezekiel 2*, 23.

17. Corral, *Ezekiel's Oracles*, 64–141. Rainey and Notley read Ezek 27 as a window into the economic world of the sixth century. See Anson F. Rainey and R. Steven Notley, *The Sacred Bridge: Carta's Atlas of the Biblical World* (2nd ed.; Jerusalem: Carta, 2006), 28–29.

18. John T. Strong, "In Defense of the Great King: Ezekiel's Oracles Against Tyre," in *Concerning the Nations: Essays on the Oracles Against the Nations in Isaiah, Jeremiah, and Ezekiel* (ed. E. K. Holt, H. C. P. Kim, and A. Mein; LHBOTS 612; London: Bloomsbury T&T Clark, 2015), 185–86.

19. See C. L. Crouch, "Ezekiel's Oracles against the Nations in Light of a Royal Ideology of Warfare," *JBL* 130 (2011): 486; H. J. Van Dijk, *Ezekiel's Prophecy on Tyre (Ez. 26:1–28:19): A New Approach* (BibOr 20; Rome: Pontifical Biblical Institute, 1968), 89–90; John B. Geyer, *Mythology and Lament. Studies in the Oracles About the Nations* (SOTSMS; Aldershot: Ashgate, 2004), 57–74; Margaret O'Dell, *Ezekiel* (Smyth & Helwys Bible Commentary; Macon: Smyth & Helwys, 2005), 434. However, John Strong has noted, "May [and more recently those previously mentioned] has proposed that מַיִם רַבִּים ('Abundant Waters') were always to be identified with Chaos, and thus, an evil force opposing YHWH. This is not universally true, and in fact, it is never the case in Ezekiel's prophecies (cf. 17:5, 8—a plant; 19:10—a vine; 31:5, 7—the World Tree). In every case, Abundant Waters denotes a source of prosperity." See John T. Strong, "Ezekiel's Oracles Against the Nations within the Context of His Message" (PhD diss., Union Theological Seminary, 1993), 205.

the nations. However, some have approached the topic as though this is Ezekiel's only message: YHWH conquers the chaos-symbolizing nations. Crouch argues that in Ezekiel's Oracles against the Nations (OANs) Tyre and Egypt both symbolize chaotic forces which YHWH conquers, thus demonstrating his rightful place as king.[20] Crouch and I end up at many of the same conclusions as to the main message of these OANs, but we get there in different ways.

There is little doubt that Daniel Block is correct when he comments on ch. 27, "This is the language of affluence and luxury, not mythology."[21] Carley Crouch concedes: "At times it is difficult to distinguish the extent to which the water language used of the city constitutes a deliberate cosmological allusion and the extent to which it is merely a consequence of geographical reality."[22] The metaphors continually portray a picture of globally recognized opulence and influence. The woods selected for the building of the vessel are of the finest quality and the sail is Egyptian linen with blue and purple coverings. While these certainly did not characterize most ships of that time, there is nothing about these materials that is strikingly odd or sends us looking for allegorical meanings for each of the parts of the ship. Instead, Carol Newsome notes that the materials of the ship were intentionally used to highlight the commodities most associated with Tyrian trade.[23] "Trade indeed built Tyre."[24] Utilizing the cognitive approach to metaphor theory,[25] the ship functions as the source domain, while the city is the target domain. This being the case, we would expect none other than city leaders at the helm of this massive metaphorical vessel ship. The dominant cognitive metaphor then is: TYRE IS A SHIP, and the ship is going down.

20. Crouch, "Ezekiel's Oracles Against the Nations," 478.

21. Daniel I. Block, *Ezekiel 25–48* (NICOT; Grand Rapids: Eerdmans, 1998), 53 n. 7. So also, Corral, *Ezekiel's Oracles*, 154–55.

22. Crouch, "Ezekiel's Oracles Against the Nations in Light of a Royal Ideology of Warfare," 484.

23. Carol Newsom, "A Maker of Metaphors—Ezekiel's Oracles Against Tyre," *Int* 38, no. 2 (1984): 157.

24. Ibid.

25. Cognitive linguistics seeks to understand the relationship between language and the human mind. See Job Y. Jindo, "Toward a Poetics of the Biblical Mind," *VT* 59 (2009): 225; Bonnie Howe and Eve Sweetser, "Cognitive Linguistics and Biblical Interpretation," in *The Oxford Encyclopedia of Biblical Interpretation* (ed. S. L. McKenzie; 2 vols.; Oxford: Oxford University Press, 2014), 1:121–31; George Lakoff and Mark Johnson, *Metaphors We Live By* (Chicago: University of Chicago Press, 2003), 5; Zoltán Köveces, *Metaphor: A Practical Introduction* (Oxford: Oxford University Press, 2002).

The crew of the ship includes the citizenry[26] and leadership of the neighboring Phoenician port cities. Eichrodt notes that it is likely an "exaggerated metaphor expressing how the richest maritime cities of Phoenicia were her vassals."[27] The wise, or skilled, of Tyre and Gebal (also Byblos) symbolized the stature and significance of the great metaphorical city-ship. Van Dijk rightly notes that these individuals were not simply skilled seamen. He writes: "The wise men are not seamen, but senators, counsellors or noble people contributing to the splendour of the ship."[28] The ship is guided and cared for by the wisest men in and around the city. "Tyre has the helm in her own hands,"[29] and her wise men are steering. The wisdom and skill of those on board also contributes to the apparent success and strength of the city. The city-ship is also guarded by the great armies of the east and shields adorn her walls, proclaiming strength and beauty to all who look upon her. To mix the metaphors, Tyre appears to be an unsinkable city!

As the extended metaphor continues, the reader quickly learns that even the city's beauty, opulence, and wisdom are not enough to prevent her downfall. As the waves of irony crash against the mighty vessel, the same sea that made Tyre great brings about her demise. Interestingly, were this oracle to be read in isolation, it would be difficult to discern whether the lament records a judgment that is the result of divine punishment or simply prophetic commentary on the state of the situation in Tyre. Several commentators have noted the sense of sincerity presented among those who mourn the fall of the great city, and certainly Tyre's destruction would have profound economic effects throughout the region. However, three times the reader is told that Tyre is perfect in beauty (כְּלִילוּ יָפְיֵךְ, vv. 3, 4, and 11), and in the first one of these instances the words are placed in the boastful mouth of the city.[30] The city-ship is described as possessing splendor (v. 10), great wealth (vv. 12, 18, 27, 33), and abundant

---

26. Reading the MT and avoiding the unnecessary emendations proposed by many commentators.

27. Walther Eichrodt, *Ezekiel: A Commentary* (OTL; Philadelphia: Westminster, 1970), 383.

28. Van Dijk, *Ezekiel's Prophecies on Tyre*, 69. Sweeney offers an interesting interpretation of the ship lament drawing from ancient Near Eastern flood stories. In this text, however, instead of the protagonist delivering his vessel through the waters and saving its passengers, the ship meets its demise (Sweeney, "Myth and History in Ezekiel's Oracle," 138–39).

29. Zimmerli, *Ezekiel 2*, 54.

30. Ian Douglas Wilson, "Tyre, a Ship: The Metaphorical World of Ezekiel 27 in Ancient Judah," *ZAW* 125 (2013): 255.

goods (vv. 16, 18).[31] The implications and message of the text are twofold: (1) the lament serves as an indictment upon the hubris that boasts in human achievements of beauty, strength, wealth, and wisdom, and (2) the lament serves as a warning to all great cities—even Jerusalem—that there are no unsinkable cities.[32]

Does the disastrous demise of the city-ship give us any indication of the prophetic perspective of the wise and skilled leaders steering it? Is this metaphor presenting wisdom as one of the characteristics that elicited judgment? The portrait of the wise men aboard the great city-ship is not necessarily negative. Their role seems to emphasize the grandeur of the city, highlighting the apparent strength of the vessel so that no one could conclude that the city ultimately fell due to foolish leadership. The wisdom of those guiding the ship is also a likely component and precursor to the beauty and wealth of the city. That wisdom precludes beauty and opulence is explicitly revealed in ch. 28, but here the relationship is present, albeit implied. However, the text indicates that wisdom has its limits. Even with wise men at the helm, the ship's pride-induced destruction cannot be averted. Wisdom cannot undo the consequences of immorality, and this is true for Tyre and Jerusalem.[33]

31. John T. Willis, "National 'Beauty' and Yahweh's 'Glory' as a Dialectical Key to Ezekielien Theology," *HBT* 34 (2012): 11. Wilson argues that references to items transported from Tyre such as cedar trees, cypress trees, and fabrics of blue and purple point the reader toward associations with the temple in Jerusalem (see Wilson, "Tyre, a Ship," 256–57). It is difficult to discern whether or not these items truly reflect an intentional—and more importantly understood—allusion to the temple as opposed to indicating wealth and power. However, Wilson rightly notes that in the centuries following the exile, the reception of the fall of Tyre was transformed from a present-day reality to a transgenerational object lesson to all those wise enough to listen.

32. Block, *Ezekiel 25–48*, 86–87.

33. Robert R. Wilson argued that the Tyrian oracle in ch. 28 is a disguised judgment against the priesthood in Jerusalem (R. R. Wilson, "The Death of the King of Tyre: The Editorial History of Ezekiel 28," in *Love and Death in the Ancient Near East: Essays in Honor of Marvin H. Pope* (ed. J. H. Marks and R. M. Good; Guilford: Four Quarters, 1987), 217. While I do not find his analysis of the oracle in ch. 28 convincing, the proposal does raise interesting questions with regard to the Tyre–Jerusalem association in ch. 27. The indictment against the Tyrian percep- tions of inviolability would have been equally appropriate in addressing the Judean misconceptions of Jerusalem.

In this epic, metaphorical scene of the wisdom of humans struggling against the immutable divine plan, a small glimpse of the prophet's perspective on wisdom becomes visible. The glimpse reveals wisdom within Tyre as a skill or ability that resulted in wealth and power but did not shelter the city from arrogance and pride. In examining Ezekiel's use of "wisdom" it is helpful to ask: How might the directions of this oracle line up with what is found in perhaps the most agreed-upon wisdom text—Proverbs?[34] In commenting on these verses, Block notes the significance of Prov 16:18–19, which states: "pride goes before destruction, and a haughty spirit before a fall. It is better to be of a lowly spirit with the poor than to divide the spoil with the proud."[35] Proverbs 11:2 states: "When pride comes, then comes disgrace, but with the humble is wisdom," and Prov 29:23 "One's pride will bring him low, but he who is lowly in spirit will obtain honor." The wisdom found aboard the Tyrian city-ship was not *true* wisdom—i.e., wisdom rooted in the fear of YHWH.[36] Tremper Longman notes, "Wisdom is not simply a matter of learning certain principles of life and applying them mechanistically. Wisdom begins with a relationship with God. That this relationship is characterized by fear means that the sages understood their place in the universe."[37] Therefore, the wise leaders of Tyre did not prevent the immoral arrogance that leads to the ship's destruction. In fact, if there is Proverbs-like wisdom to be found in this passage, it is embedded within the prophet's indictment of such faulty wisdom.

---

34. Katharine J. Dell, *"Get Wisdom, Get Insight": An Introduction to Israel's Wisdom Literature* (Macon: Smyth & Helwys, 2000), 5.

35. I am not arguing for a precise intertextual (i.e., lexical) relationship between these books. I am focusing on shared theological themes and concepts that could have easily flowed in either direction diachronically.

36. It is difficult to summarily describe the unique phrase "the fear of YHWH" in a way that captures all of the contextual nuances of its varied usage, which at times can point to an ethical, intellectual, or emotional connotation (see Bruce K. Waltke, *The Book of Proverbs, Chapters 1–15* [NICOT; Grand Rapids: Eerdmans, 2004], 100–103; Henri Blocher, "The Fear of the Lord as the 'Principle' of Wisdom," *TynBul* 28 [1977]: 3–28). However, many have noted the significance of the concept for Israelite wisdom, seeing it as closely linked to YHWH's work as Creator and Sovereign (Daniel J. Estes, *Hear, My Son: Teaching and Learning in Proverbs 1–9* [NSBT 4; Downers Grove: InterVarsity, 1997], 35–38). While the use of "fear" in this phrase should not be equated with terror, it does not mean merely to "worship" (Tremper Longman III, *Proverbs* [BCOTWP; Grand Rapids: Baker, 2006], 57–58). True wisdom always grows out of a proper response and relationship to YHWH.

37. Longman, *Proverbs*, 57–58.

The Wise and Wealthy Prince of Tyre (Ezekiel 28:1–10)

In ch. 28 the subtlety of ch. 27 has vanished. The words of the prince are brash and clear against the backdrop of the Ezekiel's recognition formula. He says, "I am a god," and it is possible that the king of Tyre viewed himself as an incarnation of the city god Melkart.[38] As a personification of the city of Tyre, the prince exudes an appalling sense of hubris for any respectable ancient Near Eastern worshiper. Similar to 27:3, the first-person statements are placed in the mouth of the prince and dripping with vainglory. The term "heart" (לֵב) here is mentally oriented so that the prince claims to have the "mind" or "intellect" of a god[39] and concludes that he can assume a position among the gods. However, Ezekiel's message is plain: "you are a man and not a god."

Verses 3–5 present the logic of how the prince became so proud. The wisdom of the prince allowed for the wealth which led to hubris. He is described as wiser than Daniel,[40] and nothing is "shut up" or "concealed" from him. By wisdom and understanding he acquires his wealth (v. 4a), and he possesses great wisdom in trade, which led to his abundance.[41] It is perhaps here that we see the notion of wisdom commercialized as it applies to the royal personification of the great Phoenician port-city. However, because of the prince's ensuing hubris, YHWH will bring ruthless nations against the beauty of his wisdom (v. 7).

Again we are presented with a similar question regarding the prophet's perspective on wisdom. Is this an indictment upon wisdom and the wise? Similar to what was observed in ch. 27, the prophet here is rebuking a certain kind of wisdom. The wisdom embodied in the prince of Tyre

---

38. Corral, *Ezekiel's Oracles*, 6.

39. "The heart is the seat of wisdom (= mind), as in Exod 31:6; Prov 23:15. Divine wisdom is mentioned in Isa 31:2 (outstrips human devices), Jer 10:7 (outstrips all sages), and Dan 2:20; 5:11 (a divine possession)" (Moshe Greenberg, *Ezekiel 21–37* [AB 22A; New Haven: Yale University Press, 1997], 573).

40. The apparent references to Daniel in Ezekiel are notoriously debated, with some arguing the individual in view is the sage of Ugaritic lore, Dan'el. See Harald-Martin Wahl, "Noah, Daniel und Hiob in Ezechiel XIV 12–20 (21–3): Anmerkungen zum Traditionsgeschichtlichen Hintergrund," *VT* 42 (1992): 542–53. Margaret O'Dell overplays the idea of intercessor in Ezek 14:14 and concludes that it is odd that Daniel is included since he is not perceived as a righteous father who intercedes or protects his children. However, the emphasis of the text is on individual righteousness, not intercession. Cf. Joyce, "'Even if Noah, Daniel, and Job Were in It,'" 120–22.

41. Moshe Greenberg comments on the present depiction of wisdom: "Here a genius for commerce is meant, and for making money" (Greenberg, *Ezekiel 21–37*, 574).

is ultimately devoid of the moral and religious fiber woven throughout Israel's wisdom tradition. Moshe Greenberg noted: "The universal principle against which the leader of Tyre has offended is stated succinctly where we should expect it—in the wisdom literature."[42] The heart of the proud prince could not be any more in opposition to the heart of the wise as portrayed in Proverbs. "Trust in YHWH with all your heart, and do not lean on your own understanding" (Prov 3:5); "Everyone who is arrogant in heart is an abomination to YHWH; be assured, he will not go unpunished" (Prov 16:5). The Lord's argument against Job in the whirlwind is also striking in light of ch. 28: "Adorn yourself with majesty and dignity; clothe yourself with glory and splendor. Pour out the overflowings of your anger and look on everyone who is proud and abase him. Look on everyone who is proud and bring him low and tread down the wicked where they stand" (Job 40:10–12). Analyzing Job and Proverbs, one quickly sees that there is nothing as unwise as claiming equality with YHWH. Fathers taught it to their sons as recorded in Proverbs and the book of Job demonstrates in dramatic fashion that the mind and wisdom of God is higher than human thought.

Primeval Wisdom in the Garden (Ezekiel 28:11–19)
Many have noted the mythological overtones of Ezekiel's condemning lament over the king of Tyre in vv. 11–19, despite the notoriously thorny Hebrew text.[43] While it is not uncommon for commentators to amend the text with the aid of the LXX, Matthieu Richelle has argued that there is a consistency and thematic coherence evident within the LXX translation that seems to be based upon the translator's interpretation of the Hebrew text in light of the garden narrative in Gen 2–3. The issue is quite significant

42. Ibid., 577.
43. For more recent proposals, see Hector M. Patmore, *Adam, Satan, and the King of Tyre: The Interpretation of Ezekiel 28:11–19 in Late Antiquity* (Jewish and Christian Perspective Series 20; Leiden: Brill, 2012); idem, "Did the Masoretes Get It Wrong? The Vocalization and Accentuation of Ezekiel XXVIII 12-19," *VT* 58 (2008): 245–57; Lydia Lee, "'You Were the (Divine) Cherub': A Potential Challenge to YHWH's Sole Divinity in Ezekiel 28:14," *JSOT* 41 (2016): 99–116; Matthieu Richelle, "Le portrait changeant du roi de Tyr (Ezéchiel 28, 11-18) dans les traditions textuelles anciennes," in *Phéniciens d'Orient et d'Occident: Mélanges J. Elayi* (ed. A. Lemaire; CIPOA 2; Paris: Maisonneuve, 2014), 113–25; James Barr, "'Thou Art the Cherub': Ezekiel 28:14 and the Post-Ezekiel Understanding of Genesis 2–3," in *Priests, Prophets, and Scribes: Essays on the Formation and Heritage of Second Temple Judaism in Honour of Joseph Blenkinsopp* (ed. Eugene Ulrich et al.; JSOTSup 149; Sheffield: JSOT Press, 1992), 213–23.

because the MT identifies the king of Tyre as an anointed cherub on the mountain of God, and the LXX identifies the figure as a prince (i.e., man) of Tyre who seems to be accompanied by a cherub. However, whether the character in the oracle is a cherub or a human accompanied by a cherub, the depiction of a royal figure associated with the divine realm is clearly in view.[44] In fact, provided Ezekiel's inaugural vision, the reader should not be surprised to encounter a human-like cherub in close proximity to YHWH's presence.[45] Lee notes, "To describe the Tyrian king as the cherub that protects the most intimate place of divine presence thus emphasizes the vicinity between the Tyrian king and the divine."[46]

The prophet presents the cherub-king as the seal (possibly referring to a cylinder seal) of perfection, full of wisdom and perfect in beauty, similar to the description in ch. 27. Here again the relationship between wisdom and beauty is noteworthy. This king stands as the paragon of royalty on earth—he is created by YHWH (v. 13) and placed in the garden of Eden,[47] but he is a guardian cherub, distinct from humanity. The placement of the king in the garden says as much about YHWH as it does about the king. Early Mesopotamian traditions believed that kingship—while mediated through dynastic progression in later millennia—descended from heaven and had a divine origin.[48] Commentators have continually wrestled over

---

44. Lee, "'You Were the (Divine) Cherub,'" 108–14.

45. Richelle, "Le portrait changeant du roi de Tyr (Ezéchiel 28, 11-18)," 123.

46. Lee, "'You Were the (Divine) Cherub,'" 113.

47. Much has been said with regard to Eden and the Garden of YHWH. For fuller treatments, see Henrik Pfeiffer, "Der Baume in der Mitte des Gartens: Zum überlieferungsgeschichtlichen Ursprung der Paradieserzählung (Gen 2,4–3,24), Teil II: Prägende Tradition und theologische Akzente," *ZAW* 113 (2001): 2–16; Konrad Schmid and Christoph Riedweg, eds., *Beyond Eden: The Biblical Story of Paradise (Gen 2–3) and Its Reception History* (FAT 2/34; Tübingen: Mohr Siebeck, 2008); Ziony Zevit, *What Really Happened in the Garden of Eden?* (New Haven: Yale University Press, 2013); Howard N. Wallace, *The Eden Narrative* (HSM 32; Atlanta: Scholars Press, 1985); T. N. D. Mettinger, *The Eden Narrative: A Literary and Religio-historical Study of Genesis 2–3* (Winona Lake: Eisenbrauns, 2007); T. Stordalen, *Echoes of Eden: Gen 2–3 and Symbolism of the Eden Garden in Biblical Hebrew Literature* (CBET 25; Leuven: Peeters, 2000); Karl Jaroš, "Die Motive der Heiligen Bäume und der Schlange in Gen 2–3," *ZAW* 92 (1980): 204–15; James Barr, *The Garden of Eden and the Hope of Immortality* (Minneapolis: Fortress, 1992); Alan R. Millard, "The Etymology of Eden," *VT* 34 (1984): 103–6; Hermann Spieckermann, "Eden, Garden of," *EBR* 7:362–64.

48. William W. Hallo, "The Birth of Kings," in Marks and Good, eds., *Love and Death in the Ancient Near East*, 45–52.

the complex compilation of the garden tradition found in Gen 2–3,[49] priestly and cultic elements (e.g., the gem stones and stones of fire), and ancient Near Eastern mythological themes found in Ezek 28. It is as if the text presents us with a three-colored tapestry, and unfortunately some have thought that the way forward is to pull each colored thread out of the tapestry and analyze it by itself.[50] I am convinced that the prophet has clearly borrowed and undoubtedly transformed the materials from which he is drawing to the extent that the origin or source can no longer be isolated without destroying the finished product.

The significance for the present discussion is seen in v. 17. "Your heart was proud because of your beauty; you destroyed your wisdom for the sake of your splendor." The prophet here clarifies that such primeval wisdom and beauty were not inherently problematic or wrong. Yet, the cherub-king destroyed his wisdom on account of his beauty and splendor. According to the prophet and the book of Proverbs, true wisdom and pride cannot coexist.

While there is certainly no hint of divine beings, the so-called royal experiment recorded in Eccl 2 presents us with an alternate picture of an awe-inspiring wise king in the midst of a garden. In this chapter Qohelet records his attempt at finding pleasure and delight in the creation of his

---

49. The relationship between the garden narrative in Gen 2–3 and the prophetic literature of the Old Testament is inherently linked to one's view of authorship and composition of the Genesis texts and the prophets (Mettinger offers a helpful survey of the various compositional strategies proposed in *The Eden Narrative*, 5–11). If it is the case that Ezekiel predates the composition of Gen 2–3 as some propose, then there is no reason to read the prophet's reference to the garden of YHWH or Eden in light of the narrative recorded in Gen 2–3. However, many source critics are willing to assign parts of the garden narrative to a preexilic period (see M. Vervenne, "Genesis 1,1–2,4: The Compositional Texture of the Priestly Overture to the Pentateuch," in *Studies in the Book of Genesis* [ed. A. Wénin; BETL 155; Leuven: Peeters, 2001], 61). Zevit also sees a much earlier tradition than the postexilic community when he writes: "After all the theorizing and close analysis that almost four centuries of scholarship have produced, the Garden story considered below, regularly assigned to the J source, is considered the distillation of a literary tradition whose oral antecedents took shape around two centuries earlier, around 1100 BCE, close to some of the dates proposed by the Mosaic-authorship approach" (Zevit, *What Really Happened*, 42).

50. E.g., Zimmerli identifies multiple examples of "secondary retouching" throughout the Tyre oracle based upon his form-critical analysis and views of thematic developments. See Walther Zimmerli, *Ezekiel 2: A Commentary on the Book of the Prophet Ezekiel Chapters 25–48* (trans. James D. Martin; Hermeneia; Philadelphia: Fortress, 1983), 87–95.

own mini-cosmos. The depiction of the royal garden found in Eccl 2 is not merely a large architectural project; the king's garden in the ancient Near East symbolized the king's empire and his reign.[51] Parks were constructed (2:5), exotic trees planted (2:5), and streams of water channeled (2:6). Not unlike the creation account in Gen 1, once this royal realm was formed it was then filled with slaves and herds of animals (2:7).

The final verses of the experiment reveal that despite Qoheleth's limitless foray in the pursuit of pleasure by exercising his wealth and power, the end result was *hebel* and chasing the wind because Qoheleth is not YHWH (2:11). Qoheleth's picture of wisdom and wealth aligns with that found in Ezekiel's oracle against the king of Tyre, albeit with a different emphasis. Read together, Qohelet's garden experiment reveals the deeper folly of the king of Tyre in looking to beauty, wealth, and pleasure as a source of pride and self-satisfaction. Both garden portraits reveal that when a person is in the midst of beauty and power through divinely acquired position, true wisdom resists pride by remembering the fleeting nature of beauty, wealth, and power under the sun.

Conclusion

This exploration into wisdom and prophecy in Ezekiel in many ways affirms Hamilton's conclusion that in engaging both concepts in the Hebrew Bible we must "think of interlocking intellectual circles that created, preserved, reused, and reinterpreted texts as fit representations of their ideas about the world, or at any rate the ideas they thought worthy of interaction and commentary."[52] Ministering within the small Judean exilic community, Ezekiel does indeed reuse and reinterpret several ideas represented in those books most often associated with Israel's wisdom writings.

Is Ezekiel opposed to wisdom? If we were to conclude that Ezekiel is anti-wisdom because of his indictments against Tyre, we could equally conclude that he is anti-prophecy because of 13:9: "My hand will be against the prophets who see false visions and who give lying divinations." Obviously the prophet is not anti-prophecy because of the reality of false prophets. It is equally wrong to conclude that he is anti-wisdom because of the reality of false wisdom. False prophets prophesied "a declaration of YHWH" when there was indeed no word from the Lord.

51. See William R. Osborne, *Trees and Kings: A Comparative Analysis of Tree Imagery in Israel's Prophetic Tradition and the Ancient Near East* (BBRSup 18; University Park, PA: Eisenbrauns, 2018), 51–54.
52. Hamilton, "Riddles and Parables, Traditions and Texts," 242.

Similarly, the priests carried out the form of religion while they departed from the instruction of the Lord. And kings, elders, and sages among the nations spoke and acted in wisdom that failed to guard against a haughty and arrogant spirit.

Who is the sage in the book of Ezekiel? I believe it is the prophet himself. Just as much as his own truly inspired prophecies exposed the deception of the false prophets, Ezekiel's depiction of false wisdom is critiqued by his insistence that YHWH will bring down the arrogant, thus demonstrating that *their* wisdom is empty and foolish.

Daniel as Wisdom in Action

Andrew E. Steinmann

Biblical wisdom literature, especially the book of Proverbs, offers advice on becoming wise and behaving wisely. But wisdom literature presents its own challenge: is it even proper to speak of a biblical wisdom literature—whether that entails a genre or literature with a certain outlook or literature written by sages?[1] Some have argued that wisdom is recognizable, though a precise definition of a wisdom genre is elusive.[2] Others have implied that wisdom literature as a genre is simply a modern construct.[3] Without belaboring the point, I would like to suggest that there is a cluster of biblical books that have been consistently grouped together since antiquity and whether one wishes to label them "wisdom" or something else, this phenomenon alone demonstrates that learned readers have shared an opinion that these books are more like each other than they are like other books of the Hebrew Bible. Thus, Josephus mentions four books that he describes as "hymns to God and counsel for the conduct of life" that probably were Psalms, Proverbs, Ecclesiastes, and Song of Songs.[4] Philo,

---

1. For instance, Sneed has argued that wisdom literature was not the product of a guild of sages. See Mark Sneed, "Is the Wisdom Tradition a Tradition?," *CBQ* 73 (2011): 50–71.

2. This includes arguments in papers prepared for previous SBL sessions: Mark Sneed, "'Grasping After Wind': The Elusive Attempt to Define Wisdom" (paper presented at the annual meeting of the SBL, Chicago, IL, 18 November 2012); Russell L. Meek, "Prophet and Sage in Dialogue: History and Methodology" (paper presented at the annual meeting of the SBL, Baltimore, MD, 22 November 2013), esp. 11–13.

3. E.g., Will Kynes, "'Wisdom' as Mask and Mirror: Response to Russell L. Meek" (paper presented at the annual meeting of the SBL, Baltimore, MD, 22 November 2013). Kynes traces the modern concept of biblical wisdom literature to Johan Fredrich Bruch's *Weisheits-Lehre der Hebräer*, published in 1851. See Kynes, "'Wisdom' as Mask and Mirror," 3.

4. Josephus, *Ant.* 12.43; Andrew E. Steinmann, *The Oracles of God: The Old Testament Canon* (St. Louis: Concordia, 1999), 116; John Barton, "The Law and the

in *The Contemplative Life*, speaks of the sacred books of the Therapeutae as "Law and words spoken by God through the prophets and Psalms and *the other books that foster and perfect knowledge and piety.*"[5] Vulgate codices frequently grouped together Job, Psalms, Proverbs, Ecclesiastes, Song of Songs, Wisdom, and Ecclesiasticus as *libiri didactici.*[6] If we are to tolerate suggestions that because these books were not called "wisdom" by the ancients, the entire concept is simply an ill-defined modern conceit, then we might want to be consistent and deny the concept of the biblical prophetic books as currently conceived or the concept of biblical historical books, perhaps also the books often labelled "Deuteronomistic History," since they along with the wisdom books were most often simply lumped together as "the prophets" by the ancients.[7] Moreover, if we want to become bogged down in arguments about genre, let us concede that the concept of *genre* itself is a slippery one that literary critics have always struggled to define.[8] Thus, I will assume for the purposes of this essay that there is a constellation of Old Testament books of wisdom or, if one prefers ancient characterization: books that promote pious and efficacious thought and life.[9] These books share enough similarities to set them apart

Prophets: Who Are the Prophets?," in *Prophets, Worship and Theodicy: Studies in Prophetism, Biblical Theology and Structural and Rhetorical Analysis and on the Place of Music in Worship: Papers Read at the Joint British-Dutch Old Testament Conference Held at Woudschoten 1982* (OTS 23; Leiden: Brill, 1984), 3–4.

5. Philo, *Contempl. Life* 25, emphasis added; see also the discussion in John Barton, *Oracles of God: Perceptions of Ancient Prophecy in Israel After the Exile* (New York: Oxford University Press, 1986), 58.

6. These include Codex Amiatinus Biblioteca Medicea Laurenziana in Florence; Codex Cavensis at the abbey of La Trinita della Cava, Italy; Codex Corbeiense in the Russian National Library, St. Petersburg; and Codex Turonensis in the National Library of France, Paris.

7. E.g., 2 Macc 15:9; Matt 5:17; 7:12; 11:13; 22:24; Luke 16:16, 29, 31; 24:27; John 1:45; Acts 13:15; 24:14; 26:22; 28:23; Rom 3:21; from Qumran one could also include the *Damascus Document* (CD-A, col. 7, lines 14–18) and *The Rule of the Community* (1QS col. 8, lines 15–16).

8. This has been acknowledged for quite some time. See the now classic studies such as Jacques Derrida, "The Law of Genre," *Critical Inquiry* 7 (1980): 55–82; Stanley Fish, *Is There a Text in This Class?* (Cambridge, MA: Harvard University Press, 1980); Alastair Fowler, *Kinds of Literature* (Cambridge, MA: Harvard University Press, 1982); Thomas Kent, *Interpretation and Genre* (Lewisburg: Bucknell, 1986).

9. I would include Job, Proverbs, and Ecclesiastes, as well as certain wisdom Psalms in this classification. Song of Songs in my opinion is marginally wisdom/ didactic. The apocryphal/deuterocanonical books of Ben Sira and Wisdom might also be considered as sharing the same orbit with these books.

from the other biblical literature and invite us also to observe how they interact with other types of biblical literature.

Yet, when we look at these books as a whole we find that with the exception of a few short passages in Ecclesiastes (Eccl 4:13−16; 5:13−17; 9:13−16) and perhaps the narrative portions of Job (Job 1:1−2:13; 42:7–17), there are no examples of wise persons in action in wisdom literature, no extended biblical case studies of wise people.[10] This is partly a consequence of the nature of wisdom literature—it tends to be poetic, epigrammatic, and aphorismic. It is not often or primarily a narrative genre.

So to find a biblical example of a wise person we have to turn to books with more extensive narrative accounts that seek to portray the protagonists in their storylines as wise.[11] I believe that the book of Daniel seeks to depict Daniel and his three Judean companions in precisely this way. One rough indication of this is the concentration of wisdom-related terms in Daniel. By "wisdom-related terms" I mean terms that are used with some frequency in biblical wisdom literature as characterizing a wise person or wise behavior and attitudes and that share a fair degree of semantic

10. By "extended case study" I mean the presentation of someone as wise followed by tracing his wise thoughts, observations, and acts over a lifetime or at least over a significant portion of his life. Certainly, 1 Kgs 3 first declares Solomon wise by using YHWH's own words (1 Kgs 3:1–15; 2 Chr 1:6–13) and then by giving *one* example of his wisdom in action (1 Kgs 3:16–28). No other actual examples of wise acts or even wise writings by Solomon are given, although such acts and writings are mentioned (1 Kgs 4:29–34; 10:3–4; 2 Chr 9:1–2, 22). Solomon's words at the dedication of the temple could be argued to be an example of his wisdom (1 Kgs 8:12–53; 2 Chr 6:1–42), but there are other examples of prayer in the Old Testament that show similar piety and theological acumen where the speaker had not been labelled as wise (e.g., Ezra 9:6–15). Solomon can barely be seen as a case study of a wise person, and certainly not an *extended* case study. If anything, in 1 Kings he is a case study of a wise person turned foolish—he spent more time building his house than YHWH's (1 Kgs 6:38; 7:1), and he turned from YHWH (1 Kgs 11).

11. The other place in Old Testament narrative one might look for wisdom lived out is in the life of Joseph (Gen 37; 39–50). See the comparison between Joseph and Daniel in Andrew E. Steinmann, *Daniel* (Concordia Commentary; St. Louis: Concordia, 2008), 37–39; Matthew S. Rindge, "Jewish Identity Under Foreign Rule: Daniel 2 as a Reconfiguration of Genesis 41," *JBL* 129 (2010): 85−104; Wendy L. Widder, "The Court Stories of Joseph (Gen 41) and Daniel (Dan 2) in Canonical Context: A Theological Paradigm for God's Word Among the Nations," *OTE* 27 (2014): 1112−28. For studies on Joseph, see Mignon R. Jacobs, "The Conceptual Dynamics of Good and Evil in the Joseph Story: An Exegetical and Hermeneutical Inquiry," *JSOT* 27 (2003): 309−38; Yigal Levin, "Joseph, Judah and the 'Benjamin

overlap with the term "wisdom" (חָכְמָה). In Daniel we find a number of these Hebrew terms or their Aramaic cognates:

Hebrew Terms

Term	Occurrences in Daniel	In Daniel	In OT Poetry/ Wisdom[12]
Verbal root בין *understand*	Dan 1:4, 17; 8:5, 16, 17, 23, 27; 9:2, 22, 23; 10:1, 11, 12, 14; 11:30, 33, 37; 12:8, 10	19 (11%)[13]	84 (49%)
Noun בינה *understanding*	Dan 1:20; 8:15; 9:22; 10:1	4 (11%)	23 (61%)
Noun דעת *knowledge*	Dan 1:4; 12:4	2 (2%)	61 (68%)
Noun מדע *understanding*[14]	Dan 1:4, 17	2 (33%)	1 (17%)
Noun חכמה *wisdom*	Dan 1:4, 17, 20	3 (2%)	91 (61%)
Verbal root שכל (H stem) *act sensibly; have insight*	Dan 1:4, 17; 9:13, 22, 25; 11:33, 35; 12:3, 10	9 (15%)	27 (46%)
Noun שכל *good sense, insight*	Dan 8:25	1 (6%)	8 (50%)

Conundrum,'" *ZAW* 116 (2004): 223–41; Christoph Levin, "Righteousness in the Joseph Story: Joseph Resists Seduction (Genesis 39)," in *The Pentateuch: International Perspectives on Current Research* (ed. Thomas B. Dozeman, Konrad Schmid, and Baruch J. Schwartz; FAT 78; Tübingen: Mohr Siebeck, 2011), 223–40; Yonatan Grossman, "The Story of Joseph's Brothers in Light of the 'Therapeutic Narrative' Theory," *BibInt* 21 (2013): 171–95; J. G. McConville, "Forgiveness as a Private and Public Act: A Reading of the Biblical Joseph Narrative," *CBQ* 75 (2013): 635–48; Konrad Schmid, "Josephs zweiter Traum: Beobachtungen zu seiner literarischen Funktion und sachlichen Bedeutung in der Josephsgeschichte (Gen 37–50)," *ZAW* 128 (2016): 374–88.

12. Job, Psalms, Proverbs, Ecclesiastes. None of these terms occur in Song of Songs, but I consider it only marginally a wisdom book (see n. 8 above).

13. Percentages are based on the number of occurrences in the OT.

14. The infrequently used noun מדע occurs only six times in the OT. Interestingly, half of these are used in 2 Chr 1:10–12 in Solomon's request to God for wisdom (but not in the parallel in 1 Kgs 3:9–14). Yet 2 Chronicles does not contain the account of Solomon's demonstration of his wisdom as found in 1 Kgs 3:16–28 or the description of his wisdom as in 1 Kgs 4:29–34.

Aramaic Terms

Term	Occurrences in Daniel
Noun בינה *discernment*	Dan 2:21; 4:31, 33; 5:12
Adjective חכים *wise*	Dan 2:12, 13, 14, 18, 21, 24, 27, 48; 4:3, 15; 5:7, 8, 15
Noun חכמה *wisdom*	Dan 2:20, 21, 23, 30; 5:11, 14
Noun מנדע *knowledge*	Dan 2:21; 4:31, 33; 5:12

Some comparison with the wisdom and poetic books is also revealing. Judging from vocabulary alone, Daniel is most closely related to Proverbs and Job and somewhat more weakly related to Ecclesiastes:[15]

Term	Daniel	Job	Psalms	Proverbs	Ecclesiastes
Verbal root בין *understand*	19 (11%)	23 (13%)	26 (15%)	34 (20%)	1 (<1%)
Noun בינה *understanding*	4 (11%)	9 (24%)	0 (0%)	14 (37%)	0 (0%)
Noun דעת *knowledge*	2 (2%)	10 (11%)	4 (4%)	40 (44%)	7 (8%)
Noun מדע *understanding*	2 (33%)	0 (0%)	0 (0%)	0 (0%)	1 (17%)
Noun חכמה *wisdom*	3 (2%)	18 (12%)	6 (4%)	39 (26%)	28 (19%)
Verbal root שׂכל (H stem) *act sensibly; have insight*	9 (15%)	3 (5%)	11 (19%)	13 (22%)	0 (0%)
Noun שׂכל *good sense, insight*	1 (6%)	1 (6%)	1 (6%)	6 (38%)	0 (0%)

I will argue below that upon closer inspection, Daniel has a much closer relationship with Proverbs than with other biblical wisdom literature.

Clearly, the Hebrew portions of Daniel, which comprise just over half of the book, have more than their share of the occurrences of these terms. A statistical comparison of the vocabulary of the Aramaic portions of Daniel with the biblical wisdom books would require much more

15. The relationship to Psalms is more complicated since not all Psalms can be characterized as wisdom literature, although a number of Psalms explore or expound on wisdom or wise attitudes and behavior and could be characterized as wisdom psalms.

sophisticated methods.[16] However, it is noteworthy that the Hebrew terms derive from four roots (בין, ידע, חכם, and שׂכל) and that the four Aramaic terms derive from three of these (all except שׂכל). These Aramaic roots are true cognates of the Hebrew counterparts—that is, the semantics of the Aramaic roots substantially correspond to those of the similar Hebrew roots. In Daniel it is difficult, if not impossible, to distinguish the use of these Aramaic roots from their Hebrew cognates.

At the same time, Daniel lacks explicit discussion of the polar opposite terms so frequently employed in the antithetical parallelism of Proverbs—it does not use vocabulary related to foolishness.[17] This lack of interest in directly describing foolishness highlights that the book of Daniel is more about depicting action than it is about describing wisdom in more objective terms as is done, for instance, in Proverbs or Ecclesiastes. Instead, when foolishness is described in Daniel it is ultimately shown to be imprudent and thoughtless but never labeled as such. Thus, the folly of those who worshiped Nebuchadnezzar's idol (Dan 3), Nebuchadnezzar's unwise arrogance (Dan 4), and Belshazzar's drunken disrespect for Israel's God (Dan 5) are shown to be foolish by the outcome of the narrative, not by calling these behaviors foolish. However, this is not surprising since in each instance the foolish behaviors are by pagans who have no dedicated relationship to Yahweh, a prerequisite for possessing biblical wisdom (e.g., Job 28:28; Prov 1:7, 29; 2:1–5; 3:5, 25–26; 9:10; Eccl 12:3). To highlight these behaviors as foolish would be almost pedantic, stating what ought to be obvious to the knowledgeable reader. However, by letting these foolish acts go unlabeled, the author all the more powerfully highlights for the reader the explicitly labelled wisdom of Daniel. The text allows readers to conclude that some behavior by pagans is foolish so that they can appreciate all the more the wise behavior of Daniel and others as flowing from their relationship with Israel's God. More importantly, a major focus of the book is how to live among the nations and continue to live the pious life of a worshiper of Yahweh.[18] The emphasis on godly wisdom fits with this focus and explains also the lack of any accenting of foolish behavior that might detract from the author's message.

So, what exactly is the relationship between the wisdom of the Old Testament and Daniel?

---

16. I am not aware of any studies that attempt to do this. However, I am confident that linguists could devise such methods.

17. Such as the noun פתי, the nouns כסיל and בסילות, the nouns אויל and אולת, the noun and verbal root נבל, the phrase חסר־לב, the adjective בער, the noun, adjective, and verbal root גבה, the noun רמיה, or the nouns לץ and לצון.

18. See the discussion in Steinmann, *Daniel*, 30–31.

Attributes of Biblical Wisdom

Before we can investigate Daniel as wisdom in action, we must first understand what biblical wisdom is. First and foremost, biblical wisdom is an attribute of God. This is stated most directly in Prov 3:19:[19]

> YHWH founded the earth by wisdom; he established the heavens by understanding.

However, this is also implied elsewhere. For instance, the poem about the way to wisdom in Job 28 speaks of wisdom as God's since only he knows the way to it:

> But God understands the way to it [wisdom]. He knows its location, for He looks to the ends of the earth and sees everything under heaven. When God fixed the weight of the wind and established the water by measure, when He determined a limit for the rain and a path for the lightning, He considered wisdom and evaluated it; He established it and examined it. (Job 28:23–27)

Later in Job when YHWH challenges Job from the whirlwind, he also claims wisdom as his own:

> Can you send out lightning bolts, and they go? Do they say to you: "Here we are"? Who put wisdom in the inner organs or gave the mind understanding? Who can number the clouds using wisdom? (Job 38:35–37a)

This passage in Job also highlights that true wisdom is a gift from God, as also explicitly stated in Proverbs:

> YHWH gives wisdom; from his mouth [come] knowledge and understanding. (Prov 2:6)

More importantly, wisdom is linked with righteousness, specifically the active righteousness of a person who trusts God.[20] Consider the following proverbs:

> Do not warn a mocker, otherwise he will hate you. Warn a wise person, and he will love you. Give [advice] to a wise person, and he will become even wiser. Teach a righteous person, and he will add [to his] wisdom. (Prov 9:8–9)

19. All translations are the author's.
20. For further on the link between wisdom and righteousness in Proverbs see Sun Myung Lyu, *Righteousness in the Book of Proverbs* (FAT 2/55; Tübingen: Mohr Siebeck, 2012); Bruce K. Waltke, "Righteousness in Proverbs," *WTJ* 70 (2008): 225–37.

The father of a righteous person will cheerfully rejoice. The man who begets a wise person will find joy in him. (Prov 23:24)

This righteousness places an emphasis on character that is unique to ancient Israel. Clifford has noted that at least when speaking of Prov 1–9 Israelite wisdom is unique in the ancient Near East:

> Taken as a whole, the instructions of Prov 1–9 are distinctive… They are less specific than their Egyptian and Mesopotamian prototypes. They urge the reader to seek wisdom rather than to do or not do particular actions. To put it another way, Proverbs emphasizes character rather than acts.[21]

Whatever theory one expounds about the relationship of Prov 1–9 to the rest of the book, in its present setting this section serves to set the tone for the concise sayings that follow and place in the reader's mind that these shorter aphorisms ought to be read in the context of character-shaping action.[22]

Thus, real wisdom according to the Old Testament stems from a relationship with YHWH and is often captured in the phrase *the fear of YHWH* (יראת יהוה).[23] This phrase at times may denote fear of punishment, although such uses are rare in the Hebrew Bible. For example:

---

21. Richard J. Clifford, *Proverbs: A Commentary* (OTL; Louisville: Westminster John Knox, 1999), 18.

22. For various theories about the origin of Prov 1–9 see Daniel Estes, *Hear, My Son: Teaching and Learning in Proverbs 1–9* (NSBT 4; Downers Grove: InterVarsity, 1997); Michael V. Fox, *Proverbs 1–9: A New Translation with Introduction and Commentary* (AB 18A; New York: Doubleday, 2000); idem, "The Social Location of the Book of Proverbs," in *Texts, Temples, and Traditions: A Tribute to Menahem Haran* (ed. Michael V. Fox et al.; Winona Lake: Eisenbrauns, 1996), 227–39; Leo G. Perdue, "Wisdom Theology and Social History in Proverbs 1–9," in *Wisdom, You Are My Sister: Studies in Honor of Roland E. Murphy, O. Carm., on the Occasion of His Eightieth Birthday* (ed. Michael L. Barré; CBQMS 29; Washington, DC: Catholic Biblical Association of America, 1997), 78–101; Patrick W. Skehan, "A Single Editor for the Whole Book of Proverbs," *CBQ* 9 (1947): 190–98; Andrew E. Steinmann, "Proverbs 1–9 as a Solomonic Composition," *JETS* 43 (2000): 659–74; R. N. Whybray, *The Book of Proverbs: A Survey of Modern Study* (History of Biblical Interpretation 1; Leiden: Brill, 1995); idem, *The Composition of the Book of Proverbs* (JSOTSup 168; Sheffield: Sheffield Academic Press, 1994).

23. On this phrase see Karl Barth, "Fear of the Lord Is the Beginning of Wisdom," *Int* 14 (1960): 433–39; Henri Blocher, "The Fear of the Lord as the 'Principle' of Wisdom," *TynBul* 28 (1977): 3–28; John Bowman, "The Fear of the Lord," in *Studies in Wisdom Literature* (ed. W. C. Van Wyk; Hercules, South Africa: NHW,

Fear Yahweh, my son, and [fear] a king. Do not associate with those who are rebellious, because their disaster will happen suddenly, and who knows what ruin both of them will cause? (Prov 24:21–22)

Do not let your mouth lead you to sin. Do not say in the presence of the messenger, "It was a mistake." Why should God be angry with your statement and ruin the work of your hands? For many dreams [result in] pointless actions, and so do many words. Therefore, fear God. (Eccl 5:5–6; EV 5:6–7)

In both cases "fear" denotes dread of God's punishment that brings ruin.

However, the fear of YHWH more frequently does not denote fear of punishment but instead a positive relationship with God that leads one to shun evil. This is especially in evidence in Deut 6:2–13 and Deut 10:12, where the fear of YHWH is linked with love for him, appreciation for his deliverance of Israel from Egypt, and willingness to "walk in his way." In Proverbs this positive relationship leads to wisdom and shunning of evil behavior.

1981), 9–12; William P. Brown, "'Come, O Children...I Will Teach You the Fear of the Lord' (Psalm 34:12): Comparing Psalms and Proverbs," in *Seeking Out the Wisdom of the Ancients* (ed. Ronald L. Troxel et al.; Winona Lake: Eisenbrauns, 2005), 85–102; Daniel Castelo, "The Fear of the Lord as Theological Method," *JTI* 2 (2008): 147–60; Robert L. Cate, "The Fear of the Lord in the Old Testament," *Theological Educator* 35 (1987): 41–55; David J. A. Clines, "'The Fear of the Lord Is Wisdom' (Job 28:28): A Semantic and Contextual Study," in *Job 28: Cognition in Context* (ed. E. J. Van Wolde; Biblical Interpretation 64; Leiden: Brill, 2003), 57–92; Alexander A. Di Lella, "Fear of the Lord and Belief and Hope in the Lord Amid Trials: Sirach 2:1–18," in Barré, ed., *Wisdom, You Are My Sister*, 188–204; Alexander A. Di Lella, "Fear of the Lord as Wisdom: Ben Sira 1, 11–30," in *The Book of Ben Sira in Modern Research: Proceedings of the First International Ben Sira Conference 29–31 July, 1996, Soesterberg, Netherlands* (ed. Pancratius C. Beentjes; BZAW 225; New York: de Gruyter, 1997), 113–33; Walter C. Kaiser, Jr., "Wisdom Theology and the Centre of Old Testament Theology," *EvQ* 50 (1978): 132–46; Roland E. Murphy, "The Fear of the Lord: The Fear to End All Fears," in *Overcoming Fear Between Jews and Christians* (ed. James H. Charlesworth et al.; New York: Crossroad, 1992), 172–80; Zóltan Schwáb, "Is Fear of the Lord the Source of Wisdom or Vice Versa?" *VT* (2013): 652–62; Dawn Lyn Spies, "The Fear of the Lord in Numbers 13–14," *Lutheran Forum* 44 (2010): 10–12; Andrew E. Steinmann, *Daniel*, 27–28; Anneke Viljoen and P. M. Venter, "An Exploration of the Symbolic World of Proverbs 10:1–15:33 with Specific Reference to 'the Fear of the Lord,'" *HTS* 69 (2013): 1–6; Bruce K. Waltke, "The Fear of the Lord," *Journal of the Christian Brethren Research Fellowship* (1992): 12–16.

Do not consider yourself wise. *Fear YHWH*, and turn away from evil. (Prov 3:7)

The *fear of YHWH* is discipline that leads to wisdom. (Prov 15:33)

Do not allow your heart to envy sinners. Instead have *the fear of YHWH* all the time. (Prov 23:17)

He [YHWH] said to mankind, "Note: *The fear of YHWH*—that is wisdom. And to turn from evil is understanding." (Job 28:28)

These two meanings are not unrelated. While fear of YHWH as a motivation to escape his punishment is dread of God's wrath, the fear of YHWH that denotes a positive relationship is a much more subtle fear— fear of the loss of relationship with a loving and gracious God who brings blessings on those who fear him. Possessing the fear of YHWH, therefore, brings comfort and reassurance in that relationship:

The fear of YHWH is strong confidence, and his children will have a refuge. (Prov 14:26)

The fear of YHWH [leads] to life, and [one who has it] rests content. He will not be disturbed by trouble. (Prov 19:23)

Thus, understanding this more subtle fear of YHWH is wisdom, something that sinners and fools cannot attain (cf. Prov 2:1–5).

Finally, we ought to note that true wisdom is sometimes counterintuitive from the perspective of those who do not possess it. That is, those who possess godly wisdom act in ways that are pleasing to God even if it appears to threaten their well-being in this life. For instance, consider this proverb:

A person's good sense makes him slow to anger, and it is to his credit that he overlooks an offense. (Prov 19:11)

Those who do not possess divine wisdom might view this advice as harmful, since overlooking an offense appears to put one in a weaker, more vulnerable position—a person who is easily imposed upon. Yet, the wise person understands that being longsuffering is being godlike (Exod 34:6; Num 14:18; Neh 9:17; Pss 86:15; 103:8; 145:8; Joel 2:13; Jonah 4:2; Nah 1:3).

A good reputation is to be chosen rather than great wealth. Favor is better than silver and gold. (Prov 22:1)

Many suppose that one cannot be too rich, that riches are an unalloyed blessing or at least more blessing than bane—but this saying runs counter to such thinking.[24] The person without godly wisdom may reason that great wealth can buy a good reputation and curry favor with others. However, a person with godly wisdom knows that this kind of reputation and favor is ephemeral, lasting only as long as one's wealth is present, and it certainly is of no value before God (cf. Zeph 1:18; Jas 5:1–6; 1 Pet 1:18). Instead, the wise person values God's instruction (Ps 119:72).

> Don't give me poverty or riches. Feed me [only] my allotted food. Otherwise I may feel satisfied and deny you and say, "Who is YHWH?" Or on the other hand, I may become poor and steal and profane the name of my God. (Prov 30:8b-9)

This prayer of Agur only makes half-sense to the worldly wise person: it certainly is not good to be poor, since it deprives a person of the means to support one's life. However, Agur's concern is less on poverty as threatening life and more on it threatening one's relationship with God. More importantly, while great wealth may seem like a good problem to have, Agur sees it as dangerous because it can damage one's relationship with God by making that relationship seem unnecessary (cf. Matt 19:24; Mark 10:25; Luke 18:25). The wise person prays only that his physical needs be met (cf. Matt 6:11; Luke 11:3).

As we turn to the narratives in Daniel, we see that the actions and aptitudes of Daniel, Azariah, Hananiah, and Mishael illustrate a number of passages in Proverbs that speak of kings and service to kings.

Daniel Demonstrates Wisdom Through Service to Overlords

All the narratives of Dan 1–6 involve service to kings—by Daniel (Dan 3–6), by Azariah, Hananiah, and Mishael (Dan 2), or by all four men (Dan 1). Proverbs has much to say about serving kings (e.g., Prov 14:35;

24. For a wider discussion of wealth and poverty in Proverbs see Timothy J. Sandoval, *The Discourse of Wealth and Poverty in the Book of Proverbs* (Biblical Interpretation 77; Leiden: Brill, 2006); Raymond C. Van Leeuwen, "Wealth and Poverty: System And Contradiction In Proverbs," *HS* 33 (1992): 25–36; Harold C. Washington, *Wealth and Poverty in the Instruction of Amenemope and the Hebrew Proverbs* (SBLDS 142; Atlanta: Scholars, 1994); R. N. Whybray, "Poverty, Wealth, and Point of View in Proverbs," *ExpTim* 100 (1989): 332–36; H. G. M. Williamson, "A Christian View of Wealth and Possessions: An Old Testament Perspective," *ExAud* 27 (2011): 1–19; G. H. Wittenberg, "The Situational Context of Statements Concerning Poverty and Wealth in the Book of Proverbs," *Scriptura* 21 (1987): 1–23.

16:12–15; 19:12; 20:2, 8; 21:1; 22:11, 29; 24:21–22; 25:2–27), and Daniel and his Judean companions demonstrate wisdom as applied to serving one's master—in this case monarchs. It is interesting to note that especially Prov 25:2–27 is in the form of advice for kings and those who serve them.[25] Some seem especially apt as general descriptions of Daniel's dealings with Nebuchadnezzar. For instance, Prov 25:15 says, "By patience a ruler can be persuaded, and a soft tongue can break a bone." Daniel and his companions repeatedly show patience in dealing with the pagan Nebuchadnezzar constantly referring him to the "God of Heaven" (Dan 2:18–19, 37, 44) or "the Most High God" (Dan 3:26; 4:2; 5:18, 21) without directly upbraiding him for his pagan beliefs and practices.

Wisdom Leads to Prominence

> Do you see a person who is efficient in his work? He will serve kings. He will not serve unknown people. (Prov 22:29)[26]

This proverb notes that being competent earns recognition and reward.[27] It encourages learning one's craft well instead of focusing on one's advancement. Those who seek success without expending the effort to increase their competence risk losing any advantages and offices they may have acquired when it becomes obvious to those who promoted them that they are not worthy of their position.

---

25. Glendon E. Bryce, "Another Wisdom 'Book' in Proverbs," *JBL* 91 (1972): 145–57; Raymond C. Van Leeuwen, *Context and Meaning in Proverbs 25–27* (SBLDS 96; Atlanta: Scholars Press, 1998), 36, 39, 72–73, 101, 146.

26. It is interesting to note that this proverb is not treated as Solomonic in proverbs but is from the "words of wise people" (Prov 22:17–24:22; see esp. Prov 22:17; see also *ANET*, 424 n. 46, and D. C. Simpson, "The Hebrew Book of Proverbs and the Teaching of Amenophis," *JEA* 12 [1926]: 232–39). This particular saying has a parallel in the Wisdom of Amenomope. Thus, it comes from what theologically might be seen as natural knowledge of God's law. See John Ruffle, "The Teaching of Amenemope and Its Connection with the Book of Proverbs," *TynBul* 29 (1977): 29–68; Paul Overland, "Structure in the *Wisdom of Amenemope* and Proverbs," in *"Go to the Land I Will Show You": Studies in Honor of Dwight W. Young* (ed. Joseph E. Colleson and Victor H. Matthews; Winona Lake: Eisenbrauns, 1996), 271–91.

27. Roland E. Murphy, *Proverbs* (WBC 22; Nashville: Thomas Nelson, 1998), 171; Richard J. Clifford, *Proverbs* (OTL; Louisville: Westminster John Knox, 1999), 208.

Daniel 1 contains the account of Daniel and his companions refusing to eat the king's rich food. However, we also find in that "In every matter of wisdom and understanding about which the king consulted them, he found them ten times better than all the diviners and mediums in his entire kingdom" (Dan 1:20). This sets the stage of the promotion of these men in Dan 2:48–49:

> Then the king promoted Daniel and gave him many generous gifts. He made him ruler over the entire province of Babylon and chief governor of all the wise men of Babylon. At Daniel's request, the king appointed Shadrach, Meshach, and Abednego to manage the affairs of the province of Babylon. But Daniel remained at the king's court.

A Wise Person Avoids Sinful Behavior

> It is a disgusting thing to kings to do wickedness, for a throne is established by righteousness. (Prov 16:12)

This proverb encourages kings and those who serve them to think about the long-term stability of their position rather than the immediate wealth and power that can be gained through corruption. The stability of the throne and the positions of those who serve it can only be achieved if the king knows that it is in the interest of the royal house to rid the court of schemers and malefactors.[28]

In Dan 6 King Darius clearly was upset when he discovered that he had been manipulated into issuing a decree that endangered Daniel (Dan 6:14).[29] Darius clearly acknowledges Daniel's piety (Dan 6:17)—a sign of Daniel's righteousness—and Daniel himself declares the righteousness of his actions (Dan 6:23). The narrative also portrays Darius as bothered by the unrighteous act of condemning the loyal Daniel to the lions' den (Dan 6:15–16). Darius's night without food and sleep are a consequence of the severe anxiety he experienced. It would be tortuous for a ruler to be pressured into condemning an innocent man whom he has regarded favorably. With a guilty conscience, Darius is unable to enjoy entertainment or pleasures, so he refrains from them. This characterization of

---

28. Clifford, *Proverbs*, 159.

29. Note that this is another example of foolishness of a king—he can be manipulated by appeal to his vanity into actions that he later regrets (Dan 6:7–10). Note, however, that Darius is not called foolish, and a casual reader might miss his foolishness altogether and focus only on the ultimate foolishness of Darius's officials who talk him into unwise behavior.

Darius serves to emphasize further the righteousness of Daniel's action and the wisdom of his behavior.

In the end, the king not only rejoices in the rescue of the righteous Daniel (Dan 6:25–27) but also shows his disgust for the wicked scheming of his officials as he condemns them to the punishment they had prepared for Daniel (Dan 6:25). The punishment for Daniel's accusers is the fate they had designed for him. The legal practice of imposing upon those who make a false accusation the penalty that they would have imposed on the accused was common in the ancient Near East (see Esth 7:10) and was even endorsed in Old Testament law (Deut 19:16–21; Ps 7:15–17; Prov 19:5, 9; 21:28). The ravenous actions of the lions (Dan 6:25) was a vivid demonstration of what the absence of God's protection means. In the end, the wisdom of Daniel's actions is highlighted by the contrasting results for the righteous Daniel versus the foolish and scheming officials.

Wisdom Results in a Master's Favor Toward His Servants

> A king's favor is toward a servant who has insight, but his fury is for one causing shame. (Prov 4:35)

> There is life in the light of a king's face; his favor is like a cloud of [that brings] spring rain. (Prov 16:15)

> The person who loves a pure heart—his lips are gracious; a king will be his friend. (Prov 22:11)

> The favor of kings is toward righteous lips. He loves a person who speaks upright things. (Prov 16:13)

Daniel's God-given insight into kings' dreams and his wise advice leads to blessings for himself and his fellow Judeans. He not only interprets dreams (Dan 2 and Dan 4) but also advises kings (Dan 4:24) and is known to be absolutely trustworthy in the faithful execution of his office (Dan 6:3). All of these result in Daniel being favored by both Nebuchadnezzar and Darius. This is already hinted in Dan 1:17 where Daniel "understood every kind of vision and dreams," granting him a specialization that went beyond that of his Judean companions, though it was of the same kind of divine favor and wisdom with which they were endowed.[30]

---

30. John J. Collins, *Daniel* (Hermeneia; Minneapolis: Fortress, 1993), 144.

A Wise Person Can Know When to Defy a Master's Anger

> A king's fearful anger is like a lion's growl; whoever intrudes on him
> endangers his life. (Prov 20:2)

> The king's anger is like a lion's growl, but his favor is like dew on grass.
> (Prov 19:12)

Shadrach, Meshach, and Abednego risk the full rage of Nebuchadnezzar
(Dan 3). Their wisdom in preferring to live in the fear of YHWH rather
than in fear of royal reprisal ultimately leads to royal favor. This narrative,
more than any other in Daniel, demonstrates the counterintuitive nature
of divine wisdom granted to God's people. While the book of Proverbs
recognizes the anger of a king, Daniel and his friends show the complexity
of wisdom in fearing the wrath of YHWH—the true king—over the king
of Babylon. Their actions actually incite the Babylonian king's anger but
for a very wise reason—to maintain their reliance on God and the gracious
relationship he has established with them. They flatly state that they have
no need to answer the king (Dan 3:16). But more importantly, they state
that if their God exists, it follows that he has the ability to save them—and
their wisdom is shown, since they fear God more than they fear the king's
wrath.[31]

A Wise Person Can Allay His Master's Anger

> A king's anger is a messenger of death, but a wise person can assuage it.
> (Prov 16:14)

Daniel's reaction when he understood Nebuchadnezzar's dream of a large
tree (Dan 4) also shows wisdom in action. Daniel knew that telling the
king bad news was a frightening prospect, and Nebuchadnezzar even
recognized the fear on Daniel's face (Dan 4:16). Daniel immediately
sought to assuage the king's anger while also moving to a frank portrayal
of the dream's meaning (Dan 4:21–23). The wisdom of Daniel's action is
exhibited in that he subtly rather than directly reinforces a key theological
point: God is in charge (Dan 4:21). This subtlety is then wisely made

---

31. Steinmann, *Daniel*, 185–87; Peter W. Coxon, "Daniel III 17: A Linguistic and
Theological Problem," *VT* 26 (1976): 400–409; Ariel A. Bloch, "Questioning God's
Omnipotence in the Bible: A Linguistic Case Study," in *Semitic Studies in Honor of
Wolf Leslau on the Occasion of His Eighty-fifth Birthday*, vol. 1 (ed. Wolf Leslau and
Alan S. Kaye; Wiesbaden: Harrassowitz, 1991), 174–88.

more explicit when Daniel tells Nebuchadnezzar that he would remain demented until the king acknowledges God's absolute rule, not his own (Dan 4:22). Finally, Daniel is wise to avoid details of Nebuchadnezzar's dreams—such as the iron and brass bands on the stump (Dan 4:12)—thereby sparing the king embarrassment of implying that he may have to be restrained physically (cf. Dan 4:23).

Daniel also displays a related ability—the capacity to allay a master's fear. In Dan 1 he overcomes fear of the king's chief eunuch by appealing to the steward whom the chief eunuch had placed in charge of Daniel and his companions (Dan 1:11–14). The ten-day trial of a vegetarian diet not only proved successful, it was also a master stroke in that it did not require permanent rejection of the king's rich food. At the same time it allowed the four young Judeans to avoid breaking any of the dietary laws found in the Pentateuch, as the Torah did not consider any edible plants to be unclean. Daniel wisely avoids any need to give a long explanation of which type of meat the Judeans could and could not eat (cf. Lev 11).

A Wise Person Understands That God Controls Human Authorities

A king's heart in Yahweh's hand is streams of water: He directs it wherever He desires. (Prov 21:1)

In the well-known account of the handwriting on the wall, Daniel for the first and only time in the book directly challenges and chastises a ruler. Unlike the more deferential attitude he displayed before Nebuchadnezzar, when he is called upon to interpret the inscription on the wall he is confrontational: he rejects the rewards that the king had proffered (Dan 5:17).[32] Daniel then reminds Belshazzar that he ought to have learned a lesson from Nebuchadnezzar's arrogance as recorded in Dan 4 (Dan 5:18–21). He then upbraids Belshazzar for his lack of humility before the Lord of Heaven (Dan 5:22–23). Only after making the king listen to this stern condemnation does Daniel deign to interpret the dream.

---

32. Miller argues that Daniel rejected Belshazzar's gift not out of rudeness but to avoid any misconceptions that God's services could be bought. See Stephen R. Miller, *Daniel* (NAC 18; Nashville: Broadman & Holman, 1994), 162. Though that may be true, Daniel's rejection of the reward borders on rude behavior and is probably a purposeful signal to the king that Daniel considered his acts foolish and arrogant and meriting God's disapproval. See Steinmann, *Daniel*, 283.

Daniel's actions display his wisdom in recognizing that God has directed Belshazzar's thoughts and emotions (cf. Dan 5:6–7). Not only will the king be patient and tolerate Daniel's words, he will even impose upon the prophet the rejected gifts (Dan 5:29). Though Daniel's defiance of Belshazzar and his interpretation of the handwriting might have been deemed worthy of death under other circumstances, Daniel was wise enough to understand the situation and the truth that God's will was at work. The fright of the king and the promise he had made in front of his guests probably forced him into honoring Daniel instead of executing him. In the narrative this serves to emphasize the wisdom of Daniel's actions.

A Wise Person Advises Kings to Be Merciful

> Mercy and truth protect a king; and he maintains his throne with mercy.
> (Prov 20:28)

This proverb is an observation that rulers cannot make their position secure through tyranny, corruption, or bloodshed. The only way a ruler can remain truly secure is to show mercy while upholding truth, just as divine mercy and truth protect all.[33]

When Daniel was asked by Nebuchadnezzar to interpret his dream of the large tree, Daniel does not only interpret the dream, he also offers advice: "…break away from your sins with righteousness and from your iniquities by showing mercy to the poor. Perhaps your prosperity will be prolonged" (Dan 4:24). Nebuchadnezzar apparently does not take Daniel's advice and for a time loses his throne (Dan 4:25–30), demonstrating the wisdom of Daniel's counsel by negative example.

Throughout the accounts of Daniel, Azariah, Hananiah, and Mishael and their interaction with kings, they exhibit wise behavior as advocated in Proverbs and summarized in Eccl 8:1–4:

> Who is like the wise person, and who knows the interpretation of a matter? A man's wisdom lights up his face, and his stern face is transformed. Keep the king's command because of your oath made before God. Do not be in a hurry and leave his presence, and do not persist in a bad cause, since he will do whatever he wants. For the king's word is authoritative, and who can say to him, "What are you doing?"[34]

33. Clifford, *Proverbs*, 186.

34. It is interesting to note that Eccl 8:4b is almost an exact match to Job 9:12, where God—not the king—is the referent. Therefore, the wisdom admonition to fear YHWH includes a healthy fear of the king. See Roland E. Murphy, *Ecclesiastes* (WBC 23A; Dallas: Word, 1992), 83.

Daniel's Prayer—Daniel 2:19–23

Daniel not only demonstrates wisdom in his interaction with kings. He also displays it in his relationship to God, as is shown in his prayer after having received the revelation of Nebuchadnezzar's dream and its interpretation.[35] In this prayer Daniel includes the following concepts found in biblical wisdom literature, especially Proverbs:

Wisdom belongs to God (Dan 2:20)

God controls time and establishes worldly authorities (Dan 2:21)

God grants wisdom (Dan 2:21, 24)

Is Daniel's Depiction of Wisdom Reliant on Proverbs?

So, are we to conclude that the narratives of Daniel are somehow reliant upon Proverbs or biblical wisdom books more generally? I suppose the answer to this question depends on what one understands as reliance of one text upon another. If by *reliance* we understand close verbal affinities between texts, easily detected parallels in thought, structure, theme, or plot, then the answer would certainly be that Daniel is not reliant on Proverbs (or Job or Ecclesiastes). However, if by *reliance* we include a more indirect and understated influence of one text upon another, then I would argue that there is a certain reliance in that the author of Daniel has internalized the wisdom of Proverbs (and at times Job and Ecclesiastes)— especially the wisdom needed to serve in a royal court—and has shaped his account of the actions of Daniel and the three Israelite young men to foreground their wisdom. The author never gives readers the impression that he is at pains to illustrate the aphorisms in Proverbs or passages in Job and Ecclesiastes in his narratives. However, by his use of selected wisdom vocabulary, he signals to the reader that some connection exists with Israelite wisdom concepts. When one compares the situations in Dan 1–6 with situations addressed in more general terms in biblical wisdom books, especially Proverbs, the reliance—or influence, if you prefer that term—can be perceived.

35. On the importance of this prayer to the entire account in Dan 2, see G. T. M. Prinsloo, "Two Poems in a Sea of Prose: The Content and Context of Daniel 2.20–23 and 6.27–28," *JSOT* 59 (1993): 93–108.

More importantly, why is Daniel portrayed as a wise courtier who exhibits wise behavior in the mode of the advice given in Proverbs? No matter when one dates the book of Daniel—from the early Persian period to the late Hellenistic era[36]—it was a book written to Jews living under foreign domination, and perhaps even persecution.[37] For such readers there had to have been an important question concerning their piety: Was it possible to accept such domination, serve foreign overlords, and still maintain one's faith and even live as a wise worshiper of YHWH? Daniel's example tells readers that they can within certain limits. While there are absolutes to the ancient Israelite faith that cannot be compromised (cf. Dan 3 and 6), with God-given wisdom one can negotiate the sometimes treacherous churning waters between service to human masters and service to God.

Wise People in Daniel's Visions

While attention to the actions of wise people seems to be missing in most of the visionary sections of Daniel, it is present in its closing vision, Dan 10–12. God's people are also depicted as wise. They exhibit the behaviors that characterize their wisdom as of divine origin, since they lead others to knowledge and righteousness:

> Those of the people who have insight will make many understand, but they will stumble by sword, flame, captivity, and plunder for some time. (Dan 11:33)

> Those who have insight will shine like the brightness of the king, and those who bring many to righteousness like the stars forever and ever. (Dan 12:3)[38]

Moreover, their wisdom is—from a worldly viewpoint—counterintuitive (cf. Prov 19:11 cited above): they must fall, be purified, and cleansed, and they will understand this while the wicked will not:

36. For discussions of various positions on the date of the composition of Daniel see Steinmann, *Daniel*, 1–19, and the various commentaries and articles referenced there.

37. For further discussion see ibid., 28–31.

38. There is general agreement by commentators of all stripes that "those who have insight" at Dan 11:33 are in the first instance faithful Jews who opposed the oppressive forced Hellenization of Judea by Antiochus IV Epiphanes. See Louis F. Harman and Alexander A. Di Lella, *The Book of Daniel: A New Translation with Introduction and Commentary* (AB 23; New York: Doubleday, 1977), 299; Miller, *Daniel*, 302; Steinmann, *Daniel*, 531. Collins (*Daniel*, 385) believes that they were more specifically those who resisted but did so by nonviolent means.

Some of those who have insight will stumble in order to refine them, purify [them], and make [them] white until the time of the end, for it is still for an appointed time. (Dan 11:35)

Many will be purified, be made white, and be refined, but the wicked will behave wickedly. The wicked will not understand, but those who have insight will understand. (Dan 12:10)

These wise persons—those with insight—will accept their persecutions as pleasing to God even as it threatens their well-being in this life. It is their *actions*, not their cognitive awareness, that demonstrates their wisdom. They, like Daniel, display sagacity by their life and, unlike Daniel, even by their death.

Retribution in Proverbs and Daniel— Is There a Link Between the Two Books?

Is there another wisdom link connecting Daniel and Proverbs? Daniel 12:10 might seem to open the door for such an exploration. Standing in antithetical parallelism to "those who have insight" are "the wicked." Most pointedly this is *not* "the foolish" (see the discussion above on Daniel's avoidance of terms in the semantic domain of foolishness). However, it does suggest that the righteousness of the wise (see discussion above) is matched by the wickedness of the foolish in Daniel. It is a commonplace in Proverbs that the wicked may face retribution for their acts. At times this is simply a poetic justice that they are ensnared in their own schemes:

The person who digs a pit will fall into it. The person who rolls a stone—it will roll back on him. (Prov 26:27).

Much more often the actions of wicked people lead them to eventual ruin (e.g., Prov 10:7, 16, 24; 11:2, 3, 6, 17, 19, 27, 31; 12:21).[39] However, in a few cases Yahweh will bring retribution on the wicked:

---

39. This is often characterized as "act–consequence" after the theory propounded by Klaus Koch, "Gibt es ein Vergeltungsdogma im Alten Testament," *ZTK* 52 (1955): 1–42. However, Koch's theory has been called into question by Peter T. H. Hatton, *Contradiction in the Book of Proverbs: The Deep Waters of Counsel* (SOTSMS 13; Aldershot: Ashgate, 2008). See also Peter Hatton, "A Cautionary Tale: The Acts–Consequence 'Construct,'" *JSOT* 35 (2011): 375–84.

> The way of YHWH is a fortress for the person of integrity, but destruction
> for evildoers. A righteous person will never be moved, but wicked people
> will not dwell on earth. (Prov 10:29)

In some cases YHWH is not mentioned as the source of retribution, but
his work is implied:

> When the storm has passed, the wicked are no more, but the righteous
> person [has] an everlasting foundation. (Prov 10:25)

Perhaps the most ominous expressions of this theology of retribution is
found in sayings with the phrase לֹא יִנָּקֶה, "he will not go unpunished"
(Prov 6:29; 11:21; 16:5; 17:5; 19:5, 9; 28:20).[40] Two of these in particular
appear to connect that punishment with YHWH:

> Everyone with an arrogant attitude is an abomination to YHWH. Be sure of
> this: that person will not go unpunished. (Prov 16:5)

> Someone who makes fun of a poor person insults his Maker. A person who
> rejoices over [someone else's] misfortune will not go unpunished. (Prov
> 17:5)[41]

What makes these passages about YHWH's retribution interesting is that
they do not specify *when* one might expect YHWH to act against the
wicked.[42] When will the wicked not dwell on earth (Prov 10:29)? Could
the storm that carries away the wicked be eschatological or is it simply
temporal (Prov 10:25)? Since the wicked "will not go unpunished," when
will their Maker mete out retribution? Any thoughtful, observant person
who has lived a good number of years knows that some evildoers seem
never to have gotten their comeuppance in this life. For every Adolph
Hitler who died a coward's death in a bunker or every Osama bin Laden
who was killed in a hail of bullets, there are just as many Josef Stalins who

---

40. Shamir Yona, "The Influence of Legal Style on the Style of Aphorism: The
Origin of the Retribution Formula and the Clause *Lō' Yinnāqeh* 'He Will Not Go
Unpunished' in the Book of Proverbs," in *Birkat Shalom.* Vol. 1, *Studies in the Bible,
Ancient Near Eastern Literature, and Postbiblical Judaism Presented to Shalom M.
Paul on the Occasion of His Seventieth Birthday* (ed. Chaim Cohen et al.; Winona
Lake: Eisenbrauns, 2008), 413–23.

41. This same theme is found in the Wisdom of Amenemope 25 (24:9–10). See
ANET, 424.

42. Interestingly, many commentators fail even to notice or comment upon the
implied threat of God's punishment in these proverbs. See Clifford, *Proverbs*, 158,
164; Murphy, *Proverbs*, 121, 129.

never had to face justice for atrocities committed under their direction. So are these proverbs reliable? Will the wicked get their just desserts? One solution to the conundrum of whether such Proverbs are reliable is the oft-stated position that the proverbs are intended to be generally, but not universally, true.[43] Yet, Prov 16:5 is quite emphatic and does not seem to allow for such an interpretation. Note the idiom יָד לְיָד, "hand to hand" (i.e., "be sure of this") that is used only one other time, also with the phrase לֹא יִנָּקֶה (Prov 11:21).[44]

However, another option might be to understand Proverbs as implying that YHWH's retribution will be primarily eschatological rather than strictly temporal. It appears that Daniel may be developing wisdom in that direction in two passages: Dan 7:9–28 and Dan 12:1–13. In Dan 7 the Ancient of Days comes for judgment and "the books are opened" (Dan 7:10), presumably in service of the judgment on the kingdoms of the world and in giving an everlasting kingdom to "the people of the saints of the Most High" (7:27)—in essence dividing between the righteous and the wicked. In Dan 12 we again find a book, this time with the names of those who will be delivered (Dan 12:1). Then in the resurrection there is a division between those who will receive everlasting life and those who have everlasting shame and contempt (Dan 12:2), between those who have insight (הַמַּשְׂכִּלִים) and the wicked (רְשָׁעִים; Dan 12:10). In both Dan 7 and Dan 12 the wicked receive judgment, and there is no suggestion that there is any escape from it. The eschatological retribution associated with the wicked is contrasted with the blessings given to those who have insight. Daniel is not offering a direct interpretation of the retribution depicted in Proverbs. However, he is developing an eschatological retribution that in Dan 12 is tied to wisdom vocabulary and cannot help but affect how his readers will understand Proverbs that speak of YHWH's retribution on the wicked.

Despite this, the author of Daniel does not focus on retribution of the wicked—it is mentioned only once as shame and contempt (Dan 12:2), but not the blessing for the wise. This is in keeping with his general trend foregrounding wise behavior and placing foolish/wicked behavior in the background.

43. E.g., as espoused in Fredrick Carlson Holmgren, "Barking Dogs Never Bite, Except Now and Then: Proverbs and Job," *AThR* 61 (1979): 341–53. See also Christine Roy Yoder, "Forming 'Fearers of Yahweh': Repetition and Contradiction as Pedagogy in Proverbs," in Troxel et al., eds., *Seeking out the Wisdom of the Ancients*, 167–83.

44. This idiom most probably means "surely, certainly, without a doubt" (see *HALOT*, s.v. יָד, 3). It may derive from the practice of sealing an agreement with the striking of hands together (Prov 11:15; 17:18; 22:26).

Conclusion

I have argued that wisdom is an important motif in Daniel, although it is not the sapiential, proverbial, epigrammatic wisdom that is so common in the biblical wisdom literature. Instead, the book of Daniel shows its readers how wise people act and display the wisdom of God in modes most clearly delineated in Proverbs but also occasionally found in Job and Ecclesiastes. Moreover, the book encourages wisdom by highlighting it as an attainable attribute for the faithful person who reveres Israel's God. Nevertheless, this wisdom, like the wisdom of Proverbs, is often counter-intuitive, since having it may lead to temporal trials and even death (Dan 11:33, 35; cf. the three young men in Dan 3 or Daniel in Dan 6). Precisely because their wisdom is demonstrated by action that can be observed by others, it simultaneously shows itself to be godly sagacity and exposes the faithful to persecution. For Daniel, wisdom is as wisdom does.

WHERE SHALL WISDOM BE FOUND
(IN THE BOOK OF THE TWELVE)?*

Daniel C. Timmer

Introduction

In searching for wisdom in the Book of the Twelve, one soon feels rather like the author of Job 28 before he arrives at his conclusion. To repeated queries as to wisdom's whereabouts in the Book of the Twelve, the various books reply one after the other, "It is not in me!" and "It is not with me!" (Job 28:14). This impression is neither rare nor difficult to explain. Norman Whybray concluded three decades ago that "it is doubtful whether any direct literary connections between the prophetical and wisdom books can be found earlier than Ecclesiasticus."[1] This lack of explicit literary connections is aggravated by methodological challenges. As Raymond Van Leeuwen observes, since arguments for the presence of wisdom in the prophetic corpus[2] can base themselves on no "explicit claims" in these texts, they are "heavily dependent upon presuppositions regarding wisdom and its history."[3] The highly variegated nature of the

* I express my thanks to the Priscilla and Stanford Reid Trust for the generous support that made possible the research underlying this chapter and its initial presentation before the Institute for Biblical Research.

1. R. N. Whybray, "Prophecy and Wisdom," in *Israel's Prophetic Tradition* (ed. R. Coggins et al.; Cambridge: Cambridge University Press, 1982), 196.

2. Specifically in its pre-redactional form, since Van Leeuwen identifies Hos 14:10 [9] and Isa 1:2–3 as redactions.

3. R. C. Van Leeuwen, "The Sage in the Prophetic Literature," in *The Sage in Israel and the Ancient Near East* (ed. J. G. Gammie and L. G. Perdue; Winona Lake: Eisenbrauns, 1990), 298. In terms of "explicit presence," the Twelve contain almost no clear wisdom elements (note only Hos 13:13; 14:10; Obad 8; Mic 6:9; Zech 9:2), so we cannot proceed as Van Leeuwen does ("Sage in Prophetic Literature," 300) by asking "what is the social role or roles of the sage as portrayed in the prophetic

Book of the Twelve also renders the quest difficult, since at first glance its heterogeneity reduces the likelihood of finding any consistent wisdom presence in it.[4]

These challenges compel us to pose several questions at the outset of our study. First, can the wisdom literature be treated as a literarily or conceptually coherent corpus? Second, how should we define "wisdom" for whatever sapiential work(s) we take as a point of reference? Third, on what grounds can we plausibly identify correspondences between the wisdom literature and the prophetic corpus? And fourth, how can we determine the significance of correspondence or dissonance between our chosen texts?[5]

To begin with the first question, the wisdom corpus is clearly not a literary unity. But while its conceptual coherence is the subject of debate, many scholars recognize the consistency of its subject matter, pedagogical goal, and vocabulary, so that Proverbs, Ecclesiastes, and Job form a sort of nuclear sapiential family. Although some have suggested that Job may be only a cousin, I envision a more diverse nuclear family than that constituted by Proverbs and Ecclesiastes alone for reasons that are not controversial but are too extensive to review here.[6] On the basis

literature" without making the Book of the Twelve hermeneutically subservient to prophetic books that do mention Israelite sages. In terms of method, note the predominantly negative answers given by the contributors to the question posed by the volume edited by M. R. Sneed, *Was There a Wisdom Tradition? New Prospects in Israelite Wisdom Studies* (AIL 23; Atlanta: SBL, 2015).

4. On the question of how the Twelve might cohere, contrast J. Wöhrle, *Der Abschluss des Zwölfprophetenbuches: Buchübergreifende Redaktionprozesse in den späten Sammlungen* (BZAW 389; Berlin: de Gruyter, 2008) and D. C. Timmer, *The Non-Israelite Nations in the Book of the Twelve: Thematic Coherence and the Diachronic–Synchronic Relationship in the Minor Prophets* (Biblical Interpretation 135; Leiden: Brill, 2015). I do not explore here whether the wisdom material I identify might correlate with an orderly redaction like the one R. C. Van Leeuwen proposed since I am not convinced that Exod 34:6–7 and its context have "wisdom affinities"; R. C. Van Leeuwen, "Scribal Wisdom and Theodicy in the Book of the Twelve," in *In Search of Wisdom* (ed. L. Perdue, B. B. Scott, and W. J. Wiseman; Louisville: Westminster John Knox, 1993), 31–49.

5. K. Dell rightly stresses that the resemblance between wisdom and other writings can be due either to a common "early formative influence" or to later redaction. See "Wisdom in Israel," in *Text in Context: Essays by Members of the Society for Old Testament Study* (ed. A. D. H. Mayes; Oxford: Oxford University Press, 2000), 350–53.

6. K. Dell suggests that Job may be a cousin. "Deciding the Boundaries of 'Wisdom': Applying the Concept of Family Resemblance," in Sneed, ed., *Was There*

of this general but not absolute consensus, the following exploration of the Twelve's relationship to wisdom will be carried out in terms of those prophetic books' similarity and difference with respect to the book of Job, although the same could be done with respect to Proverbs or Ecclesiastes.[7]

Second, defining "wisdom" remains difficult. It is wise to avoid definitions that focus primarily on a strong interest in creation, righteousness, or the like, since those emphases also appear in other biblical corpora and genres. The definition proposed by Van Leeuwen is more nuanced and puts us on solid ground. He suggests that wisdom "presupposes the 'fear of Yahweh/God,'...entails insight into and practice of the *generic* patterns and norms for creation and creatures" and "knowledge of and appropriate action with reference to *particular* circumstances, institutions, persons, and other creatures," and "is traditional," being mediated generationally but taking account of what is new.[8]

Next, regarding the identification of correspondences between prophecy and wisdom, J. William Whedbee argued several decades ago that the influence of wisdom on prophecy may be claimed when there is the "coincidence of distinctively wisdom-like form and content."[9] As sensible as this method is, the criterion of "wisdom-like form" will

---

a Wisdom Tradition?, 156. Contrariwise, see L. Perdue, "Wisdom in the Book of Job," in Perdue, Scott, and Wiseman, eds., *In Search of Wisdom*, 73–98, and T. Römer, *La sagessse dans l'Ancien Testament* (Cahiers Bibliques 3; Aubonne: Moulin, 1991).

7. If Habakkuk is compared with Proverbs, the juxtaposition of proverbs that promise wealth to the righteous on the one hand and proverbs that recognize divine discipline of the righteous on the other raises the question of divine justice in the present in a way similar to Habakkuk's questions. Again, Habakkuk's concerns with the delay in divine justice fall somewhere between Qohelet's affirmations of a divine judgment that cannot dispense with vanity (Eccl 3:17–20) and the frame narrator's concluding perspective that puts human existence in the context of a relationship with God that involves divine "evaluation" or "judgment" (מִשְׁפָּט, Eccl 12:13–14).

8. R. C. Van Leeuwen, "Wisdom Literature," in *Dictionary for Theological Interpretation of Scripture* (ed. K. J. Vanhoozer; Grand Rapids: Baker Academic, 2005), 848–49 (emphasis original). Note also W. Kynes, "The Modern Scholarly Wisdom Tradition and the Threat of Pan-Sapientialism: A Case Report," in Sneed, ed., *Was There a Wisdom Tradition?*, 31, who considers Job, Proverbs, and Ecclesiastes to be "wisdom literature" on the basis of their common subject matter but without presuming shared literary forms or origins.

9. J. W. Whedbee, *Isaiah and Wisdom* (Nashville: Abingdon, 1971), as summarized by H. G. M. Williamson, "Isaiah and the Wise," in *Wisdom in Ancient Israel: Essays in Honour of J. A. Emerton* (ed. J. Day, R. P. Gordon, and H. G. M. Williamson; Cambridge: Cambridge University Press, 1995), 134.

soon put an end to any such quest in the Twelve. That concern aside, approaching the question of how wisdom and prophetic texts interrelate in a way that privileges their semantics allows us to avoid the significant difficulty involved in establishing convincing links between them on the basis of reconstituted and largely hypothetical social settings or other historical arguments.[10] No less importantly, if we limit our investigation to passages in which formal wisdom elements are present, we eliminate from consideration beliefs, claims, and arguments that can be expressed in any number of modes or genres, not only in wisdom parlance.[11] Both James Barr's dictum that "The linguistic bearer of the theological state- ment is usually the sentence and the still larger literary complex and not the word or the morphological and syntactical mechanisms"[12] and the realization that intertextuality produces meaning through "adapta- tion" and "appropriation" of levels of discourse higher than individual words prove that larger units of discourse merit correspondingly greater attention than isolated words and phrases when comparing prophecy and wisdom.[13] In what follows I hope to show via several case studies that a semantic basis for such comparisons puts them on firmer footing than other approaches, especially as we explore the significance of the ways in which different modes or genres of discourse correspond. If I am able to do so with some success, the outlines of an answer to the fourth question posed above should become apparent.[14]

---

10. In this study I cannot even begin to construct a historical model in which a given direction of influence might have prevailed, nor is such a task as feasible as was once thought. Note the wide-ranging critiques of arguments for influence or dependence based on historical, generic, or social factors in Sneed, ed., *Was There a Wisdom Tradition?*. In any case, it seems better to propose a historical reconstruction after, and not before, the semantic relationships between the two corpora are clear, so that task is subsequent to the one undertaken here.

11. Cf. S. Weeks, "Wisdom, Form and Genre," in Sneed, ed., *Was There a Wisdom Tradition?*, 161–77, esp. 175.

12. J. Barr, *The Semantics of Biblical Language* (Oxford: Oxford University Press, 1961), 269.

13. J. Sanders, *Adaptation and Appropriation* (The New Critical Idiom; London: Routledge, 2006), 17–21. The semantic focus of intertextuality is demonstrated by M. Wilcox, "Text Form," in *It is Written: Scripture Citing Scripture* (ed. D. A. Carson and H. G. M. Williamson; Cambridge: Cambridge University Press, 1988), 193–204.

14. K. Dell ("Deciding the Boundaries," 151) similarly elevates "content" over "form" in determining the proximity or resemblance of wisdom and non-wisdom texts.

A Semantic-Intertextual Method

While any investigation of the relationship between literary works is "intertextual" in a general sense, the method employed here is intertextual in the specific sense that it attends to conceptual rather than lexical or formal parallels (hence the qualifier "semantic").[15] Not only are clear verbal and formal correspondences between the Twelve and the wisdom literature extremely rare, but an interest in what the text is saying promises to yield more substantial results than an approach limited to surface features.[16] Notably, the type of intertextuality examined here can be either synchronic or diachronic, despite the complexity that lies behind this pair of terms.[17] This methodological flexibility is important in light of the often elusive historical location of the correspondences between the prophetic and wisdom texts considered here.[18]

This Study's Objective: Influence, Confluence, or Something Else?

Given the frequency with which scholars propose a particular and often detailed course of development for Israelite wisdom literature or the wisdom tradition, the factors that complicate such undertakings merit more attention than they have received. First, the varied and vague (if not completely unspecified) historical settings of the various wisdom and prophetic books highlight the hypothetical nature of any such undertaking. Further, most of the data that contributes clarity to questions of historical development is late, so that only the latest stage of any proposed development of the sapiential tradition possesses a relatively

---

15. On conceptual intertextuality, see Sanders, *Adaptation and Appropriation*. On the distinction between the "soft" methodological intertextuality explored here and the "hard" theoretical sort that sees all texts as related, see J. Barton, "*Déjà lu*: Intertextuality, Method or Theory?," in *Reading Job Intertextually* (ed. K. Dell and W. Kynes; LHBOTS 574; London: Bloomsbury T&T Clark, 2013), 1–18.

16. Kynes ("The Modern Scholarly Wisdom Tradition," 32–33) also favors intertextuality as a way to focus on semantics without imposing an accompanying historical reconstruction.

17. See G. D. Miller, "Intertextuality in Old Testament Research," *CurBR* 9 (2010): 283–309, for further discussion of the terms, and J. Barton, "*Déjà lu*," for an exploration of their interdependence and complexity.

18. See B. D. Sommer, "Dating Pentateuchal Texts and the Perils of Pseudo-Historicism," in *The Pentateuch: International Perspectives on Current Research* (ed. T. B. Dozeman, K. Schmid, and B. W. Schwartz; FAT 78; Tübingen: Mohr Siebeck, 2011), 85–108.

solid textual basis.[19] The same difficulty applies to study of the Book of the Twelve, since only some of its books are internally dated while others could be placed almost anywhere between the eighth and fifth centuries, not to mention the vexed question of those books' possible development individually and as a group.

Second, since scribes were involved in the production and copying of texts of various genres for millennia across the ancient Near East,[20] this common social-literary matrix makes it possible that wisdom and prophetic literature would reflect at least superficial similarities.[21] Third, contrary to a simplistic reading of Jer 18:18 as a sociological description of three distinct groups with diverse and perhaps incompatible worldviews, Sneed and others have made clear that this text speaks of three types of spokespersons for God and offers no sociological or ideological analysis of their interrelation.[22] Consequently it is ill-advised to presuppose distinct, separate groups operating in "strictly separated milieus, separated from each other."[23] Finally, the question of a more or less fixed "wisdom tradition" with a fixed worldview that differs sharply from much of the other material in the Hebrew Bible can be questioned for reasons related to the selectivity of the constituent books and the fact that no single genre or mode "tells it all." The collective contribution of law, narrative, prophecy, wisdom, and other primary genres offers a more or less full-orbed picture of ancient Israelite thought, but no single corpus should be expected to do so singlehandedly, nor should certain constellations of ideas be tied rigidly or exclusively to one genre.[24] For these reasons and those mentioned earlier, this study will focus on identifying the degree of semantic or conceptual correspondence of

19. These include the explicit mentions of revelation in 4QInstruction[a] (cf. 4Q418 123 ii 4), the increasingly porous boundary between wisdom and apocalypticism in other Dead Sea Scrolls, and Ben Sira's explicit assertion that wisdom and prophecy are equivalent (Sir 24:33; 39:6).

20. Y. Cohen, *Wisdom from the Late Bronze Age* (WAW 29; Atlanta: SBL, 2013).

21. Kynes ("The Modern Scholarly Wisdom Tradition," 22–23) rightly notes that this historical matrix should not be used to argue that the entire Hebrew canon came under wisdom influence.

22. Sneed, "Is the 'Wisdom Tradition' a Tradition?," 57–58.

23. R. Kessler, "Amos and Wisdom" (paper presented at the annual meeting of the Society of Biblical Literature, San Diego, CA, 23 November 2014), 2. This point was made several decades ago by R. Murphy, "Assumptions and Problems in Old Testament Wisdom Research," *CBQ* 29 (1967): 407–18 (411).

24. Sneed, "Is the 'Wisdom Tradition' a Tradition?," 60, 75.

several passages in the Twelve with wisdom material rather than on corresponding literary forms, vocabulary, or general "ideas" tied to specific historical settings and the possible influence or confluence of the respective corpora.[25]

Case Studies on the Interrelation of Prophetic Writings and Wisdom Literature

On the basis of verbal and especially thematic correspondences between the books of Job and Habakkuk, we will first examine these books' treatments of the theme of human behavior and well-being in relation to divine justice (or its absence). Why this theme? Most would agree that the value of pursuing well-being through appropriate action and the attendant presupposition of an ordered, relatively predictable world lie behind many proverbs,[26] are a source of significant irritation in Ecclesiastes by virtue of their absence,[27] and are a central concern for Job and his friends.[28] Since a theme is the statement that a work makes about its subject matter, a shared theme means that different authors are doing similar things with similar subject matter, which in this case involves *problematizing the relationship of divine justice to human behavior.*[29]

After noting similarities and differences between Job's and Habakkuk's development of this theme, we will investigate the degree to which the treatment of the same theme in the adjacent book of Nahum converges with, or diverges from, those of Habakkuk and Job. Since there is no

25. J. L. McLaughlin, "Is Amos (Still) Among the Wise?," *JBL* 133 (2014): 281–303, summarizes past arguments for wisdom "influence" on Amos under these headings as he critiques suggestions of influence. For similar methodological conclusions regarding the limited value of forms, vocabulary, and social setting, see D. Miller, "Wisdom in the Canon: Discerning the Early Intuition," in Sneed, ed., *Was There a Wisdom Tradition?*, 106–7.

26. B. Waltke, *Proverbs 1–15* (NICOT; Grand Rapids: Eerdmans, 2004), 73–76, 107–9.

27. L. Perdue, *Wisdom and Creation: The Theology of the Wisdom Literature* (Nashville: Abingdon, 1994), 193–94, 238–42.

28. K.-J. Illman, "Theodicy in Job," in *Theodicy in the World of the Bible* (ed. A. Laato and J. C. de Moor; Leiden: Brill, 2003), 304–33.

29. See J. T. LeCureux, *The Thematic Unity of the Book of the Twelve* (HBM 41; Sheffield: Sheffield Phoenix, 2012), 27. Since subject and theme can be articulated using a variety of lexemes, the same message or purpose can appear in works that do not share significant amounts of vocabulary.

appreciable presence of formal wisdom elements in Nahum, the degree to which its treatment of the chosen theme corresponds to Habakkuk's, and especially to Job's, will determine the degree to which an approach focused more on semantics than on formal features can illuminate questions of these books' correspondence.

A Sapiential Point of Departure: Job

I approach the book of Job as a literary unity because it has been transmitted to us only in that form and because cogent arguments exist for the coherence of the frame with the dialogue sections.[30] In terms of our chosen theme of human behavior and well-being in relation to divine justice (or its absence), Job is of course the *cas par excellence*. Job's behavior is impeccable (Job 1:1), yet terrible trials fall upon him. His initial reactions to his suffering clear God of wrongdoing (1:20–22; 2:9–10) and so recognize that the suffering of the innocent is consistent with divine justice. Eventually, however, Job begins to argue on the basis of his empirical observation that there is something gravely amiss in the cosmos (ch. 3), and he goes on to accuse God of wrong both generally (9:22–24) and regarding his particular case (19:7; 27:2).

YHWH's reply to Job counters Job's accusations by asserting that they have obscured his divine "plan" (עצה, 38:2) and have wrongly condemned him as unjust (40:8, with the Hiphil of רשע). YHWH's answer to Job's charges highlights the limits of Job's wisdom but also offers an oblique answer, based on revelatory epistemology, to Job's questions concerning divine justice. On the one hand, the limits of Job's wisdom mean that a justification of God's treatment of Job in all its particulars is not possible on empirical grounds.[31] On the other, the extended surveys of how YHWH's wisdom and justice manifest themselves in the cosmos show that they are highly varied and do not *immediately* produce perfect justice and order. This is especially clear in YHWH's self-identification as the righteous judge of the wicked in 38:12–15:

---

30. See V. Kubina, *Die Gottesreden im Buche Hiob* (Freiburger Theologische Studien 115; Frieberg: Herder, 1979), 115–23; D. Timmer, "God's Speeches, Job's Responses, and the Problem of Coherence in the Book of Job: Sapiential Pedagogy Revisited," *CBQ* 71 (2009): 286–305; D. Frankel, "The Speech About God in Job 42:7–8: A Contribution to the Coherence of Job," *HUCA* 82 (2011–2012): 1–36.

31. J. Lévêque, "L'interprétation des discours de YHWH (Job 38,1–42,6)," in *The Book of Job* (ed. W. A. M. Beuken; BETL 114; Leuven: Leuven University Press, 1994), 222.

Have you ever in your life commanded the morning, and made the dawn know its place, that it might grasp the ends of the earth so that the wicked are shaken out of it? It is changed like clay under a seal, and all becomes tinted like a garment.[32] From the wicked their light is withheld, and the uplifted arm is broken.

In this passage YHWH asserts that the world does not contain zones in which his justice is not active.[33] At the same time, the *progressive* images in 38:12–15 add an essential detail by depicting "the gradual transition from the world of darkness to the domain of Dawn."[34] These images represent God's justice coming to *gradual* realization and thus show that Job's conclusion that God has abandoned his responsibilities of retribution and vindication was premature (e.g., 9:24; 12:6; 24:17).

Although the first divine speech had no discernible effect on Job, the second evidently did. Although the sense of 42:6 continues to be debated, it most likely describes Job's repentance in the sense that he retracts his former accusations against God and contents himself (albeit not without difficulty) with the indirect explanation of his case offered in the divine speeches.[35] This explanation asserts that it is possible for the innocent to suffer and that not all cases of suffering or injustice can be fully understood on an empirical basis (at least not in the present).[36] Job's restoration brings a degree of moral order back into Job's experience even though YHWH's promise to punish the wicked remains unfulfilled at that point.[37]

---

32. Reading וְתִצָּבַע instead of MT's וְיִתְיַצְּבוּ, as proposed by many; cf. D. J. A. Clines, *Job 38–42* (WBC 18B; Nashville: Thomas Nelson, 2011), 1057.

33. H. H. Schmid shows that in the ancient Near East "legal order belongs to the order of creation." See "Creation, Righteousness, and Salvation: 'Creation Theology' as the Broad Horizon of Biblical Theology," in *Creation in the Old Testament* (ed. B. W. Anderson; Issues in Religion and Theology 6; Philadelphia: Fortress, 1984), 104.

34. N. Habel, *The Book of Job: A Commentary* (OTL; Philadelphia: Westminster, 1985), 540.

35. See the survey of interpretative issues in T. Krüger, "Did Job Repent?," in *Das Buch Hiob und seine Interpretation: Beiträge zum Hiob-Symposium auf dem Monte Verità vom 14.19. August 2005* (ed. T. Krüger et al.; ATANT 88; Zurich: TVZ, 2007), 217–29, and the similar conclusion of R. S. Fyall, *Now My Eyes Have Seen You: Images of Creation and Evil in the Book of Job* (NSBT 12; Downers Grove: InterVarsity, 2002), 53.

36. I agree with E. W. Nicholson that Job "is not only humbled but enlightened and reconciled with God." "The Limits of Theodicy as a Theme of the Book of Job," in Day, Gordon, and Williamson eds., *Wisdom in Ancient Israel*, 80.

37. Here I am building on D. Miller's ("Wisdom in the Canon," 102) observation that Job's story emphasizes resolution in the narrative past.

It is noteworthy that Job's repentance constitutes an implicit acceptance, *prior to* his restoration, of God's revelatory claims that he will eventually settle accounts with the wicked and the just alike. This underlines the importance of this *eschatological* resolution for Job's relationship with YHWH in the *present*.[38]

A First Prophetic Compare and Contrast: Habakkuk

We begin our search for wisdom elements in prophetic literature in Habakkuk, where a number of interpreters find the coincidence of sapiential form and content that Whedbee saw as essential to claims of wisdom influence on prophecy.[39] For example, Habakkuk begins with a complaint that closely resembles both the language and the thought of Job 19: "How long shall I...cry to you, 'Violence!' and you will not save?" (1:2; cf. Job 19:7).[40] Habakkuk 1–2 also contains protest dialogue with God (Hab 1:2–4; 1:12–2:1), offering a rough parallel with the various discourses in which Job addresses God. Further, if we modify Gowan's assertion that Habakkuk "begins with a complaint and ends with a theophany" to include the prophet's reaction to the theophany at the end of ch. 3, we can suggest that both books share structures that include a complaint based on perceived injustice, a divine response to the complaint in a vision or theophany, and a reaction to the vision or theophany that resolves the complaint without full justice being realized in the present.

Most importantly, however, the relation between human behavior and well-being in the context of divine justice is Habakkuk's primary concern no less than it is Job's.[41] Habakkuk is troubled by the empirical

---

38. By "eschatological" I mean future circumstances that are discontinuous with the present "to such an extent that one can speak of an entirely new state of reality." D. L. Petersen, "Eschatology (Old Testament)," *ABD* 2:575. In the passages under consideration here, elements of finality are added to the newness and communal and cosmic facets that Petersen notes (576).

39. Whedbee, *Isaiah and Wisdom*. Figuring among those who continue to see formal and material reasons for postulating a wisdom–prophecy overlap in Habakkuk are D. E. Gowan, "Habakkuk and Wisdom," *Perspective* 9 (1968): 157–66; G. A. Tuttle, "Wisdom and Habakkuk," *Studia Biblica et Theologica* 3 (1973): 3–14; and G. T. M. Prinsloo, "Life for the Righteous, Doom for the Wicked: Reading Habakkuk from a Wisdom Perspective," *SK* 21 (2000): 621–40.

40. On the possible relevance of the opening *mass'a* for the prophecy–wisdom relationship, see Mark Sneed, "Inspired Sages: *Mass'a* and the Confluence of Wisdom and Prophecy," in *Schreiber als Weisheitslehrer und Propheten: Prophetische une weisheitliche Traditionen in dem Wiesheitsschriften une im Zwölfprophetenbuch* (ed. Jutta Krispenz; BZAW 496; Berlin: de Gruyter, forthcoming).

41. Cf. Prinsloo, "Life for the Righteous," 629.

absence of punishment for Judeans whose behavior he summarizes as violence (חמס), iniquity (און), wrong (עמל), destruction (שד), strife (ריב), and contention (מדון) (1:2–4). When God announces that he will punish Judean wrongs using Babylon as his instrument (1:5–11), Habakkuk's concern is aggravated rather than assuaged, since he considers Judah "more righteous" than Babylon (1:13). Yet when God associates Babylon with "violence" (חמס) in 1:9, he merely puts Babylon on a par with the segment of Judean society that Habakkuk has already defined as "violent" (also with חמס) in 1:2. While these two statements do not equate all Judeans with all Babylonians, they do suggest that being Judean entails no inherent moral or spiritual superiority with respect to non-Israelites. This perspective is similar to wisdom literature's attenuated emphasis on Israel's special status.[42]

The resolution of the two-fold problem that Habakkuk finds in the non-punishment of guilty Judeans and Babylonians can be realized only through God's judgment of the proud and deliverance of the just. This divine intervention is promised both in the immediate future in the limited context of Judah (1:5–11) and Babylon (2:2–20), and eschatologically in the global theophanic judgment of 3:1–15. In the eschatological setting, the only parties are the "wicked" (רשע, 3:13, in parallel with the "nations") on the one hand and God's people and anointed (עמך, משיחך, 3:13) on the other. These universal, binary categories; YHWH's direct confrontation with the nations and its definitive outcome (3:13–14); and the theophanic context for YHWH's intervention that integrates elements from the exodus, crossing of the Reed Sea, and the entry into Canaan (3:3–11) contribute the newness, finality, and global perspective that constitute the passage's eschatological orientation.[43]

Habakkuk, like Job, presses his empirical standard of justice by demanding that God immediately punish and reward. YHWH, on the other hand, reveals his plan to accomplish his justice *gradually*, dealing first with sinners in Judah, then with Babylon, and finally with the "wicked" and the "nations."[44] As Ben Zvi has noted, in prophetic literature neither God's plan for Israel and the nations nor his attributes "can be abstracted from common experience; they are not universal knowledge. Instead, they are the particular knowledge of communities of readers and

42. Cf. Miller, "Wisdom in the Canon," 91.

43. See further Timmer, *The Non-Israelite Nations in the Book of the Twelve*, 143–47, regarding the eschatological perspective of Hab 3.

44. See the discussion of most of the relevant passages in Timmer, *The Non-Israelite Nations in the Book of the Twelve*, 136–50.

interpreters of books which claim to represent God's speech."[45] In both
Habakkuk and Job a divine plan governs the administration of justice, and
neither its timing nor its degree are known to or satisfy Habakkuk and Job
apart from their acceptance of the revelatory content of divine speech.[46]

To summarize, we can return to the structure of Habakkuk, this
time by way of Prinsloo's observation that Hab 1 consists of despair
or questioning, ch. 2 introduces the prophet's transformation based on
divine speech, and ch. 3 presents the anticipation of eschatological deliverance for YHWH's people and punishment for his enemies. Apart from
Job's initial acceptance of his suffering, this movement from questioning
through transformation to hope closely parallels that of Job, with the
added qualification that in Habakkuk resolution is exclusively future
while in Job some measure of closure appears in the present when his
fortunes are restored. Both books emphasize that the final resolution of the
human behavior / well-being / divine justice problem will only appear at
some future point, and they share this knowledge with the reader through
the channel of divine revelation, not sapiential reflection.

The correspondence of the central themes of Job and Habakkuk
suggests that the overall purpose of the two books is quite similar and
that they therefore share a family resemblance. It is important to notice
that the correspondence between the books does not hinge on the presence
of isolated wisdom elements in Habakkuk but is integral to all its parts
taken together. This suggests that formal wisdom elements have a real but
limited value as indicators of a relationship between a given work and
the wisdom corpus, while semantic or conceptual intertextuality is more
significant.[47]

45. E. Ben Zvi, "Understanding the Message of the Tripartite Prophetic Books,"
RQ 35 (1993): 93–100. In context, he refers to Isaiah, LXX Jeremiah, and Zephaniah.
46. The language of "watch/see" in Habakkuk might be "pedagogic," as in "Here
is the lesson: study it and reflect on it," something the prophet does at the end of ch.
3. Note also M. Floyd, "Prophetic Complaints About the Fulfillment of Oracles in
Habakkuk 1:2–17 and Jeremiah 15:10–18," *JBL* 110 (1991): 397–418.
47. This is so mainly because the meaning of a text is the aggregate of its
statements (phrase, section, and discourse level) rather than of discrete elements at the
lexical or structural level considered apart from the text's propositional content. Note
S. Weeks's ("Wisdom, Form and Genre," 175) critical observation that "scholarly
discussions have tended to bind the formal features of texts to their thought, so that
texts with the same ideas or assumptions are expected not to have different forms,
while texts with similar forms are presumed to have the same ideas and assumptions...
In many respects, these assumptions are akin to the sort of illegitimate totality transfer
about which James Barr complained." Weeks's argument suggests that no single,

A Second Prophetic Compare and Contrast: Nahum

If compelled to suggest some external resemblance between wisdom literature and Nahum, one might point very tentatively to parallels between Nahum's taunts and those in Prov 1 and 9, but there is no commonly recognized evidence of wisdom elements in Nahum.[48] Despite this fact, and even though Nahum's structure is the inverse of Habakkuk's (with the final divine acts of retribution and deliverance presented at the beginning of the book rather than at the end), Nahum's presentation of YHWH's future deliverance of Judah (sinful but assumed to be penitent and so on the cusp of liberation from Assyria) and punishment of Assyria (roundly condemned and so ripe for judgment) constitutes a primary theme that can be fruitfully compared with Habakkuk's and, *mutatis mutandis*, with Job's.

Nahum's description of the status quo in the author's present finds Judah and all other nations in Assyria's orbit under Assyrian oppression. Only in Judah's case, however, is this referred to as YHWH's "affliction" for her (unstated) misdeeds.[49] Though covenantal discipline of Judah does not draw YHWH's justice into question, his grace makes it possible for that punishment to end in the immediate future. As a result, Assyria will soon receive her due, and Judah and the other nations she has oppressed will be liberated from her clutches (Nah 1:15). Notably, this revelation-based claim flies in the face of empirical epistemology, which rightly recognizes that in the book's seventh-century setting Assyria was at full strength (1:12) and Judah was under its thumb (1:15).[50]

While most of Nahum elaborates on the anticipated fall of Nineveh and Assyria, that complex of events is only a faint shadow of the eschatological judgment sketched in 1:2–8. Like the theophany of Hab 3, a number of features of Nahum's so-called hymn give it a perspective

---

fixed relationship exists between form and content and so corroborates our focus on content (i.e., semantics or overall message) here. Still, if the semantic overlap of two texts is established, the more explicitly one text's formal features resemble those of the other, the more comprehensive their similarity will be.

48. An exception appears in J. J. M. Roberts, *Nahum, Habakkuk, and Zephaniah: A Commentary* (OTL; Louisville: Westminster John Knox, 1991), 73: "like intercourse with a harlot (Prov. 7:27), involvement with Assyria led eventually to death."

49. For God as subject of עָנָה (Piel) with the sense of punish/afflict, see 1 Kgs 11:39 (limited punishment of the Davidic line); Pss 88:7 (punishment // wrath); 90:15 (punishment // experience evil); 107:17 (punishment for iniquities, Hithpael); Isa 64:12 (punishment defined as exile and destruction of Jerusalem). The Qal and Pual appear in Ps 119:67, 71.

50. J. Oates, "The Fall of Assyria," *CAH* III.2:62–93.

characterized by finality and radical newness with respect to the rest of the book. YHWH's arrival concerns the "earth and all who dwell in it" (1:5d), and its avoidance of all political and ethnic categories makes the divine act of global judgment and deliverance described in 1:2–8 applicable to all humanity. Further, the passage assigns binary, ultimate fates to YHWH's anonymous "enemies" (who are pursued into darkness, ירדף־חשך, and brought to an end by an overwhelming flood, בשטף עבר כלה יעשה, 1:8) and those who "seek refuge in him" (note the echo of the exodus in YHWH's "great power," Exod 32:11, and that the deliverance here must be no less definitive than the judgment one escapes), so that no subsequent changes appear to be possible or necessary.[51] In contrast to the rest of Nahum, which deals with the perceived problem of Assyria's continued dominance despite her highly objectionable behavior (cf. 1:9–11, 13–15; 2:2; 3:14–16, 19), the opening theophany thus focuses instead on the fate of all humanity in light of God's final intervention. In that context the hymn's point of departure is the incomplete resolution of the problematic relation between human behavior and well-being as shown by YHWH's *presently unrequited* enemies.[52] YHWH will resolve this problem in a final eschatological act by showing mercy to those who trust him and retribution to those who remain his enemies.

Although very cursory, this survey of Nahum gives ample reason to conclude that its primary theme overlaps significantly with those of Habakkuk and Job, although Nahum problematizes the relation between divine justice and human experience as an observer rather than a participant (i.e., there is no first-person speech of the prophet) and does so against the backdrop of the initially revealed assurance in 1:2–8 that all wrongs will eventually be fully requited. This conclusion also demonstrates that a semantically focused intertextual study of early Israelite religious writings allows fruitful, well-grounded comparison that transcends the inevitable but ultimately distracting boundaries of genre.

51. These features have prompted a number of interpreters to date it later than most of the rest of the book; cf. K. Seybold, *Profane Prophetie: Studien zum Buch Nahum* (SBS 135; Stuttgart: Katholisches Bibelwerk, 1989); L. Perlitt, *Die Propheten Nahum, Habakkuk, Zephanja* (ATD 25/1; Göttingen: Vandenhoeck & Ruprecht, 2004), 3–4; and A. Hagedorn, *Die Anderen im Spiegel: Israels Auseinandersetzung mit den Völkern in den Büchern Nahum, Zefanja, Obadja und Joel* (BZAW 414; Berlin: de Gruyter, 2011), 72–80.

52. Notably, this is necessary even after the fall of Assyria and Judah's consequent liberation.

Conclusions

The books of Job, Habakkuk, and Nahum exhibit some intriguing similarities and differences:

1. In these books the cosmos is currently under God's control but is not without mystery or unpunished sin.
2. These books approach the timing and/or degree of realized divine justice as a problem to be examined and explained.
3. All three books recognize YHWH as the global judge while focusing on smaller-scale situations, whether nations, parts of a nation, or an individual.
4. Job, Habakkuk, and Nahum anticipate one or more future resolutions to the incomplete realization of divine justice in the present, but only Job includes vindication here and now.
5. While empirical observation is sometimes accurate in these books, only by revelation can Job and the prophets grasp the way in which the theodicy problem they discuss will be resolved.
6. In all three books a specific kind of relationship with YHWH, with trust and submission at its center, is inseparable from understanding how YHWH's justice works in the present and to surviving its full manifestation in the future.[53]

Admittedly, all biblical books dealing with Israel's history will intersect our chosen theme to some degree, since the Sinai covenant makes the divinely orchestrated act–consequence calculus prominent. However, not all books *problematize* the timing and/or degree of divine punishment or deliverance, nor do they all attend to this problem outside Israel. Job, Habakkuk, and most of Nahum thus have a shared and dominant thrust that inclines "toward wisdom."[54] In Van Leeuwen's terms, they problematize the occasionally incongruous relationship between the "*generic* patterns and norms for creation and creatures" and "*particular* circumstances" in

---

53. Habakkuk is initially exasperated but waits in faith, impatience is only hinted at in Nahum (Nah 1:15), and Job's response developed from initial submission to the confidence he was right and God was not before finally accepting the divine explanation that (partially) resolved the question of theodicy.

54. Here I adapt the thought of S. C.-C. Cheung, *Wisdom Intoned: A Reappraisal of the Genre "Wisdom Psalms"* (LHBOTS 613; London: Bloomsbury T&T Clark, 2015), 29. His observation that "variations" on a theme still allow recognition of the theme expresses well the proximity to the wisdom tradition (especially Job) that I see in Nahum and Habakkuk.

which those patterns seem to be absent or even contradicted. It is also significant that the highlighted theme is the *dominant* theme throughout each of these compositions rather than appearing only intermittently.[55] We may conclude therefore that Habakkuk and Nahum bear an essential family resemblance to the wisdom literature.[56]

On the other hand, it is interesting to compare these books on the basis of the three characteristics that Douglas Miller argues are definitive of Israelite wisdom literature. While Habakkuk and Nahum could be said to represent a sort of "primarily epideictic rhetoric" that reinforces values "but also challenges toward new understandings," these two prophetic books do not "put more emphasis on the present realization of God's blessings than a future catastrophic inbreaking," nor is their epistemology "broadly based on the potential for insight through creation…with primary attention to ongoing divine communication through life experiences."[57] By the same token, however, and as many have noted for these and other reasons, Job is not a perfect fit in the wisdom category due to its interest in revelatory wisdom and eschatological justice with respect to wickedness on a global scale (e.g., Job 38:12–15) alongside Job's vindication in the narrative past (42:7–17).

---

55. Cf. the similar conclusion of Cheung, *Wisdom Intoned*, 36–37.

56. Van Leeuwen, "Wisdom Literature," 848–49.

57. D. Miller, "Wisdom in the Canon," 108. Despite the arguments of T. J. Johnson, *Now My Eyes See You: Unveiling an Apocalyptic Job* (HBM 24; Sheffield: Sheffield Phoenix, 2009) and whether one defines apocalyptic literature materially (as expressing "the belief that human life is largely shaped by supernatural forces, and bounded by the expectation of a final judgment, including the judgment of the dead" J. J. Collins, "What Is Apocalyptic Literature," in *Oxford Handbook of Apocalyptic Literature* [ed. J. J. Collins; Oxford: Oxford University Press, 2014], 1) or formally ("a genre of revelatory literature with a narrative framework, in which a revelation is mediated by an otherworldly being to a human recipient, disclosing a transcendent reality which is both temporal, insofar as it envisages eschatological salvation, and spatial insofar as it involves another supernatural world," ibid., 2), Job can hardly be called apocalyptic. However, there is no reason to deny that wisdom literature can have an eschatological horizon, whether in a limited role, as in Job 38:12–15, or in a larger role, as in Eccl 12:9–14 or elsewhere; cf. J. G. Gammie, "From Prudentialism to Apocalypticism: The Houses of the Sages Amid the Varying Forms of Wisdom," in Gammie and Perdue, eds., *The Sage in Israel and the Ancient Near East*, 489. The eschatological nature of Eccl 12:1–8, however, seems doubtful in light of 12:8, which forms an *inclusio* with 1:2, *pace* C. L. Seow, "Qohelet's Eschatological Poem," *CBQ* 118 (1999): 209–34. See further on the relationship between Ecclesiastes and wisdom the essay by R. Schultz in this volume.

Where then is wisdom to be found in the Twelve? I propose that wisdom is present (among other places) in passages or books of any genre that *problematize* the timing and/or degree of divine punishment or deliverance vis-à-vis human behavior, or, in Van Leeuwen's terms, the perceived difference between "*generic* patterns and norms for creation and creatures" and "*particular* circumstances."[58] Here it is helpful to return to the metaphor of family resemblance, understanding that the physical resemblance of the metaphorical family refers to the semantic or theological resemblance of the books in question. Just as a collection of undated photos of individuals in the same intergenerational family would reveal various facial and physical similarities while leaving undetermined the chronological relationship between them, so the messages of Habakkuk and Nahum share much with the so-called wisdom family while giving little if any hint of their temporal relationship to it. Habakkuk's combination of formal and material correspondence with Job makes its message slightly closer to the semantic nucleus of the sapiential family than Nahum's, but a conclusive judgment on this point depends in turn on the relationship of Job to the rest of the wisdom literature. While that is a question for another time, it seems clear that Habakkuk and Nahum share prominent thematic and semantic features with well-known members of the sapiential family, even if these data do not allow plausible arguments as to the location or precise genetic makeup of each family member in the family tree.[59] This conclusion is corroborated by and reinforces the argument of Weeks and others that form and content should not be too closely linked and encourages further reflection on the relationship of the wisdom "category" to the various genres of the Hebrew Bible.[60]

58. Van Leeuwen, "Wisdom Literature," 848–49.

59. Note also the theophany-like response to the Yehudite complaint that God's justice is not clearly visible: Mal 2:17–3:6.

60. E.g., Weeks, "Wisdom, Form and Genre." The "category" label is used by Dell, "Deciding the Boundaries," 158. Even appraisals of the wisdom–prophecy relationship that accord primary importance to the diachronic nature of their interaction can propose that they interacted in "eines wechselseitigen Fortschreibungsprozesses" and that "Weisheit und Prophetie stehen ineinander und untereinander in einem vielfältigen Gespräch über Grunderfahrungen menschlicher Existenz in ihrer sozialen als auch religiösen Dimension" (W. Urbanz, "Weisheit und Prophetie" [paper presented at the annual meeting of the Arbeitsgemeinschaft der Assistentinnen und Assistenten an bibelwissenschaftlichen Instituten, Österreich, Salzburg, 2013], 13).

Part III

PROPHECY AMONG THE SAGES

A Prophet in the Sage's House?
Origins of the Feminine Metaphors in Proverbs

Ryan O'Dowd

Fifty years ago Norman Whybray said that the "wisdom books say *nothing whatever* about Israel, its history…laws, priesthood, or prophets."[1] While many scholars still embrace this sentiment today, Whybray's phrase "say nothing whatever" is simply too broad and ambiguous to support what actually emerges from the sum of his life's work. Recent trends in scholarship, moreover, demand a more detailed assessment of the biblical sages and the source of their inspiration.[2] This essay visits one parcel of this old territory to consider anew if and how the sages might have drawn on prophetic sources.

Hermeneutical Foundations

Dating

Most scholars agree that Proverbs came into its final form in the postexilic period but also acknowledge the paucity of evidence for such a date. Since the purpose of this paper is to explore prophetic influence in Proverbs, we must assume that the final form of Proverbs postdates the prophetic writings—a safe assumption given the fact that this essay focuses on Prov 1–9, which is generally regarded as a later addition to the collection. Future discoveries may allow a refinement of the conclusions here.

---

1. R. N. Whybray, *Wisdom in Proverbs* (London: SCM, 1965), 14, emphasis added.
2. E.g., Bernd U. Schipper, *Hermeneutik der Tora: Studien zur Traditionsgeschichte von Prov 2 und zur Komposition von Prov 1–9* (BZAW 432; Berlin: de Gruyter, 2012).

Genre, Office, Person

It is also necessary to define as clearly as possible the authors and the nature of the literature they wrote. When one thinks of the prophets and prophecy, the poetic books of the Three and the Twelve are probably the first things that come to mind. But prophecy also includes the narrative prophets like Samuel, Nathan, Elijah, and Elisha, as well as less obvious ones such as Abraham, Moses, Aaron, Miriam, and Huldah. Daniel muddies the waters, sitting ambiguously in and out of this group.

This matter is further complicated by the fact that the word "prophet" is not Hebrew at all but comes from the Greek word προπετής, which has become a catch-all for the Hebrew terms נָבִיא and נְבִיאָה ("prophet"), חֹזֶה ("seer"), רֹעֶה ("diviner or seer"), and אִישׁ הָאֱלֹהִים ("man of God"). While it is fairly clear that these figures had independent functions in preexilic and post-monarchical eras, by the Second Temple period they had come to be aligned under a single word, whether προπετής or נָבִיא.[3] This broad group was known not only for prediction and foresight but also for performed signs, intercessions, and critiques of laypersons, kings, and other prophets.

In addition to prophetic books and personalities, we have to remain aware of prophetic stories, rhetoric, style, tropes, content, and the canonical shape of prophetic texts in our Hebrew and Christian Bibles.[4] All of this to say that one cannot avoid the fact that prophets and prophecy mark out a broad territory with fluid boundaries.

"Sage," like "prophet," is an extrabiblical word that covers the broad scope of scribes, experts, and counselors. The closest Hebrew term is חָכָם ("the wise"), who, as described by David Daube, has "a grasp of the ways of God, men, and nature," "a comprehension of man's position in society and the scheme of things," and "the conduct to be adopted by a person of such understanding."[5] The sage, in sum, has mastery of *the ways of things* in every domain of human life, thought, and conduct.

"Wisdom" is also like "prophecy" in that it describes a broad and loosely defined body of traditions and sayings. More will be said about the methodological approaches to genre below. For now, I highlight Roland Murphy's observation that wisdom literature is best identified

3. See Michael H. Floyd, "Introduction," in *Prophets, Prophecy, and Prophetic Texts in Second Temple Judaism* (ed. Michael H. Floyd and Robert D. Haak; LHBOTS 427; New York: T&T Clark International, 2006), 3–5.

4. Christopher Seitz, *Prophecy and Hermeneutics: Toward a New Introduction to the Prophets* (Grand Rapids: Baker Academic, 2007).

5. David Daube, *Law and Wisdom in the Bible: David Daube's Gifford Lectures* (ed. Calum Carmichael; West Conshohawken: Templeton Press, 2010), 4.

by its view of reality and emphasis on human life within cosmic order.[6] In this way, wisdom literature is explicitly concerned with practical matters of life, teaching and learning, and the means to—and limits of—knowledge. Many types of texts could be said to fit loosely within this description, of course, and so the best practice is to label a book "wisdom literature" when no other genre is more suitable. And, as many scholars have observed, the label "wisdom" is most suitable where we find terms like דַּעַת ("knowledge"), חָכְמָה ("wisdom"), בִּינָה ("understanding"), and מוּסָר ("instruction") in their highest density: Job, Proverbs, Ecclesiastes, Wisdom of Solomon, Sirach, and the wisdom psalms.[7]

Literary Citations of Sages and Prophets
The breadth and ambiguity of sages and prophets requires us to identify some criteria by which to judge the possibility of influence between them. Three helpful criteria are provided by David Petersen's introduction to prophetic literature. First, the core feature of the prophet is its position between God and humans—the "mouthpiece of the deity" as Petersen calls it.[8] Sages, priests, and some kings share this role as well.[9] But prophets and sages stand apart in this group in their function as *public voices* concerned with the health, well-being, and ethical direction of society, which shows that either of them would be justified in borrowing from the other.[10]

Second, Petersen observes that the prophet arises within historically situated contexts and is concerned with Israel's social situation in light

---

6. Roland Murphy, "Wisdom—Theses and Hypotheses," in *Israelite Wisdom: Theological and Literary Essays in Honor of Samuel Terrien* (ed. John G. Gammie, Walter A. Brueggemann, W. Lee Humphreys, and James M. Ward; Missoula: Scholars Press, 1978). Cf. also Leo G. Perdue, *Wisdom Literature: A Theological History* (Louisville: Westminster John Knox, 2007), 2, 8–11, 15–36.

7. For further discussion, see "Introduction" in Ryan P. O'Dowd, *Proverbs* (Story of God Bible Commentary; Grand Rapids: Zondervan, 2017).

8. David L. Petersen, *The Prophetic Literature: An Introduction* (Louisville: Westminster John Knox, 2002), 7, 28.

9. In fact, the prophet-priest role overlaps at points, as Jeremiah, Ezekiel, Joel, and Zephaniah all have priestly lineages. See ibid., 7–8.

10. It should be added here that prophets speak rhetorically from outside the protection and power of the throne, whereas the sage speaks from within the power and authority of royal courts. One might argue that prophets like Samuel, Nathan, and Ahijah speak from within the court, as Petersen does (ibid., 12–13). But it is truer to say that prophets' roles are independent and often critical of kingship. See Joseph Blenkinsopp, *Sage, Prophet, Priest: Religious and Intellectual Leadership in Ancient Israel* (Louisville: Westminster John Knox, 1995), 138.

of the past and the future.[11] This is not true of the sage, particularly in any explicit sense. Josephus and the Talmudic rabbis recognized this distinction, noting that the sage did not have the functions of writing scripture or recording history.[12] But this does not mean, as is often held among modern scholars, that the sages were unaware of, or uninterested in, Israel's cultic and covenant life and history (e.g., Prov 2:16; 3:9–10; 7:14; 17:1; 21:3).

This leads to a third criterion in Petersen's work, which is that the poetic prophets favor the uses of symbolic signs and language to include a common interest in metaphor.[13] As we will see below, this is significant because it helps distinguish prophets like Jeremiah, Ezekiel, Hosea, and Malachi from the narrative prophets in Samuel–Kings and elsewhere.

A fourth criterion can be found in the fact that the sage has the world at his disposal in his lectures and loses nothing by appealing to law, politics, nature, or prophecy in the interest of adorning his portrait of an ideal world. Proverbs 29:18a, for example, which reads, "Where there is no prophetic vision חָזוֹן, the people cast off restraint," freely makes use of language that is used elsewhere only of prophets.[14] Michael Fox rightly comments on this verse, "there is no reason to imagine that at any stage the 'wise man' repudiated either [cult or prophecy]."[15]

The prophet, on the other hand, has a particular interest in social critique and avoiding associations with established religion, the so-called wise, the cult, and royal courts. Isaiah, Jeremiah, and Obadiah all specifically critique groups known as חֲכָמִים ("the wise"), רֹאִים ("diviners"), and הַחֹזִים ("seers").[16] Wisdom, moreover, even in its ties to kingship and appeals to creation and the cosmic Woman Wisdom, does not carry the same authoritative weight as Moses or the prophets, who speak directly

---

11. Petersen, *Prophetic Literature*, 5–13, 22–24. Petersen does not phrase things in this way, but it is true to his analysis in these contexts. Cf. also Louis H. Feldman, "Prophets and Prophecy in Josephus," in Floyd and Haak, eds., *Prophets, Prophecy, and Prophetic Texts*, 219–20.

12. Feldman, "Prophets and Prophecy in Josephus," 219–20.

13. Petersen, *Prophetic Literature*, 123.

14. By my count חָזוֹן is used thirty-five times in the Hebrew Bible, of which only Ps 89:19 does not explicitly mention a prophet. The psalm nevertheless certainly alludes to Samuel or Nathan. See John Goldingay, *Psalms*. Vol. 2, *Psalms 42–89* (BCOTWP; Grand Rapids: Baker Academic, 2007), 696. Cf. Tremper Longman III, *Proverbs* (BCOTWP; Grand Rapids: Baker Academic, 2006), 507, who does not see any prophetic allusion in Prov 29:18.

15. Michael V. Fox, *Proverbs 10–31* (AB 18B; New Haven: Yale University Press, 2009), 840.

16. Isa 5:21; 19:11; 29:10; 30:10; 44:24; Jer 4:4; 8:8–9; Obad 8.

from God. A prophet's overt citation of a wisdom text, or allusions lending weight to the wisdom movement, could undermine the prophetic authority and its claim to direct divine revelation.[17] It is thus more likely that a sage would borrow from prophecy than a prophet from wisdom, but little more can be said in this regard.

On Method and Allusion

Most modern efforts that address influence and allusion in biblical texts rely on methodological frameworks.[18] Such approaches are helpful in that they furnish us with a demand for logic and the vocabulary of historical, form-critical, linguistic, theological, and other related disciplines.

But methodologically driven research is often conspicuously silent in the face of Hans Gadamer's critique of method and his parallel emphasis on the "art" of interpretation.[19] In his arguments in *Truth and Method*, Gadamer demonstrates that methodological approaches entered biblical studies as a result of the scientific and philosophical developments of the Enlightenment with the hope that new positivist methods would yield objective insight into the intentions of the original author and thus to the singular meaning of a text.[20] While the belief in a singular meaning of a text and the ability to discover the author's original intentions have largely run their course, the status quo of strict methodological readings, oddly enough, has not. This methodological bent—driven as it is by scientific epistemologies—has the unfortunate tendency of distorting or flattening literary artifacts in search of certainty, especially those with a high degree of aesthetic form. And so whatever might be gained from methodologies will have to be balanced by an aesthetic epistemological reading as well.[21]

---

17. The book of Daniel is a clear exception to this assumption, as the book freely makes use of wisdom themes and motifs. Contrary to other prophets, Daniel is not combating Israelite society and religion, at least not directly. Instead, Israelite religion and wisdom in Daniel prove more powerful and truer than the wisdom and rule of Israel's conquerors.

18. See the summary essay in this volume by Russell L. Meek.

19. Hans-Georg Gadamer, *Truth and Method* (2nd ed.; New York: Crossroad, 1985).

20. There is some irony in the fact that the turn to method in an effort to resolve literary ambiguities has left behind a guild of scholars mired in endless and virtually irresolvable debates about their methods. The tacit skill of reading texts, meanwhile, is receding slowly into the background.

21. For an excellent discussion of analytical and aesthetic or narrative epistemologies, see Eleanore Stump, *Wandering in Darkness: Narrative and the Problem of Suffering* (Oxford: Oxford University Press, 2010), 23–63.

The following study of influence and allusion thus makes these three assumptions. One, these biblical texts were written in a fairly small, well-contained culture where cross-pollination of texts, language, symbols, and traditions was likely if not unavoidable.[22] Two, and more importantly, we are dealing with *literature*, most of it allusive poetry. These works of art, as Gadamer and others have argued, are always in an "unfinished process" of signification and symbolization where meaning is thick and robust rather than narrow and thin.[23]

Three, as Gadamer observes in a related vein, written words, especially those composed in another era, always say more and less than the author intended.[24] Umberto Eco similarly concedes this point about the encoded symbols and allusions in his own work: "one notices, I think, that the plurality of meanings is a phenomenon that is set up in a text even if the author was not thinking about it at all and has done nothing to encourage a reading on a multiplicity of levels."[25] In reality, authors, texts, and readers exist in mutually dependent relationships where the reader cannot help but read through a subjective and historically determined lens and the author cannot help but say more and less than is needed for others to understand her perfectly. This point will become important below when we examine the meaning resident in the canonical shape of the Old Testament.

All this to say that one usually seeks in vain to try and *prove* that authors borrowed this or that text for such and such a reason, and we are much better off asking if the associations we find between two similar texts *honor* and *fit* with the style of the author, historical background, and shape of the text within the canon and its history as a whole. And, if so, how this influence shapes the meaning of the passage in its immediate and broader contexts.

The Prophets in Proverbs

We now turn to the specific question of how prophecy *might* have influenced the composition of Proverbs, or at least fits with the content in Proverbs. We begin with the obvious point that Prov 10–29 and the prophetic books share common concerns with justice, honesty and lying,

---

22. Cf. Nancy Nam Hoon Tan, *The "Foreignness" of the Foreign Woman in Proverbs 1–9: A Study of the Origin and Development of a Biblical Motif* (BZAW 381; Berlin: de Gruyter, 2008), 167.

23. Gadamer, *Truth and Method*, 88.

24. Ibid., 264–65.

25. Umberto Eco, "Intertextual Irony and Levels of Reading," in *On Literature* (New York: Mariner, 2005), 226.

diligence and laziness, and generosity and greed. Little of substance can be said about these parallels, since most of them can be found in law, psalms, and public life in general. Even the example about Prov 29:18 above reveals little more than that the sage enjoyed tremendous freedom in drawing upon prophetic ideas and writings.

There are also several points in Prov 30 where Agur echoes prophetic texts, whether consciously or unconsciously. I have discussed Prov 30 elsewhere,[26] so the remainder of this chapter explores what I take to be the third major place where prophetic influence is most likely: the *femme fatale* in Prov 1–9. It is critical, in this light, to recognize that these nine chapters represent the prologue for the book of Proverbs and consist of two groups of carefully interwoven poems: instructions from the father to the son and poems about wisdom and folly. Notice in Table 1 that the feminine language and symbols introduced in ch. 1 become increasingly central and even gradually merge with the father's instructions in chs. 4, 5, 7, and 9. Bearing this structure in mind will allow us to appreciate the striking role of feminine figures and imagery in these chapters.

Table 1. Poetic Structure of Proverbs 1–9

Instructions from the Father	Wisdom Interludes
1:1–19	
	1:20–33: Wisdom Poem
2:1–22	
3:1–12	
	3:13–18: Wisdom Poem
3:21–35	
4:1–9: Wisdom as a Wife	
4:10–19	
4:20–27	
5:1–23: The Wife and Adulteress	
6:1–19	
6:20–35: Portraits of Foreign Women I	
7:1–27: Portraits of Foreign Women II and Wisdom as a Sister	
	8:1–36: Wisdom Poem
9:1–18: Wisdom and Folly	

26. Ryan O'Dowd, "Poetic Allusions in Agur's Oracle in Proverbs 30:1–9," in *Inner-Biblical Allusion in the Poetry of Psalms and Wisdom* (ed. Mark J. Boda, Beth Tanner, and Kevin Chau; London: Bloomsbury T&T Clark, forthcoming).

On the whole chs. 1–9 create a stark portrait of polar opposites: life, Woman Wisdom, her ways, her house, wisdom, and the wife of one's youth on one side, and death, Dame Folly, her ways, her house, and the collection of "foreign" women in chs. 5–7 on the other. While these polar oppositions and the metaphor of the "path" are evident in chs. 10–31, they are only stated explicitly in a handful of proverbs.

Furthermore, while the father's instructions address many issues, they focus most intently on sexual temptation. Again, by comparison, sexual temptation is only mentioned four more times in the five hundred individual sayings in chs. 10–31 (18:22; 22:14; 23:27; 31:3).

The father's instructions can be further divided between invitations and warnings. The invitations use lover's language to call the son to embrace the "wife of his youth" just as they entreat him to love and grasp Wisdom as a sister, wife, and lover. Far more space is given to the father's warnings, which address the dangers of what may be as many as four or five distinct women: the זָרָה ("forbidden/wayward woman"), זוֹנָה ("harlot"), נָכְרִיָּה ("foreign woman"), the זָרָה נָכְרִיָּה ("foreign or strange woman"), and the אֵשֶׁת רָע ("evil woman").

The translations for זָרָה and נָכְרִיָּה are mired in endless debate. In her study of these women in Prov 1–9, Nancy Nam Hoon Tan convincingly demonstrates that the meaning of זָר in the Hebrew Bible is usually fluid and determined by its context.[27] Her argument proceeds to show that in the context of Prov 1–9 זָר has been carefully paired with נָכְרִי ("foreigner") in its first and last appearances (2:16; 7:5), which, she suggests, leads us to read not only the זָר as foreign by association but the rest of the forbidden women in these contexts as well. In this way, these women all depict human temptation as a whole and not just a series of coincidental types of women that appeal to a young man.[28]

Tan's work also relies on recent developments in linguistic theory and the study of ethnicity. She observes that the word "foreign," while having geographical and national origins, is often applied figuratively to things that are in many other ways *different*—just as we are accustomed to saying, "that's foreign to me" or "that's a foreign concept." Using "foreign" as a metaphor in this way, the authors/editors of Proverbs could indicate differentness at the same time as they tie the women in chs. 1–7 to the semantic origins of foreign women in Israel's past.[29]

---

27. Tan, *Foreign Woman*, 18. See Isa 29:21; 61:5; Jer 5:19; Pss 69:8; 81:10; Job 19:15; Prov 2:16; 5:10; 20:16; 27:2, 13; Obad 11; Lam 5:2.

28. See Leo G. Perdue, *Proverbs* (Interpretation; Louisville: John Knox, 2000), 87.

29. Roland E. Murphy, *Proverbs* (WBC 22; Nashville: Thomas Nelson, 1998), 15, makes a similar argument for staying with the literal rendering of a word when other options are not obvious.

Still many scholars refuse to translate זָר as "foreign" in this way not only because the women in chs. 1–9 are sometimes depicted as neighbors but also because these scholars feel inclined to understand נָכְרִי solely in terms of national and geographical foreignness, which does not apply to all of the women in these chapters in Proverbs.[30] Fox is one of the more strident opponents of this reading, favoring a literal understanding of the women in chs. 2–7: "this is another man's wife...this identification alone is correct."[31] Anything more is an "egregious, if productive, overreading."[32] For those who share Fox's opinion, the symbolic or personified Dame Folly in ch. 9 should in no way be tied to, or read into, the presentation of these other forbidden women in chs. 2–7.

In answer to such objections, I will expand on Tan's research to present eight pieces of cumulative evidence that demonstrate both the intricacy and pervasiveness of the symbolic metaphors in Prov 1–9 but, even more, the way this symbolism links the foreign women to Dame Folly and wisdom and the wife to Woman Wisdom:

1. Words, poetic language in particular, speak along the broad spectrum of meaning between the literal (semantic) and allegorical senses, with the wide area of symbolic and metaphorical meaning in between.[33] In the *context* of chs. 1–9, the foreign women can very naturally represent concrete temptations in daily life *and* poetic/cosmic expressions of human desire.

2. Over half of the verses in Prov 1–9 address women and/or feminine imagery.[34] Adultery also receives more attention in these chapters than any other topic. Egyptian wisdom literature by comparison rarely addresses sexual ethics, and adultery only appears four times in all of chs. 10–31—over half of the rest of Proverbs (18:22; 22:14; 23:27; 31:3). Roland Murphy is right to describe the emphasis in chs. 1–9 as "striking, even oppressive," and "all out of

30. Cf. Richard J. Clifford, *Proverbs: A Commentary* (OTL; Louisville: Westminster John Knox, 1999), 48; and Longman, *Proverbs*, 124.

31. Fox, *Proverbs 1–9* (AB 18A; New York: Doubleday, 2000), 34. Cf. also Arndt Meinhold, *Die Sprüche* (Zurich: Theologischer Verlag, 1991), 6:68–69.

32. Fox, *Proverbs 1–9*, 252.

33. On this understanding of metaphor and symbol, see Paul Ricoeur, *Interpretation Theory: Discourse and the Surplus of Meaning* (Fort Worth: Texas Christian University Press, 1976), 54–69.

34. Or 135 of 256 verses, compared to only 4 of 659 similar references in chs. 10–31.

proportion to the importance of sexual conduct."[35] Indeed, as we will see below, sexual desire is highlighted in the prologue because it uniquely represents the role of desire in all human behavior.

3. The sexual imagery in Prov 1–9 sits within a larger network of metaphorical opposites: two paths, two women and their two houses, two doors, two sets of lips, and two kinds of words. There are also antithetical sets of feet and two sources of natural fluids that function as sexual metaphors. These erotic metaphors together portray a system or map of reality that places desire at the fork in the road between wisdom/life and folly/death.[36]

4. The centrality of *eros* in this network of metaphors—loving, desiring, hating, and despising—exists at every level of the feminine imagery: the adulteress, the wife of one's youth, the harlot, wisdom, and cosmic/personified Woman Wisdom and Dame Folly.

5. The four figures on the wisdom/life side of this polarity—wisdom (lower case), the wife of one's youth, Woman Wisdom, and the valiant woman—are intricately connected: all have children, all are worth more than "gold" and "jewels," all are to be loved, all have wise "words" and "speech," and all live by, or encourage, "the fear of Yahweh."[37]

6. On the other side of the polarity, Dame Folly and the foreign women also share undeniable parallels: both call out (7:14–21; 9:13), both are loud (7:11; 9:13), both have houses (7:12; 9:14), and both lead to death and Sheol (5:23; 6:32; 7:27; 9:18).[38] Fox oddly concedes that the foreign woman in 7:25–27 is depicted in "superhuman terms…a mass murderer and affiliate of the underworld."[39] But to allow for such a symbolic portrayal, Fox has to believe that this woman is neither the same as the woman in the previous nineteen verses of the same chapter nor the same as the symbolic woman Dame Folly in ch. 9—a reading that seeks to close down the natural allusivity of poetry in these chapters.

---

35. Murphy, "Wisdom and Eros," *CBQ* 50 (1988): 600–601.

36. See Raymond Van Leeuwen, "Liminality and Worldview in Proverbs 1–9," *Semeia* 50 (1990): 111–44.

37. See Christine Roy Yoder, "Proverbs," in the *Women's Bible Commentary* (ed. Carol A. Newsome, Sharon H. Ringe, and Jacqueline E. Lapsley; Twentieth Anniversary ed.; Louisville: Westminster John Knox, 2012), 241.

38. Tan (*Foreign Woman*, 101) says there is "no doubt that [these women] are one and the same."

39. Fox, *Proverbs 1–9*, 253–54.

7. The foreign women in chs. 2–9 all seduce the man by cunning words rather than actions.[40] This definitively sets the foreign woman not only against the wife but also against wisdom and Woman Wisdom at the same time (cf. 6:24). In chs. 5–7 the father similarly prepares his son to resist foreign women by tuning his ear to sapiential terms: "wisdom," "torah," "understanding," "discretion," and "knowledge" (5:1–2; cf. 6:20–24; 7:1–3), all of which terms emanate from Woman Wisdom as well (8:5, 9–12).[41]

8. Finally, marriages to foreign women develop in their symbolic depth throughout the progress of Israel's history as it is portrayed canonically. Esau defiantly married a Canaanite against his father's wishes (Gen 28:1, 9), which is repeated by Judah in his marriage to Shua (Gen 38:2). The prohibitions and warnings against foreign wives in Deut 7 and 23 reappear in the stories of Solomon and his foreign wives as well as of Jezebel, the foreign wife of Ahab in 1 Kings, and the prohibitions and penalties against the foreign wives taken in Ezra–Nehemiah. Tan shows that the patterns of foreign women in these passages are not meant to disparage particular foreign nations or deride other ethnicities in general but to draw upon the increasingly popular motif that equated foreign marriages with apostasy, particularly in the prophets and especially among Israel's kings.[42]

Tan relies on similar evidence to argue that Prov 1–9 draws upon the "poetic shorthand" of foreign women in Deuteronomy and the Deuteronomic History—particularly Ezra–Nehemiah—in its depiction of "these symbolic characters and their speeches."[43] Reinhard Kratz offers some support to Tan's thesis, stating that Ezra was a transitional figure between the age of the prophet and that of the sage.[44] Blenkinsopp,

40. Murphy, "Wisdom and Eros," 602.

41. Interestingly, Potiphar's wife (Gen 39:7–18), Samson's unnamed wife and Delilah (Judg 14:16–17; 16:1–22), and Jezebel (1 Kgs 21:25) are all foreign women who are known for their deceptive and cunning speech. Cf. Tan, *Foreign Woman*, 86. This may suggest that the symbolic role of women was a common trope for the majority of biblical writers.

42. Ibid., 166. See also See Joseph Blenkinsopp "The Social Context of the 'Outsider' Woman in Proverbs 1–9," *BibInt* 42 (1991): 463.

43. Tan, *Foreign Woman*, 167.

44. Reinhard G. Kratz, "Ezra—Priest and Scribe," in *Scribes, Sages, and Seers: The Sage in the Eastern Mediterranean World* (ed. Leo G. Perdue; FRLANT 219; Göttingen: Vandenhoeck & Ruprecht, 2009), 163–88.

meanwhile, is among those who identify the strange woman primarily as foreign goddesses in ancient fertility cults, though he also sees those figures addressed in the situations in Ezra–Nehemiah, Isaiah, Zechariah, and Malachi.[45]

It does appear as if the ideas of foreign women and goddesses were prevalent in Israel's late postexilic period. But when it comes to asking what inspired the sages who wrote Prov 1–9, it is to be acknowledged that Ezra and Nehemiah are better characterized as memoirs than wisdom or prophetic writings, and their language tends more toward historical commentary than poetic symbolism and figuration. Are these narratives really the most likely source for the women in Prov 1–9?

The Prophets as the Origin of the Foreign Women in Proverbs 1–9

In what follows I seek to show that, while the sages may have been influenced by narrative accounts of foreign women in the Deuteronomic history, it is the poetic prophets—Jeremiah, Ezekiel, Hosea, and Malachi in particular—who provided the inspiration for the sages to weave together themes of harlotry, folly, and covenant infidelity in Prov 1–9. Consider these words in Mal 2:11, 14–16:

> …Judah has been faithless and abomination has been done in Israel and in Jerusalem. For Judah has polluted the sanctuary of YHWH, which he loves, and has married the daughter of a foreign [נֵכָר] god.
>
> But you say, "Why?" It is because YHWH is witness between you and *the wife of your youth* against whom you were faithless, though she is your companion and your wife by covenant.
> …guard yourselves in your spirit, and do not be faithless to *the wife of your youth.*
> For he hates his wife, who sends her away, says YHWH, the God of Israel, covers his garment with violence, says YHWH of hosts. So guard yourselves in your spirit, and do not be faithless.[46]

Tan observes that Malachi blends into one the accusation against Judah for covenant unfaithfulness, the divorce of wives, and the marrying of pagan worshipers.[47] But in her conclusion Tan makes an unsupported claim that "The motif of the Foreign Woman is distinct from the depictions for

45. Blenkinsopp, "Social Context," 464–65.

46. My translation. Verse 15a presents many difficulties for translation, but this has no bearing upon the argument here.

47. Tan, *Foreign Woman*, 59–63.

adulterous women in the prophetic literature, who constitute a separate set of 'bad women' images in the Bible."[48] But she says nothing more about this "separate set" of women in the prophets or why their metaphors would not have provided inspiration for the sages.

This lacuna takes us back to make three points about Malachi and its metaphorical representation of covenant unfaithfulness as adultery. First, the metaphor is charged with emotions of animosity, fear, and resentment of foreign nations and their gods, which bears a striking resemblance to the language and emotion in the introduction to the foreign woman in Prov 2:16–18:

> So you will be delivered from the strange woman, from the foreign woman with her smooth words,
>> who has forsaken the companion of her youth and forgotten the covenant of her God;
>> for her house sinks down to death, and her paths to the spirits of the dead.

In both Proverbs and Malachi we have foreign women, sacred covenants with God, and consequences spelled out in cosmic terms.[49] Elsewhere, Proverbs and Malachi also share a conspicuous contrast in their appeals, one to "rejoice in the wife of your youth," אֵשֶׁת נְעוּרֶךָ (Prov 5:18), and the other to resist being unfaithful to "the wife of your youth," אֵשֶׁת נְעוּרֶיךָ (Mal 2:14–15). It is highly significant that this phrase אֵשֶׁת נְעוּרֶיךָ, which also appears in Isa 54:6 and in a related form in Jer 2:2, has no parallel in Ezra–Nehemiah or Samuel–Kings. This reinforces the close connections between the metaphors in Proverbs and the poetic prophets.[50]

Second, in addition to Malachi, the prophets Isaiah, Jeremiah, Ezekiel, and Hosea all express the breaking of Israel's covenant with YHWH in symbolic terms of marital unfaithfulness to foreign wives.[51] These poetic prophets also portray God as a "fountain of living water" (Jer 2:13; cf. Prov 5:15–18) and one who gives gifts of wine and vineyards (Hos 2:8–13) to an unfaithful wife who has committed adultery and prostitution (Jer 3:2–6; Ezek 16:28, 32)—images that are strewn throughout Prov 5–9 (cf. 5:15–23; 6:23–29; 7:16–20; 9:2, 17).

---

48. Ibid., 169.

49. See Blenkinsopp, "Social Context," 462, 471–72.

50. Not to say that these "latter" prophets are strict poetic verse, but their style of terse phrases, metaphors, and symbols is certainly more *poetic* than the narrative prophets.

51. Isa 54:5–6; Jer 2:2, 13, 32–33; 3:1–25; 9:1–2; Ezek 16 and 22; Hos 2:2; 5:1–15; 6:7.

Third, the connections between the prophets and Proverbs take on an additional significance from the perspective of canon criticism. At this level, the intentions of the authors and their sources are secondary to the meaning located in poetics of the texts in their collected form. Note how early Christians intentionally reordered the books in the Hebrew Writings, placing Ecclesiastes and Song of Songs between Proverbs and Isaiah. Brevard Childs observes that in its earlier place in the Hebrew Bible, Song of Songs fit most naturally with the emphasis of the wisdom literature and the pursuit of life in the this world, "the mystery of love within the created order."[52] But in the Christian canon's relocation of Song of Songs next to Isaiah, "the book is made to symbolize the prophetic themes of God's love for his people, of the new Exodus, etc....themes which are missing in the wisdom corpus."[53] Childs thus helpfully shows that the feminine metaphors in Song of Songs had a pliability and degree of play, yet his broad statement about the wisdom literature fails to take note of Proverbs and its use of feminine symbols.

Indeed, by distinctly naming Solomon the author of Proverbs (1:1; 10:1; etc.)—despite the clear fact that the collection includes other sources (22:17; 24:23; 25:1; 30:1; 31:1)—Prov 1–9 creates a diptych portrait of Solomon made up of poetic and narrative sources.[54] The *poetic Solomon* speaks his sayings alongside Ecclesiastes, Song of Songs, and the poetic prophets while the *narrative Solomon* situates the proverbs within the broader story of Solomon's life: his prayer for wisdom (1 Kgs 2:4–15), his wise rule (1 Kgs 3:16–4:34), and his many proverbs (1 Kgs 4:32). The narrative Solomon collects "silver," "gold," and "precious stones" (1 Kgs 10:25), which the poetic Solomon views as barriers to getting wisdom (Prov 3:14–15; 8:10, 19). Furthermore, just as narrative Solomon's love for foreign women turns his heart away from God (1 Kgs 11:4), so we find in poetic Solomon that the strange woman, the adulteress, and Dame Folly compete with the young man's pursuit of wisdom and Woman Wisdom (Prov 2:16–19; 5:1–23; 6:20–35; 7:6–27; 9:1–18). In the end, the love that narrative Solomon gives to his foreign wives and their foreign religions (1 Kgs 11:1–2), the poetic Solomon directs to the pursuit of wisdom and Woman Wisdom (Eccl 7:25–29), the "wife of [his] youth" (Prov 4:6; 5:15–19; Song 3:11; 4:9–10), and "the fear of Yahweh" (Prov 1:7).

---

52. Brevard S. Childs, *Introduction to the Old Testament as Scripture* (Philadelphia: Fortress, 1979), 576.
53. Ibid., 575.
54. See Blenkinsopp, "Social Context," 457.

In sum, the vibrant field of erotic metaphors in the poetic prophets and their association with marriage and covenant faithfulness provide the likely inspiration for the sages' portrayal of wisdom, Woman Wisdom, the *femme fatale*, and Dame Folly in Proverbs. Even more, once we see these women in both the poetic and narrative texts in the broader canon, it is impossible not to make these connections and conclude that Proverbs in its final form offers both narrative and poetic/prophetic images of Solomon, love, women, and the pursuit of wisdom. In this way the sages and prophets can be seen to root religious life and moral learning within the very same thirst for fruit and knowledge that haunted Adam and Eve in the garden in Gen 3. This should not surprise us, for, as the Swiss philosopher Denis de Rougemont observes in his work on love and passion in the Western traditions, the woman provides the ideal symbol for both "sexual attraction" and "*eternal* desire," both the "divine and prophetic."[55] The prophets' apocalyptic imagery of divorce and judgment, in fact, manifests the same pattern of two ways of wisdom and life and folly and death that we find in Gen 1–3 and Prov 1–9.

55. Denis de Rougemont, *Love in the Western World* (Princeton: Princeton University Press, 1983 [1940]), 63–64, 74–75.

You Can't Get a Sage to Do a Prophet's Job: Overcoming Wisdom's Deficiency in the Book of Job

Martin A. Shields

Introduction

Although the book of Job is typically identified as wisdom literature, it doesn't take much to realize that one of its features is the way it depicts the inadequacy of wisdom and the need to look elsewhere for answers to life's most vexing questions. This is apparent in several ways. First, those ostensibly identified as sages (Job and his friends, but in particular Eliphaz and Elihu) appear to sense the inadequacy of arguing purely from a wisdom perspective by appealing to special revelation. Second, Job's three older friends fail, in their wisdom, to explain the true basis for Job's suffering. Indeed, their "wisdom" is explicitly denounced by YHWH in the epilogue. Third, the book moves to a theophany where direct special revelation takes place and which (appears to) ultimately answer Job's complaint and (perhaps) explain his sufferings. Fourth, the book contains clear intertextual links with prophetic literature and, in particular, to the servant of Isa 40–55.

So Job is not an archetypal wisdom text in the way that Proverbs is, although Job is clearly styled as wisdom literature, albeit wisdom literature that has to look beyond the scope of wisdom to find its answers. After all, the book of Job employs more wisdom terminology than any other book in the Bible outside Proverbs and Qohelet.[1] When Job speaks

---

1. Searching for a list of distinctive wisdom terms puts Job third after Proverbs and Qohelet and well above other biblical books. For example, a search for חכם, חָכָם, ־ידע, ידע, סְכְלוֹת, סֶכֶל, סָכָל, סכל, בְּסְלָה, כֶּסֶל, ־בסל, בִּינָה, בין, ־בִּינָה, חִכְמוֹת, ־חָכְמָה, חָכְמָה, עֲצֵלְתַּיִם, עֲצְלוּת, עָצְלָה, עָצֵל, עצל, עָצָה, ־מָשָׁל, משל, ־מָשָׁל, מוֹסָר, מוּסָר, ־דֵּעַת, דַּעַת in Accordance lists Proverbs with 28.60 hits/1000 words, Qohelet with 25.36, then Job with 13.04. After

in chs. 27 and 29 his words are described as a משל (proverb, wisdom saying). And even the theophany—the portion of the text which would appear to be most obviously *not* something we'd normally expect to see in wisdom literature—is unusual (at least so far as we can describe any theophany as "usual"). If anything, we might be able to describe it as a *wisdom* theophany because so much of it consists of questions about wisdom matters. For example, many of YHWH's questions in chs. 38–41 are questions about the natural world, and this appears to have been one particular subject of study for the sages if 1 Kgs 5:13 [ET 4:33] is any indication: "[Solomon] produced manuals on botany, describing every kind of plant, from the cedars of Lebanon to the hyssop that grows on walls. He also produced manuals on biology, describing animals, birds, insects, and fish" (NET).

Yet clearly Job is not Proverbs nor even Qohelet. Just about everyone has noted some form of prophetic influence in Job. James Crenshaw wrote, for example, that "Job is not free of prophetic influence, both stylistically and theologically, so that the continuity between Job and prophecy cannot be denied."[2] Hence the prophetic elements of Job identified above bear further examination.

Job's Friends' Appeals to Prophecy

First, then, the significance of the apparent claims to special divine revelation made by Job's friends warrants investigation. Whether or not wisdom can legitimately incorporate prophecy and still be classified as wisdom, direct special revelation is prophecy whether it appears in wisdom or any other literary genre. Furthermore, since prophecy does not appear regularly in wisdom literature (being entirely absent and perhaps even disparaged in Qohelet and not clearly present in Proverbs), instances of clearly prophetic material embedded in wisdom texts are worthy of examination. It is thus necessary to determine precisely what each character is claiming for their speech and then to ascertain the significance of those claims for the relationship between wisdom and prophecy in the book of Job.

this are Daniel with 8.21, then Hosea with 7.19, and so on. Affirming my claim that the Song of Songs should not be counted among the wisdom literature is the fact that these terms are almost entirely absent from it (with the exception of two words related to ידע in Song 1:8; 6:12).

2. J. L. Crenshaw, *Prophetic Conflict: Its Effect on Israelite Religion* (BZAW 124; New York: de Gruyter, 1971), 108–9.

Eliphaz

Very early on in the debate between Job and his friends we find Eliphaz implying that his words are derived from a special revelation which he received in a dream. Thus in Job 4:12–13 we read:

ואלי דבר יגנב

ותקח אזני שמץ מנהו

בשעפים מחזינות לילה בנפל תרדמה על אנשים

A word was secretly brought to me,
and my ear received a fragment of it.[3]
In the troubling thoughts of the visions of the night when a deep sleep falls
on men…

Dreams were typical means by which God (or, in the ancient Near East, gods) revealed himself directly to prophets and others.[4] In this case Eliphaz unsurprisingly notes that this revelation endorsed his argument that Job's circumstances arise because he is not righteous nor pure before God (Job 4:17).[5]

Now, while this passes Jeremiah's test for prophecy (i.e., that prophets invariably bear bad news, cf. Jer 28:8–9), in the epilogue YHWH makes it clear that Eliphaz's words are false. Hence, while revelation mediated by a prophet may be supposed to carry greater authority than the outworking of human intellect represented by the arguments of the wise, even prophecy is not infallible. Furthermore, Eliphaz is vague about the source of his revelation. In light of the story's non-Israelite setting, we ought to be wary of assuming the source of his revelation is YHWH.

What is surprising, however, is that what is ostensibly a wisdom text so quickly departs from any pretense of presenting any argument derived from wisdom as commonly understood to appeal to a more prophetic methodology founded upon direct revelation. There are a couple of possible reasons for this. First, it might indicate that the disjunction between wisdom and prophecy is somewhat artificial. The ease with

3. The term שמץ appears only in Job 4:12; 26:14; Sir 10:10; 18:32. It seems to mean "a little" and so here suggests that Eliphaz may have only heard part of the message being conveyed to him. See D. J. A. Clines, *Job 1–20* (WBC 17; Dallas: Word, 1989), 111.

4. E.g., Num 12:6; Deut 13:1–5.

5. For an alternate reading of Eliphaz's vision, see K. Brown, *The Vision in Job 4 and Its Role in the Book: Reframing the Development of the Joban Dialogues* (Studies of the Sofja Kovalevskaja Research Group on Early Jewish Monotheism 4; Tübingen: Mohr Siebeck, 2015).

which Eliphaz can appeal to revelation as an adjunct to his use of wisdom may be surprising to the modern scholar who presupposes a compartmentalism that is ultimately artificial, though it may not have been to the ancient audience of Job.

Second, it likely reflects a tacit acknowledgment that divine revelation carries greater authority than human wisdom alone. Whatever conclusions Eliphaz may have drawn based exclusively on his application of the basic presuppositions of the sages relating to retributive justice remain ultimately subject to the vicissitudes of human reason, whereas a direct word from God circumvents that particular problem. In all likelihood, both factors are at play in Job 4.

Elihu

The only other of Job's friends with any serious claim to the prophetic is Elihu. Opinions about Elihu vary—he's young and brash and perhaps attractive to younger readers while older readers see him as a bit of an upstart. Many scholars are, however, too quick to condemn Elihu.[6] What is widely noted, however, is that Elihu invokes prophetic revelation rather than simply arguing from a wisdom perspective. The major impetus for this comes from Elihu's words in Job 32:7–9:

> I said to myself, "Age should speak,
>> and length of years should make wisdom known."
> But it is a spirit in people,
>> the breath of the Almighty,
>> that makes them understand.
> It is not the aged who are wise,
>> nor old men who understand what is right. (NET)

These words in particular prompt many to understand Elihu to be making prophetic claims for himself. For example, William Brown says that,

> Elihu rejects the traditional picture of the sage, whose head is hoary and back is bent, and comes close to a prophetic understanding of wisdom, whose source is unmediated revelation... Wisdom is not inherited from the preceding generations; rather it is received immediately and directly as inspiration.[7]

---

6. See M. A. Shields, "Was Elihu Right?," *JESOT* 3, no. 2 (2014): 155–70.

7. W. P. Brown, *Character in Crisis: A Fresh Approach to the Wisdom Literature of the Old Testament* (Grand Rapids: Eerdmans, 1996), 85. For a similar understanding see T. Longman, *Job* (BCOTWP; Grand Rapids: Baker, 2012), 380–82. Longman also characterizes Elihu's speech as though Elihu were saying "Thus says the Spirit

Elihu also refers to God speaking in dreams or visions of the night (Job 33:15–16). He characterizes the content of these revelations as warnings, probably against sins or actions yet to be committed.[8] Further still, Elihu expands the nature of divine warning beyond dreams and visions to include suffering itself (Job 33:19; cf. 36:21 where Elihu explicitly delivers the warning, "Watch out! Do not turn to sin").

However, it is not quite so clear that Elihu is really claiming divine inspiration for his own words. The reference to "the spirit in a man, the breath of Shaddai" (Job 32:8) comes in a context wherein Elihu suggests that worthwhile contributions to the discussion should not be restricted to the elders because of their presumed wisdom, but that wisdom is shared by all the living. He argues that he ought not to be discounted simply because he is young, for he, like the older friends, embodies the breath of God. Furthermore, the noun נשמה is almost always used in reference to life, not revelation, even in Isaiah—the only prophet to use the word (e.g., Isa 2:22; 30:33; 42:5; 57:16).[9] Later, Elihu uses similar language quite clearly to affirm no more than that he is alive (רוח אל עשתני ונשמת שדי תחיני, "The Spirit of God has made me, and the breath of the Almighty gives me life," Job 33:4).[10] That language is likely an allusion to Gen 2 where the man is given breath after being formed from dust.[11]

There are also a number of other places where both רוח and נשמה appear together as they do in Job 32:8. In Gen 7:22 we find the expression

---

of God" (382). For more on revelation to Elihu, see J. E. Hartley, *The Book of Job* (Grand Rapids: Eerdmans; 1988), 427; A. Postell, "Wineskin or Windbag? Elihu and the Problem of Justice in the Book of Job," *Ramify* 2, no. 1 (2011): 42. L. G. Perdue, *Wisdom in Revolt: Metaphorical Theology in the Book of Job* (London: Sheffield Academic Press, 1991), 249 understands Elihu's claim to be that this "prophetic" wisdom "is the universal possession of humans in whom the spirit of God dwells."

8. See Shields, "Was Elihu Right?"

9. Furthermore, when used in parallel with רוח in Isaiah, it is clearly not a reference to God's Spirit nor to special revelation, cf. Isa 42:5. The use of רוח in Eccl 3:21 is clearly not God's Spirit, nor is it God's Spirit throughout the wisdom literature. D. J. A. Clines, *Job 21–37* (WBC 18A; Nashville: Thomas Nelson, 2006), 718 also argues that this is not a claim to inspiration.

10. This point is repeated in v. 6. Longman concedes that Elihu may simply be saying that "he is a creature just like Job" (Longman, *Job*, 385). Clines notes that Elihu "regards himself...as laying claim to no authority over [Job] and as being no more than a fellow creature with Job." D. J. A. Clines, *Job 38–42* (WBC 18B; Nashville: Thomas Nelson, 2011), 726.

11. Job 33:6 uses "mortar: (חמר), although the allusion to ancient Near Easter creation ideas seems clear.

נשמת רוח חיים, "breath of the spirit of life," which again simply refers to a living creature. In Isa 42:5 the terms are used in parallel, again simply to refer to life and not any special prophetic revelation:

Thus says the God Yhwh:	כה אמר האל יהוה
Who created the heavens and spread them out,	בורא השמים ונוטיהם
Who stretched out the land and its offspring,	רקע הארץ וצאצאיה
Who gives breath to the people on it,	נתן נשמה לעם עליה
And spirit to those living in it.	ורוח להלכים בה

Yet there is nowhere that these terms appear together where the reference is to the Spirit of God as the agent of special revelation.

Finally, if Elihu is claiming to be making a prophetic speech, it seems odd that his reasoning is essentially that he has refrained from speaking God's words because old men should have priority! That never appears to have prevented any Old Testament prophet from speaking.

The other passage that warrants examination is Elihu's claim in Job 36:2 that the NET renders as "...I still have words to speak on God's behalf." Is Elihu here claiming a prophetic role? Once again, it's easier to make more of this than is actually warranted, and the Hebrew is far from clear. The text reads:

כתר לי זעיר ואחוך כי עוד לאלוה מלים

Wait with me a little and I will tell you that there are still words for God.

Is Elihu actually claiming to speak God's words or merely claiming to speak more words in God's defense? Job 36:3–4 continues Elihu's introductory words leading into his final speech, but the content is particularly relevant:

I will carry my knowledge from afar	אשא דעי למרחוק
and to my maker I will give righteousness.	ולפעלי אתן צדק
For my words are certainly not false,	כי אמנם לא שקר מלי
one of impeccable knowledge is with you.	תמים דעות עמך

If Elihu is claiming to have "impeccable" knowledge, then his claim clearly sounds rather presumptuous. Indeed, Clines notes that the last clause causes many to remonstrate over Elihu's apparently excessive boast. However, Clines argues that perhaps Elihu is really saying little more than "a man sincere in his ideas stands before you."[12] The other

---

12. Clines, *Job 38–42*, 854–55.

possibility, however, is that Elihu is claiming that the quality of his knowledge is founded upon its divine origins, as possibly implied in v. 2. Then knowledge born from afar (v. 3) could feasibly refer to knowledge from the heavenly realm.[13]

Clines is probably right to be cautious about claiming too much here.[14] For one, a dominant theme of Elihu's speech is the defense of God's righteousness, and his claims here still to have "words for God" and then "to my maker I will give righteousness" fit this well. Since the remainder of Elihu's speech is largely just such a defense of God, his claim in v. 2 makes better sense as an affirmation that he has more to say in God's defense. Nor does Elihu's claim about bearing knowledge from afar necessarily imply its source is God. For one, while we're not sure precisely where Job is set, we do know it is not set in Israel (indeed, it is probably set before Israel existed), yet Elihu has a rather Hebraic sounding name.[15] As wisdom was a truly international phenomenon, perhaps Elihu is merely claiming that his contribution represents an outsider's view in his present company.

So Elihu probably doesn't claim to be a prophet, although he does make the point that the application of wisdom alone is insufficient to explain all human suffering. Hence he does make an appeal to revelation in Job 33: "God does speak," he says. It would appear that, in contrast to Job's friends, Elihu realizes that the principle of retributive justice is insufficient to explain all human suffering, and that dreams or other special revelation might be necessary if an explanation is to be sought (or, alternatively, suffering itself may *be* the revelation).

Conclusion

Among Job's friends, then, there is only one who claims anything approaching prophetic revelation, and that is Eliphaz. And although his prophetic claims in his first speech are spurious, in the epilogue it turns out that he finally does become a prophet, for in Job 42:7–9 we read:

> After YHWH had said these things to Job, YHWH said to Eliphaz the Temanite, "I've become angry with you and your two friends because you have not spoken truthfully about me as my servant Job has. Now take for yourselves seven bulls and seven rams and go to my servant Job and offer a burnt offering for yourselves. Then my servant Job will intercede for you so I do not do what your folly deserves, for you have not spoken right about me as has my servant Job."

13. So Hartley, *Job*, 468.
14. Clines, *Job 38–42*, 854.
15. See n. 35 below for factors indicating the ancient setting of Job.

Here YHWH speaks specifically to Eliphaz with a message for all three friends. This meets all the basic definitions of prophecy, even announcing what is potentially bad news and calling the men to repent.

Ultimately, however, it is from both Eliphaz and Elihu that we see that the sages could be open to incorporating the prophetic in their understanding of the world. While Eliphaz appears either to have been misled or else set out to mislead in his claim to have received a prophetic word, Elihu makes no such claim but instead highlights the place of prophecy in seeking to understand Job's situation.

Is Job a Prophet? The Theophany in Job

There is also a history of some readers identifying Job himself as a prophetic figure. For one, Islam recognizes Job as a prophet, but the tradition is broader than that. As Seow has noted:

> Hermann Cohen…accepted the claim of Maimonides that Job is in some sense a prophet and that suffering is a form of prophecy and, hence, full of purpose. Rejecting the cause-and-effect arguments of Job's friends and their assumption that Job's suffering must be a punishment for sins, Cohen followed the medieval commentators in arguing that suffering may, in fact, be a manifestation of divine providence. Suffering may be redemptive, a part of God's plan of salvation not for the sufferer alone, but also for all humanity.[16]

Early Christian interpreters often saw Job as a prophet of the Christ and drew upon various allegorical readings to justify this claim.[17] These identifications of Job as a prophet, however, tend to be too light on specific details to warrant making the connection from an exegetical perspective. There is, however, one element of Job's story that could be construed as support for the claim that the man Job takes on a prophetic role: the theophany of Job 38–41.

The primary account of direct, special revelation in the book of Job arrives in the form of the theophany where YHWH speaks directly to Job. Now, while theophanies are definitely not staples of wisdom literature, the relationship of this theophany with prophecy is also a little tenuous. For one, a prophet is typically a human intermediary conveying a message obtained from the deity to the intended recipients. Here, however, the intermediary is bypassed. While that may be partly because we've already had at least one spurious claim to prophetic revelation made by

---

16. C. L. Seow, *Job 1–21: Interpretation and Commentary* (Grand Rapids: Eerdmans, 2013), 151.

17. See ibid., 174, 179, 180.

Eliphaz, it is also likely a response to Job's insistence that God answer his charges directly. Job, however, appears to get both more and less than he expected—less in that he receives no explicit explanation for his suffering and loss, and more in that the invariable outcome of such an encounter with YHWH throughout the Bible always results in the human witness being well and truly put in their place, as George Savran explains:

> One of the chief distinguishing characteristics of theophany stories is the reaction of the protagonist to the appearance of the divine. Though they may differ in the form of expression, these responses are characterized by an unusual display of humility or fear, an awareness of "creature consciousness." The external contours of these reactions include bowing (Exod. 24:1, 34:8; Num. 22:31; Josh. 5:14; Judg. 13:20), hiding the face (Exod. 3:6), exclamation (Gen. 28:16), or even the simple הנני, "ready," as a statement of willingness to respond to the divine (Gen. 46:2, Exod. 3:4, 1 Samuel 3). In certain cases, these expressions are coupled with a sense of thankfulness for not having perished as a result of the encounter with the divine, sometimes coupled with an explicit fear of death.[18]

There is a case to be made, however, for associating a theophany with a prophetic call.[19] Such theophanies do occur in Isa 6:1–13 and Ezek 1:1–3:15 (cf. also Moses, Exod 3:1–4:7). So although these theophanies have some prophetic connection, most theophanies occur outside the prophetic books in other contexts, and it is clear that a theophany alone does not indicate that a prophetic call has been made. Indeed, while Isaiah and Ezekiel experience a theophany, what makes these distinctively call events are God's words and their appeal to the recipient to fulfill a specific, prophetic role. So while Job is confronted by God in a theophany, that event does not call Job to a prophetic role and so the event itself cannot be understood prophetically in that sense. Job is not made out to be a prophet by his encounter with God.[20]

18. G. Savran, "Theophany as Type Scene," *Prooftexts* 23, no. 2 (2003): 130–31. This is also reflected in Job's final response to his encounter with YHWH in Job 42:5.

19. Although most prophetic calls do not include the physical manifestation of God which is requisite for a true theophany but rather take the form of "the word of YHWH came to me..." (e.g., Jon 1:1–2). Cheol-Woo Park has suggested that the latter chapters of the book of Job have a number of parallels to prophetic call narratives, in particular with Isa 6:1–13, although I don't think his argument is compelling. See C.-W. Park, "Central Contents of Job 38–42 Reconsidered in Relation to the Call Narrative (Isaiah 6)," *Korean Journal of Old Testament Studies* 20, no. 2 (2014): 94–126.

20. Phinney notes four characteristics of call narratives: (1) A direct proclamation by YHWH or his messenger to the called person; (2) a response of the called

Yet a significant factor in an analysis of prophetic connections in the book of Job lies in the issue of why there is a theophany at all, as opposed to the arrival of a prophet or seer or man of God, or why God doesn't merely speak to Job, as is frequently reported by the prophets themselves (i.e., "the word of YHWH came to..." e.g., Isa 38:4; Jer 1:4, 11, 13; 2:1; 7:1; 11:1; Ezek 1:3; 6:1; 7:1; Jonah 1:1; 3:1; Hag 1:3; Zech 1:1). Theophanies include both a vision of God and a message from God, thus adding an extra element to a direct word from God and removing the mediated nature of words spoken by prophets. Thus, while a vision itself could be ambiguous, and while words spoken through a prophet themselves offered no final guarantee of the ultimate divine origin of the message nor its faithful transmission by the mediating prophet, the theophany conveyed a message directly from God in a context wherein its authority could not be questioned. In the book of Job it would appear that all these considerations come into play given Eliphaz's prior claim to revelation.

Furthermore, what should also be noted is that the resolution to Job's problems comes not through the considered wisdom of the sages but rather via direct revelation. In this way the book of Job reflects some prophetic element. Any definitive diagnosis of the causes of suffering for any individual can only be made with the benefit of special divine revelation.

Intertextual Connections Between Job and the Prophets

There are also various literary and thematic parallels between the book of Job and various prophetic books. For example, James Harding highlights some of the issues which are found in both Job and various prophetic books:

> The relationship between theodicy and prophetic access to the divine council is a key issue in Jeremiah, and likewise in Job. The problem for traditional theodicy raised by the possibility of divine actions committed "without good cause" (*ḥinnām*) is a concern in Ezekiel (esp. Ezek. 14:23), and also in Job. Finally, the nexus between theodicy and the revealed attributes of Yhwh (cf. Exod. 34:6–7) is a concern throughout the Twelve, as it is in Job, and at the end of the Twelve, in Malachi, the problem of the relationship

regarding their inadequacy for the task; (3) reassurance by YHWH; and (4) a sign is given. See D. N. Phinney, "Call/Commission Narratives," in *Dictionary of the Old Testament: Prophets* (ed. Mark J. Boda and J. G. McConville; Downers Grove: IVP Academic, 2012), 65.

between divine justice (Mal. 2:17) and fearing (*yr'*) or serving (*'bd*) Yhwh
"for naught" (*šāv'* in Mal 3:14) is raised, the latter arguably being the theme
around which the book of Job ultimately revolves.[21]

Beyond these, Harding notes other parallels such as Job's lament over his
birth (Job 3:3–10) and Jeremiah's seventh lament (Jer 20:14–18), together
with the prophetic lawsuits against Israel, which are inverted in Job's
accusations against YHWH.[22]

Although the existence of such links is readily apparent, their
significance is perhaps less so. For Harding, the book of Job is "a work
that draws on themes and ideas present in the prophetical books, in order
to wrestle with the assumptions underlying them."[23] Foundational for this
reading of Job, however, is the assumption that the insight granted the
reader into the heavenly realm in Job 1–2 is meant to offer a comprehensive explanation for the cause of Job's suffering, an assumption which
I have elsewhere questioned.[24]

Rather more likely is that Job addresses similar problems in more
particular circumstances. The prophets focus on the question of theodicy
as it applies to the entire nation or even the known world. Job, in common
with the other wisdom literature, particularizes the problem to the case of
the individual. For the prophets, national apostasy rightly attracts divine
censure and the principle of retributive justice established in the Torah
stands. For Job, such an analysis cannot be extended to the lives of each
individual person. The prophets spoke to the nation, the sages—and Job
in particular—to the individual.

Job and the Suffering Servant

Of all the intertextual connections between the book of Job and the
prophets, it is that between the man Job and the Suffering Servant of
Isaiah which has perhaps attracted most comment.[25] In 1927 Robert
Pfeiffer wrote that "[t]he fundamental conceptions of Second Isaiah

21. J. E. Harding, "The Book of Job as Metaprophecy," *Studies in Religion/
Sciences Religieuses* 39, no. 4 (2010): 526.

22. Cf. ibid., 526; D. Wolfers, *Deep Things Out of Darkness: The Book of Job,
Essays and a New English Translation* (Grand Rapids: Eerdmans, 1995), 49.

23. Harding, "The Book of Job as Metaprophecy," 528.

24. See M. A. Shields, "Malevolent or Mysterious? God's Character in the
Prologue of Job," *TynBul* 61 (2010): 255–70.

25. In addition to those quoted below, see also J. C. Bastiaens, "The Language of
Suffering in Job 16–19 and in the Suffering Servant Passages of Deutero-Isaiah," in
Studies in the Book of Isaiah: Festschrift Willem A. M. Beuken (ed. J. Van Ruiten and

represent a development of the views of the Book of Job."[26] Hartley similarly considers that "Isaiah was so inspired by the account of Job that Job served as one of his models in his portrait of the Suffering Servant."[27] However, not everyone has seen Isaiah as a development from Job. Gordis argued that the author of Job applied a nationalistic view of suffering to the individual, a notion he derived from the suffering servant songs of Deutero-Isaiah.[28]

If there is any direct connection between Job and Second Isaiah, the direction in which that connection occurs is difficult to demonstrate. Scholars generally date Job to one of three periods: the early seventh century during the time of Hezekiah; the mid-sixth century after the fall of Jerusalem; or the Second Temple period of the fourth to third centuries.[29] Now, if all of Isaiah shares an eighth-century origin, clearly the flow must be from Isaiah into Job. However, few scholars would date all of Isaiah to that period and most would place Second Isaiah around the sixth century—so potentially the link could go either way.

Will Kynes has recently looked into intertextual connections between Job and Isa 40–55.[30] He notes the presence of the phrase כי יד יהוה עשתה זאת ("that the hand of YHWH has done this") in Job 12:9 and Isa 41:20 and its implications for the direction of borrowing, suggesting that Job may be quoting Isaiah because this is the only place in Job's dialogues where the name יהוה appears whereas it is quite common in Isa 40–55.[31]

M. Vervenne; BETL 132; Leuven: Peeters, 1997). In particular, note the recent work in K. Dell and W. Kynes, eds., *Reading Job Intertextually* (New York: Bloomsbury T&T Clark, 2013).

26. R. H. Pfeiffer, "The Priority of Job over Is. 40–55," *JBL* 46 (1927): 202–6. Pfeiffer writes that "[t]he parallels in thought and expression between the Book of Job and Is. 40–55 are sufficiently numerous and close to make it reasonably certain that one of the two authors was acquainted with the other." He proceeds to argue that Isaiah was dependent upon Job. See also S. Terrien, "Quelques Remarques sur les Affinités de Job avec le Deutéro-Ésaïe," in *Volume du Congrès: Genève 1965* (ed. P. A. H. de Boer; VTSup 15; Leiden: Brill, 1966), 295–310 (cited in K. J. Dell, *Job: Where Shall Wisdom Be Found?* [Sheffield: Sheffield Phoenix, 2013], 23).

27. J. E. Hartley, *The Book of Job* (Grand Rapids: Eerdmans, 1988), vii.

28. R. Gordis, *The Book of God and Man* (Chicago: University of Chicago Press, 1965); cf. Dell, *Job*, 23.

29. Hartley, *Job*, 18; W. Kynes, "Job and Isaiah 40–55: Intertextualities in Dialogue," in Dell and Kynes, eds., *Reading Job Intertextually*, 95–96.

30. Kynes, "Job and Isaiah 40–55."

31. Ibid., 97. However, the expression יד יהוה is itself quite common and so may have contributed to its presence in Job despite a general aversion to the use of the divine name in the speeches.

Kynes himself argues that Job's use of parody places Job's speeches later than Isa 40–55:

> While the negative meaning of Job's accusations would linger and spoil the confident praise in Isa 40–55 were the author of the latter text alluding to them, it is precisely the contrast between the positive message of Isa 40–55 and Job's reversal of it that would give his use of the parallel language its bite.[32]

and later,

> ...based on the analogy of Job's "bitter parody" of Ps 8 in Job 7, a synchronic comparison of the external coherence of the possible allusions between Job and Isa 40–55 strongly suggests the diachronic conclusion that Job is the later text. Thus, Job attacks the message of Isa 40–55 in light of his experience, unremitting and unexplained affliction that does not accord with the prophet's confident proclamations of God's goodness.[33]

An immediate difficulty with Kynes's analysis here, however, is that Isa 40–55 does not actually present quite such a one-sided view of God's goodness. For example, Isa 45:7 reads:

> I am the one who forms light
> > and creates darkness;
> the one who brings about peace
> > and creates calamity. (NET)

Clines says of Job 12:9 that "Strangely enough, Job too agrees that 'Yahweh's hand has done this,' but he cannot consent to the friends' conception of what 'this' is: it is not for him the inexorable outworking of a moral law of nature but the willful act of a malign deity."[34] In Isaiah, the hand of YHWH achieves great things:

> I will make streams flow down the slopes
> and produce springs in the middle of the valleys.
> I will turn the desert into a pool of water
> and the arid land into springs.
> I will make cedars, acacias, myrtles, and olive trees grow in the wilderness;
> I will make evergreens, firs, and cypresses grow together in the desert.
> (Isa 41:18–19, NET)

---

32. Ibid., 98.
33. Ibid., 99.
34. Clines, *Job 1–20*, 294.

However, in Job it is the terrible things that have befallen Job that are done by the hand of YHWH. The quotation in Job thus expresses the same idea found in Job's words in the prologue: "YHWH gave and YHWH has taken away, may the name of YHWH be blessed" (Job 1:21). Or perhaps, more precisely, Job 1:21 encompasses both Isa 41:20 (the good) and Job 12:9 (the bad)!

While Kynes makes a good argument for the chronological sequence of composition of Job and Isaiah, any reading of the texts built on this overlooks a significant detail: the implied literary historical location of each text. If we take our chronological cues from each text's own implied historical context, then it is clear that Job is a story that is set well before Isaiah and this development from innocent suffering to vicarious suffering is reflected in a more canon-conscious reading of the intertextual connections. Put another way, the author of Job has projected his tale back into Israel's pre-history and by doing so has established it as a background not simply to the vicarious suffering of Isaiah's servant, but even to Solomon's wisdom as found in Proverbs.[35] The intertextual links with Isaiah's suffering servant function to place Job's innocent suffering on a clear trajectory leading to the vicarious innocent suffering of the Servant and, ultimately, to Jesus the Messiah.[36]

---

35. A similar phenomenon can be seen in modern cinema where, for example, *Star Wars* episodes 1–3 are set before episodes 4–6 despite being written and produced well after them. So also Job and Isaiah, although thankfully without either Jar-Jar Binks or midi-chlorians.

Job's temporal location is established by (1) the non-Israelite setting of the book; (2) Job's wealth being measured in animals and servants; (3) Job offers sacrifices without a priest; (4) Job lives well over 140 years; (5) the land of Uz may refer to Gen 10:23; (6) the unit of money used in Job 42:11 is only used in ancient times (Gen 33:19; Josh 24:32); (7) the phrase האיש ההוא גדול מכל בני קדם in Job 1:3 may play on a deliberate ambiguity in קֶדֶם as "in ancient times" (cf. Gen 2:8).

An objection to this approach might be that the Job's use of parody requires that Job be read after that which is parodied (in this case, Isa 41:20). However, once the two texts are combined into a single corpus their individual ideas play against one another without specific reference to the actual order in which they were written. Furthermore, the idea that YHWH stands behind suffering and evil is also present in Isa 40–55 (cf. Isa 45:7), so the strength of the supposed parody by Job's author is somewhat undermined.

36. This agrees with Pfeiffer and Terrien above as well as Hartley. Kynes ("Job and Isaiah 40–55," 96 n. 10) notes that this could go either way: "those who argue for the dependence of Isa 40–55 on Job often point to the lack of explicit mention of vicarious suffering in Job as an answer to the problem of innocent affliction

The Message of Job and the Message of the Prophets

Some scholars have suggested that the exile provided the impetus for the composition of the book of Job.[37] This association implies that the national tragedy of the exile takes place not because of the sinfulness of Israel and Judah as the prophets and the Deuteronomistic Historian had asserted, but rather was inflicted upon Israel for some unknown reason just as Job's suffering was inflicted upon him for an unknown reason—with the one caveat that it *was not* inflicted because of sin. If this is the case then Job stands in opposition to the prophets who so vehemently claimed that the sin of Judah led inevitably to its exile and destruction.

It needs to be said that some aspects of this line of interpretation are quite attractive. The prophetic appeal by Eliphaz that is shown to be false functions as repudiation of the prophets' claim that Israel suffered a just punishment at the hands of an angry God for its sins. The final theophany crushes the inherent authority associated with prophetic speech with a far greater and irrefutable authority implicit in the direct appearance of God. In short, the book of Job becomes an attack on the authority of the prophets of ancient Israel.

This interpretation is not without some difficulties. First, where prophets did readily point to specific and undeniable examples of Israel's and Judah's sin, it seems difficult to see how the exceptional character of Job presented in the prologue could easily prompt any ancient Judean exile to see in Job's plight their own when there already existed competing explanations for the exile which highlighted the nation's sinfulness. Job is simply too upright for any reader to be able to easily identify with him on either a personal or a national scale. Second, Pope discounts this interpretation since there are no hints of nationalistic concerns in the text

---

prominent in both texts (see, e.g., Terrien 1966, 309; Hartley 1988, 15), assuming that if the author of Job had known Isa 40–55, he would have incorporated this solution more prominently into his work. In response, however, some have argued that the author of Job has applied the nationalistic view of suffering in Isa 40–55 to the individual (e.g., Gordis 1965, 216). Naish (1925, 41) claims Job omits vicarious suffering because he does not find it comforting. Peake (1904, 38–39) similarly observes, 'Israel may suffer for the nations, but what would Job's vicarious suffering avail?'"

37. For example, L. G. Perdue, *Wisdom Literature: A Theological History* (Louisville: Westminster John Knox, 2007), 78–80; Wolfers, *Deep Things Out of Darkness*; S. Cook, "A Reading of Job as a Theatrical Work: Challenging a Retributive Deuteronomistic Theodicy," *Literature & Aesthetics* 24, no. 2 (2014): 39–62.

and an Edomite main character would be unlikely to prompt a Judean audience to associate themselves with the main character in light of Edom's involvement in the fall of Jerusalem.[38] Third, David Clines writes,

> Some have thought that the inexplicable suffering of Job may have been intended to be symbolic of the suffering of the Jews in Babylonian exile in that century, and therefore to have been composed at about that period. But the author has so convincingly located his narrative in the patriarchal world that there are no clear contemporary allusions of any kind to the period contemporary with the author.[39]

Fourth, the assumption that such literature can *only* arise from social trauma on a grand scale is misplaced—without a footnote in the autograph and a clear date for the composition of the book, who can really tell whether the author was prompted by national tragedy, personal tragedy, or even just philosophical curiosity?

Of course, these points do not undermine the notion that the book of Job sets out to question the doctrine of retributive justice, but it is clear that it is difficult to maintain the notion that it is a specific attack on the prophetic and deuteronomistic claim that the nation was exiled because of its apostasy and sin.

Conclusions

Although the connections between the book of Job and wisdom literature are clear, its author has nonetheless made quite clear that wisdom and the sages who propounded it in the ancient world find themselves at a loss when faced with difficult individual circumstances such as those of the character Job. Whereas wisdom could provide general principles and broad ideals, Job's author knew that accounting for individual circumstances was well beyond the means of even the most exceptional sage without the benefit of divine guidance.

In Eliphaz we find a sage who, without any apparent hesitation, suggests that some of the wisdom he propounds finds its origins in direct special revelation. The lack of hesitation itself suggests that the traditional notion that wisdom operated solely out of the operation of the human

---

38. E. B. Smick, "Job," in *The Expositor's Bible Commentary* (ed. F. E. Gæbelein; Grand Rapids: Zondervan, 1988), 4:852, points to the book of Obadiah as evidence of this. See M. H. Pope, *Job* (AB 15; New York: Doubleday, 1973).

39. Clines, *Job 1–20*, lvii.

intellect is rather reductionistic. Rather, the claim of Eliphaz suggests that the sage would not scorn revelation if it came, but rather would integrate it into his or her understanding of the world. So Eliphaz works both with the traditional wisdom notion of retributive justice together with insight gained via a dream. If this is the case we should not be surprised to find prophetic elements within the book of Job (nor even in other wisdom literature).

This conclusion is, to some extent, borne out by later parts of the book. For one, Elihu goes on to suggest that suffering functions in a manner equivalent to visions and dreams (Job 33:14–30). Second, the ultimate answer to Job's complaint comes not through the words of his wise friends but in a direct revelation from YHWH who goes on to repudiate the words of the sages. Intellectual wisdom is supplanted by revelation. The author of Job has turned his back on the way of wisdom and appealed to prophecy to provide the final answer for Job. Indeed, the book of Job's answer goes beyond even this, for the revelation to Job is not mediated by a fallible human prophet but is imparted directly by YHWH through the theophany. In some sense, then, the author highlights not only the inadequacy of the human intellect but even the shortcomings of prophecy.

Finally, as the character Job appears as an upright and blameless individual, the book establishes a canonical background to Isaiah's prophetic account of the Suffering Servant. In Job we learn that the innocent can suffer and yet truly be innocent. They can be afflicted by God and yet have committed no sin that warrants that affliction. Job and the Suffering Servant of Isaiah thus stand together, their places established only through the prophetic voice of their authors.

In these ways the book of Job is a bridge between the sages and the prophets. The true sages must, as Elihu insists, listen to their own wisdom as well as to the voice of YHWH. They must cross the bridge into the prophetic world of direct revelation without which their wisdom will invariably fail when it encounters individuals living in the complex mess that is the real world.

WAS QOHELET AN ESCHATOLOGICAL OR AN ANTI-APOCALYPTIC SAGE? *HEBEL*, THE EVIL DAY, AND DIVINE JUDGMENT IN THE BOOK OF ECCLESIASTES

Richard Schultz

One benefit of the recent increased attention to biblical intertextuality is that verbal and conceptual relationships between diverse books of the Hebrew Bible are being examined afresh utilizing an explicit and refined methodology.[1] For example, in considering the conceptual relationship between the prophetic and wisdom writings,[2] one notes that an earlier research emphasis on wisdom influences on the prophetic corpus[3] has

1. See the helpful survey of various approaches to the subject in G. D. Miller, "Intertextuality in Old Testament Research," *CurBR* 9 (2011): 283–309.

2. Despite studying Isaiah and Ecclesiastes for several decades, I never had considered the intertextual relationship between these two books until I was invited to devote an essay to the topic, and I wrongly did not expect to find much relevant secondary literature. See Richard Schultz, "Qoheleth and Isaiah in Dialogue," in *Reading Ecclesiastes Intertextually* (ed. Katherine Dell and Will Kynes; LHBOTS 574; London: Bloomsbury T&T Clark, 2014), 57–70. Some of the material in the present essay was discussed, either more briefly or in greater detail, in my 2014 essay.

3. For much of the twentieth century, ancient Hebrew wisdom literature was understood to be essentially independent of the other major literary genres and theological traditions of Israel. Furthermore, it was considered to be the product of careful observation of life experiences and decisively influenced by the wisdom writings of its neighbors, especially Egyptian instruction texts. Accordingly, when wisdom terms, forms, and concepts were identified in the prophetic corpus, this usually was evaluated as "wisdom influence," with Gerhard von Rad even claiming that wisdom gave rise to apocalyptic. This "pan-sapientializing" approach has been critiqued appropriately by James Crenshaw, Stuart Weeks, and others (Crenshaw, *Old Testament Wisdom: An Introduction* [2nd ed.; Louisville: Westminster John Knox, 1998], 29–30, 33–34; Weeks, *An Introduction to the Study of Wisdom Literature* [London: T&T Clark International, 2010], 135–42).

been supplemented recently by a perhaps less-noted effort to identify prophetic influences on the wisdom corpus.

This essay will focus on an aspect of the latter investigation, reviewing and evaluating the evidence in Ecclesiastes (and as expressed by its dominant voice, Qohelet) for such prophetic influence, primarily from the book of Isaiah, since Isaiah is the prophetic book most often cited by scholars as having influenced Qohelet. I will begin with some examples of claimed prophetic elements in Ecclesiastes, considering the distinctiveness of these features.[4] Most of the essay, however, will be devoted to summarizing and assessing two divergent suggestions: (1) that Qohelet, particularly in Eccl 12:1–8, utilizes eschatological language neutrally (i.e., without a strong commitment to an eschatological ideology) in blending a description of the end of the world with the end of an individual's life, and (2) that Qohelet, especially in Eccl 1:3–11, alludes to key aspects of the "apocalyptic vision" in order to reject, refute, or reconstruct it.

"Prophetic" Elements in Ecclesiastes

It certainly is plausible that an Israelite sage such as Qohelet, especially if he were situated in Jerusalem in the early to late postexilic period (the majority scholarly viewpoint today), might be familiar with Hebrew prophetic literature.[5]

There are several prominent themes that are found in both Isaiah and Ecclesiastes. Divine judgment is announced and portrayed from beginning (Isa 1:19–20, 24–25) to end (Isa 66:1, 4, 6, 14–16, 24) in—and throughout—the book of Isaiah. Although such judgment is usually national or even universal in scope, specific groups are frequently singled out as well (e.g., Isa 5:8, 11, 18, 20, 21, 22). Ecclesiastes likewise speaks of divine judgment in 3:16–17; 11:9; 12:13–14; and possibly 8:5–8 (cf. 8:11–12), each time using the word מִשְׁפָּט. The word מִשְׁפָּט occurs forty-two times in Isaiah, although it is less clear than in Ecclesiastes where it denotes the act of judgment rather than the justice that results from this action.[6] Here one also must distinguish between temporal and

---

4. That is, are these elements merely found in (or even derived from) prophetic books, or are they distinctively prophetic in nature?

5. However, even a "monarchial" Qohelet could have been familiar with some classical and pre-classical prophetic traditions now preserved in the prophetic corpus of the Hebrew Bible.

6. The former is likely in Isa 3:14; 4:4; 5:16; 28:6; 34:5; 53:8; and 54:17. See also Isa 66:16, where the related verb שָׁפַט is used.

eschatological (or final) judgment, and it is debated which one is in view in each cited Ecclesiastes text—except for 12:14, which is more likely eschatological.[7] Also at issue is whether Qohelet actually expects divine judgment to be carried out someday rather than merely lamenting its delay or absence, although Eccl 8:12–13 appears to assume it ("I know that it will go better with those who fear God, who are reverent before him. Yet because the wicked do not fear God, it will not go well with them").[8]

Due to these disputed issues, it is difficult to state with any degree of certainty that the discussion of divine judgment in Ecclesiastes, which focuses more on the actions of individuals than of nations, has been influenced by a prophetic book like Isaiah. This, of course, begs the question of from where the sages in general derived their belief in divine, especially final, judgment (see also, for example, texts such as Prov 3:33; 15:25; 16:5; 19:17; 20:22; and 22:23, as well as Job 8:3; 21:22; 34:12; 37:23), since the prophetic writings of the Hebrew Bible certainly would be a possible, perhaps even the most likely, source.

A related prophetic emphasis, especially in the eighth-century prophets, is the lack of justice in Israelite society, blaming the leaders and the powerful wealthy class for perpetrating injustice (e.g., Isa 1:23; 10:1–2). A similar claim is made in Eccl 5:8 [MT 5:7] and 8:9–14. Both books describe incompetent rulers, using נער pejoratively (Isa 3:4–5, 12; Eccl 10:16–17),[9] as well as immature and self-indulgent officials who drink at inappropriate times (Isa 5:11, 22–23 and Eccl 10:16–17):

> Woe to the land whose king was a servant (נער) and whose princes feast in the morning. Blessed is the land whose king is of noble birth and whose princes eat at a proper time—for strength and not for drunkenness. (Eccl 10:16–17)

---

7. Eccl 12:13–14, however, is usually—and largely for that reason—viewed as a later redactional addition. Aarre Lauha, *Kohelet* (BKAT 19; Neukirchen–Vluyn: Neukirchener Verlag, 1978), 6, labels 12:12–14 "a dogmatic correction," also attributing 2:26a.ba; 3:17a; 5:18; 7:26b; 8:12b, 13; and 11:9b to the same "orthodox" (*rechtgläubig*) editor.

8. All biblical quotations in this essay, unless noted, are from the New International Version 2011.

9. C. L. Seow notes the conceptual parallel to Eccl 10:16 in Isa 3:4, 12 but does not suggest that any direct influence is involved. *Ecclesiastes: A New Translation with Introduction and Commentary* (AB 18C; New York: Doubleday, 1997), 329. Only Isa 3, however, describes these individuals as holding an office as a result of divine judgment.

I will make mere youths (נערים) their officials; children will rule over them... People will oppress each other—man against man, neighbor against neighbor. The young (הנער) will rise up against the old, the nobody against the honored... Youths oppress (מעולל) my people, women rule over them. My people, your guides lead you astray; they turn you from the path. (Isa 3:4, 5, 12)

Woe to those who rise early in the morning to run after their drinks, who stay up late at night till they are inflamed with wine... Woe to those who are heroes at drinking wine and champions at mixing drinks, who acquit the guilty for a bribe, but deny justice to the innocent. (Isa 5:11, 22–23)

The latter parallel is noted by Thomas Krüger, who suggests that Eccl 10 "perhaps alludes to the reproaches in Isa 5:11, 22."[10]

The common description of rulers in both Eccl 10 and Isa 3 as a נער could reflect the fact that it "was simply against convention for a *na'ar*, either as one who is not yet of age [i.e., the emphasis in Isa 3] or as one who is not of the right status or character [i.e., the emphasis in Eccl 10], to be king."[11] The reference to inopportune drinking in Eccl 10 and Isa 5, even though the latter individuals are not explicitly described as royalty or even governmental officials, is more likely to involve influence or dependence. The fact that four features (i.e., a woe, leaders, feasting and drinking, and an inappropriate time of day for such actions) occur in both texts offers a sufficient textual basis for claiming an allusion here. The fact that the description in Isa 5 is more general and more poetically evocative than in Eccl 10, which focuses more narrowly on royal misbehavior, supports Krüger's suggestion that it is Ecclesiastes rather than Isaiah doing the alluding.

Several scholars discussing Isaianic influence on Qohelet cite the striking confluence in Eccl 1:9–11 of the words "former" (ראשנים; also 7:10), "latter/later" (אחרנים; also 4:16), "new" (חדש), and "remembrance" (זכרון; see also 2:16; 5:20 [MT 19]; 9:5, 15; 11:8; 12:1), terms that occur repeatedly in Isa 40–66 (42:9; 43:9, 18–19; 46:9; 48:3, 6; 65:16–17; 66:22).[12] The references in Ecclesiastes to the "evil day" or "day of

10. Thomas Krüger, *Qohelet* (trans. O. C. Dean, Jr.; Hermeneia; Minneapolis: Fortress, 2004), 188.

11. Seow, *Ecclesiastes*, 329.

12. See especially the discussion by Seow in *Ecclesiastes*, 116–17: "Indeed the words of Qohelet in 1:9–11 echo the protoapocalyptic proclamations of Deutero-Isaiah that new things were about to happen, which would be unlike the former things (Isa 42:9)." Seow's claim will be discussed later in this essay.

adversity" (ביום רעה, Eccl 7:14), "evil time" or "time of calamity" (לעת רעה, 9:12), and "evil days" or "days of trouble" (ימי הרעה, 12:1) call to mind the prophetic announcement of the day of the LORD. In Isaiah this is referred to more often simply as "in that day" (ביום ההוא; ninety-two times in the book with various time referents; cf. "in that time" (בעת ההיא; only in Isa 18:7 and 20:2). Expressions similar to Eccl 9:12 are found within the prophetic corpus in Jer 2:27–28; 11:12; 15:11; and Mic 2:3 (עת רעה היא), however.

Given the almost ubiquitous occurrence of the word רע throughout the Hebrew Bible and its wide range of nuances (i.e., bad, evil, unfortunate), even its occurrences with a specific time referent, as in the passages listed above, do not necessarily demonstrate a dependence of Ecclesiastes on Isaiah or other prophetic traditions. Weighing against this assumption is that in Ecclesiastes the "evil day" is primarily described as one that will affect individuals rather than a nation or humanity as a whole, although a focus on the individual is a distinctive feature of Old Testament wisdom literature. Nevertheless, this parallel element, as well as the "former/ latter" and "old/new" language in Ecclesiastes and Isaiah, warrant and will receive further discussion below.

Three additional shared features between Ecclesiastes and Isaiah probably should be viewed as wisdom elements in Isaiah rather than the reverse, if any interrelationship involving dependence exists. Inter- estingly, Qohelet's favorite, though enigmatic, descriptor, הבל (NIV: "meaningless"), occurs three times in Isaiah (30:7; 49:4; 57:13). Of these three texts, only 49:4 exhibits a use of הבל that is similar to Ecclesiastes. There the servant (v. 5) complains, "But I said, 'I have labored in vain; I have spent my strength for nothing at all'" (ואני אמרתי לריק יגעתי לתהו והבל כחי כליתי). Note also the initial phrase, which parallels the prominent introductory verb in Ecclesiastes, ו/אמרתי ("and/I said"; 2:1, 15; 3:17, 18; 9:16) reinforced by the independent pronoun אני ("I").[13] The observation that only one of three occurrences of הבל in Isaiah parallels Qohelet's usage already suggests that no influence of the latter upon the former is present here. More significantly, although the servant's assessment of his labors seems to echo that of Qohelet, his personal relationship with YHWH could not be more of a contrast—divinely chosen before birth (v. 1), equipped (v. 2), designated to glorify God (v. 3), confident of receiving his due (v. 4; משפטי), divinely honored and strengthened (v. 5), and commissioned to restore Israel and illumine the Gentiles (vv. 5–6).

---

13. Unlike in Isa 49:4, in Ecclesiastes the pronoun follows the verb. Note, as well, that the Hebrew root יגע ("weary") in Isa 49:4 also occurs in Eccl 1:8 and 10:15.

Thus Qohelet's self-assessment of his efforts is usually viewed by interpreters as being accurate, whereas the servant's evaluation proves to be
premature and mistaken.

Furthermore, the call in Isa 22:13 ("Let us eat and drink, for tomorrow
we die") sounds remarkably similar to the refrain-like call to eat and drink
in the face of the transience of everything "under the sun" in Eccl 2:24;
3:13; 5:18 [MT 17]; 8:15; and especially 9:7(–10). However, the phrase in
Ecclesiastes is expressed as Qohelet's sage counsel to his readers (or his
charge, in 9:7) in light of the ephemeral nature of everything "under the
sun," while in Isa 22:13 it represents the words of a sinful and blatantly
rebellious people, which directly counter God's command to fast and
mourn (Isa 22:12–14). Given the very different moods indicated in each
text, any influence is unlikely.

In addition to these thematic and verbal parallels, Murphy identifies a
"woe oracle," a typical prophetic form, in Eccl 4:10 and 10:16.[14] However,
it is unclear that the label "oracle" fits the contents of 10:16–17. Both Eccl
4:10 and 10:16 begin with אי rather than the typical הוי or אוי,[15] and the
latter text addresses the victim of the faulty behavior (the "land," ארץ;
LXX: the "city," πόλις) rather than the guilty party (unlike 4:10), and there
is no announced punishment. The following verse, 10:17, however, begins
with אשרי ("blessed"; 8× in Proverbs and Ecclesiastes, 3× in Isaiah), an
expression that is clearly at home in wisdom circles.

In sum, of the various verbal and formal features that the books of
Isaiah and Ecclesiastes share, only a few involve prophetic features that
can be found in Ecclesiastes, and it would be difficult to demonstrate that
the latter are the result of prophetic influence on Qohelet. Just because a
word is found more frequently in canonical prophetic literature than in
wisdom literature does not qualify it as a prophetic term that is somehow
typical or distinctive of the prophetic genre. Even if a word, word pair,
or a set of related words occurs frequently or prominently in a particular
book or book section, such as "former/latter" and "old/new" in Isa 40–66
or "meaningless" in Ecclesiastes, this is an inadequate basis for claiming
that its use elsewhere is dependent on or influenced by the former unless
there is some contextual indication that a later author is clearly (i.e.,
intentionally) echoing it. Even as distinctive a word as הבל in Ecclesiastes
(38×) may not be claimed, without further argument, to have influenced

---

14. Roland E. Murphy, *Wisdom Literature: Job, Proverbs, Ruth, Canticles,
Ecclesiastes, and Esther* (FOTL; Grand Rapids: Eerdmans, 1981), 130. He also,
apparently mistakenly, lists 2:16.

15. For a discussion of this form in 4:10 and 10:16, see Seow, *Ecclesiastes*, 182.

the formulation of Isa 49:4 when הבל also occurs in the books of Genesis (in the name "Abel"), Deuteronomy, 1–2 Kings, Job, Psalms, Proverbs, Jeremiah, Lamentations, Jonah, and Zechariah.[16] Too many intertextual studies give the impression of operating within a closed linguistic world, that is, the assumption that, whenever we discover an identifiable verbal parallel within the Hebrew Bible, one text is most likely the source and the other the borrower of that expression rather than both texts drawing independently on the shared linguistic resources of their culture.

Eschatological Imagery in Ecclesiastes 12:1–7

The concluding poem of Ecclesiastes in 12:1–7 continues to taunt interpreters seeking to offer a coherent explanation of its diverse imagery since it appears to combine meteorological and even cosmic imagery with a portrayal of cessation of business as usual and possibly domestic ruin, as well as with a partially figurative or symbolic and partially literal description of the process of an individual's aging and death.

A number of recent commentators suggest a prophetic or eschatological source for the description in Eccl 12:2 ("before the sun and the light and the moon and the stars are darkened and the clouds return with the rain," NRSV). According to Michael Fox, "two events—the end of a world and the end of a person—resonate in each other" in 12:1–8, but his comments regarding the source remain vague: "Some motifs in the poem *resemble* the disastrous day of judgment described in the Prophets and called 'the day of the LORD' and equivalent terms."[17] In his view, both "Qohelet and the prophets draw upon images of mourning and universal cataclysm. In the prophets, these depict the disaster to a nation or the world. Qohelet uses them to represent the demise of the individual."[18] In other words, Fox does not actually state that Qohelet is drawing on prophetic imagery here; rather, both draw on similar images familiar to both from everyday life in the community (i.e., mourning) and from portrayals of cosmic disaster, although the latter clearly are more prominent in prophetic than in wisdom texts.

---

16. Although a significant number of these, especially in the Prophets, are used to denigrate idols as "worthless."

17. Michael V. Fox, *Ecclesiastes* (JPS Bible Commentary; Philadelphia: Jewish Publication Society, 2004), 77, emphasis added.

18. Michael V. Fox, *A Time to Tear Down and a Time to Build Up: A Rereading of Ecclesiastes* (Grand Rapids: Eerdmans, 1999), 342. In other words, "Koheleth is not describing the actual day of judgment or the world's end; he is depicting the death of an individual human with overtones of cosmic disaster" (Fox, *Ecclesiastes*, 76).

Seow makes a stronger claim, labeling Eccl 12:1–7 "Qohelet's eschatological poem." Like Fox, he sees Eccl 11:9–12:1 as referring to aging,
but, in his view, beginning with 12:2, Qohelet "recasts the vision of the
end through a radical revision that is reminiscent of the prophetic eschatology," painting "a picture of the end of the world."[19] Seow offers three
primary lines of support: (1) He sees 12:1–7 as offering a concluding
contrast to the book's opening poem in 1:4–11, both through contrasting
the continuous processes of nature and human activity with the end of
the world and all human possibilities and through reusing a number of
words from 1:4–11 (e.g., שֶׁמֶשׁ, עוֹלָם, סוֹבֵב, and רוּחַ) in 12:1–7, but in a
strikingly different manner. For example, in 1:5 the sun rises and sets,
while in 12:2 it is darkened never to shine again. (2) He claims that the
language of a cosmic blackout in Eccl 12:2 "belongs to the rhetoric of
prophetic eschatology and the description of widespread destruction,"
as found in Isa 5:30; 13:10; Ezek 32:7–8; Amos 5:8; 8:9; Mic 3:6; Joel
2:10; 3:4; 4:15; Job 3:9; 18:6; Matt 24:29; Mark 13:24; Luke 23:45; and
Acts 2:20.[20] Isaiah 13:10 offers one of the closest parallels ("The stars
of heaven and their constellations will not show their light. The rising
sun will be darkened and the moon will not give its light"), while Joel
2:2 and Zeph 1:15 associate "clouds" with the "darkness" of the "day
of the LORD," which is lacking in Isa 13:10 (although these two verses
use a different Hebrew word for "clouds" [עָנָן] than occurs in Eccl 12:2
[הֶעָבִים]). (3) Seow proceeds systematically through 12:1–7, seeking
to find an eschatological backdrop for nearly every word, phrase, or
image. (For example, "the rare sight of a disgusting almond tree" in 12:5
portrays the "languishing of nature" and thus is "evidence of a cosmic
catastrophe.")[21]

Seow's detailed analysis and effort to offer a coherent interpretation of
the concluding poem is impressive, and he offers a persuasive argument
for seeing prophetic sources for the imagery of Eccl 12:2. However, the
closest parallel for this language is found in Eccl 11:1–8, which similarly
refers to "disaster" (v. 2), "clouds" (vv. 3, 4), "rain" (v. 3), "light" (v. 7),

---

19. C. L. Seow, "Qohelet's Eschatological Poem," *JBL* 118 (1999): 234. See
the similar descriptions by Krüger (*Qohelet*, 201–2): "the description of a universal
cosmic catastrophe" as "world judgment"; Norbert Lohfink (*Kohelet* [2nd ed.; Die
Neue Echter Bibel; Stuttgart: Echter, 1980], 84, my translation): "here Kohelet relates
apocalyptic *topos* regarding the end of the world to the life of an individual"; and
Roland E. Murphy (*Ecclesiastes* [WBC 23; Dallas: Word, 1992], 116): "eschatological
overtones that point to the end of the world."

20. Seow, "Qohelet's Eschatological Poem," 213.

21. Ibid., 223.

"sun" (v. 7), and "darkness" (v. 8) in a clearly non-eschatological context.[22] Furthermore, not all of the prophetic references to a future day of national or universal judgment cited by Seow clearly describe the end of the world. For example, in Isa 5:30 the backdrop is probably the imminent invasion of the Assyrian army. In light of this and other prophetic texts using similar cosmic language, what is strikingly missing from Eccl 12:2–7 is any reference to divine wrath or divine agency in the coming destruction. (Contrast the repeated description of these in Isa 13.) Jennie Barbour therefore argues, contrary to the common interpretation, that the imagery of Eccl 12:2–7 as a whole more closely resembles city laments (e.g., Lam 3:2, 6; Isa 15:4) than prophetic "day of the LORD" language and that the mood in these verses is more "elegiac" than panic-stricken, as would be expected in a cosmic-judgment setting.[23]

Even if one grants that one hears echoes of prophetic eschatological language in Eccl 12:2–7, it remains unclear what this would indicate. Since interpreters commonly deny that Qohelet expects any individual divine judgment in the next world, as traditionally conceived,[24] despite lamenting the delay or absence of divine judgment in the present, the claim that Qohelet concludes his treatise by invoking "divine judgment" imagery seems rather incongruous. Furthermore, if cosmic judgment is falling on the individuals described in 12:2–7, on what basis are they being judged? Krüger points to the mention of God's judgment in 11:9b as anticipating this and explains that this divine judgment "over human beings consists precisely in their transitoriness (11:10b)," and this judgment is inescapable "because no one is completely innocent."[25]

There is certainly more than one option for understanding the imagery employed in 12:2–7. In a 1999 publication Fox explains that, although prophetic eschatology uses "hyperbolic, end-of-the-world imagery to suggest the extremity of the day's horror,"[26] such as caused by an enemy

---

22. The relationship between these terms in 11:1–8 and their recurrence in 12:1–7 is intentional, according to Daniel C. Fredericks, "Life's Storms and Structural Unity in Qoheleth 11.1–12.8," *JSOT* 52 (1991): 95–114.

23. Jennie Barbour, *The Story of Israel in the Book of Qohelet: Ecclesiastes as Cultural Memory* (Oxford Theology and Religion Monographs; Oxford: Oxford University Press, 2012), 152–57.

24. This assumes, of course, that Eccl 12:14 is the work of a later editors, not the summary words of Qohelet.

25. Krüger, *Qohelet*, 197, 201. Somewhat surprisingly, he suggests that this "judgment" will strike harder "the man who in 'good times' failed to rejoice and enjoy his life" (197).

26. Fox, *A Time to Tear Down*, 341.

invasion or natural disaster, these verses are not actually describing an "end times" day.[27] Rather, as Fox elaborates in his 2004 commentary, "Koheleth is not describing the actual day of judgment or the world's end; he is depicting the death of an individual human with overtones of cosmic disaster. It is as if Koheleth is saying, when you die, a world *is* ending—*yours*."[28]

Seow conceives of the end here in more comprehensive and more literal terms. In his view, Qohelet concludes by affirming that it is imperative to enjoy life in the "here and now because there will come a time when there will no longer be any possibility of enjoyment by anyone, because creation will be taken back," since, ultimately, everything is הבל (12:8).[29] This "uncreation" scenario, however, is unexpected here, especially in light of Qohelet's initial claim in 1:4 that "the earth remains forever" (לעולם עמדת). The second-person-singular address in 12:1 and concluding claim that "the spirit returns to God who gave it" (12:7) more likely speak of individual rather than corporate eschatology in a manner that is absent from prophetic eschatology. The closest conceptual parallel for this in the Hebrew Bible is found in Ps 104:29—"when you take away their breath (רוחם), they die and return to the dust."

In sum, it certainly is possible, perhaps even likely, to see the influence of prophetic imagery in Eccl 12:2–7, but this should not be understood as a more comprehensive affirmation of prophetic eschatology by Qohelet.

Ecclesiastes as a "Deconstruction" or "Ambiguation" of Late Prophetic Eschatology or an Anti-Apocalyptic Polemic

A contrasting approach to the issue of prophetic influence on Qohelet has been put forth by a number of scholars, including Thomas Krüger, Gregor Reichenbach, Leo Perdue, and Jerome Douglas. These scholars propose that Qohelet's primary disputation partner or "opponents" are eschatological prophets, apocalyptic seers, or apocalyptic sages. In general, this approach relies on a number of presuppositions: (1) a clear distinction between the characteristics of prophetic eschatology and

---

27. Although Eccl 12:1 refers to "the evil days" (ימי הרעה; but see "bad days"—NJB; "days of trouble"—NRSV; "days of sorrow"—TNK), the evil day (וביום רעה) or time (לעת רעה) referred to, respectively, in Eccl 7:14 and 9:12 is not an "end times" day.
28. Fox, *Ecclesiastes*, 76, emphasis in original.
29. Seow, "Qohelet's Eschatological Poem," 234.

those of apocalyptic, (2) a third-century BCE date for the composition of Ecclesiastes at a time when the prophetic corpus was undergoing inter-pretive expansion (i.e., *Fortschreibung*), both of these literary processes taking place in Jerusalem so that Qohelet's intimate familiarity with such traditions is assured, (3) the validity of what is commonly referred to in New Testament studies as a "mirror reading," that is, an interpreter's ability to identify the (usually unstated) views being countered in a text on the basis of what the author does say (and does not say),[30] coupled with (4) the accuracy of a composition-critical analysis that identifies where an author is quoting an opponent in order to refute their position, where one's own position is being articulated, and where potentially contrary expressions are best labelled later redactional additions.

In this essay I can only sketch briefly these variant positions and offer some initial responses. Due to the terminological overlap (noted in the first section of this paper), Krüger posits a literary allusion in Eccl 1:9–10 to Isa 43:18–19 and 65:17.[31] Here Qohelet offers a critical (or "decon-structive") re-reading of the latter: Whereas, according to Isa 43 one can "forget" what was "earlier" because the "new" has come, according to Eccl 3 the so-called new only appears new because one has forgotten what was "earlier." Similarly, Qohelet offers an ironic-critical reception of the hope promised in Isa 65:13 of a new world where God's servants will eat, drink, and rejoice. But this imminent expectation has not been fulfilled yet, and Qohelet doubts that anything "fully new" will ever arrive and thus encourages others to be content to eat, drink, and enjoy life in the "old world."[32] As noted in the previous section, according to Krüger Qohelet also offers a critical reconstruction in Eccl 11:9 and 12:1–7 of the prophetic-eschatological conception of a cosmic-universal judgment of God on the basis of his own creation-theological conception in terms of the contingency and certitude of death that every individual encounters.[33]

---

30. See, for example, Nijay K. Gupta, "Mirror-Reading Moral Issues in Paul's Letters," *JSNT* 34 (2012): 361–81.

31. Thomas Krüger, "Dekonstruktion und Reconstruktion prophetischer Escha-tologie im Qohelet-Buch," in *"Jedes Ding hat seine Zeit…" Studien zur israelitischen und altorientalischen Weisheit. Diethelm Michel zum 65. Geburtstag* (ed. Anja Diesel et al.; BZAW 241; Berlin: de Gruyter, 1996), 111–12.

32. Ibid., 114.

33. Ibid., 116, 124.

Reichenbach agrees with Krüger that Qohelet takes up the prophetic tradition of divine judgment in its late eschatological form but rejects the latter's claim that the sage "deconstructs" or critically reconstructs it.[34] Since, according to Reichenbach, the wisdom tradition lacks a concept of divine judgment, a statement like Eccl 3:17 ("I said in my heart, God will judge the righteous and the wicked, for he has appointed a time for every matter, and for every work") must be derived from prophetic texts like Isa 66:15–17 and Joel 4:2 [ET 3:2]. However, according to Reichenbach, the divine judgment texts in Ecclesiastes (3:16–17; 8:5–7; 11:9; 12:13–14) become ambiguous in the process of being merged with the wisdom tradition of "the changing times," thus leaving unresolved the question of the claim being made by these combined traditions.

Perdue, after reviewing four other possible opponents of Qohelet, concludes that he is countering the teachings of apocalyptic sages, that is, those who "combined apocalyptic language and thought with traditional wisdom and the Torah."[35] In other words, the type of person whom Reichenbach identifies with Qohelet himself, Perdue instead sees as Qohelet's foes, whose perspective is most clearly evident in Eccl 2:1–26; 3:10–15, 18–22; 4:1–5:19; 6:10–7:14; 9:1–10; and 11:1–9—in other words, nearly half of the book![36] Thus, in Eccl 7:1–10, Qohelet is citing and refuting an apocalyptic "theology of despair" that claims that the present is worse than the past, so that the wise cannot rejoice in the present world and therefore should be mourning.[37] Accordingly, Perdue understands Eccl 3:17 ("I said to myself, 'God will bring into judgment both the righteous and the wicked, for there will be a time for every activity, a time to judge every deed'") and 12:9–14 as redactional additions by the apocalyptic sages. Qohelet rejects the apocalypticists' foundational affirmations of divine justice, earthly retribution, moral dualism, and one's ability to correlate time and event for a successful outcome.[38]

---

34. Gregor Reichenbach, "'Zeit und Gericht' (Koh 8,5f): Anmerkungen zu Kohelets prophetischen Erbe," in *Mensch und König: Studien zur Anthropologie des Alten Testaments* (ed. Angelika Berlejung and Raik Heckl; Herders Biblische Studien; Freiburg im Breisgau: Herder, 2008), 192.

35. Leo Perdue, "Wisdom and Apocalyptic: The Case of Qohelet," in *Wisdom and Apocalypticism in the Dead Sea Scrolls and in the Biblical Tradition* (ed. F. García Martínez; BETL 168; Leuven: Leuven University Press/Peeters, 2003), 245.

36. Ibid., 245. The total number of verses listed here by Perdue is 109 out of 222 verses in the book.

37. Ibid., 246.

38. Ibid., 247.

He also opposes the apocalyptic themes of one's ability to know the divine character, eschatological judgment, and life after death.[39]

Douglas essentially expands on Perdue's thesis to monograph length by offering detailed discussions of three texts previously identified by Perdue, which Douglas labels as belonging to "an anti-apocalyptic genre": Eccl 3:10–22; 7:1–10; and 9:1–10.[40] According to Douglas, Qohelet "desires to turn his audience away from the grandiose expectations of the apocalyptic eschatology of his day... He focuses their attention on this absurd, meaningless, vain life and encourages them to enjoy it."[41]

In light of these four representative studies of prophetic influence on Qohelet and the shaping of the book of Ecclesiastes, one might conclude that this sage not only was familiar with but also primarily motivated by prophetic eschatological or apocalyptic visions to offer his perspective as a counter-proposal or corrective. However, a number of questions can be raised. First of all, are their overall interpretations of the book and of its individual texts sound? Ecclesiastes is a literary text for which, to a greater extent than most other books in the Hebrew Bible, one's overall interpretation of the book dramatically influences or even determines one's interpretation of its individual texts. This begins with the meaning and implications of the repeated use of הבל throughout the book. Is the author's point that, in light of his denial of a knowable God, one's ability through wisdom to influence one's destiny or even one's life now, a final judgment, and a life beyond the grave, life is senseless or worthless, except for the brief moments of joy which one may be able to grasp? Or is he claiming rather that, although all human actions and influences "under the sun" are ephemeral and can be ineffective, there is nevertheless a dimension to life that actually matters, that sooner or later will be judged by God, and that thus endures because the eternal God has placed it in the human heart (Eccl 3:11)? The authors of the four publications summarized above are dependent on the former interpretation for their thesis to be valid.

---

39. Ibid., 251.

40. Jerome N. Douglas, *A Polemical Preacher of Joy: An Anti-Apocalyptic Genre for Qohelet's Message of Joy* (Eugene: Pickwick, 2014), 113–33. Douglas differs from Perdue in that Perdue considers Qohelet's opponents to be "apocalyptic sages" while Douglas views them as "apocalyptic seers." "Qoheleth speaks against special revelation, the ability to change one's life and status, and a final judgment understanding of retribution" (ibid., 111).

41. Ibid., 134. It is unusual to characterize a literary genre merely by negation. He offers the following definition of "genre": "Genre is flexible, anchored to authorial will, and centered on the *foci* of setting and function" (44).

Second, the question of the relationship between prophecy and wisdom is being answered by Perdue and Douglas primarily in terms of extrabiblical and post-prophetic texts, which makes the analysis of such influence more difficult than when Krüger notes a literary allusion in Eccl 1:9–10 to Isa 43:18–19 and 65:17. This is not to dispute the list of key apocalyptic features or themes that scholars such as John Collins have noted in multiple publications,[42] but it is not obvious that Qohelet explicitly rejects all of these. For example, Collins notes that the apocalyptic genre commonly involves "a revelation [that] is mediated by an otherworldly being to a human recipient, disclosing a transcendent reality,"[43] whereas it is commonly claimed that, for Qohelet, there is no possible knowledge of God because the deity does not communicate with humanity. Is this a necessary inference, for example, from texts like Eccl 3:11b (בלי אשר לא־ימצא האדם את־המעשׂה אשר־עשׂה האלהים מראשׁ ועד־סוף; "but without man ever guessing, from first to last, all the things that God brings to pass," TNK; compare NRSV: "yet they cannot find out what God has done from the beginning to the end"); 7:14 (על־דברת שׁלא ימצא האדם אחריו מאומה; "consequently, man may find no fault with Him," TNK; compare NRSV: "so that mortals may not find out anything that will come after them"), or 5:1 [ET 2] (כי האלהים בשׁמים ואתה על־הארץ על־כן יהיו דבריך מעטים; "For God is in heaven and you are on earth; that is why your words should be few," TNK)? In light of the book of Proverbs, one might suggest that the Hebrew sage simply did not address this subject (but see Prov 29:18—"Where there is no prophecy, the people cast off restraint, but happy are those who keep the law," NRSV; cf. also Eccl 8:5). Must a third-century BCE Qohelet necessarily take a stance on the issue?

Third, with regard to the confluence of the terms former, latter, new, and remembrance in both Isa 40–66 and Eccl 1 and the resultant claim that Qohelet is thereby "clearly distancing himself from a hopeful expectation" and making an "anti-eschatological" point, as Barbour claims,[44] it must be noted that these parallel terms have very different referents in the two books. Ecclesiastes 1:9–11 concerns the "defectiveness of the collective memory"[45] and "earlier" and "later" probably refer to people and their achievements (as in 4:11, rather than to "days" as in 7:10), since "not remembering" elsewhere in Ecclesiastes always refers to humans and

---

42. Ibid., 83–88, relying primarily on John Collins, "Towards the Morphology of a Genre," *Semeia* 14 (1978): 1–20.

43. Cited by Douglas, *A Polemical Preacher of Joy*, 59–60.

44. Barbour, *The Story of Israel*, 51.

45. Fox, *A Time to Tear Down*, 169.

their deeds (2:16; 5:20 [MT 19]; 9:5, 15). In Isaiah, however, these terms refer to eras or events resulting from divine action, which either are to be remembered or not remembered (Isa 43:18; 44:12; 46:8–9; 54:4; 63:10; 65:17). Whether or not the "new" in Eccl 1:9 simply refers to progress and innovation through human effort, the use of this word here should not be construed as denying the possibly of God the Creator (12:1) creating something new.

Finally, the claim that Qohelet's concept of (or denial of) "universal judgment" is derived from (or rejects) prophetic or apocalyptic eschatology needs further clarification. Reichenbach claims that Old Testament wisdom literature never speaks of divine judgment (*ein Gericht JHWHs*).[46] However, this may be suggested in Prov 29:26 (וּמֵיהוה מִשְׁפַּט־אִישׁ, "but it is from the LORD that one gets justice") as well as in Job 36:17 ("But now you are laden with the judgment due the wicked; judgment and justice have taken hold of you," cf. 34:5, 23). According to John Hartley: "Elihu states that God has found it necessary to devastate Job's former tranquil life for his own good. In an effort to discipline him, God has brought upon him the kind of *judgment due to the wicked, a just judgment.*"[47] In support of his claim, Reichenbach cites Isa 66:15–17; Joel 4:2; Zeph 3:6–8; and Mal 3:1–5. However, the key features of these texts (e.g., divine wrath, conflagration, slaying the wicked, the judging of the nations on the basis of their treatment of Israel, laying waste entire cities, a divine agent carrying out judgment, a refining of the people, and the listing of specific misdeeds) are all strikingly missing in Ecclesiastes, which appears to refer to both pre-mortem (5:6 [MT 5]; 7:17; 8:5–6, 12–13) and post-mortem (3:15–17; 11:9; 12:14) judgment, although distinguishing between the two is difficult.[48] Accordingly, it remains unclear that either Qohelet (or the editor of the book of Ecclesiastes, with regard to Eccl 12:14) is directly depending on or interacting with prophetic eschatology as developed in the Hebrew Bible.

In an intriguing 2002 essay, Eep Talstra asks regarding Second Isaiah and Qohelet: "Could one get them on speaking terms?" and concludes his nuanced affirmative response by noting that "Qohelet would agree with

---

46. Reichenbach, "Zeit und Gericht," 194.

47. John E. Hartley, *The Book of Job* (NICOT; Grand Rapids: Eerdmans, 1988), 474, emphasis original.

48. Richard Schultz, "'Fear God and Keep His Commandments' (Eccl 12:13): An Examination of Some Intertextual Relationships Between Deuteronomy and Ecclesiastes," in *For Our Good Always: Studies on the Message and Influence of Deuteronomy in Honor of Daniel I. Block* (ed. Jason S. DeRouchie, Jason Gile, and Kenneth J. Turner; Winona Lake: Eisenbrauns, 2013), 332–33.

Second Isaiah on the large gap between God's knowledge and human knowledge."[49] Qohelet clearly utilizes a number of terms, themes, and concepts that are more fully developed in prophetic texts like the book of Isaiah. However, a careful examination of the textual evidence cited by the scholars noted in this essay indicates that the extent of prophetic influence on Qohelet's thought as well as the degree to which his teaching reflects a fundamental polemic against prophetic or apocalyptic traditions is considerably less than has been claimed.

---

49. Eep Talstra, "Second Isaiah and Qohelet: Could One Get Them on Speaking Terms?," in *New Things: Eschatology in Old Testament Prophecy: Festschrift for Henk Leene* (ed. P. Postma et al.; ACEBT; Maastricht: Uitgeverij Shaker, 2002), 235.

From Where Should Apocalyptic Be Found?
The Book of Job as Key to Von Rad's Theory

Timothy Johnson

Introduction

Most accept that apocalypticism emerged from prophecy while wisdom has served as a distant, though significant, alternative.[1] However, Gerhard von Rad popularized the notion that wisdom served as the more likely source of apocalypse than prophecy.[2] Assuming a tradition-historical interpretive scheme, von Rad questioned whether prophecy could be the satisfactory womb out of which apocalypses came forth:

> The decisive factor, as I see it, is the incompatibility between apocalyptic literature's view of history and that of the prophets. The prophetic message is specifically rooted in the saving history, that is to say, it is rooted in definite election traditions. But there is no way which leads from this to the apocalyptic view of history.[3]

Thus, the Israelite history so central to prophecy but diminished in apocalyptic functioned as the key stumbling block to the primacy of prophecy. For von Rad, it was unlikely that prophecy could serve as the predecessor to apocalyptic because traditions build on that which precedes.

---

1. For a review of the relationship between apocalypses and prophecy, see my entry, "Apocalypticism, Apocalyptic Literature," in *Dictionary of the Old Testament: Prophets* (ed. Mark J. Boda and J. Gordon McConville; Downers Grove: Intervarsity, 2012).

2. For an excellent history of scholarship on the relationship of wisdom and apocalypse see the second chapter of Elizabeth Johnson, *The Function of Apocalyptic and Wisdom Traditions in Romans 9–11* (Atlanta: Scholars, 1989). She indicates the first discussion of this relationship occurred in the early twentieth century (56).

3. Gerhard von Rad, *Old Testament Theology* (trans. D. M. G. Stalker; New York: Harper & Row, 1965), 2:303.

While von Rad's ideas yielded an exciting crop of fresh research, contemporary scholars remain unconvinced primarily because wisdom lacks overt eschatology, which Matthew Goff notes is prevalent in postexilic prophecy.[4] However, this rejection fails to address von Rad's insistence that eschatology is not the most elemental feature of apocalypses. More will be said on this aspect of von Rad's theory later, but to reject his hypothesis without addressing this critical assertion cannot bury the theory once and for all.

Goff then points out that von Rad's reliance on Ecclesiastes and Ben Sira to support his theory was flawed because these two wisdom books existed after modern scholarship had determined the oldest apocalypses emerged in the third century BCE in "The Book of the Watchers" and the "Astronomical Book of 1 Enoch."[5]

While Goff is correct to recognize an exemplar pre-dating the Hellenistic growth of apocalypses is required to make von Rad's case, the earlier phase of the rise of apocalypse during the postexilic period allows for the possibility that a postexilic wisdom text could also function as the source for an exemplar.[6] I would also add that Ecclesiastes and Ben Sira are not effective exemplars because neither reveals core generic features readily associated with apocalypses such as a narrative framework, cosmological conflict, or, especially, direct revelation.[7]

I suggest the book of Job is a better candidate for von Rad's elusive exemplar because of its quasi-wisdom status, its postexilic dating, and most significantly because it may evidence an early form of apocalypse as its governing genre.

---

4. Matthew Goff, "Wisdom and Apocalypticism," in *The Oxford Handbook of Apocalyptic Literature* (ed. J. J. Collins; Oxford: Oxford University Press, 2014), 52, who then states, "the view that one should choose wisdom rather than prophecy to understand the origins of apocalypticism problematically minimizes the view that the prophetic tradition is foundational in the development of apocalypticism" (59–60).

5. Ibid., 60.

6. See for example, Paul Hanson, "Apocalyptic Consciousness," *Quarterly Review* 4 (1984): 28–39.

7. Several regular features associated with apocalypses will be discussed later in the essay of which these three are more or less central. In a recent work that may also undermine von Rad's choice of Ecclesiastes, Jerome Douglas argues Ecclesiastes reflects an "anti-apocalyptic" genre. *A Polemical Preacher of Joy: An Anti-Apocalyptic Genre for Qoheleth's Message of Joy* (Eugene: Pickwick, 2014).

Job as Candidate for Von Rad's Thesis

Since most have held that the book of Job is ensconced in the wisdom corpus, such a seemingly alien suggestion may seem absurd. However, the proposal is not entirely novel. Indeed, several leading voices have intimated a friendly relationship between Job and apocalypse exists, and my own research has sought to put some flesh on those suggestive bones.

I do not argue that Job is a fully developed apocalypse, per se. I argue that various literary and thematic indicators reveal extremely close resemblances to what modern scholars now recognize as apocalypse.[8] A brief illustration may help to make my point.

Near my town is a wonderful place called "Old World Wisconsin," where mid-nineteenth-century Wisconsin is recreated in the form of communities reflecting the look and feel of that period. A game is played there called "Rounders," which consists of two nine-man teams on an unkempt field containing four bases in the shape of a diamond. A small, crude ball made of old shoe-rubber scraps encased in leather and stitches is tossed underhanded to a man with a wooden bat who tries to hit the ball and then run as many bases as possible before being deemed out.

Naturally, the modern observer identifies "Rounders" as the precursor to baseball. Rounders was a less developed form of baseball, with no fences over which a ball could be hit to earn what is now called a homerun and no fireworks that punctuated such hits. No one could steal bases, curve balls did not exist, and one umpire observed the game to the side of the field, only speaking when the teams could not agree on disputes. There were no food vendors to season the air and parking was never a problem. Much has changed in over 150 years, and while the old form of baseball did not include the spectacular sights, sounds, and smells we have come to expect with modern-day baseball, the core features of the modern game were already present.

I argue that Job is to an apocalypse what Rounders is to baseball: something different, but something with sufficiently shared characteristics as to conclude they are members of the same family. I suggest Job represents an early stage of what has come to be called apocalypse.

---

8. To date most reviewers seem unpersuaded but are nevertheless intrigued and many suggest my research merits further attention. For example, see Katharine J. Dell's review in *JSOT* 35 (2011): 121–22, which states the work "deserves to have an important place in the discussion of the genre of the ever-enigmatic book of Job" (122).

Those who insist Job can only be considered a part of Wisdom literature must reconcile the fact that Job is not conveniently classified as wisdom, and that is also not a particularly new revelation. Roland Murphy, one of the most influential authorities on Wisdom literature, recognized that "the author of the book of Job moved outside of strict wisdom genres."[9]

Equally authoritative, James Crenshaw commented that "a case can be made against Job as a wisdom writing," and in his important introduction to Wisdom literature he lists Job as part of the collection of wisdom texts "with reservations."[10]

No book in the Bible has received more generic attention with an eye toward discovering a more fitting hermeneutical category than the book of Job. It is therefore proper to take a moment to reflect on genre.

A Word on Genre

John Collins reminds us the terms apocalypse and apocalyptic "are modern analytical categories that coincide only partially with ancient generic labels. There was little sustained generic analysis in either ancient Judaism or early Christianity."[11]

Goff joins Collins in applying this caution to both apocalypse and wisdom, observing that some even question whether we can usefully deploy generic labels at all. He notes that since both wisdom and apocalypse are "modern constructs," interpreters need to be "cautious and careful" in how they impose the generic categories on the ancient texts.[12] These are telling words.

Along those lines, it is worth noting the term apocalypse is derived from the Greek word ἀποκαλύπτω, which generally means to reveal or disclose. Employed in the book of Revelation, which older Bibles entitled "The Apocalypse of John," the use of the generic term apocalypse is therefore historically and organically grounded in that canonical work. Yet in several instances the Apocalypse of John self-identifies as a prophecy (1:3; 22:7, 10, 18, 19).

---

9. Roland Murphy, *Wisdom Literature: Job, Proverbs, Ruth, Canticles, and Esther* (FOTL 13; Grand Rapids: Eerdmans, 1981), 3.

10. James Crenshaw, *Old Testament Wisdom: An Introduction* (Atlanta: John Knox, 1981), 16–17.

11. John J. Collins, "What Is Apocalyptic Literature?," in Collins, ed., *The Oxford Handbook of Apocalyptic Literature*, 1.

12. Goff, "Wisdom and Apocalypticism," 66.

Have we crossed some sacred boundary by imposing a modern label of apocalypse onto a self-described prophecy? What would it mean for us to interpret Revelation as prophecy instead of apocalypse, assuming we could understand what John meant by prophecy? Do we know better? Generic labels must be approached with greater measures of humility than certainty.

To be sure, having some understanding of genre is absolutely critical for developing a responsible approach to interpretation, even if pursued cautiously. Concerning Job's genre, Claus Westermann noted, "the whole question of literary form would become significant only if the judgment concerning literary classification were to have a decisive effect upon the exegesis of the book."[13] Thus, the pursuit of an overarching genre for Job is worth the effort.

As testimony to the challenge of discerning Job's literary classification, some of the most helpful discussions on its genre occur among those who dare to stand on the floating log that is the genre of Job;[14] all will get wet in the process and expend much energy seeking balance.

While an oversimplification, studies in genre tend toward two approaches. Some prefer classification that seeks objective criteria by which to determine a work's genre. Such studies tend to stem from Gunkel's program to categorize various forms in order to establish an appropriate *Sitz im Leben*.[15] Various works are compared and often help winnow away those that fit the criteria and those that do not.

Others prefer less objective paradigms and instead emphasize the process of communication as the determinant locale for genre.[16] In this case the reader is privileged, and developing a sense of genre while reading is more of a subjective process than a final declaration. Such approaches resist efforts to superimpose genre on interpreters, preferring instead to extend the possibilities.

---

13. Claus Westermann, *The Structure of the Book of Job: A Form-Critical Analysis* (trans. Charles Meunchow; Philadelphia: Fortress, 1981), 1.

14. For example, see Katharine J. Dell, *The Book of Job as Sceptical Literature* (BZAW 197; Berlin: de Gruyter, 1997), and Tremper Longman III, "Form Criticism, Recent Developments in Genre Theory, and the Evangelical," *WTJ* 47 (1985): 46–67.

15. Hermann Gunkel, *The Psalms: A Form-Critical Introduction* (Philadelphia: Fortress, 1967; translation of *Die Religion in Geschichte und Gegenwart* [2nd ed.; J. C. B. Mohr (Paul Siebeck), 1930]).

16. For example, see Alastair Fowler, *Kinds of Literature: An Introduction to the Theory of Genres and Modes* (Cambridge, MA: Harvard University Press, 1982), 20–23.

In my estimation, E. D. Hirsch continues to hold the high ground in arguing that meaning is genre bound, and, as such, the pursuit of a work's genre is paramount if we are to establish basic community-wide rules for interpretation.[17] This is essential since readers naturally intuit genres when they interpret, even if they cannot commit to a particular interpretive genre. Carol Newsom notes readers best discern a genre by recognizing "[p]atterns of similarity and dissimilarity, that is, the recognition that the text at hand is like these and not those."[18] John Collins notes that this phenomenon is part of the natural process of reading:

> An interpreter always begins with an assumption about the genre of a text. If our expectations are fulfilled, the assumptions will reveal no revision. If they are not fulfilled, we must revise our idea of genre or relinquish the attempt to understand. There can be no understanding without at least an implicit notion of genre.[19]

While we must proceed cautiously in discerning Job's genre, we must continue to attempt.

Why Job Is Not Easily Categorized as Wisdom

Over the centuries scholarship has been remarkably uncomfortable identifying Job as wisdom, and the number of alternative suggestions testifies to it.[20] This indicates the need for revision, and my research proffers that while the book of Job conveys elements of wisdom, the overarching pattern of the book is more like proto-apocalypse and less like formal wisdom.

Due in large part to the presumption that the book of Job's purpose is to examine unjust suffering, scholarship has tended to consider it a wisdom text. However, prophets such as Habakkuk, and some chapters in Psalms, also engage the question of unjust suffering and yet they are not considered part of the wisdom corpus.

---

17. Eric Donald Hirsch, *Validity in Interpretation* (New Haven: Yale University Press, 1967), 71–77.

18. Carol Newsom, *The Book of Job: A Contest of Moral Imaginations* (Oxford: Oxford University Press, 2003), 4, 11.

19. John J. Collins, *The Apocalyptic Imagination: An Introduction to Jewish Apocalyptic Literature* (2nd ed.; Grand Rapids: Eerdmans, 1998), 8.

20. For a brief survey see Timothy Johnson, *Now My Eye Sees You: Unveiling an Apocalyptic Job* (Sheffield: Sheffield Phoenix, 2012), 23–37.

Having said that, Job is not without significant wisdom features. For example, Job 28 addresses the search for wisdom in personified form, a theology of retribution is on display throughout, and the term "wisdom" seasons the story. Still, many question if the combined weight of those clues is sufficient to declare Job wisdom. Murphy denied Job easily aligns with wisdom, and instead noted that applying wisdom to Job is "merely a term of convenience."[21]

By contrast, most recognize Proverbs, Ecclesiastes, and the Deuterocanonical books Sirach and Wisdom of Solomon as the best representatives for Wisdom literature. These didactic books demonstrate proverbial, aphoristic, and axiomatic elements designed to provide concentrated training that do not reveal any hint of a narrative plot.

There are other important reasons Job does not easily conform to wisdom. For example, Job does not address the reader directly.[22] Similarly, one easily observes that Job does not offer explicit instruction to the reader, and direct divine speech is absent in the classic wisdom books.

Martin Shields characterizes well the conundrum scholarship has faced when declaring Job as wisdom literature: "Job is not an archetypal wisdom text in the way that Proverbs is, although Job is clearly styled as wisdom literature, albeit wisdom literature which has to look beyond the scope of wisdom to find its answers."[23]

Wisdom is an insufficient host and needs something else to bear fully the weight of Job's message. Shields appeals to prophecy as the antidote and in so doing contributes to a long line of scholars dissatisfied with wisdom. While his argument cannot overcome the non-existent prophet in Job who would mediate a direct word from the Lord, Shields does emphasize the importance of direct revelation in Job as a way to resolve the issue.[24] Direct revelation is also found in apocalyptic literature, which, in its earliest stages, may be a better designation for Job.

21. Murphy, *Wisdom*, 3.

22. Gerhard von Rad, *Wisdom in Israel* (trans. J. D. Martin; Nashville: Abingdon, 1972), 46.

23. See in this collection of essays M. Shields, "You Can't Get a Sage to Do a Prophet's Job: Overcoming Wisdom's Deficiency in the Book of Job" (p. 182).

24. Shields acknowledges prophecy's shortcomings in his proposal as well as the tenuous connection between Yahweh's theophany and the conventional requirement of a human mediator (ibid.). Richard Schultz concludes that prophetic influences on Ecclesiastes are "considerably less than has been claimed" (p. 214) perhaps indicating that the sages exhibit no clear dependence on the prophetic corpus; see in this collection, "Was Qohelet an Eschatological or an Anti-Apocalyptic Sage? *Hebel*, the Evil Day, and Divine Judgement in the Book of Ecclesiastes" (pp. 197–212).

Why Job Could Be Categorized as Apocalyptic

I am not the first to notice apocalyptic features in Job, and the list of those who have is impressive. John Collins indicates that of all the wisdom books in the Hebrew Bible, Job is most closely associated with apocalypse because the book's content orients its readers to find order where chaos has emerged. Furthermore, by employing a divine revelation via God's speech from the whirlwind, the book of Job reveals the key form associated with apocalypse.[25]

Richard Sewall suggests Job cannot be considered a tragedy because an apocalypse exists in Job.[26] Katharine Dell argues that Eliphaz's dream account in Job 4:12–21 may represent an apocalyptic form.[27] Commenting on the presence of a Paleo-Hebrew text of Job, which was the only non-Pentateuchal book discovered at Qumran in that ancient script, Frank Moore Cross found it intriguing that "Job's importance was not forgotten in apocalyptic circles."[28] Most significantly, the apocalyptic scholar Christopher Rowland declared that "the whole structure of the book of Job offers an embryonic form of the later apocalypse."[29] Like Collins, Rowland also recognizes the central apocalyptic feature of divine revelation present in the whirlwind, but he also draws attention to the fact that the reader is not addressed directly in the book.[30]

While none of these scholars either fully investigated Job's relationship to apocalypse or explicitly declared Job an apocalypse, the initial evidence the book of Job could represent an early, undeveloped form of apocalypse is provocative.

To explore this possibility further I compared both the content and various forms of Job to the master paradigm on apocalyptic established by the Society of Biblical Literature's Genres Project Study Group, which likely represents the most objective test of whether or not a book can be considered a member of the apocalyptic family.[31]

25. John J. Collins, "Cosmos and Salvation: Jewish Wisdom and Apocalyptic in the Hellenistic Age," *History of Religions* 17 (1977): 140 n. 3.

26. Richard Sewall, *The Vision of Tragedy* (enlarged ed.; New Haven: Yale University Press, 1980), 23.

27. Dell, *Sceptical Literature*, 104.

28. Frank Moore Cross, "New Directions in the Study of Apocalyptic," *JTC* 6 (1969): 163.

29. Christopher Rowland, *The Open Heaven: A Study of Apocalyptic in Judaism and Early Christianity* (New York: Crossroad, 1982), 207.

30. Ibid., 206.

31. John J. Collins, "Introduction: Towards the Morphology of a Genre," *Semeia* 14 (1979): 1–20. I chose the master paradigm as my point of departure for

The Apocalyptic Matrix

The study group condensed their work into the following definition:

> Apocalypse is a genre of revelatory literature with a narrative framework, in which a revelation is mediated by an otherworldly being to a human recipient, disclosing a transcendent reality which is both temporal, insofar as it envisages eschatological salvation, and spatial, insofar as it involves another, supernatural world.[32]

The master paradigm represents a classificatory approach to discerning whether or not a particular work identifies as an apocalypse. I present the paradigm so readers may follow my brief comparison of Job to the paradigm and judge for themselves. It is important to note not all apocalypses share every feature listed in the paradigm. However, any work commonly considered an apocalypse will exhibit several of the traits listed. The paradigm consists of thirteen main features:[33]

Master Paradigm

Manner of Revelation
1. Medium by which the revelation is communicated
    1.1. Visual revelation in the form of:
        1.1.1. Visions, or
        1.1.2. Epiphanies (describing apparition of mediator)
    1.2. Auditory revelation usually clarifies the visual by:
        1.2.1. Discourse (uninterrupted speech by mediator), or
        1.2.2. Dialogue (between mediator and recipient)
    1.3. Otherworldly journey (heaven, hell, remote places)
    1.4. Writing (revelation contained in written document)
2. Otherworldly mediator communicates revelation
3. The human recipient
    3.1. Pseudonymity
    3.2. Disposition of recipient (circumstances, emotions)
    3.3. Reaction of recipient (often awe and/or perplexity)

comparison because it is the result of rigorous efforts on the part of respected scholars to help bring clarity to an otherwise murky field of study. For critiques of the master paradigm, see Robert Webb, "Apocalyptic: Observations on a Slippery Term," *JNES* 49 (1990): 115–26, and David Hellholm, "The Problem of Apocalyptic Genre and the Apocalypse of John," *Semeia* 36 (1986): 1–12.

32. Collins, "Morphology," 9.
33. Ibid., 5–8.

Content of Revelation: Temporal Axis
  4. Protology (pre-history or beginning of history)
     4.1. Theogony and/or Cosmogony (origin of God/Pleroma, and/or cosmos)
     4.2. Primordial events having paradigmatic significance
  5. History, viewed as:
     5.1. Explicit recollection of the past, or
     5.2. *Ex Eventu* prophecy
  6. Present salvation through knowledge (in Gnostic texts)
  7. Eschatological crisis, in the form of:
     7.1. Persecution, and/or
     7.2. Other eschatological upheavals (disturbing the order of nature or history)
  8. Eschatological judgment and/or destruction upon:
     8.1. The wicked, or the ignorant (in Gnostic texts)
     8.2. The natural world
     8.3. Otherworldly beings
  9. Eschatological salvation, may involve:
     9.1. Cosmic transformation (renewal of entire world)
     9.2. Personal salvation
          9.2.1. Resurrection in bodily form, or
          9.2.2. Other forms of afterlife (such as exaltation to heaven with angels)
Content of Revelation: Spatial Axis
  10. Otherworldly elements
     10.1. Otherworldly regions (described usually in otherworldly journeys)
     10.2. Otherworldly beings (angelic or demonic)
Paraenesis
  11. Paraenesis (by mediator to the recipient)
Concluding Elements
  12. Instructions to the recipient
  13. Narrative conclusion

Does Job Conform to the Master Paradigm?
The reader familiar with Job will notice several areas where the story fits this classification, some more easily than others. Sprinting through the master paradigm,[34] none can dispute Job contains at least one important revelation (Section 1): the whirlwind speech whereby God discloses

---

34. Each section of the paradigm receives greater attention in Johnson, *Now My Eye Sees You*, 47–65.

important lessons on creation and his sovereignty. However one interprets this message, it is a revelation and it does lead to a substantial change in Job's disposition.

As noted earlier, Dell sees Eliphaz's vision as an apocalyptic form, and such a form, like the whirlwind speech, is inconsistent with wisdom books. Eliphaz is confronted by a supernatural voice that transcends his own historical framework.[35]

Drawing on Stephen Geller's work, I argued Job 28 also represents a revelation since it reveals the futility of discovering wisdom on earth. Geller understands Job 28:23b "almost as much a theophany as the divine speech out of the whirlwind."[36] Some are not convinced, but the mysterious mine and the magnitude of the content of the revelation should not be easily dismissed.[37]

God's whirlwind speech (Job 38–41) and Eliphaz's vision (Job 4:12–21) more than satisfy the paradigm's demand for a revelation and all the attendant features typically associated with apocalyptic revelations as indicated in sections 1.1–1.4 of the master paradigm.[38]

In each case, there is an otherworldly mediator (section 2) and a human recipient (section 3) whose reactions and dispositions are detailed for the reader. Eliphaz is terrified at the vision and Job is awed after God's message is completed.

All three of the proposed revelations display protological impulses (section 4). Eliphaz's vision wonders if humans can be considered pure before their Maker (Job 4:17b), God is disclosed as the source of wisdom in Job 28:23–28, and the whirlwind speech is rife with creation imagery as God challenges Job. Job's frequent remembrances of his former life may conform to historical recollections of the past (section 5).

---

35. See also Shields's essay in the present volume, who considers Eliphaz's vision a "special revelation" (p. 184).

36. Stephen Geller, '"Where Is Wisdom?': A Literary Study of Job 28 in Its Setting," in *Judaic Perspectives on Ancient Israel* (ed. J. Neusner, B. Levine and E. Frerichs; Philadelphia: Fortress, 1987), 165.

37. In his review of my work, Michael Moore is most critical of my assessment labeling Geller's claim as an "off-the-cuff remark" in *RBL* 06/2012. However, C. R. A. Morray-Jones seems to accept my proposal on the basis of Job 28's "revelatory qualities...which have been ably pointed out by Stephen A. Geller" ("The Opening of Heaven in the Book of Job," in *Revealed Wisdom: Studies in Apocalyptic in Honour of Christopher Rowland* [ed. J. Ashton; Ancient Judaism and Early Christianity 88; Leiden: Brill, 2014], 31).

38. In his review of my work, Scott Jones suggested that Elihu's speeches could also be treated as revelation, *RBL* 02/2011, 223.

While the story does not seemingly point to salvation through knowledge (section 6), the character Job nevertheless arrives at a better place after he received important knowledge. For example, after Job's confrontation with God he recognizes his inferiority and repents. Key corrections ensue, such as God rebuking the friends, God restoring Job's fortunes, and Job dying at a ripe old age. While not eschatological salvation, Job's life improves dramatically.

It is true an overtly eschatological crisis is lacking in the story (section 7). However, the master paradigm suggests two important characteristics of this crisis: persecution and upheaval. These are present in Job, albeit without obvious eschatological nuances.

Job is unrelentingly persecuted by his friends, who seek to convince him he has done something to merit his punishment, and Job resists. It is a crisis for Job, if not for the reader who, unlike Job, knows God has put Job forward because of his blamelessness.

Job's life is a full-blown upheaval from that which was normal. He has lost everything of material and personal value, questions his own existence (Job 3), and critiques the predictable theology of retribution to which both he and his friends subscribe.

In a similar fashion, we do not see eschatological judgment in Job (section 8), but insofar as judgment plays a part in the story, we cannot deny its presence. Eliphaz is singled out among the friends for judgment in the epilogue for not speaking about Yahweh correctly, and Job receives his own judgment of restoration after he retreats.

A final eschatological feature of salvation (section 9) accords with what has been said about Job concerning sections 7 and 8, namely, while the overt eschatological dressings are not obviously present, an early apocalyptic pattern does present itself again.

Job is "saved" insofar as his possessions are restored and he lives to be an old man. However, the master paradigm does specify a personal resurrection could be present, and in fact the LXX version of Job portrays Job as resurrected.[39] While space does not allow for a detailed discussion on the priority of the LXX vis-à-vis the MT, Job's resurrection was the accepted understanding in the early Christian church where it was the authoritative Old Testament text.

---

39. See Albert Pietersma and Ben Wright, eds., *A New Translation of the Septuagint* (New York: Oxford University Press, 2007) where Job 42:17a (alpha) reads, "And it is written that he will rise again with those the Lord raises up."

Otherworldy elements (section 10) abound in Job, from the prologue's depiction of the satan and the heavenly court to Eliphaz's dream to the mysterious mining location to the theophany. Rare is the apocalypse that includes paraenesis (section 11), but the messages concerning human sin in Eliphaz's vision, the location of wisdom in Job 28, and other various ethical admonitions such as those in Job 29–31 may serve as legitimate candidates.

When God instructs Eliphaz to offer a sacrifice to atone for his and the other two friends' errors, the placement of specific instructions that contribute to the close of the story emerges (section 12). Finally, the narrative conclusion (section 13) conforms undeniably.

Taken as a whole, the degree to which the framework, theme, and story of Job conform to the master paradigm should surely force an objective reader to take notice. If one is able to set aside the initially anticipated apocalyptic furnishings of fantastic beasts, eschatological clashes, and the consummation of time associated with later apocalypses and instead note that shared but less developed principles undergird the story, more might give serious consideration to the suggestion that Job may represent an early fossil of the growth of apocalypse that seemed to reach beyond the close of the Old Testament canon and was preserved in later writings.

Traditions' Evidence of an Apocalyptic Job
As mentioned, the LXX's depiction of a resurrected Job may be evidence of an apocalyptic understanding of Job. The *Testament of Job* also includes various eschatological strands such that Collins suggested it "shows certain affinities with Jewish apocalyptic" whose "deeper structures...might be more purposefully located in a class of works which mediate an opposition between heavenly reality and earthly illusion, than in the class of 'testaments' to which it superficially belongs."[40]

Preserving the essential story of Job, the *Testament of Job* seems to elaborate the main storyline and shape it more toward an apocalyptic interpretation. Resurrection plays a heightened role, as does the satan, an angelic presence, and more explicit cosmic imagery.

---

40. John J. Collins, "Structure and Meaning in the Testament of Job," in *Society of Biblical Literature Seminar Papers, 1974* (ed. George MacRae; 2 vols.; SBLSP; Cambridge: Scholars Press, 1974), 1:49, 51.

In the New Testament Job only appears in Jas 5:1–11, which is a passage containing sufficient eschatological and apocalyptic influences that scholarship suggests an apocalyptic worldview is present.[41] Job is the only biblical figure identified by name, and he is regarded as a model for how to endure in the midst of suffering.

This portrait of Job in James was replicated in the third-century apocryphal discussion of heaven and hell in the *Apocalypse of Paul*, where Job is encouraged by the devil, instead of Job's wife, to "speak a word against the Lord and die."[42] That the story of Job lent itself to apocalyptic interpretations can also be seen in later medieval works.[43]

Thus, some Jewish and Christian traditions reveal a strong witness to Job's association with key apocalyptic markers such as perseverance, resurrection, and eschatology, thereby indicating that the story allows for an apocalyptic interpretation.[44]

A Brief Reading of an Apocalyptic Job

A more apocalyptic interpretation of Job picks up on the cosmological crisis in which Job finds himself and the question of whether or not he will endure. I have proposed the following outline for the story, pivoting on the three suggested revelations that serve to unify the book around my proposed intrinsic genre of nascent apocalypse:[45]

41. Patrick Hartin, *A Spirituality of Perfection: Faith in Action in the Letter of James* (Collegeville: Liturgical Press, 1999), 11, 54–55 n. 51.

42. See Hugo Duensing, "Apocalypse of Paul," in *New Testament Apocrypha* (ed. E. Hennecke and W. Schneemelcher; trans. R. Wilson; 2 vols.; Philadelphia: Westminster, 1964), 2:755–98.

43. My research suggests Cynewulf's *Ascension* (lines 633–658) and the *Phoenix* (lines 546–575a) both portray Job as an important witness to Christ's resurrection and resurrection in general. Another example is in the Old French paraphrase of Job where he testifies to the promise of resurrection and judgement day. See Johnson, *Now My Eye Sees You*, 100.

44. Dell's *JSOT* review of my work appreciates the insight into how some of tradition has read Job in more apocalyptic ways, but she correctly points out that just because later interpreters viewed Job this way does not confirm that was the original author's intent (121). See also Jones's *RBL* review, which found this part of my research to be "the most important contribution of the book" (226).

45. The idea of an intrinsic genre is taken from Hirsch (*Validity*, 86), who recognized that while more than one genre can be deployed in a literary work, there exists a guiding genre for the whole of the work that functions as a "means of which an interpreter can correctly understand any part in its determinacy." Having said that, I do assume a final-form reading of MT Job and am therefore seeking to understand

1:1–4:11	Job's Demise and Challenge
4:12–28:22	Revelation of Humanity's Unrighteousness: Job Persecuted
28:23–37:24	Revelation of Humanity's Lack of Wisdom: Job Encouraged
38:1–42:6	Revelation of Humanity's Powerlessness: Job Repents
42:7–42:17	Job's Victory and Rewards

I suggest the main plot revolves around whether or not Job will curse God to his face, as twice predicted by the satan (Job 1:11; 2:5). The reader is aware Job is blameless in God's eyes and not deserving the catastrophes that follow. Thus, the reader awaits a time when Job will have an audience with God to see if in fact he will curse God to his face.

As Job suffers in the cosmologically originating crisis in which he finds himself, the friends enter the scene as unwitting conduits of the satan. Eliphaz's revelation concerning humanity's unrighteous standing before God (Job 4:17–21) initiates the battle for Job's soul as the friends level charges against Job, whom they incorrectly deduce has claimed to be righteous himself, seeking to persuade Job to repent of something he's done and so return to a life of bliss.[46] But by capitulating to these entreaties, Job would prove the satan correct, namely, that Job only serves God because God has blessed him so richly. The reader wonders if Job will persevere.

Even as Job finds comfort in ch. 28's revelation that wisdom cannot be found on earth, least of all with his so-called friends, he nevertheless persists in his self-justifying claim of innocence, seeking an audience with God. Elihu's entrance serves as a final snare to condemn Job's desire to defend himself in God's presence, but the reader both anticipates and pines for that encounter with God, for only in that exchange will we learn if Job will actually curse God to his face.

---

either the original author's intention or a final redactor's. In his review of my work, J. Huddleston felt "this attempt to read Job in conversation with apocalypse does shed interesting light on the book's unity" (*Biblical Interpretation* 21 [2013]: 425).

46. C. R. A. Morray-Jones, "The Opening of Heaven in the Book of Job," in *Revealed Wisdom: Studies in Apocalyptic in Honour of Christopher Rowland* (ed. John Ashton; Boston: Brill, 2014), 10–36 (32), while critical of various aspects of my research, still seems to accept the overall trajectory of the project, suggesting that some of the readings I offer "may advance our understanding of the apocalyptic dimension of Job as the book now stands." Morray-Jones offers that Eliphaz's vision is not from God, but from the satan instead (32). This intriguing suggestion does not detract from an apocalyptic reading and may instead advance it.

When Yahweh presents himself to Job in the great theophany (Job 38–41), he ends the battle for Job's soul, saving Job from the friends and himself, but in so doing he reveals Job is wrong to question his ordering of the universe, including, by implication, the place of suffering. Laden with creation imagery, God reinforces his sovereignty over all the nuances of life, good or bad.

Humbled, if not humiliated, Job concedes he had no right to challenge God and therefore retreats. In accepting God's control over all the affairs of life, Job is rewarded while the friends are condemned. Justice is meted out.

Such a reading emphasizes the role of persevering in the midst of an attack on one's faith. If at any point Job capitulated to the friends or Elihu, the satan would have been able to claim victory. However, the most critical question is whether or not Job would actually curse God to his face, which does not happen. In that victory for Job, the satan is defeated. God wins, Job wins, and the satan's unwitting minions are judged.

This storyline follows nicely the major lines of apocalyptic plots. The hero's faith is put to the test in the midst of substantial conflict. For the one who perseveres, life and rewards await.

While pure eschatological drama is seemingly absent, the core elements of an apocalypse exist and thereby offer a generic framework from which one can see the main point of Job, which is to maintain one's faith in the battles of an upside-down world where good appears as evil and evil appears as good. A future eschatological judgment is not explicitly addressed, but even the restoration of Job's possessions is future to his struggles. An implicit message for readers may very well be to fix their eyes on God's future righteous judgment in the midst of their personal suffering.[47] In every epoch of human history, such a message resonates.

One Implication Is That Wisdom Could Be a Source for Apocalypse

If this treatment of Job is plausible, it opens up the possibility that Job may serve as a canonical artifact of the transition from wisdom to apocalypse. As noted earlier, Job certainly contains wisdom ideas, but the book of Job is different than traditional wisdom in that it transports the reader beyond reflection and into urgent action. It is more exhortation than instruction as our author has done something unique with those sagacious questions.

---

47. I am indebted to Russell Meek for this insight.

The story may give us a glimpse into the cradle of "apocalyptic," which, if reflected in the story of Job as I suggest, emerged out of a search for the meaning of life that transcended the limited Israelite history that otherwise dominates the Old Testament. That Job the non-Israelite is preserved in the Jewish canon is itself worthy of attention, but perhaps the story's potential missional role as a bridge between philosophical specu-lation and belief in the God of Israel through sustained faith in the midst of chaos merits even further consideration.

Perhaps anticipating that wisdom's lack of eschatological contours would weaken his proposal, von Rad argued early on that "knowledge" instead of history is the "nerve-centre of apocalyptic literature," suggesting the "real matrix" for apocalyptic is wisdom.[48] Rowland also recognized the apocalypticists "depended on the disclosure from God of the answers to questions which were impossible to elucidate by human reason alone."[49]

Later, in his *Wisdom in Israel,* von Rad acknowledged an "eschatologi-cal orientation" was important to apocalypses, but still not the most essen-tial. Instead, it is the divine determination of times that is more central.[50]

Succeeding research such as that by Michael Stone helped promote von Rad's theory, but the lack of an exemplar has hindered the proposal.[51] Still, if von Rad's theory is to be rejected, it must first account for his efforts to situate an apocalypse's fundamental feature in knowledge and divine determination of times instead of critiquing it on purely eschato-logical expectations.

While neither of these traits are overtly enumerated in the master paradigm, they are both present in the book of Job. For example, the knowledge revealed about humanity's sin in Eliphaz's dream and lack of wisdom in the mine provide essential information apparently lacking. Additionally, Yahweh's declared sovereignty over all of life, including time and determined moments in life (Job 38:4, 12, 17, 23), indicates that both of von Rad's apocalyptic markers appear in Job, thereby qualifying it as a possible exemplar for his suggestion.

48. von Rad, *Old Testament Theology,* 2:306.

49. Rowland, *The Open Heaven,* 75. This theme is found in the classic apocalyptic works of Daniel and Revelation. For example, see Dan 7:15–28 and Rev 1:20. See also Matt 24:36 and Mark 13:32, where Jesus also acknowledged the need for divine disclosure.

50. von Rad, *Wisdom,* 278.

51. See Michael Stone, "List of Revealed Things in the Apocalyptic Literature," in *Magnalia Dei: The Mighty Acts of God: Essays on the Bible and Archaeology in Memory of G. Ernst Wright* (ed. F. Cross, W. Lemke, and P. Miller; Garden City: Doubleday, 1976), 414–52.

As a book widely believed to have been completed in its final form some time after the exile, Job would be a candidate for a canonical book that exhibits both mature questions associated with wisdom and structural features of a nascent form of apocalypse that pre-dates the Hellenistic burst of apocalypses.

Cross argues that Job is a sixth-century work that was heavily influenced by the "catastrophe of the exile," which was the period out of which the apocalyptic mind emerged.[52] This suggestion coincides with Paul Hanson's observation that the sixth-century exile was the first of two apocalyptic seasons, with the other being the Hellenistic explosion.[53]

The sixth century was a traumatic period of upheaval and turmoil in Judaism that Hartley claims stimulated the need for a book such as Job.[54] It is worth repeating that Cross, commenting on Job's influence at Qumran, considered Job "a major force in the evolution of Israel's religion" whose "importance was not forgotten in apocalyptic circles."[55]

Thus, the book of Job emerged in the first season of apocalyptic development after the exile and then again later in the second season as it deeply influenced the apocalyptic scribes crafting the Dead Sea Scrolls, the LXX, and the *Testament of Job*.

Perhaps there was an ancient tale of a non-Jewish man named Job, who, like other ancient Near Eastern wisdom characters, wrestled with the problems of evil, theodicy, retribution, and the location of wisdom. During the Babylonian captivity, Jewish scribes who seriously questioned whether or not historical Israel was ended may have looked beyond their own history and into the future. Finding a compatible partner in the sagacious story of Job, they may have framed that ancient tale into a narrative with its hero, protagonists, revelations, long conflict, and rewarding resolution into an exhortation to persevere in the midst of unexpected suffering and its attendant chaos, as Israel itself discovered it needed to do.

---

52. Frank M. Cross, "The Development of the Jewish Scripts," in *The Bible and the Ancient Near East: Essays in Honor of William Foxwell Albright* (ed. G. Ernst Wright; London: Routledge & Kegan Paul, 1961), 161–63.

53. Hanson, "Apocalyptic Consciousness." Hanson's seminal work that advocates for the primacy of prophecy in the growth of apocalyptic continues to serve as an influential and invaluable contribution to the discussion, *The Dawn of Apocalyptic: The Historical and Sociological Roots of Jewish Apocalyptic Eschatology* (rev. ed.; Philadelphia: Fortress, 1979).

54. John Hartley, *The Book of Job* (NICOT; Grand Rapids: Eerdmans, 1988), 50.

55. Cross, "New Directions," 163.

Part IV

RESPONSES

Response on Methodological Matters Regarding Wisdom Influence and on the Relationship Between Wisdom and Prophecy

Katharine J. Dell

"If the danger of a 'pan-chokmism' is to be avoided, care must be taken with definitions of wisdom and with inferences drawn from the texts about social milieu."[1] This quotation from van Leeuwen flags up the importance of a clear methodology when it comes to discussing biblical wisdom and its influence. These two aspects of definition on the one hand and social milieu on the other have come to define this particular discussion and are reflected in four of the five essays that I am responding to here. Meek cites this same article by van Leeuwen and says that "methodology is the critical issue in determining the relationship between wisdom and prophecy"—in fact the point that van Leeuwen makes, and that Meek draws out, is that we have the complication of dealing with two literary stages in our consideration of all these texts—that of the final "canonical" form of the corpus or that of "the original life and literary settings."[2] Whilst modern leanings are toward final redactional stages and canonical shaping, much of the older discussion of links between wisdom and prophecy has focused on form-critical concerns, and it seems that we are unwilling to let go of this method when it comes to discussing the relationship between wisdom and prophecy. This tension also characterizes much of the discussion in these four essays. The issues are slightly different in the fifth essay on the ancient Near Eastern material, and so I devote a separate section to it at the end of my article.

---

1. R. van Leeuwen, "The Sage in the Prophetic Literature," in *The Sage in Israel and the Ancient Near East* (ed. John G. Gammie and Leo. G. Perdue; Winona Lake: Eisenbrauns, 1990), 297.
2. Van Leeuwen, "The Sage in the Prophetic Literature," 295.

I have isolated four main areas of concern that seem to me to arise from a consideration of these four essays on methodology and of the wider topic: genre issues, the definition of wisdom, the nature of wisdom influence, and discussion of scribal culture and what that entailed. I shall therefore divide this response into these four areas and then add a fifth on the ancient Near Eastern discussion. It is a great pleasure for me to be invited to respond in this way, and any criticisms of perspectives not my own are simply reflections of my own "wisdom worldview."

Genre Issues

It is clear that the form-critical method dominated this discussion of possible wisdom influence in the prophetic literature, and indeed many other discussions, for a long time, as Meek makes clear. Its legacy casts a long shadow. Discussion of "genres" is a direct result of the form-critical method that defines a genre or *Gattung* according to the three categories of form, content, and context.[3] It is increasingly clear that the "form" category as applied in this definition is too narrow and restrictive and that talk of genre is best released from this particular straightjacket, i.e., the title "form criticism." Kynes makes this point, citing Blum,[4] that strictly form categories do not work. I would agree that they should not be given priority over other categories, but they do "work" to a certain degree in that they help us to classify material. Meek suggests that we seek a "more refined methodology" and indicates that the answer lies in pursuing an intertextual method. This raises the question for me whether intertextual method has in fact replaced genre analysis? There is always a danger that we find new techniques more to our liking and are quick to throw out the old. I would say that, if we are careful in our employment of genre analysis, both this method and intertextuality can be complementary approaches. Intertexts are also defined by genre connections as well as shared vocabulary and ideas, so that genre is often a subset of intertextuality.[5] In fact what Meek calls for in his opening paragraphs is a "more refined methodology for determining literary influence between

3. H. Gunkel, *The Psalms: A Form-Critical Introduction* (trans. Thomas Horner; Philadelphia: Fortress, 1967).

4. Erhard Blum, "Formgeschichte—a Misleading Category? Some Critical Remarks," in *The Changing Face of Form Criticism for the Twenty-First Century* (ed. Marvin A. Sweeney and Ehud Ben Zvi; Grand Rapids: Eerdmans, 2003), 32–45.

5. See K. Dell and W. Kynes, eds., *Reading Job Intertextually* (LHBOTS 574; New York: Bloomsbury T&T Clark, 2012); idem, *Reading Ecclesiastes Intertextually* (LHBOTS 587; New York: Bloomsbury T&T Clark, 2014).

prophet and sage," and this draws out another potential problem: that we transition too easily between the language of "the literature" or "the text," which we are approaching in genre or intertextual terms, and the language of persona, a historical role, a socially contextual person, i.e., prophet or sage. In the strict terms of this discussion of relationships between texts we should surely be focusing on a literary analysis rather than Fichtner's "shared culture,"[6] which is, at best, a woolly term. And yet we seem, at least here in the work of Sneed and Weeks, to be getting back to "shared culture" type ideas. The path from literary material to ideas about the nature of the culture that created it is a slippery one.

Genres are not static, and this is one of the aspects that makes them complex and makes the quest for parallels also complex. Meek cites Fishbane on the point that genres are transformed by re-use in another context, the example here being transformation of a prophetic oracle by a legal genre.[7] This is an intentional allusion to an existing genre in order to transform another genre and say something fresh that nonetheless alludes to and is shaped by what came before. Even Weeks says that such allusions are what we are examining here, even though he wants to say that the nature of allusion is not always a deliberate literary link but rather a product of a wider cultural literary interaction. Such interactions may be lost to us today on one level both because of our cultural and time distance and also because we cannot get inside the scribe's head, but on another level we are emboldened to make the attempt both in the areas of genre and of allusion/intertext with the tools we do have at our disposal. Weeks suggests that intertextuality has gone mad in the search for literary parallels to the detriment of recognizing that there may be a whole raft of allusions that are less easy to pin down, the product of wider culture and ideas. But that leaves us with an uneasy feeling that we can never know the exact thought processes that generated these texts. Kynes too makes the point that the search for genres is itself a modern literary phenomenon. We have to ask whether the writers themselves thought in this way. Our quest is subjective and time distanced. But isn't that the case with all efforts to understand a culture so far removed from our own? All we can do is use our own methods to try to understand the past, even if it is "another country." So the problem of cultural distance needs to be acknowledged, but it should not stop us trying to say anything useful about texts that, after all, do continue to speak to us today in our very different and varying contexts.

6. J. Fichtner, "Jesaja unter den Weisen," *TLZ* 74 (1949): 75–80.
7. Michael Fishbane, "Revelation and Tradition: Aspects of Inner-Biblical Exegesis," *JBL* 99 (1980): 343–61.

Kynes notes that there is a misguided tendency in this debate to regard genres as static and as universally applicable. It is clear that genres change over time—my own work on parody in the way the book of Job re-uses and indeed mis-uses psalmic genres is a case in point.[8] Kynes also mentions an unfortunate tendency in the literature on wisdom and prophecy to begin with form criticism and questions of genre when in fact there may be better approaches. The quest for relationships between texts is, for him, a better way forward. He proposes considering "types" of literature last, after individual connections have been identified and analyzed. Along the lines that Weeks calls for, Kynes says we need to look at individual texts, although Weeks sees "connections" as part of a wider cultural literacy and ultimately as a set of social and contextual connections, thus blurring the boundary between literary and contextual or, to put it another way, the move from literary genre to "shared culture." This relates to the point about familiarity with texts (made by Kynes). This is important—texts, ideas, images can only have been preserved and transmitted and indeed transformed if authors were aware of them. An obscure reference to something very few would understand would be lost on the average reader. If the author of Job was parodying, what better than to use psalmic texts that would have been familiar in the context of worship? Or was there a context of worship? It is all too easy to move from genre to context. Were there just occasional wisdom genres, or was that part of a wider wisdom tradition or movement that made up a consistent social entity?

Kynes remarks that form criticism was "content to assume that meaning is produced through the interactions of texts," but I would contend that form criticism was not actually looking for exact interactions of texts (as in the case of intertextuality or inner-biblical criticism) but rather for common structures that cut across many types of texts and that may have had an oral or written prehistory before its "placement" in the text that we now receive. Sneed in his article makes the point that genres tend to be systemic—genres do not do double duty. On one level a genre needs to have a certain fixity otherwise we cannot identify it, but on the other we can also recognize one genre in another and the transformative power of prophetic re-use or Joban parody. It raises the question of what makes a genre—just what it contains or also what it does not contain. Genre classifications can be too restrictive. A good example is the way psalms have been divided

---

8. Katharine J. Dell, *The Book of Job as Sceptical Literature* (BZAW 157; Berlin: de Gruyter, 1991).

into different genres.[9] This is fine until we encounter a psalm with two genres within it. Does this mean that two different "interest groups" got to work on the same psalm? Does it mean that one genre is dominant, the other an afterthought? Does this translate into two incompatible worldviews represented in one psalm? Genre classifications include within their remit the question of context. Does a partial wisdom psalm indicate some encroachment of the wisdom worldview on a psalm that is essentially of another genre?[10] It is the same with prophecy—is an oracle dominated by legal genres any longer an oracle? Has a different worldview encroached upon a more purist assumption of what context tended to produce prophetic oracles? Is there a standard genre against which to measure such "offcuts"? Such discussions and the assumptions upon which it is based are also largely dependent, it seems to me, on the idea of groups/interest groups/authorial groups producing different types of material within society.

So it seems that the idea of fixity of genres is definitely a mistake, not only in literary terms but also in terms of the cultures which produced them—we need to take account of the fact that genres change over time. Sneed mentions that "form or genre is the same" in the case of modern blues music, even if the content is different—but form and genre are themselves not the same! Form is a subset of genre along with content and context.[11] Sneed goes on to make the point that since genres change and evolve it is hard to say anything about their original form and function—the proverb emerging from a folk society for example. In its final form the proverb is not functioning as such, and so, Sneed asks, can we really reconstruct a former context like this? Proverbs are now "like epigrams coined by famous people" (cf. superscriptions to books). I am not sure this is what they are like now—they are certainly appropriated by more elevated circles in that they find literary expression and there is the capacity for them to be "retweeted." Sneed argues that twice-told proverbs also mitigate against a folk setting. Sneed points to a scribal phenomenon of making new maxims out of old ones. But this is not an either/or in my view. These could be both genuine folk proverb doublets and scribal remakings. Can we necessarily rule one out in favor of the other? Ultimately we don't know whether a twice-told proverb is a citation of an older proverb or a later composition made to appear old.

9. As by Gunkel, *The Psalms*.

10. See discussion in S. Cheung, *Wisdom Intoned: A Reappraisal of the Genre "Wisdom Psalms"* (LHBOTS 613; London: Bloomsbury T&T Clark, 2015).

11. As I argued in Dell, *The Book of Job as Sceptical Literature*.

We might cite Ecclesiastes' "quotation" of proverbs that he probably made up himself.[12] We don't know whether such proverbs were passed down in a long tradition that nurtured the "genre" of folk proverb or whether we have them due to scribal reworking or composition.

Sneed makes a very helpful distinction between *Sitz im Leben* and *Sitz im Literatur*, which goes some way to avoiding the grey area between the two mentioned above. He is using this distinction as a useful one to distinguish between original (cultural) setting and literary setting. Sneed suggests though that both of these are distinct from the originally oral *Sitze im Leben* of the prophecies. So we are back to the tension Meek noticed, citing van Leeuwen, of "canonical" stage versus "original" social setting.[13] Sneed is making a clear distinction between written and oral, but we don't in fact know that all the original *Sitze im Leben* were oral—much could have been written in earlier sources (or is this too Wellhausian a suggestion?). Sneed makes the point that by the later "scribal" period all the literati could read and write in the various genres of their culture. This suggests that overlap would be very likely (so maybe, I might add, explaining intertextual links), but it doesn't address the basic conundrum that we find in the wisdom literature, and that is why national history—so key in the understanding of the prophetic literature—is not in the biblical wisdom literature. Why, if this was the case, are "links in" from the wider culture with its history and all the allusions tied up with that history so few? Why is the wisdom literature so distinctive if indeed it is the product of such a wide and educated scribal culture as immersed in prophecy and law as it is in wisdom?

Sneed harks back to the language of genre when he is talking of the relationship between the prophetic books and prophets in the Deuteronomistic History—messengers are repeating the words given to them by those who sent them (i.e., messenger formulas) in both types of literature. He harks back to genre when he talks of prophetic and wisdom genres in different parts of the scribal brain. Sneed poses an interesting challenge when he writes: "questions, such as how the differing conventional worlds of each type of literature rhetorically functioned to persuade scribes and others to accept various theological and ideological positions, need to be addressed." Isn't that though where intertextuality with its rhetorical re-use of one text by another comes in?

---

12. Quotations were argued for by R. Gordis, *Koheleth —the Man and His World: A Study of Ecclesiastes* (New York: Schocken, 1968).
13. Van Leeuwen, "The Sage in the Prophetic Literature."

Defining Wisdom

Some of the contributors focus on defining wisdom, but Weeks decisively moves away from a question that he sees as unproductive. It is noted that the broadest definitions of wisdom as "an approach to reality" (von Rad[14]) or "shared culture" (Fichtner[15]) (cf. also Murphy's "shared approach to reality"[16]) is less than helpful. Meek writes that the quest for shared vocabulary and themes (as by Terrien[17]) is problematic as it "can easily be attributed to wisdom as a shared reality unless an intentional textual relationship can be established." Some clarity is needed here—whilst I agree that shared vocabulary and ideas can be unhelpfully broad in the same way that the "shared reality" definition (an amalgam of the definitions of others?) is broad, I would not see that quest for shared vocabulary and themes only becoming important once an intertextual relationship has been established. There can also be narrower attempts to isolate significant vocabulary and thematic overlaps between books, done on the basis of genre. Meek goes on to comment on links between Amos and Job and the consequent category of "wisdom influence," following Crenshaw.[18] This seems to be a second-tier category after "wisdom" or "wisdom literature" for those books or parts of books that show some overlaps of vocabulary and theme but not enough to categorize them entirely as wisdom literature. This is the category normally ascribed to the prophets—they are first prophetic in genre, but second they may show "wisdom influence." Weeks argues that too much emphasis has been placed by scholars on the definition of wisdom and not enough on the nature of "wisdom influence" (see below).

14. G. von Rad, *Wisdom in Israel* (trans. James D. Martin; Harrisburg: Trinity, 1993).

15. Fichtner, "Jesaja."

16. Roland E. Murphy, "Wisdom—Theses and Hypothesis," in *Israelite Wisdom: Theological and Literary Essays in Honor of Samuel Terrien* (ed. John G. Gammie, Walter Brueggemann, W. Lee Humphreys, and James M. Ward; Missoula: Scholars Press, 1978), 35–42, esp. 39–40.

17. Samuel Terrien, "Amos and Wisdom," in *Israel's Prophetic Heritage: Essays in Honor of James Muilenburg* (ed. Bernard W. Anderson and Walter J. Harrelson; London: Harper, 1962), 108–15; repr. in *Studies in Ancient Israelite Wisdom* (ed. James L. Crenshaw; Library of Biblical Studies; New York: Ktav, 1976), 448–55.

18. James Crenshaw, "The Influence of the Wise Upon Amos: The 'Doxologies of Amos' and Job 5:9–16; 9:5–10," *ZAW* 79 (1967): 42–52; idem, "Method for Determining Wisdom Influence Upon 'Historical' Literature," *JBL* 88 (1969): 129–42.

This raises the issue of Job—is Job wisdom? Kynes critiques Meek here, arguing that one cannot start with wisdom literature and then define a wisdom tradition and wisdom "approach to reality." Meek "perpetuates many of the unquestioned presuppositions of previous approaches" says Kynes. I agree, but Kynes is more critical about the way Meek moves from genre to tradition than I would be (although I agree that they are separate items) and about the value of genre as an approach. Kynes says that interpretation of Job has been drowned in its existential message through the wisdom categorization, itself essentially a philosophical classification. Kynes asks whether there are any "safe" scholarly consensuses or starting points any more. It seems von Rad got there first, though, when it comes to questioning the wisdom category: "[t]he question is therefore justified whether the attractive codename 'wisdom' is nowadays not more of a hindrance than a help, in so far as it disguises what stands behind it rather than depicts it properly."[19]

The problem of definitional boundaries extends to prophecy as a genre—there is the same problem with grouping texts under this heading as there is with the wisdom categorization. Where does prophecy change into apocalyptic (or is that a wisdom influence too)? Is prophecy really too broad a genre classification anyway for anything useful to be said about the detail of any of the books that make up the category? The same can be said for wisdom as a genre classification. One could start with defining the prophetic genre more precisely! Sneed provides a helpful definition of each—he sees prophecy as divinatory literature, wisdom as practical instruction: "Its sphere of operation is that of ethics and dealing with the problem of evil, again, as it relates to individuals. Prophetic literature focuses more on the sphere of politics and also on the problem of evil, but as it applies to the nation."

Wisdom Influence

Meek complains in a footnote that there is a dearth of research on the influence of prophecy on wisdom, but that is not so. One might refer to the work of Claudia Camp on woman wisdom portrayed as a prophetic figure in Prov 1:20–33 for example.[20] There is no evidence for the idea either that the prophets viewed wisdom with suspicion (apart perhaps from Jer 18:18). Whedbee made a good point about the cumulative nature

19. von Rad, *Wisdom in Israel*, 7–8.
20. Claudia Camp, *Wisdom and the Feminine in the Book of Proverbs* (Bible and Literature; Sheffield: Almond, 1985), 141–43.

of evidence in Isaiah of wisdom interaction.[21] Macintosh successfully demonstrated the partial influence of wisdom on Hosea.[22] It seems that the eighth-century prophets are our most useful source of such possible interactions. So what does wisdom influence really mean? Is this simply about literary style rather than any kind of broader literary (or contextual) dependence?[23] Weeks and Sneed seem to be moving down this path too. Furthermore, is it really about proverbial genres when it comes to prophecy and wisdom rather than about any link with Job or Ecclesiastes? Van Leeuwen challenges that a detailed comparison between prophetic material and Job and Ecclesiastes is yet to be undertaken.[24]

Kynes writes, "where wisdom influence ends and wisdom membership begins is a question yet to be satisfactorily answered"—this is a good point and a helpful distinction. Wisdom influence is a woolly term that could cover any text that shows the smallest link to a wisdom genre. Yet it seems that full-blown wisdom membership is restricted to very few texts, possibly not even to Job. Maybe then we are simply speaking of Proverbs and Ecclesiastes in this category?[25] Kynes makes an important point about the groupings of material made by pre-critical interpreters. There was the division into Writings; there was an "attribution to Solomon" grouping— the canonical as well as the genre cake can be cut many ways.[26]

Sneed speaks of prophecy and wisdom as "modes" of literature treating different domains. "Modes" is a good word but aren't we just replacing one word with another, i.e., genre with mode? It is an interesting suggestion that each mode has a differing, even slightly contradictory, theology and "job to do" and that both are necessary for Israelite culture as a whole. Sneed helpfully tries to contextualize the prophecy side of the debate.

21. J. W. Whedbee, *Isaiah and Wisdom* (Nashville: Abingdon, 1971).

22. Andrew A. Macintosh, "Hosea and the Wisdom Tradition: Dependence and Independence," in *Wisdom in Ancient Israel: Essays in Honour of J. A. Emerton* (ed. John Day, Robert P. Gordon, and Hugh G. M. Williamson; Cambridge: Cambridge University Press, 1995), 124–33.

23. As J. A. Soggin, "Amos and Wisdom," in Day, Gordon, and Williamson, eds., *Wisdom in Ancient Israel*, 119–23.

24. Van Leeuwen, "The Sage in the Prophetic Literature."

25. As argued in Katharine J. Dell, "Ecclesiastes as Mainstream Wisdom (without Job)," in *Goochem in Mokum/Wisdom in Amsterdam* (ed. George J. Brooke and Pierre Van Hecke; OTS 68; Leiden: Brill, 2016), 43–52.

26. See Katharine J. Dell, "Deciding the Boundaries of Wisdom: Applying the Concept of Family Resemblance," in *Was There a Wisdom Tradition? New Prospects in Israelite Wisdom Studies* (ed. Mark R. Sneed; AIL 23; Atlanta: SBL, 2015), 145–60.

He makes a distinction between inspired divination rather than deductive divination (as also Hilber). Interpretation of dreams and oneiromancy come into the picture under what is often described as "mantic wisdom." Sneed points to the overlap between prophecy and wisdom in sapiential parables in Ezekiel—but there are few who would classify Ezekiel's very extended parables as wisdom as they are very unlike the short comparison sayings we have in the biblical wisdom literature.

Weeks sees allusions as part of what it is to be educated and cultured—not every reference is specific or deliberate or citing another text, rather it is as one might cite literature today—not even a conscious activity. He speaks of the cultural heritage of the scribal elite. Of course this is no doubt true, but it is difficult for us to distinguish as we are not inside the scribe's head! We need some data for what that scribal heritage might entail. Weeks uses the example of Ecclesiastes and its citation of both Lamentations and the Song of Songs—it is interesting he doesn't choose Gen 1–11, with which most allusions with Ecclesiastes have been found. Weeks states that any quest for wisdom influence will always be inclined to separate the fact of allusions out from the purposes of the texts in which they are found (part of his argument for starting with the text instead)—and yet my thought is that part of intelligent comment on texts is knowing about these broader categories and trends. He makes a good point here though. We are to stop seeing wisdom genres as an alien presence in other works—we might learn more about the nuances of texts if we stop looking for this. I agree, but this approach still doesn't explain why so much of other genres in texts—notably historiography—has been left out of Proverbs. Weeks looks at pseudonymity practices across prophetic and wisdom texts in order to try to look at new links so as to get away from the older questions of "influence." "Wisdom influence," he says, indicates links that are not supposed to exist because of the neat lines of demarcation. However, I would say that it is only because of our training genre analysis and intertextuality that we are able to unpick these distinctions that "are not supposed to exist." Weeks says that "allusion" just becomes an assembly of decontextualized data. We need to ask what resemblances in each of our texts mean in the context of interpreting these texts. I would add though that we need to focus on what is *not* there as well as what is there in relation to why so many genres are not in wisdom literature which is presumably why it seems to be distinctive and have a different flavor.

A Scribal Culture

Have we just replaced "the wise"[27] with "scribal culture," a broader term? Sneed talks of "coteries of scribes" composing epigrams—famous people who, if they spoke them orally, did so for like-minded people (like in academic debate) without disseminating outside these circles. This is a nice idea, but where is the evidence for it? Sneed defines scribes sufficiently broadly to mean that different types of material are accommodated. An academic setting, proverbs designed to puzzle young scribes—this almost sounds like a return to the scribal training ideas promoted by those of the Solomonic enlightenment persuasion, but of course placed in a much later period. Emphasis is again put on the educational setting based on ancient Near Eastern parallels. The example of Baruch (Jer 36:10) is used—he has access to the royal scribal chamber, which means he was known by fellow scribes. Another nice vignette, but where is the evidence in the text? Sneed inquires, who controls the production of each type of material, i.e., who controls the genre? Was there a kind of genre police?! Sneed suggests high ranking scribes controlled both genres of literature—prophecy and wisdom. He has effectively replaced two groups—sages and prophets—with one—scribes! This still doesn't answer my persistent question of why there is more overlap in the wisdom to prophecy direction than the other way around.

The small number of the educated is stressed. Sneed suggests that all the literati could read and write in the genres of their cultures. He tries to link prophets with kings—kings would be interested in prophetic criticism of them (or would they?). Sneed employs a good quotation from Ben Sira 38–39 showing overlap of activities, but this is a much later text from a time when these different "genres" were coming together in a much closer way. At one point Sneed says that political sages are different from wisdom literature composers. This seems to contradict Sneed's convergence arguments where scribes cover many of these tasks. Scribes, he says, "could have certainly composed 'prophetic' oracles." Well, anything is possible, but this is a big assumption that totally undercuts the contextual differences between genre composition! The old argument about the small size of the Israelite state is wheeled out here—it may have been small, but it was certainly productive! Literate/illiterate seems to be the main divider between "groups" here in Sneed's analysis. He argues that they shared

---

27. Johannes Lindblom, "Wisdom in the Old Testament Prophets," in *Wisdom in Israel and in the Ancient Near East* (ed. Martin Noth and D. Winton Thomas; VTSup 3; Leiden: Brill, 1955), 192–204. Lindblom argued this mainly based on Jer 18:18.

the same supernatural worldview, and yet the supernatural is somewhat lacking in biblical wisdom books unless I have missed something.

Overall it would have been nice to have more textual examples in these four articles—they all tended to be a bit abstracted from the texts themselves. My key point is that these explanations—whether literary or contextual—don't explain why Proverbs in particular is so different from prophecy in its genres. If these are "synaptic reflexes" in the scribal brain (so Sneed), then why is there such a strong division in the use of material? It is likely that wisdom material was imported out and that in some sense prophets were influenced by wisdom genres, but why, oh why, was material generally not imported in? That omission, it seems to me, makes at least Proverbs and Ecclesiastes very different from many other books across the canon, and we might go so far as to call them "wisdom literature" on some definitional ticket or other.

Wisdom and Prophecy in the Ancient Near East

Speaking of textual examples, these are well represented in this essay from across the ancient world, providing a very helpful introduction to the material. What comes across very strikingly is the very different nature of the ancient Near Eastern material from its biblical counterparts. The main point of linkage seems to me to be more in the realm of "intention"—to teach, to educate a small group, and so on—rather than in the content of the material, which is much more revelatory, be that through tradition or immediate inspiration. Hilber makes a key distinction near the beginning of his piece between intuitive and technical revelatory processes, i.e., between "mechanical inducement of the revelatory experience and the intuitive reception of an associated message." It is the latter that relates more to biblical wisdom literature, and yet there is a strong tradition of mantic wisdom that relates to the former. This is found in biblical texts often seen to have wisdom influence, such as Daniel. These two categories mix together when looking at the ancient Near Eastern "wisdom" material and so makes the distinction from prophecy more complex. Having said this, Hilber concludes that there is little mixing of these two genres within the textual examples themselves. He writes, "the integration of wisdom traditions into prophetic material is scarce," and similarly "there is little evidence of the incorporation of prophetic messages into wisdom texts." Maybe the ancient Near Eastern genre differences are therefore clearer. It is only in the tendency of wisdom toward divination that the boundaries become more blurred. The apocalyptic category in its overlap with both of these also muddies the waters. Hilber shows how different genre-classification labels are often given to the same texts by different scholars, perhaps indicating that the texts themselves do not fit neatly into one genre (e.g., the Marduk prophecy he cites).

It is interesting that, citing Cohen,[28] Hilber finds three categories of form, content, and context that make appropriate the drawing of links with biblical wisdom literature—these are the very three criteria that make up "genre" as traditionally defined. The context includes the nature of the task at issue—the didactic nature and interest in "the question of skillful living." Hilber delineates a class of sages from prophets, one relying on technical skill and tradition, the other on intuitive perception of divine messages. Whilst some Egyptian wisdom texts, for example, foretell the future, it is based on tradition passed down or secrets, including magical arts, held by scribes rather than on intuitive divine experience. Whilst in the distant past the old traditions and techniques might have been divinely revealed by the gods to humankind, this was no longer the case in the wisdom arena—scribes had to be professionally trained with these skills—skills for life to be passed on from one generation to another. Ancient Near Eastern wisdom parallels, then, do not provide supporting evidence for broadening the wisdom net to include divine revelation. Whilst tradition could be developed and the divine perceived in such developments, this was not the same as the prophetic emphasis on the divine moment of the acquisition of knowledge of and from God.

This debate seems to me to relate in particular to Sneed's discussion of the remit of the scribe. Are we defining the scribe, as both prophet and sage combined, too broadly? Rather than avoiding the narrowing of categories with such broadening, are we in danger of blurring them together? It seems to me that this distinction between wisdom and prophecy in the ancient Near East on the issue of revelation is an important one for those seeking to define what is going on in wisdom books in the biblical canon. This final article, then, is complementary to the others and helps to broaden out the biblical picture, which is in danger of being drawn too narrowly within a simply Israelite context. It seems that the ancients drew distinctions that we find difficult to interpret, but these five articles at least help us to define our task and understand its complexity and so make a significant contribution to the ongoing debate.

28. Y. Cohen, *Wisdom from the Late Bronze Age* (WAW 29; Atlanta: SBL, 2013), 13–19.

Wisdom in Prophecy: A Response

Mark J. Boda

Modern study of the Bible has always stressed the importance of context for interpretation, and this context has been understood in terms of both history and literature. Emphasis on the historical distance between the modern reader and the ancient text reminds readers that the message of the book was not directed to our contemporary world but to an ancient audience with distinct language, culture, and needs. The immediate literary context, that is, the context of pericope and book, has also been deemed important to the meaning of a particular word, phrase, or sentence.

As modern research has developed over the past few centuries, while the perception of "historical context" has remained largely static, the perception of "literary context" has undergone significant shifts. In setting the Bible within its ancient context, historical critics have read biblical texts within the literary context of ancient Near Eastern texts uncovered in archaeological digs over the past two centuries. For instance, the discovery of various treaty forms led to a rereading of the covenant texts within the Old Testament. Even before this, source criticism identified literary layers that should take precedence in inter-pretation. For example, the P document/tradition would take precedence in the interpretation of a phrase from a priestly passage even over other pericopae in the immediate literary context. In tracing certain editorial strategies within a document, redaction criticism interpreted passages in light of other passages reflecting the same redactional activity even if they were found in contexts removed from the passage under discussion. With form criticism, passages sharing the same or related form were given precedence for interpreting a text even if they were in completely different books and time periods. Tradition criticism carried on this trend, first as it traced the oral development of traditions and then with the rise of inner-biblical allusion and intertextuality, the enduring development of tradition in written form. New literary and rhetorical criticism sought to return to the unique expression of a passage within its literary context, but even then certain literary tropes and styles seen throughout the biblical literature were used to understand the text (e.g., type scenes).

There has been an enduring emphasis within biblical research to read biblical texts within a certain context, and most would agree that this is necessary for interpreting a text. We cannot isolate a text since its meaning is inextricably linked to the historical and literary contexts in which it is found. However, as we look back over this history of contextual research we realize why we need to be careful with how we define that context: it exerts a massive influence on our reading of the text.

The various essays in the prophetic section of this volume highlight the influence of conceptions of context for reading the prophetic material. This is seen in the basic assignment that was given to these fine contributors: to trace evidence of wisdom within these prophetic books. Key to fulfilling this assignment is first defining wisdom and prophecy and then adopting a strategy for identifying links between the two traditions.

The introductory section of this volume highlights well the challenge of defining "wisdom," and the presence of of the book of Daniel within the prophetic section underlines the challenge of defining "prophetic." This difficulty in definition can be discerned as Daniel Timmer brings Job into conversation with Habakkuk and Nahum, with Job considered an outlier within the "wisdom" corpus. One could say the same for a book like Jonah within the Twelve, even though there are narrative presentations of prophets within the traditional prophetic corpus, whether Haggai, Zechariah or Isaiah, Jeremiah and Ezekiel. Defining wisdom and prophecy is very important to the present project—where claims are made about the role that wisdom plays within prophecy—and yet one can discern a tension over this very issue throughout these various essays. This issue will be addressed in more detail below.

As for the strategies for creating links between these two traditions, the presence of wisdom within prophecy is largely identified by the use of lexical data which dominate the wisdom tradition, especially those related to perception and wisdom. Ortlund and Allen focus mostly on vocabulary associated with wisdom, Osborne and Steinmann look initially for vocabulary before turning to general themes, while Timmer focuses on conceptual and structural parallels rather than lexical or formal parallels (pp. 150–53).[1] Connections based on more general concepts and

---

1. Timmer encourages an analysis that focuses on "levels of discourse higher than individual words": "larger units of discourse merit correspondingly greater attention than isolated words and phrases when comparing prophecy and wisdom" (p. 150), drawing on Julie Sanders, *Adaptation and Appropriation* (New Critical

structures, however, leave these scholars open to the charge of reducing the literature to its lowest common denominator and thus forging connections where they do not exist. For this reason, I have consistently pursued lexical links, giving priority to constellations of lexical data and collocations.[2] However, there is room for all these levels of data as evidence of a literary tradition. In my own work I have talked about "word views," that is, "the variety of lexical, imagistic, and conceptual frameworks… of the many Old Testament books."[3] In that work when I introduced some of the key books of the Old Testament I tried to capture the lexical, imagistic, and conceptual range of particular books or book traditions. Nevertheless, it is important to remember that the individual elements in the lexical, imagistic, and conceptual range of a particular book or tradition should not be treated as the exclusive property of that particular book or tradition. When we see multiple features of the "word view" of a book/tradition, then we are on more certain ground in determining literary relationships.

The use of lexemes which dominate books traditionally associated with the wisdom tradition is the focus of both Ortlund's work on Isaiah and Allen's on Jeremiah. Both show the role this common wisdom vocabulary plays in key passages or motifs within their respective books and in this way reflect the agenda of intertextuality championed by Stead called "sustained allusion."[4] Ortlund moves in a different direction from previous research which created distance between the wisdom vocabulary in Isaiah and the wisdom tradition from which it supposedly arose. For Ortlund wisdom is a key quality of the restoration. Allen argues for a greater contrast between human wisdom and divine wisdom, thus

Idiom; London: Routledge, 2006), 17–21. At one point, however, Timmer refers to "verbal and especially thematic correspondences between the books of Job and Habakkuk," which suggests some attention to lexical connection. Unclear is Timmer's distinction between "conceptual correspondence" and "general 'ideas' tied to specific historical settings" (pp. 152–53).

2. Mark J. Boda, *Praying the Tradition: The Origin and Use of Tradition in Nehemiah 9* (BZAW 277; Berlin: de Gruyter, 1999), 2–3.

3. Mark J. Boda, *A Severe Mercy: Sin and Its Remedy in the Old Testament* (Siphrut: Literature and Theology of the Hebrew Scriptures 1; Winona Lake: Eisenbrauns, 2009), 7.

4. Michael R. Stead, *The Intertextuality of Zechariah 1–8* (LHBOTS 506; London: T&T Clark International, 2009), 74: "the repeated references to another 'background' passage, which stretch across multiple passages." Thus, it is the cumulative evidence of multiple passages rather than relying on concentration in one passage.

suggesting a critical stance within Jeremiah toward the wisdom tradition. Both scholars are aware of the covenantal character of the terminology and passages in view and thus seek to interlink the concepts of knowing within both wisdom and covenantal traditions as, for instance, Ortlund, who concludes that Isa 1:2–3 shows "that Israel's failure in wisdom is raised in the larger context of their failure in covenant relationship," and Allen, who argues that Jer 9:23–24 "downplays wisdom…and provides a renewed emphasis on the covenantal concerns that marked 8:8–9" (p. 102).[5] There is more work to be done on repairing the relationship between wisdom and covenant, and especially if the pursuit of wisdom should be more closely allied with the relational pursuit that dominates the covenant tradition. In this we can take our lead from Steinmann who writes: "real wisdom according to the Old Testament stems from a relationship with YHWH and is often captured in the phrase *the fear of YHWH*…," linking this to the covenantal language of Deuteronomy (p. 131).[6]

While Ortlund treats wisdom more positively, that is, he sees wisdom as key to the vision of renewal in Isaiah, he argues that wisdom is not a catalyst for restoration since wisdom can make an appeal, but when rejected wisdom is lost. Thus, "wisdom itself shows no mechanism for recovering those who have turned away" (p. 93). However, the direct appeals to the foolish and naïve to follow the way of righteous wisdom, and the subtle depictions of blessing (implicit invitations) and curse (implicit warnings) are intended to promote "an ethical lifestyle motivated by a wise interior life dominated by the fear of Yahweh and the spirit of wisdom," and for this reason I have argued that "*the penitential* lies at the heart of the way of wisdom."[7] This explains then why the purveyors of

5. See Allen's citation of Lindblom who long ago "observed that knowing Yahweh 'is of course genuinely prophetic and has nothing to do with the doctrines of the Wisdom teachers'" (p. 97), from Johannes Lindblom, "Wisdom in the Old Testament Prophets," in *Wisdom in Israel and in the Ancient Near East Presented to H. H. Rowley* (ed. Martin Noth and David Winton Thomas; VTSup 3; Leiden: Brill, 1960), 192–204 (199).

6. Although I would say that the "fear of YHWH" is not merely a "more subtle fear—fear of the loss of relationship with a loving and gracious God who brings blessings on those who fear him" (p. 133), but rather in light of its presentation in the Torah, the stance of awe before the Almighty Holy One. See further Bruce K. Waltke, "The Book of Proverbs and Old Testament Theology," *BibSac* 136 (1979): 302–17; Mark J. Boda, "The Delight of Wisdom," *Themelios* 29 (2004): 4–11.

7. Boda, *Severe Mercy*, 374.

traditional wisdom in the debates of Job speak so often of repentance.[8] It may be that the role that wisdom will play within renewal is as Ortlund has described, but this should not be based on the view that wisdom has no mechanism for recovering those who have turned away. What we see in the prophetic tradition in general is a consistent shift away from hope in human potential for renewal toward the necessity of divine intervention. This is as true for the wisdom needed as it is for the repentance that is demanded. The call to repentance will be fulfilled by a community that experiences God grace and interior renewal,[9] and this is true also for the quality of wisdom that should typify the restored community.

As with Ortlund and Allen, Osborne and Steinmann also focus on what they consider "wisdom" lexical stock to identify initial links to the wisdom tradition. But then Osborne and Steinmann proceed to identify more general connections to wisdom concepts articulated in the book of Proverbs. Although Osborne and Steinmann do not appear to claim specific reliance of the prophetic books on Proverbs, one must be careful of claims that these wisdom conceptions lie behind the depictions of wise or unwise rule in the prophetic books.[10] Certainly it is better to highlight links between these prophetic books and the ancient Israelite wisdom tradition than to create links to modern leadership literature, but as I have already noted above once one moves from lexical stock to concepts it is easy to make connections between the literature and ignore disconnections.

While there is clearly a danger within these essays to emphasize links between traditions or literary works, there is also an equal danger to emphasize contrasts. One of the temptations of teaching and researching in the academy is the tendency to simplify, creating helpful typologies to enable students and readers alike to grasp the concept being described. Hebrew Bible/Old Testament scholarship is no exception, especially in the description of traditions and their related social groups. This leads to attempts to identify clear distinctions between tradition streams related to covenant, wisdom, prophecy, and priestly/cultic material, to name a

8. Ibid., 393–94. Also, many psalms that display the influence of the wisdom tradition refer to repentance; cf. ibid., 395–451.

9. Boda, *Severe Mercy*, 354–6, as I summarize: "In each prophetic collection the ultimate hope is shifted from human response to a *divine gracious and transformative initiative*" (p. 355 [original emphasis]).

10. Steinmann is aware of his approach to "reliance," contrasting what he is doing with "more indirect and understated influence of one text upon another" from "close verbal affinities between texts, easily detected parallels in thought, structure, theme, or plot" (p. 141).

few. While these historical distinctions and tensions between traditions have often been an important counter to the theological tendency toward cohesion and continuity, it has resulted at times in the creation of caricatures for which exceptions need to be introduced in increasing number. We have already seen this in the juxtaposition of wisdom and covenant traditions above, but one can also see it in other contrasts identified between wisdom and other traditions.

For instance, Osborne cites Paul Joyce's claim that the reason there is little wisdom influence in Ezekiel is that wisdom is relatively secular whereas Ezekiel is priestly, a view that Osborne appears also to embrace when he speaks of "Ezekiel's evident priestly orientation" (p. 110). Osborne carefully notes that while Ezekiel does assess proverbial sayings negatively at times, the prophet in the end embraces wisdom and uses parables. But in making this argument one can discern the vestiges of a common caricature of Hebrew wisdom, namely, that it is secular and disconnected from priestly cult. Earlier work on wisdom has challenged this view, especially as seen in the presentation of traditional wisdom figures in Job, as well as in Ecclesiastes (e.g., 5:1–6) and Proverbs (e.g., 15:8, 29; 20:25; 21:27).[11]

Another juxtaposition based on earlier caricatures can be discerned in depictions of the epistemological modes of wisdom and prophecy. At times in these essays one finds depictions of wisdom as focused on human observation and tradition related to creation and culture contrasted with depictions of prophecy as divine revelation related to redemptive-historical concerns. This is problematic for books associated with wisdom as well as those associated with prophecy.

On the one hand, the prophets regularly employ motifs and images drawn from creation and culture. Hosea, Isaiah, Jeremiah, and Ezekiel, for instance, emphasize family relationships in their revelation of the

11. See L. G. Perdue, *Wisdom and Cult: A Critical Analysis of the Views of Cult in the Wisdom Literature of Israel and the Ancient Near East* (SBLDS 30; Missoula: Scholars Press, 1977), 345–62; John E. Hartley, *The Book of Job* (NICOT; Grand Rapids: Eerdmans, 1988), 48; William Scott Green, "Stretching the Covenant: Job and Judaism," *RevExp* 99 (2002): 569–77; Samuel E. Balentine, "Job as Priest to the Priests," *Ex auditu* 18 (2002): 29–52; idem, "I Was Ready to Be Sought out by Those Who Did Not Ask," in *Seeking the Favor of God*. Vol. 1, *The Origin of Penitential Prayer in Second Temple Judaism* (ed. Mark J. Boda, Daniel K. Falk, and Rodney A. Werline; Early Judaism and Its Literature 21; Atlanta: SBL, 2006), 1–20. Hartley notes how the speeches of Job's friends are "traditionally cultic ones" which suggests that traditional wisdom "is the handmaiden of the Israelite cult." Cf. Boda, *Severe Mercy*, 382.

relationship between Yahweh and Israel. Amos is one of many prophets who draw on creational images and motifs in their declaration of the word of God.

On the other hand, books and passages associated with wisdom do not exclusively focus on human observation of creation/culture and preservation of tradition. The figure of Wisdom in Prov 1:20–33 speaks in language reminiscent of prophecy:

> Turn (שׁוב) to my reproof
> Attention, I will pour out my spirit (רוּחִי) on you
> I will make known my words to you (v. 23)

And this promise is then followed by the warning:

> Because I called (קרא) and you refused (מָאֵן),
> I stretched forth my hand and no one paid attention (v. 24)
> …
> Then they will call (קרא) on me, but I will not answer (ענה);
> They will seek me diligently, but not find me (v. 28)

Such a warning is reminiscent of the review of the prophetic tradition in passages like Zech 7:11–14.[12] Wisdom in Prov 1, therefore, functions in a way that we have often limited to the prophetic tradition.

But this is not restricted to the book of Proverbs. The book of Job introduces us to a key stream of wisdom with the appearance of Elihu in Job 32–37.[13] Elihu's introductory remarks reflect a hermeneutic that we have typically limited to the prophetic tradition, that is, the acquisition of wisdom through divine revelation in the spirit within rather than through the patient acquisition of wisdom through years of observation of creation and inculcation of tradition. According to Elihu, wisdom is thus attainable by youth and not just by the elderly. This wisdom stream can also be discerned in the presentation of figures like Daniel, Joseph, and Solomon, all of whom we are told are given wisdom in their youth directly from God. This type of wisdom—which seems more like the revelatory mode we typically associate with the prophetic tradition—should not come as a

---

12. Interestingly, both passages also employ storm imagery.

13. Rainer Albertz, "The Sage and Pious Wisdom in the Book of Job: The Friend's Perspective," in *The Sage in Israel and the Ancient Near East* (ed. John G. Gammie and Leo G. Perdue; Winona Lake: Eisenbrauns, 1990), 243–61. Albertz notes three sources of wisdom in Job: experience, antiquity, and finally revelation, expressed especially through Elihu (251).

surprise to us in light of the lack of distinction between the divinatory and wisdom in the ancient Near Eastern world.[14] It is this that may explain the canonical conundrum regarding the book of Daniel, which is associated with the prophets within the canonical order that dominates the Christian tradition but among the Writings (where wisdom books are found) within the order that dominates the Jewish tradition.

At the same time we need to be careful not to conclude that these elements are "prophetic" elements in wisdom. Within the ancient Near East a wise figure like Daniel has access to revelation from the deity.[15] The problem has been our caricature of wisdom in terms of secular Western academic values. This caricature of wisdom at times seems to underlie Steinmann's work on Daniel[16] as well as Timmer's work on the Twelve.

Steinmann's definition of wisdom is seen in how he describes his focus. He looks to literature which "offers advice on becoming wise and behaving wisely" (p. 124) and "books that promote pious and efficacious thought and life" (p. 125). His focus on biographical presentation of

14. See Paul-Alain Beaulieu, "The Social and Intellectual Setting of Babylonian Wisdom Literature," in *Wisdom Literature in Mesopotamia and Israel* (ed. Richard J. Clifford; Leiden: Brill, 2007), 3–19.

15. See John J. Collins, "The Court-Tales in Daniel and the Development of Apocalyptic," *JBL* 94 (1975): 218–34, who distinguishes between "proverbial wisdom" (which he says dominates Old Testament wisdom books) and "mantic wisdom, as practiced by Joseph and Daniel, which includes the interpretation of dreams, signs, and vision" (232). Collins notes how mantic wisdom "is closer to prophecy than to proverbial wisdom" (232). See further idem, "The Sage in the Apocalyptic and Pseudepigraphic Literature," in *The Sage in Israel and the Ancient near East* (ed. John G. Gammie and Leo G. Perdue; Winona Lake: Eisenbrauns, 1990), 343–54. Cf. Brian A. Mastin, "Wisdom and Daniel," in *Wisdom in Ancient Israel: Essays in Honour of J. A. Emerton* (ed. John Day, Robert P. Gordon, and H. G. M. Williamson; Cambridge: Cambridge University Press, 1995), 161–69; Andreas Bedenbender, "Seers as Mantic Sages in Jewish Apocalyptic (Daniel and Enoch)," in *Scribes, Sages, and Seers: The Sage in the Eastern Mediterranean World* (ed. Leo G. Perdue; FRLANT 219; Göttingen: Vandenhoeck & Ruprecht, 2008), 258–70; Leo G. Perdue, "Mantic Sages in the Ancient Near East, Israel, Judaism, and the Dead Sea Scrolls," in *Prophecy After the Prophets?* (ed. Kristin De Troyer, Armin Lange, and Lucas L. Schulte; CBET 52; Leuven: Peeters, 2009), 133–89; Mark R. Sneed, *The Social World of the Sages: An Introduction to Israelite and Jewish Wisdom Literature* (Minneapolis: Fortress, 2015), 13–14. Perdue wisely notes (in opposition to Bedenbender) that one must "allow for Israelite and Jewish sages to shape ancient Near Eastern mantic wisdom according to indigenous theology" (189).

16. Although Steinmann does cite Prov 2:6, stating that "true wisdom is a gift from God" (p. 130)

wisdom is a welcome addition to this volume.[17] However, it appears that because Steinmann is focused on "the actions of wise people" he misses the revelatory dimension of wisdom in "the visionary sections of Daniel" (p. 142).

Of course, in the initial chapters where he does see wisdom emphasized in the activity of Daniel and his friends, it is interlaced with the "visionary" as well, yet Steinmann only mentions this revelatory dimension of wisdom in passing (p. 137), even though it is a major dimension of Daniel's wisdom. In his treatment of the latter section of Daniel, Steinmann even juxtaposes the quality of "insight" and "their actions," writing: "It is their *actions,* not their cognitive awareness, that demonstrates their wisdom" (p. 143), even though it is the revelatory experiences of Daniel that seem to be emphasized in the entire section as well as in the verses related to "insight" and "understanding" (Dan 11:33; 12:10).[18] The paucity of treatment of this dimension of wisdom can likely be traced to a certain definition of wisdom that needs revisiting.

Timmer favors Van Leeuwen's definition of wisdom, which he finds more nuanced:

> He suggests that wisdom "presupposes the 'fear of Yahweh/God,'...entails insight into and practice of the *generic* patterns and norms for creation and creatures" and "knowledge of and appropriate action with reference to *particular* circumstances, institutions, persons, and other creatures," and "is traditional," being mediated generationally by taking account of what is new. (p. 149)[19]

---

17. Steinmann's statement that wisdom literature "tends to be poetic, epigrammatic, and aphorismic" rather than "narrative" shows that his approach is dominated by Proverbs as the true core of wisdom (p. 126). Yet, in fact, two of the three core books (Job, Ecclesiastes) are dominated by narrative, with Job using narrative as the envelope to contain the wisdom speeches (the dialogue is not to be divorced from the narrative, but rather the narrative is the literary vehicle in which the dialogue occurs), and Ecclesiastes' autobiographical account lying at the core of the book. In light of this evidence, biographical wisdom as found in connection with Joseph, Solomon, and Daniel is not odd.

18. It is the wicked who will not understand (12:10), since as Collins notes: "true understanding is hidden. It is available only to the משכילים, who are privy to the revelation," John J. Collins, *Daniel: A Commentary on the Book of Daniel* (Hermeneia; Minneapolis: Fortress, 1993), 400.

19. From Raymond C. Van Leeuwen, "Wisdom Literature," in *Dictionary for Theological Interpretation of the Bible* (ed. Kevin J. Vanhoozer, Craig G. Bartholomew, Daniel J. Treier, and N. T. Wright; Grand Rapids: Baker Academic, 2005), 848–49.

What is missing from this is the revelatory dimension of wisdom that can be discerned alongside the more traditional practices of wisdom.[20] This is key to Timmer's work because he focuses on the theophanic appearance of YHWH, a revelatory moment, which he sees as more at home in our traditional view of the prophetic, but not so in the traditional view of wisdom. This is something that Timmer seems to concede near the end of his contribution when he admits that "Job is not a perfect fit for the wisdom category due to its interest in revelatory wisdom" (p. 162). This is precisely why the revelatory dimension of wisdom is important to incorporate into our view of the wisdom tradition. One may argue that Job is an outlier (as Timmer seems to suggest) within the wisdom corpus, but evidence we have seen from Proverbs and narrative wisdom depictions suggests otherwise.

This may help Timmer with the seeming frustration at the end of his contribution as he considers the status of Job within the wisdom tradition and even Habakkuk and Nahum in the prophetic tradition. Possibly this should prompt us to hold loosely our book genre and tradition designations so that we are not blinded or dissuaded from connections outside our literary designations.[21]

Timmer's work, though, raises one final point of reflection in that it highlights similar features in books traditionally associated with wisdom and prophecy. We have suggested that it may not be best to treat this as the intrusion of one tradition into the other but rather as a feature shared between the two traditions. The struggle showcased in this case may be an enduring methodological frustration from the history of form and tradition criticism. Classic form criticism assumed a direct connection between form and setting, that is, that differing settings in life gave rise to different forms appropriate for those settings. However, as scholars identified an ever-increasing number of settings for the use of single forms or an ever-increasing number of forms for a single setting, this assumption was called into question.[22] This is relevant for the present discussion because there was an assumption of discrete settings in which wisdom and prophecy arose and thus the surprise at the appearance of a form or style from what should be a discrete setting. But this assumption does not take into account the dynamic nature of communal speech and

20. Timmer is aware of what he terms "revelatory epistemology" in Job, at least in Yahweh's answer to Job (p. 154).

21. See the essay by Kynes in the introductory section of the volume.

22. See my nascent thoughts on this in Mark J. Boda, "Form Criticism in Transition: Penitential Prayer and Lament, *Sitz im Leben* and Form," in Boda, Falk, and Werline, eds., *Seeking the Favor of God*, 181–92.

the fact that while a form may arise from a particular group, that form has a life of its own and can be appropriated by a variety of groups in diverse ways and enter into the general parlance of a culture and be employed in a variety of contexts. This was brought out masterfully by Osborne in his reminder that while Ezekiel did criticize the proverbs of his day which were circulating among the people, he also employed wisdom forms to communicate his message (pp. 110–11). Furthermore, the employment of these proverbs probably had nothing to do with any purported "wisdom tradition" but was merely a form that was used among the general population apart from any tradition group. Wise also is Allen's allusion to pop psychology in Western culture loosing vocabulary from "precise professional settings" to be used in society in more general ways (p. 96).

While I have raised many concerns about the various claims made in these essays, I certainly affirm their guidance for studying these biblical books, although certain conclusions and arguments may need to be revised or abandoned. Even if the "wisdom" designation is rejected by interpreters, the identification of lexical stock, themes, forms, and structures traditionally connected to wisdom within the prophetic corpus has provided new insights into the meaning of the prophets. The challenge, however, remains to reflect wisely on what contexts we are employing for reading texts so that the texts can continue to speak prophetically to modern readers.

Prophecy and Wisdom:
Connections, Influences, Relationships

Tremper Longman III

The study of wisdom in the Hebrew Bible is at an interesting point in many ways. In the first place, as acknowledged by the authors in this collection, the whole idea of wisdom literature is under challenge. One can no longer simply assume that Job, Proverbs, and Ecclesiastes comprise the core of a distinct grouping of books that can be characterized as wisdom. And after a generation of incorporating many other books under the label of wisdom (some psalms, Song of Songs, and certain historical texts [Dan 1–6; the Joseph Story], and much more), a number of scholars are suggesting that the category has been stretched much too far.[1] In a synthetic study of the concept of wisdom in the Hebrew Bible and beyond, I have provided a rationale for continuing to consider the category of wisdom literature as a viable category and this idea seems shared by the contributors to this volume.[2]

On the other hand, there are still many scholars who believe that wisdom is not only distinctive within the Hebrew Bible but almost an alien presence there with little or no contact with the historical, legal, covenantal, prophetic, or priestly traditions. Rather than redemptive-history, the argument goes, wisdom grounds itself in creation theology. Rather than

---

1. The challenge is most forcefully articulated in W. Kynes, *An Obituary for "Wisdom Literature"* (Oxford: Oxford University Press, forthcoming); as well as chapters by Kynes ("The Modern Scholarly Tradition and the Threat of Pan-sapientialism: A Case Report"), M. R. Sneed ("'Grasping After the Wind': The Elusive Attempt to Define and Delimit Wisdom"), and others in M. R. Sneed, ed., *Was There a Wisdom Tradition? New Prospects in Israelite Wisdom Studies* (AIL 23; Atlanta: SBL, 2015).

2. T. Longman III, *The Fear of the Lord Is Wisdom: A Theological Introduction to Wisdom in Israel* (Grand Rapids: Baker, 2017).

polemicizing against pagan religion the sages incorporate ancient Near Eastern wisdom ideas, principles, and instructions uncritically. William Brown provides an example of this type of thinking when he states:

> ...ancient Israel's sages had no qualms incorporating the wisdom of other cultures. Biblical wisdom seeks the common good along with the common God. Wisdom's international, indeed universal appeal constitutes its canonical uniqueness. The Bible's wisdom corpus is the open door in an otherwise closed canon.[3]

In my aforementioned recent work on wisdom, I have provided a counter-argument to the understanding of wisdom as universal and cosmopolitan.[4] In my opinion, the sages were much more integrated into the other traditions than is often admitted. Thus, I applaud the insightful efforts of my colleagues who in this volume explore the relationship between wisdom and prophecy. Even in those places where I find myself unconvinced by their viewpoints, I was stimulated in my thinking by their insightful work.

Job: Prophet or Apocalyptic Seer?

Two of the essays provide an interesting pair to be examined together. Martin A. Shields ("You Can't Get a Sage to Do a Prophet's Job: Overcoming Wisdom's Deficiency in the Book of Job") makes the bold claim that appeals to divine revelation in the book of Job align it with prophetic literature. Timothy Johnson ("From Where Should Wisdom Be Found? The Book of Job as Key to von Rad's Theory") makes the equally striking, but different, argument that divine revelation connects the book of Job to apocalypse. Notice how both focus our attention again on the role of direct revelation in the book.

Shields correctly argues that the book of Job demonstrates the inadequacy of wisdom as a solution to human problems. I would immediately qualify this statement, however, by saying that it demonstrates the inadequacy of *human* wisdom. I characterize Job as a wisdom debate; the suffering of Job provides the foil for the real question of the book: Who is wise?[5] Wisdom should lead to a proper diagnosis of Job's situation and perhaps even a solution to his problem. Job, the three friends, and Elihu

---

3. W. P. Brown, *Wisdom's Wonder: Character, Creation, and Crisis in the Bible's Wisdom Literature* (Grand Rapids: Eerdmans, 2014), 3.

4. Longman, *The Fear of the Lord*, particularly Chapters 7–10.

5. See Longman, *The Fear of the Lord Is Wisdom*, 43–62; idem, *Job* (BCOTWP; Grand Rapids: Baker, 2012).

all have a diagnosis and prescription for his ailment. The three friends famously believe that his problem is a result of his sin and therefore the solution is repentance. Job believes the problem is God's injustice and therefore the solution is to confront God and set him straight. Elihu presents himself as a third option, but he eventually falls back to the same position of the three friends, though he does ground his view on a different source of authority (more on this below). At the end, rather than Job setting God straight, God sets Job straight by simply asserting his wisdom and his power and in effect leading Job to trust him and accept the mystery of his suffering.

According to Shields, however, the book of Job demonstrates that wisdom is inadequate and that prophecy trumps wisdom. After all, he argues, the resolution to the disputation only occurs when in the theophany in 38:1–41:34 God directly reveals himself and his message to Job. And, according to Shields, "whether or not wisdom can legitimately incorporate prophecy and still be classified as wisdom, direct special revelation is prophecy whether it appears in wisdom or any other literary genre." Or is it?

But before answering that question, we should also acknowledge that Shields recognizes at least one certain and one less certain bit of prophetic material in the book of Job, Eliphaz in 4:12–13 and Elihu. In a somewhat strange passage (4:12–13), Eliphaz appeals to a dream in which a spirit passed before his face. His description of this spirit is very mysterious as having a "form" but not one that was recognizable. There is no doubt that this form was a heavenly figure and that Eliphaz thus appeals to heavenly authority for his argument that mortals by definition (and thus Job specifically) cannot be righteous before God. But whether Eliphaz believed that this unrecognizable form was God or an angel is unclear. In any case, can we really think of this as prophecy? On Shields's understanding that any direct revelation is prophetic, it would certainly count, but is his definition too broad? There may indeed be a broad definition of prophetic that would count any divine revelation as prophetic, but then everything that is in the Bible is prophetic in that sense. The narrower definition of a prophet, I would argue, is a person who receives a message from God in order to speak it to a sinful people to elicit their repentance. I don't think Eliphaz here is claiming that this spirit-message was intended specifically for Job but rather was pronouncing a general truth about humanity that Eliphaz thinks applies to Job. In any case, it is more likely that this is not even a true revelation from heaven but either a made-up one or some kind of hallucination. If he is a prophet, then he is a false one, since he misapplies the divine message to Job.

Elihu is an interesting case. Shields thinks that Elihu is different than Eliphaz in 4:12–13 in that he does not represent himself as a prophet but rather simply allows that prophetic revelation helps in understanding Job's situation. But he is different from the three friends in that his claim is that his understanding comes directly from God ("but it is the spirit in a person, the breath of the Almighty, that gives them understanding," 32:8). However, rather than seeing this as the imposition of the prophetic on wisdom, isn't it better to think of this as yet a different basis for wisdom? In other words, we need to entertain the possibility that direct revelation does not mean there are prophetic elements in wisdom, but that direct revelation is an important source of wisdom. Granted, Shields seems to allow for this connection when he says that the inclusion of direct revelation "might indicate that the disjunction between wisdom and prophecy is somewhat artificial—the ease with which Eliphaz can appeal to revelation as an adjunct in his use of wisdom may be more surprising to the modern scholar who presupposes a compartmentalism that is ultimately artificial than it was to the ancient audience of the book of Job."

However, in spite of this recognition, much of Shields's chapter seems to speak as if there is such a compartmentalism between the two, as we can observe in his discussion of the theophany at the end of the book. He entertains the possibility that Job might be a prophet since he is a recipient of divine revelation and that theophanies usually accompany the prophetic call. He rightly concludes that Job is not a prophet because he is not commissioned for a prophetic task. In other words, a prophet receives a divine message to communicate to the people, but God's speeches to Job are to upbraid him for his charge that God was unjust (40:8). However, he does say that "the resolution to Job's problems comes not through the considered wisdom of the sages but rather via direct revelation. In this way the book of Job reflects some prophetic element." I would rather say that the book of Job shows that revelation is a source of wisdom, perhaps its most important source, as we will see below. Indeed, I think direct revelation is the ultimate source of wisdom not only in Job but also in Proverbs and Ecclesiastes.

While Shields looks at the relationship of wisdom, particularly the book of Job, and the prophetic, Timothy Johnson sees Job as the precursor to apocalyptic. In this he seeks to revitalize the thesis of von Rad that apocalyptic emerged from wisdom rather than from the prophetic.

He first of all raises the question of Job's connection with wisdom. He suggests that the primary reason the book of Job is considered wisdom is because it is dealing with the question of innocent suffering. And the presence of the theophany at the end and the ultimate appeal to divine revelation is foreign to wisdom and suggests another connection that he argues is apocalyptic.

Though he is not the only scholar today to question Job's connection to wisdom, I would disagree and say that Job's connection to wisdom is solidly based on the fact that the whole book is a discussion of where wisdom might be found. The answer isn't that wisdom is faulty or inadequate and that direct revelation, which is something different (apocalyptic), provides the solution. Rather, the book demonstrates that human wisdom apart from God's revelation is faulty, but wisdom informed by God's revelation is what humans need to seek ("The fear of the Lord—that is wisdom," 28:28).

What is an apocalypse? Johnson helpfully appeals to Collins's matrix that describes the elements that help us identify the genre.[6] Rather than list the elements I will simply describe the key elements and use the book of Daniel (chs. 7–12), the one undisputed example of the genre in the Old Testament, as an illustration, though the book of Revelation in the New Testament also illustrates these traits.

In the first place, in an apocalypse there is a seer who, unlike a prophet, never hears directly from God (in some extrabiblical apocalypses the seer is caught up into heaven and overhears the divine council). When Daniel has a dream or a vision, it is an angelic mediator, not God himself, who tells him its significance. The dream/vision looks into the future with a specific purpose that is quite different from the purpose of prophecy. The prophet receives a message from God in order to share it with God's sinful people to elicit their repentance, while the seer's vision has the function of bringing comfort to God's oppressed people.

In any case, it seems to me that the book of Job misses two essential ingredients of apocalyptic. In the first place, and Johnson admits this, the book of Job has no eschatological message. God's speech to Job does not talk about the future. It certainly does not have the purpose of comforting Job in the midst of his suffering. But in the second place, the dynamics of the divine–human interaction in the book of Job do not conform to that of apocalyptic. God speaks to Job directly (that does not happen in Daniel or apocalyptic). There is no vision or dream that needs interpretation, as there often is in apocalyptic. Johnson rightly chides Shields because there is no prophet in Job who mediates a message from God, or for that matter Job is not a prophet who mediates a message to others. But Johnson's

6. J. J. Collins, ed., *Apocalypse: The Morphology of a Genre* (Semeia 14; Missoula: Scholars Press, 1979).

thesis suffers from the fact that God speaks directly to Job in rather plain language (as opposed to apocalyptic, which is typically communicated in highly symbolic, mythically informed language) that requires no apocalyptic seer.

Were the Sages Influenced by the Prophets?

The two remaining essays take a somewhat different track to the question of the relationship between wisdom and prophecy by exploring specific cases in which wisdom teachers might have been influenced by prophetic sources.

Ryan O'Dowd ("A Prophet in the Sage's House? Origins of the Feminine Metaphors in Proverbs") is interested in the depiction of folly in the book of Proverbs as a wayward woman. He begins by navigating the difficult issues that provide background for his work. For his thesis to work, he needs to clarify what is meant by sage and prophet (as well as the genres associated with each), establish the fact that wisdom (in particular the book of Proverbs) should be dated after the prophets, and also explain what exactly constitutes an allusion.

There is much to commend in his careful consideration of these matters, but I do want to object to his viewpoint that, though the sage would have no problem citing a prophet, the reverse is not true:

> The prophet...has a particular interest in social critique and avoiding associations with established religion, the so-called wise, the cult, and royal courts. Isaiah, Jeremiah, and Obadiah all specifically critique groups known as חֲכָמִים ("the wise"), רֹאִים ("diviners"), and הַחֹזִים ("seers"). Wisdom, moreover, even in its ties to kingship and appeals to creation and the cosmic Woman Wisdom, does not carry the same authoritative weight as Moses or the prophets, who speak directly from God. A prophet's overt citation of a wisdom text, or allusions lending weight to the wisdom movement, could undermine the prophetic authority and its claim to direct divine revelation. It is thus more likely that a sage would borrow from prophecy than a prophet from wisdom, but little more can be said in this regard.

In the first place, the prophetic critique of sages (he cites Isa 5:21; 19:11; 29:10; 30:10; 44:24; Jer 4:4; 8:8–9; Obad 8[7]) should not be taken as a universal condemnation of wisdom and its practitioners any more than their condemnation of prophets entails a universal condemnation of prophets (e.g., Jer 8:8–9, which, if it was a blanket condemnation of

7. Indeed, some of these don't critique the wise at all and others Egyptian and Edomite wisdom.

all prophets, would include themselves). In other words, they are not condemning wisdom but *false* wisdom. The prophets were not avoiding association with "established religion" unless it was corrupt. In the second place, the statement that "wisdom…does not carry the same authoritative weight as Moses or the prophets, who speak directly from God" strikes me as deeply questionable and theologically problematic. In the first place, I have already questioned the idea that direct revelation is alien to wisdom (and see more below). In the second place, such a view lends itself to a canon within the canon, where accounts of direct revelation somehow supersede biblical texts that don't have them (besides wisdom, think of the book of Psalms or even the historical tradition).

That said, his main thesis that "the poetic prophets—Jeremiah, Ezekiel, Hosea, and Malachi in particular—who provided the inspiration for the sages to weave together themes of harlotry, folly, and covenant infidelity in Prov 1–9," is certainly a reasonable and well-argued, though as he admits, speculative conclusion. He prefers this explanation to the idea that the inspiration came from the Deuteronomic history (that utilizes the theme broadly) or Ezra–Nehemiah with its concern about marriage to foreign women.

Even so, one does have to wonder whether there has to be a specific inspiration for a metaphor that would have presented itself as obvious to thoughtful, faithful people. The connection between adultery and idolatry (covenant infidelity) is rooted in the fact that these two sins are both violations of the only two mutually exclusive relationships. In the same way, that a faithful person can have only one God, so a woman (in the divine–human relationship metaphor the latter is always the woman/wife[8]) can have only one husband.

Finally, but not least, Richard Schultz ("Was Qohelet an Eschatological or an Anti-Apocalyptic Sage? *Hebel*, the Evil Day, and Divine Judgment in the Book of Ecclesiastes") ably analyzes recent attempts to see either affirmation or critique of prophetic/apocalyptic thinking in the book of Ecclesiastes. He shows admirable caution in trying to determine whether there is distinct prophetic influence on the book of Ecclesiastes. Thus, he concludes in his review of comparable statements and thoughts in Isaiah and Ecclesiastes that "it would be difficult to demonstrate that the latter (that is, prophetic features in Ecclesiastes) are the result of prophetic influence on Qohelet."

---

8. The metaphor may have been grounded in the monogamous relationship described in Gen 2, but the connection between adultery and idolatry could also be understandable in a polygamous situation since while humans can have only one God, God has many worshipers.

He then moves on to examine recent studies of the magnificent reflection on growing old and dying found in 12:1–7. Some scholars (Fox and even more strongly Seow), he points out, have argued that the imagery used is related to and perhaps drawn from apocalyptic imagery of the future day of divine judgment. Schultz, while appreciating these efforts, is hesitant to fully affirm the connection and even more dubious of attempts to draw further implications. Fox believes that day of judgment imagery is simply being co-opted to describe the end of a person's life in hyperbolic terms. Seow believes that it is actually pointing to end-time imagery. Schulz again exercises admirable restraint: "It is possible, perhaps even likely, to see the influence of prophetic imagery in Eccl 12:1–7, but this should not be understood as a more comprehensive affirmation of prophetic eschatology by Qohelet."

Schultz then turns to another school of thought that, rather than seeing a co-opting of prophetic language in Ecclesiastes, sees a dispute going on between the book and prophetic thought. Here he reviews the work of Kruger, Reichenbach, Perdue, and Douglas. Schultz is convincingly even more skeptical of these claims, concluding, "a careful examination of the textual evidence cited by the scholars noted in this essay indicates that the extent of prophetic influence on Qohelet's thought as well as the degree to which his teaching reflects a fundamental polemic against prophetic or apocalyptic traditions is considerably less than has been claimed."

Wisdom and Direct Revelation

If I were to pinpoint the single most interesting and perhaps important question raised by these essays, it has to do with the role of divine revelation in books that we normally associate with wisdom. Is the direct revelation, say in the book of Job particularly the theophany at the end, a foreign element (perhaps prophetic or apocalyptic) in a book often identified as wisdom, or does direct divine revelation fit comfortably with wisdom?

I have already shown my hand on this question by favoring the latter option, and in my opinion Job is not the only wisdom book that appeals to divine revelation to establish wisdom.[9]

There is no question that, say, Proverbs recognizes that wisdom comes through study and hard effort. As the father tells the son:

---

9. I lay out my case fully in Chapter 7 ("Sources of Wisdom: Experience, Observation, Tradition, Correction, and Ultimately Revelation") of *The Fear of the Lord Is Wisdom*.

My son, if you accept my words
   and store up my commands within you,
turning your ear to wisdom
   and applying your heart to understanding—
indeed, if you call out for insight
   and cry aloud for understanding,
and if you look for it as for silver,
   and search for it as for hidden treasure,
then you will understand the fear of the Lord
   and find the knowledge of God. (2:1–5)

That said, the father quickly lets his son know that ultimately the wisdom he will accrue through his effort actually comes from God himself:

From the Lord gives wisdom;
   from his mouth come knowledge and understanding. (2:6)

Wisdom that comes through study is no less directly from God than God speaking to Job out of the whirlwind. Indeed, we can only learn from our observations because God has so gifted us ("Ears that hear and eyes that see—the Lord has made them both," Prov 20:12).

But we also need to consider the role of the figure of Woman Wisdom in Proverbs. The true sage has an intimate relationship with her and learns from her. But what or who does Woman Wisdom represent? Most scholars recognize that she is a personification of the Lord's wisdom, and that is sufficient for my point here that God is the ultimate source of true wisdom. My own view that the location of her house on "the highest point of the city" (9:3, where the temple would be located) associates her directly with God strengthens this idea.[10]

As we turn to the book of Ecclesiastes, we have what I understand to be an appeal to divinely given wisdom as opposed to human wisdom, which depends solely on observation apart from the revelation of God. Qohelet tries to find meaning in life "under the sun," apart from the revelation of God, and he ends up empty. Thus, the second wise man tells his son (12:12) to adopt what we might call an "above-the-sun" perspective: "Fear God and keep his commandments, for this is the duty of all mankind. For God will bring every deed into judgment, including every hidden thing, whether good or evil" (12:13–14).[11]

10. See T. Longman III, *Proverbs* (BCOTWP; Grand Rapids: Baker, 2006), 58–61.

11. In *The Fear of the Lord Is Wisdom* (121) I suggest that the second wise man is alluding to the Tanak here. Fear God makes one think of the Writings, obeying

Thus, the book of Ecclesiastes, along with Job and Proverbs, appeals to a divinely authorized and sourced wisdom and points out the inadequacy of wisdom acquired only through the use of human experience, observation, tradition, and so forth. After all, as all three books remind us "The fear of the Lord is the beginning of wisdom." The sages and the prophets agree that true wisdom and knowledge come only from YHWH, the God of Israel.

Conclusion

I want to conclude by first commending all the contributors for their stimulating studies of the relationship between wisdom and prophecy/apocalyptic. Such studies have many variables: the nature of genre, intertextuality, the definition of wisdom and prophecy, the roles of sages and prophets, dating of textual material, and much more. No wonder there are disagreements even among the contributors themselves. I have offered my response with deep respect and with the knowledge that when we disagree it could well be me who misconstrues the material.

the commandments the Torah, and the mention of the future judgment the Prophets. Admittedly, this point is speculative and based on the supposition that Ecclesiastes is written extremely late in the postexilic period (T. Longman III, "Determining the Historical Context of Ecclesiastes," in *The Words of the Wise Are Like Goads: Engaging Qohelet in the 21st Century* [ed. Mark J. Boda, Tremper Longman III, and Cristian Rata; Winona Lake: Eisenbrauns, 2013], 89–102).

BIBLIOGRAPHY

Allen, Leslie C. *Jeremiah: A Commentary*. OTL. Louisville: Westminster John Knox, 2008.

Alster, Bendt. *Proverbs of Ancient Sumer: The World's Earliest Proverb Collection*. 2 vols. Bethesda: CDL, 1997.

———. *Wisdom of Ancient Sumer*. Bethesda: CDL, 2005.

Alter, Robert. *The Art of Biblical Poetry*. New York: Basic, 1985.

Barbour, Jennie. *The Story of Israel in the Book of Qohelet: Ecclesiastes as Cultural Memory*. Oxford Theology and Religion Monographs. Oxford: Oxford University Press, 2012.

Barr, James. *The Garden of Eden and the Hope of Immortality*. Minneapolis: Fortress, 1992.

———. *The Semantics of Biblical Language*. Oxford: Oxford University Press, 1961.

———. "'Thou Art the Cherub': Ezekiel 28:14 and the Post-Ezekiel Understanding of Genesis of Genesis 2–3." In *Priests, Prophets, and Scribes: Essays on the Formation and Heritage of Second Temple Judaism in Honour of Joseph Blenkinsopp*, ed. Eugene Ulrich et al., 213–23. JSOTSup 149. Sheffield: JSOT Press, 1992.

Barth, Karl. "Fear of the Lord Is the Beginning of Wisdom." *Int* 14 (1960): 433–39.

Bartholomew, Craig G. *Ecclesiastes*. BCOTWP. Grand Rapids: Baker Academic, 2009.

Barton, John. '*Déjà lu*: Intertextuality, Method or Theory?' In *Reading Job Intertextually*, ed. K. Dell and W. Kynes, 1–18. LHBOTS 574. London: T&T Clark International, 2013.

———. "The Law and the Prophets: Who Are the Prophets?" In *Prophets, Worship and Theodicy: Studies in Prophetism, Biblical Theology and Structural and Rhetorical Analysis and on the Place of Music in Worship: Papers Read at the Joint British-Dutch Old Testament Conference Held at Woudschoten 1982*, 1–18. OTS 23. Leiden: Brill, 1984.

———. *Oracles of God: Perceptions of Ancient Prophecy in Israel After the Exile*. New York: Oxford University Press, 1986.

Bastiaens, J. C. "The Language of Suffering in Job 16–19 and in the Suffering Servant Passages of Deutero-Isaiah." In *Studies in the Book of Isaiah: Festschrift Willem A. M. Beuken*, ed. J. Van Ruiten and M. Vervenne, 421–32. BETL 132. Leuven: Peeters, 1997.

Baumann, Gerlinde. "Jeremia, die Weisen und die Weisheit: Eine Untersuchung von Jer 9,22f." *ZAW* 114 (2002): 59–79.

Beal, Richard H. "Hittite Oracles." In *Magic and Divination in the Ancient World*, ed. Leda Ciraolo and Jonathan Seidel, 57–81. AMD 2. Leiden: Brill, 2002.

Beaulieu, Paul-Alain. "The Social and Intellectual Setting of Babylonian Wisdom Literature." In *Wisdom Literature in Mesopotamia and Israel*, ed. Richard J. Clifford, 3–19. SymS 36. Atlanta: SBL, 2007.

Beckman, Gary. "Proverbs and Proverbial Allusions in Hittite," *JNES* 45 (1986): 19–30.

Ben Zvi, E. "Understanding the Message of the Tripartite Prophetic Books." *RQ* 35 (1993): 93–100.

Bergey, Ronald. "The Song of Moses (Deuteronomy 32:1–43) and Isaianic Prophecies: A Case of Early Intertextuality?" *JSOT* 28 (2003): 33–54.

Blenkinsopp, Joseph. *Sage, Priest, Prophet: Religious and Intellectual Leadership in Ancient Israel.* LAI. Louisville: Westminster John Knox, 1995.

Bloch, Ariel A. "Questioning God's Omnipotence in the Bible: A Linguistic Case Study." In *Semitic Studies in Honor of Wolf Leslau on the Occasion of His Eighty-fifth Birthday.* Vol. 1, ed. Wolf Leslau and Alan S. Kaye, 174–88. Wiesbaden: Harrassowitz, 1991.

Blocher, Henri. "The Fear of the Lord as the 'Principle' of Wisdom." *TynBul* 28 (1977): 3–28.

Block, Daniel I. *Ezekiel 25–48.* NICOT. Grand Rapids: Eerdmans, 1998.

Blum, Erhard. "Formgeschichte—A Misleading Category? Some Critical Remarks." In *The Changing Face of Form Criticism for the Twenty-First Century*, ed. Marvin A. Sweeney and Ehud Ben Zvi, 32–45. Grand Rapids: Eerdmans, 2003.

Boda, Mark J. *Praying the Tradition: The Origin and Use of Tradition in Nehemiah 9.* BZAW 277. Berlin: de Gruyter, 1999.

Bogaert, P.-M. "Les mécanismes en Jér. 10,1–6 (LXX et MT) et la significance des supplements." In *Le livre de Jérémie: le prophète et son milieu, les oracles et leur transmission*, ed. P.-M. Bogaert, 222–38. 2nd ed. Leuven: Leuven University Press, 1997.

Borger, Rykle. "The Incantation Series *Bīt Mēseri* and Enoch's Ascension to Heaven." *JNES* 33 (1974): 183–96

Borghouts, J. F. "Divine Intervention in Ancient Egypt and Its Manifestation (*Bꜣw*)." In *Gleanings from Deir El-Medîna*, ed. R. J. Demarée and Jac J. Janssen, 1–70. Leiden: Nederlands Instituut voor het Nabije Oosten, 1982.

Bowman, John. "The Fear of the Lord." In *Studies in Wisdom Literature*, ed. W. C. Van Wyk, 9–12. Papers Presented at the 15th and 16th Congresses of the Ou-Testamentiese Werkgemeenskap in Suid-Afrika Held in 1972 and 1973. Hercules, South Africa: NHW, 1981.

Brenner, Athalaya. "Pornoprophetics Revisited: Some Additional Reflections." *JSOT* 70 (1996): 63–86.

Brown, K. *The Vision in Job 4 and Its Role in the Book: Reframing the Development of the Joban Dialogues.* Studies of the Sofja Kovalevskaja Research Group on Early Jewish Monotheism 4. Tübingen: Mohr Siebeck, 2015.

Brown, William P. *Character in Crisis: A Fresh Approach to the Wisdom Literature of the Old Testament.* Grand Rapids: Eerdmans, 1996.

———. "'Come, O Children…I Will Teach You the Fear of the Lord' (Psalm 34:12): Comparing Psalms and Proverbs." In *Seeking Out the Wisdom of the Ancients*, ed. Ronald L. Troxel et al., 85–102. Winona Lake: Eisenbrauns, 2005.

———. *Wisdom's Wonder: Character, Creation, and Crisis in the Bible's Wisdom Literature.* Grand Rapids: Eerdmans, 2014.

Bruch, Johann. *Weisheits-Lehre der Hebräer: Ein Beitrag zur Geschichte der Philosophie.* Strasbourg: Treuttel & Würtz, 1851.

Brueggemann, Walter A. "The Epistological Crisis of Israel's Two Histories (Jer. 9:22–23)." In *Israelite Wisdom: Theological and Literary Essays in Honor of Samuel Terrien*, ed. J. G. Gammie et al., 85–105. Missoula: Scholars Press, 1978.

Bryce, Glendon E. "Another Wisdom 'Book' in Proverbs." *JBL* 91 (1972): 145–57.

Buss, Martin J. "Dialogue in and Among Genres." In *Bakhtin and Genre Theory in Biblical Studies*, ed. Roland Boer, 9–18. SemeiaS 63. Atlanta: SBL, 2007.

Camp, Claudia. *Wisdom and the Feminine in the Book of Proverbs*. Bible and Literature. Sheffield: Almond, 1985.

Campbell, Anthony F. "Form Criticism's Future." In *The Changing Face of Form Criticism for the Twenty-First Century*, ed. Marvin A. Sweeney and Ehud Ben Zvi, 15–31. Grand Rapids: Eerdmans, 2003.

Carr, David M. "Orality, Textuality, *and* Memory: The State of Biblical Studies." In *Contextualizing Israel's Sacred Writings: Ancient Literacy, Orality, and Literary Production*, ed. Brian B. Schmidt, 161–73. AIL 22. Atlanta: SBL, 2015.

———. *Writing on the Tablet of the Heart: Origins of Scripture and Literature*. Oxford: Oxford University Press, 2005.

Castelo, Daniel. "The Fear of the Lord as Theological Method." *JTI* 2 (2008): 147–60.

Cate, Robert L. "The Fear of the Lord in the Old Testament." *Theological Educator* 35 (1987): 41–55.

Cheung, Simon Chi-Chung. *Wisdom Intoned: A Reappraisal of the Genre "Wisdom Psalms."* LHBOTS 613. London: Bloomsbury T&T Clark, 2015.

Childs, Brevard. *Isaiah: A Commentary.* OTL. Louisville: Westminster John Knox, 2011.

Clifford, Richard J. *Proverbs: A Commentary.* OTL. Louisville: Westminster John Knox, 1999.

Clines, D. J. A. "'The Fear of the Lord Is Wisdom' (Job 28:28): A Semantic and Contextual Study." In *Job 28: Cognition in Context*, ed. E. J. Van Wolde, 57–92. Biblical Interpretation 64. Leiden: Brill, 2003.

———. *I, He, We, and They: A Literary Approach to Isaiah 53*. JSOTSup 1. Reprint, Sheffield: Sheffield Academic Press, 1983.

———. *Job 1–20*. WBC 17. Dallas: Word, 1989.

———. *Job 21–37*. WBC 18a. Nashville: Thomas Nelson, 2006.

———. *Job 38–42*. WBC 18b. Nashville: Thomas Nelson, 2011.

Cohen, Yoram. *The Scribes and Scholars of the City of Emar in the Late Bronze Age.* HSS 59. Winona Lake: Eisenbrauns, 2009.

———. *Wisdom from the Late Bronze Age*. WAW 29. Atlanta: SBL, 2013.

Collins John J., ed. *Apocalypse: The Morphology of a Genre*. Semeia 14. Missoula: Scholars Press, 1979.

———. *The Apocalyptic Imagination: An Introduction to Jewish Apocalyptic Literature.* 2nd ed. Grand Rapids: Eerdmans, 1998.

———. "Cosmos and Salvation: Jewish Wisdom and Apocalyptic in the Hellenistic Age." *History of Religions* 17 (1977): 121–42.

———. *Daniel*. Hermeneia. Minneapolis: Fortress, 1993.

———. "Epilogue: Genre Analysis and the Dead Sea Scrolls." *DSD* 17 (2010): 418–30.

———. "Introduction: Towards the Morphology of a Genre." *Semeia* 14 (1979): 1–20.

———. "Structure and Meaning in the Testament of Job." In *Society of Biblical Literature Seminar Papers 1974*, ed. George MacRae, 1:35–52. Cambridge: Scholars Press, 1974.

———. "Towards the Morphology of a Genre." *Semeia* 14 (1978): 1–20.

———. "What Is Apocalyptic Literature?" In *The Oxford Handbook of Apocalyptic Literature*. Edited by John J. Collins, 1–16. Oxford: Oxford University Press, 2014.

Cook, S. "A Reading of Job as a Theatrical Work: Challenging a Retributive Deuteronomistic Theodicy." *Literature & Aesthetics* 24, no. 2 (2014): 39–62.

Coombs, James H. "Allusion Defined and Explained." *Poetics* 13 (1984): 475–88.

Corral, Martin Alonso. *Ezekiel's Oracles Against Tyre*. BibOr 46. Rome: Pontifico Istituto Biblico, 2002.

Coxon, Peter W. "Daniel III 17: A Linguistic and Theological Problem." *VT* 26 (1976): 400–409.

Crenshaw, James L. "The Influence of the Wise Upon Amos: The 'Doxologies of Amos' and Job 5:9–16; 9:5–10." *ZAW* 79 (1967): 42–52.

———. "Method in Determining Wisdom Influence Upon 'Historical Literature.'" *JBL* 88 (1969): 129–42.

———. *Old Testament Wisdom: An Introduction*. 3rd ed. Louisville: Westminster John Knox, 2010.

———. "Prolegomenon." In *Studies in Ancient Israelite Wisdom*, edited by James L. Crenshaw, 1–60. LBS. New York: Ktav, 1976.

———. *Prophetic Conflict: Its Effect on Israelite Religion*. New York: de Gruyter, 1971.

———. "Qoheleth's Understanding of Intellectual Inquiry." In *Qohelet in the Context of Wisdom*, ed. A. Schoors, 205–24. BZAW 136. Leuven: Leuven University Press and Uitgeveru Peeters, 1998.

Cross, Frank Moore. "The Development of the Jewish Scripts." In *The Bible and the Ancient Near East: Essays in Honor of William Foxwell Albright*, ed. G. Ernst Wright, 170–264. London: Routledge & Kegan Paul, 1961.

———. "New Directions in the Study of Apocalyptic." *Journal for Theology and the Church* 6 (1969): 133–202.

Crouch, C. L. "Ezekiel's Oracles Against the Nations in Light of a Royal Ideology of Warfare." *JBL* 130 (2011): 473–92.

Davies, Philip R., and Thomas Römer, eds. *Writing the Bible: Scribes, Scribalism and Script*. BibleWorld. London: Routledge, 2013.

Day, John, Robert P. Gordon, and H. G. M. Williamson, eds. *Wisdom in Ancient Israel: Essays in Honour of J. A. Emerton*. Cambridge: Cambridge University Press, 1995.

Ellis, Maria de Jong. "Observations on Mesopotamian Oracles and Prophetic Texts: Literary and Historiographical Considerations." *JCS* 41 (1989): 127–86.

Dell, Katharine J. *The Book of Job as Sceptical Literature*. BZAW 197. Berlin: de Gruyter, 1991.

———. *The Book of Proverbs in Social and Theological Context*. Cambridge: Cambridge University Press, 2006.

———. "Deciding the Boundaries of 'Wisdom': Applying the Concept of Family Resemblance." In *Was There a Wisdom Tradition? New Prospects in Israelite Wisdom Studies*, ed. Mark Sneed, 145–60. AIL 23. Atlanta: SBL, 2015.

———. "Ecclesiastes as Mainstream Wisdom (without Job)." In *Goochem in Mokum/ Wisdom in Amsterdam*, ed. George J. Brooke and Pierre Van Hecke, 43–52. OTS 68. Leiden: Brill, 2016.

———. *"Get Wisdom, Get Insight": An Introduction to Israel's Wisdom Literature*. Macon: Smyth & Helwys, 2000.

———. *Job: Where Shall Wisdom Be Found?* Sheffield: Sheffield Phoenix, 2013.

———. "Review of *Now My Eye Sees You*." *JSOT* 35 (2011): 121–22.

———. "Wisdom in Israel." In *Text in Context: Essays by Members of the Society for Old Testament Study*, ed. A. D. H. Mayes, 348–75. Oxford: Oxford University Press, 2000.

Dell, Katharine J., and Will Kynes, eds. *Reading Ecclesiastes Intertextually*. LHBOTS 587. New York: Bloomsbury T&T Clark, 2014.

————. *Reading Job Intertextually.* LHBOTS 574. New York: Bloomsbury T&T Clark, 2013.

————. *Reading Proverbs Intertextually.* LHBOTS. New York: Bloomsbury T&T Clark, forthcoming.

Derrida, Jacques. "The Law of Genre." *Critical Inquiry* 7 (1980): 55–82;

Di Lella, Alexander A. "Fear of the Lord and Belief and Hope in the Lord Amid Trials: Sirach 2:1–18." In *Wisdom, You Are My Sister: Essays in Honor of Roland E. Murphy, O. Carm., on the Occasion of His Eightieth Birthday,* ed. Michael L. Barre, 188–204. CBQMS. Washington, DC: The Catholic Biblical Association, 1997.

————. "Fear of the Lord as Wisdom: Ben Sira 1, 11–30." In *The Book of Ben Sira in Modern Research: Proceedings of the First International Ben Sira Conference 29–31 July, 1996, Soesterberg, Netherlands,* ed. Pancratius C. Beentjes, 113–33. BZAW 225. New York: de Gruyter, 1997.

Dijkstra, Meindert. "Lawsuit, Debate, and Wisdom Discourse in Second Isaiah." In *Studies in the Book of Isaiah: Festschrift Willem A. M. Beuken,* ed. J. Van Ruiten and M. Vervenne, 251–71. BETL 132. Leuven: Leuven University Press, 1997.

Donn, Morgan F. "Wisdom and the Prophets." In *Studia Biblica 1978: 1, Papers on Old Testament and Related Themes,* ed. E. A. Livingstone, 209–44. Sheffield: JSOT, 1978.

————. *Wisdom in the Old Testament Traditions.* Atlanta: John Knox; Oxford: Blackwell, 1981.

Douglas, Jerome N. *A Polemical Preacher of Joy: An Anti-Apocalyptic Genre for Qohelet's Message of Joy.* Eugene: Pickwick, 2014.

Duensing, Hugo. "Apocalypse of Paul." In *New Testament Apocrypha,* ed. E. Hennecke and W. Schneemelcher, trans. R. Wilson, 2:755–98. Philadelphia: Westminster, 1964.

Duguid, Iain M. *Ezekiel and the Leaders of Israel.* VTSup 56. Leiden: Brill, 1994.

Dutcher-Walls, Patricia. "The Social Location of the Deuteronomists: A Sociological Study of Factional Politics in the Late Pre-exilic Judah." *JSOT* 52 (1991): 77–94.

Edenburg, Cynthia. "How [Not] to Murder a King: Variations on a Theme in 1 Sam 24; 26." *SJOT* 12 (1998): 64–85.

Eichrodt, Walther. *Ezekiel: A Commentary.* OTL. Philadelphia: Westminster, 1970.

Estes, Daniel J. *Hear, My Son: Teaching and Learning in Proverbs 1–9.* NSBT 4. Downers Grove: InterVarsity, 1997.

Farber, W. "Witchcraft, Magic, and Divination in Ancient Mesopotamia." In *Civilizations of the Ancient Near East,* ed. J. M. Sasson, 1895–1909. Peabody: Hendrickson, 1995.

Feldman, L. H. "Prophets and Prophecy in Josephus." In *Prophets, Prophecy, and Prophetic Texts in Second Temple Judaism.* Edited by Michael H. Floyd and Robert D. Haak, 201–39. LHBOTS 427. New York: T&T Clark International, 2006.

Fey, Reinhard. *Amos und Jesaja: Abhängigkeit und Eigenständigkeit des Jesaja.* WMANT 12. Neukirchen-Vluyn: Neukirchener Verlag, 1963.

Fichtner, Johannes. "Jesaja unter den Weisen." *TLZ* 74 (1949): 75–80.

Fish, Stanley. *Is There a Text in This Class?* Cambridge, MA: Harvard University Press, 1980.

Fishbane, Michael. *Biblical Interpretation in Ancient Israel.* Rev. ed. Oxford: Clarendon, 1988.

————. "Inner-Biblical Exegesis: Types and Strategies of Interpretation in Ancient Israel." In *Midrash and Literature,* ed. Geoffrey H. Hartman and Sanford Budick, 19–37. New Haven: Yale University Press, 1986.

————. "Revelation and Tradition: Aspects of Inner-Biblical Exegesis." *JBL* 99 (1980): 343–61.

Floyd, M. "Introduction." In *Prophets, Prophecy, and Prophetic Texts in Second Temple Judaism*. Edited by Michael H. Floyd and Robert D. Haak, 3–5. LHBOTS 427. New York: T&T Clark International, 2006.

———. "Prophetic Complaints about the Fulfillment of Oracles in Habakkuk 1:2–17 and Jeremiah 15:10–18." *JBL* 110 (1991): 397–418.

Foster, Benjamin R. *Before the Muses: An Anthology of Akkadian Literature*. Bethesda: CDL, 2005.

Fowler, Alastair. *Kinds of Literature: An Introduction to the Theory of Genres and Modes*. Cambridge, MA: Harvard University Press, 1982.

Fox, Michael V. *Ecclesiastes* קהלת. JPS Bible Commentary. Philadelphia: Jewish Publication Society, 2004.

———. "The Epistemology of the Book of Proverbs." *JBL* 126 (2007): 669–84.

———. "Ideas of Wisdom in Proverbs 1–9." *JBL* 116 (1997): 613–33.

———. "The Innterstructure of Qoheleth's Thought." In *Qohelet in the Context of Wisdom*, ed. A. Schoors, 225–38. BZAW 136. Leuven: Leuven University Press and Uitgeveru Peeters, 1998.

———. "Joseph and Wisdom." In *The Book of Genesis: Composition, Reception, and Interpretation*, ed. C. E. Evans, J. N. Lohr, and D. L. Petersen, 231–62. VTSup 152. Leiden: Brill, 2012.

———. *Proverbs 1–9: A New Translation with Introduction and Commentary*. AB 18A. New York: Doubleday, 2000.

———. *Proverbs 10–31*. AB 18B. New Haven: Yale University Press, 2009.

———. "The Social Location of the Book of Proverbs." In *Texts, Temples, and Traditions: A Tribute to Menahem Haran*, ed. Michael V. Fox et al., 227–39. Winona Lake: Eisenbrauns, 1996.

———. "Three Theses on Wisdom." In *Was There a Wisdom Tradition? New Prospects in Israelite Wisdom Studies*, ed. Mark R. Sneed, 69–86. AIL 23. Atlanta: SBL, 2015.

———. *A Time to Tear Down and a Time to Build Up: A Rereading of Ecclesiastes*. Grand Rapids: Eerdmans, 1999.

Frankel, D. "The Speech about God in Job 42:7–8: A Contribution to the Coherence of Job." *HUCA* 82 (2011–2012): 1–36.

Fredericks, Daniel C. "Life's Storms and Structural Unity in Qoheleth 11.1–12.7." *JSOT* 52 (1991): 95–114.

Frow, John. *Genre: The New Critical Idiom*. London: Routledge, 2006.

Fyall, R. S. *Now My Eyes Have Seen You: Images of Creation and Evil in the Book of Job*. NSBT 12. Downers Grove: InterVarsity, 2002.

Gammie, J. G. "From Prudentialism to Apocalypticism: The Houses of the Sages Amid the Varying Forms of Wisdom." In *The Sage in Israel and the Ancient Near East*, ed. J. G. Gammie and L. G. Perdue, 479–97. Winona Lake: Eisenbrauns, 1990.

Geller, Stephen. "'Where Is Wisdom?' A Literary Study of Job 28 in Its Setting." In *Judaic Perspectives on Ancient Israel*, ed. J. Neusner, B. Levine, and E. Frerichs, 155–88. Philadelphia: Fortress, 1987.

Gerstenberger, Erhard. "The Woe-Oracles of the Prophets." *JBL* 81 (1962): 249–63.

Geyer, John B. *Mythology and Lament: Studies in the Oracles About the Nations*. SOTSMS. Aldershot: Ashgate, 2004.

Gilbert, M. "Jérémie en conflit avec les sages?" In *Le livre de Jérémie: le prophète et son milieu, les oracles et leur transmission*, ed. P.-M. Bogaert, 105–18. 2nd ed. Leuven: Leuven University Press, 1997.

Glassner, Jean-Jacques. "The Use of Knowledge in Ancient Mesopotamia." In *Civilizations of the Ancient Near East*, ed. Jack M. Sasson, 1815–23. Peabody: Hendrickson, 2000.

Goff, Matthew. "Qumran Wisdom Literature and the Problem of Genre." *DSD* 17 (2010): 315–35.

———. "Wisdom and Apocalypticism." In *The Oxford Handbook of Apocalyptic Literature*, ed. John J. Collins, 52–68. Oxford: Oxford University Press, 2014.

Goldingay, John. *The Message of Isaiah 40–55: A Literary-Theological Commentary*. New York: T&T Clark International, 2005.

Gordis, R. *The Book of God and Man: A Study of Job*. Chicago: University of Chicago Press, 1965.

———. *Koheleth—The Man and His World: A Study of Ecclesiastes*. New York: Schocken, 1968.

Gordon, Robert P. "Where Have All the Prophets Gone? The 'Disappearing' Israelite Prophet Against the Background of Ancient Near Eastern Prophecy." *BBR* 5 (1995): 67–86.

Gowan, D. "Habakkuk and Wisdom." *Perspective* 9 (1968): 157–66.

Grabbe, Lester L. *Priests, Prophets, Diviners, Sages: A Socio-Historical Study of Religious Specialists in Ancient Israel*. Valley Forge: Trinity, 1995.

Gray, J. *The Book of Job*. The Text of the Hebrew Bible 1. Sheffield: Sheffield Phoenix, 2010.

Grayson, A. K., and W. G. Lambert. "Akkadian Prophecies." *Jcs* 18 (1964): 7–30.

Green, James N., and Peter Stallybrass. "Benjamin Franklin: Writer and Printer: Inventing Poor Richard." The Library Company of Philadelphia. Online: http://www.librarycompany.org/bfwriter/poor.htm (accessed 9 December 2015).

Greenberg, Moshe. *Ezekiel 21–37*. AB 22A. New Haven: Yale University Press, 1997.

Grossman, Yonatan. "The Story of Joseph's Brothers in Light of the 'Therapeutic Narrative' Theory." *BibInt* 21 (2013): 171–95.

Guinan, Ann K. "A Severed Head Laughed: Stories of Divinatory Interpretation." In *Magic and Divination in the Ancient World*, ed. Leda Ciraolo and Jonathan Seidel, 7–40. AMD 2. Leiden: Brill, 2002.

Gunkel, Hermann. "The Literature of Ancient Israel." Translated by Armin Siedlecki. In *Relating to the Text: Interdisciplinary and Form-Critical Insights on the Bible*, ed. Timothy Sandoval, Carleen Mandolfo, and Martin J. Buss, 26–83. JSOTSup 384. London: T&T Clark International, 2003.

———. *The Psalms: A Form-Critical Introduction*. Philadelphia: Fortress, 1967.

Habel, N. *The Book of Job: A Commentary*. OTL. Philadelphia: Westminster, 1985.

Hagedorn, A. *Die Anderen im Spiegel: Israels Auseinandersetzung mit den Völkern in den Büchern Nahum, Zefanja, Obadja und Joel*. BZAW 414. Berlin: de Gruyter, 2011.

Hallo, William W. "Akkadian Apocalypses." *IEJ* 16 (1966): 231–42.

———. "The Birth of Kings." In *Love and Death in the Ancient Near East: Essays in Honor of Marvin H. Pope*, ed. J. H. Marks and R. M. Good, 45–52. Guilford: Four Quarters, 1987.

Halton, Charles. "Allusions to the Stream of Tradition in Neo-Assyrian Oracles." *ANES* 46 (2009): 50–61.

Hamilton, Mark. "Riddles and Parables, Traditions and Texts: Ezekielian Perspectives on Israelite Wisdom Traditions." In *Was There a Wisdom Tradition? New Prospects in Israelite Wisdom Studies*, ed. Mark R. Sneed, 241–64. AIL 23. Atlanta: Society of Biblical Literature, 2015.

Hamori, Esther J. *Women's Divination in Biblical Literature: Prophecy, Necromancy, and Other Arts of Knowledge*. ABRL. New Haven: Yale University Press, 2015.

Hanson, Paul. "Apocalyptic Consciousness." *Quarterly Review* 4 (1984): 28–39.

———. *The Dawn of Apocalyptic: The Historical and Sociological Roots of Jewish Apocalyptic Eschatology*. Rev. ed. Philadelphia: Fortress, 1979.

Harding, J. E. "The Book of Job as Metaprophecy." *Studies in Religion / Sciences Religieuses* 39, no. 4 (2010): 523–47.

Harman, Louis F., and Alexander A. Di Lella. *The Book of Daniel: A New Translation with Introduction and Commentary*. AB 23. New York: Doubleday, 1977.

Hartin, Patrick. *A Spirituality of Perfection: Faith in Action in the Letter of James*. Collegeville: Liturgical Press, 1999.

Hartley, J. E. *The Book of Job*. NICOT. Grand Rapids: Eerdmans, 1988.

Hatton, Peter T. H. "A Cautionary Tale: The Acts–Consequence 'Construct.'" *JSOT* 35 (2011): 375–84.

———. *Contradiction in the Book of Proverbs: The Deep Waters of Counsel*. SOTSMS 13. Aldershot: Ashgate, 2008.

Hayes, Katherine. "'A Spirit of Deep Sleep': Divinely Induced Delusion and Wisdom in Isaiah 1–39." *CBQ* 74 (2012): 39–54.

Hays, Christopher B. "Echoes of the Ancient Near East? Intertextuality and the Comparative Study of the Old Testament." In *The Word Leaps the Gap: Essays on Scripture and Theology in Honor of Richard B. Hays*, ed. J. Ross Wagner, C. Kevin Rowe, and A. Katherine Grieb, 20–43. Grand Rapids: Eerdmans, 2008.

Hays, Richard B. *Echoes of Scripture in the Letters of Paul*. New Haven: Yale University Press, 1989.

———. *First Corinthians*. Int. Louisville: John Knox, 1997.

Heim, Knut Martin. *Poetic Imagination in Proverbs: Variant Repetitions and the Nature of Poetry*. BBRSup 4. Winona Lake: Eisenbrauns, 2013.

Hellholm, David. "The Problem of Apocalyptic Genre and the Apocalypse of John." *Semeia* 36 (1986): 1–12.

Hermisson, H.-J. "Prophetie und Weisheit." In *Weisheit in Israel*, ed. D. J. A. Clines et al., 111–30. Altes Testament und Moderne 12. Münster: Lit-Verlag, 2003.

———. *Studien zur isralitischen Spruchweisheit*. WMANT 28. Neukirchen-Vluyn: Neukirchener Verlag, 1968.

———. "Weisheit im Jeremiabuch." In *Schriftauslegung in der Schrift: Festschrift für Odil Hannes Steck zu seinem 65. Geburtstag*, ed. K. Schmidt et al., 175–91. BZAW 300. Berlin: de Gruyter, 2000.

Hilber, John W. "The Culture of Prophecy and Writing in the Ancient Near East." In *Do Historical Matters Matter to Faith?*, ed. James K. Hoffmeier and Dennis Magary, 219–42. Wheaton: Crossway, 2012.

———. "Prophetic Speech in the Egyptian Royal Cult." In *On Stone and Scroll: Essays in Honour of Graham Ivor Davies*, ed. James K. Aitken, Katharine J. Dell, and Brian A. Mastin, 39–54. BZAW 420. Berlin: de Gruyter, 2011.

Hirsch, E. D. *Validity in Interpretation*. New Haven: Yale University Press, 1967.

Holladay, William L. *Jeremiah 1: A Commentary on the Prophet Jeremiah Chapters 1–25*. Hermeneia. Philadelphia: Fortress, 1986.

Holmgren, Fredrick Carlson. "Barking Dogs Never Bite, Except Now and Then: Proverbs and Job." *AThR* 61 (1979): 341–53.

Howe, Bonnie, and Eve Sweetser. "Cognitive Linguistics and Biblical Interpretation." In *The Oxford Encyclopedia of Biblical Interpretation*, ed. S. L. McKenzie, 121–31. Oxford: Oxford University Press, 2014.

Huddleston, J. Review of *Now My Eye Sees You: Unveiling an Apocalyptic Job* by Timothy J. Johnson. *BibInt* 21 (2013): 425.

Huffmon, Herbert B. "The Covenant Lawsuit in the Prophets." *JBL* 78 (1959): 285–95.

———. "Prophecy in the Mari Archives." In *Prophecy and Prophets: The Diversity of Contemporary Issues in Scholarship*, ed. Yehoshua Gitay, 7–22. SemeiaSt 33. Atlanta: Scholars Press, 1997.

Hunter, Alastair. *Wisdom Literature*. London: SCM, 2006.

Hurowitz, Victor Avigdor. "The Wisdom of Šūpê-amēlī–a Deathbed Debate Between a Father and Son." In *Wisdom Literature in Mesopotamia and Israel*, ed. Richard J. Clifford, 37–54. Leiden: Brill, 2007.

Illman, K.-J. "Theodicy in Job." In *Theodicy in the World of the Bible*, ed. A. Laato and J. C. de Moor, 304–33. Leiden: Brill, 2003.

Irwin, William. "What Is an Allusion?" *Journal of Aesthetics and Art Criticism* 59 (2001): 287–97.

Jacobs, Mignon R. "The Conceptual Dynamics of Good and Evil in the Joseph Story: An Exegetical and Hermeneutical Inquiry." *JSOT* 27 (2003): 309–38.

Janzen, J. Gerald. *At the Scent of Water: The Ground of Hope in the Book of Job*. Grand Rapids: Eerdmans, 2009.

Jaroš, Karl. "Die Motive der Heiligen Bäume und der Schlange in Gen 2–3." *ZAW* 92 (1980): 204–15.

Jensen, Joseph. *The Use of Tôrâ by Isaiah: His Debate with the Wisdom Tradition*. CBQMS 3. Washington, DC: Catholic Biblical Association of America, 1973.

Jindo, Job Y. "Toward a Poetics of the Biblical Mind." *VT* 59 (2009): 225.

Johnson, Elizabeth. *The Function of Apocalyptic and Wisdom Traditions in Romans 9–11*. SBLDS 109. Atlanta: Scholars, 1989.

Johnson, Timothy J. "Apocalypticism, Apocalyptic Literature." In *Dictionary of the Old Testament: Prophets*, ed. Mark J. Boda and J. Gordon McConville, 36–42. Downers Grove: InterVarsity, 2012.

———. *Now My Eyes See You: Unveiling an Apocalyptic Job*. HBM 24. Sheffield: Sheffield Phoenix, 2009.

Jones, Douglas R. *Jeremiah*. New Century Bible. Grand Rapids: Eerdmans, 1992.

Jones, Scott. Review of *Now My Eye Sees You: Unveiling an Apocalyptic Job* by Timothy J. Johnson. *Review of Biblical Literature* 02/2011. Online: https://www.bookreviews.org/pdf/7514_8199.pdf (accessed 20 July 2017).

Joyce, Paul. "'Even if Noah, Daniel, and Job Were in It...' (Ezekiel 14:14): The Case of Job and Ezekiel." In *Reading Job Intertextually*, ed. Katharine J. Dell and Will Kynes, 118–28. LHBOTS 574. London: Bloomsbury T&T Clark, 2013.

———. *Ezekiel: A Commentary*. LHBOTS 482. London: T&T Clark International, 2009.

Kaiser, Walter C., Jr. "Wisdom Theology and the Centre of Old Testament Theology." *EvQ* 50 (1978): 132–46.

Kent, Thomas. *Interpretation and Genre*. Lewisburg: Bucknell, 1986.

Kessler, R. "Amos and Wisdom." Paper presented at the Society of Biblical Literature, San Diego, 23 November 2014.

Keun-Jo, Ahn. "The Trace of Wisdom in the Book of Jeremiah." In *Mapping and Engaging the Bible in Asian Cultures: Congress of the Society of Asian Biblical Studies 2008 Seoul Conference*, ed. Yeong Mee Lee and Yoon Jong Yoo, 177–93. Korea: Christian Literature Society of Korea, 2009.

Koch, Klaus. "Gibt es ein Vergeltungsdogma im Alten Testament." *ZTK* 52 (1955): 1–42.

Koole, Jan. *Isaiah III.* Vol. 2, *Isaiah 49–55*, trans. A. P. Runia. HCOT. Kampen: Kok Pharos, 1998.

Kovacs, Brian. "Is There a Class-Ethic in Proverbs?" In *Essays in Old Testament Ethics*, ed. James L. Crenshaw and John T. Wills, 173–89. New York: Ktav, 1974.

Köveces, Zoltán. *Metaphor: A Practical Introduction.* Oxford: Oxford University Press, 2002.

Krüger, Thomas. "Dekonstruktion und Reconstruktion prophetischer Eschatologie im Qohelet Buch." In *'Jedes Ding hat seine Zeit...' Studien zur israelitischen und altorientalischen Weisheit. Diethelm Michel zum 65. Geburtstag*, ed. Anja Diesel et al., 107–29. BZAW 241. Berlin: de Gruyter, 1996.

———. "Did Job Repent?" In *Das Buch Hiob und seine Interpretation: Beiträge zum Hiob-Symposium auf dem Monte Verità vom 14.19. August 2005*, ed. T. Krüger et al., 217–29. ATANT 88. Zurich: Theologischer Verlag Zürich, 2007.

———. *Qohelet.* Hermeneia. Translated by O. C. Dean Jr. Minneapolis: Fortress, 2004.

Kubina, V. *Die Gottesreden im Buche Hiob.* Freiburger Theologische Studien 115. Frieberg: Herder, 1979.

Kutsch, Ernst. "Weisheit und Prophetenwort: Zur Traditionsgeschichte des Spruches Jer 9,22–23." *BZ* NF 25, no. 2 (1981): 161–79. Reprinted in *Kleine Schriften zum Alten Testament*, ed. L. Schmidt and K. Eberlein, 197–215. BZAW 168. Berlin: de Gruyter, 1986.

Kynes, Will. *An Obituary for "Wisdom Literature."* Oxford: Oxford University Press, forthcoming.

———. "Job and Isaiah 40–55: Intertextualities in Dialogue." In *Reading Job Intertextually*, ed. K. Dell and W. Kynes, 94–105. LHBOTS 574. New York: Bloomsbury T&T Clark, 2013.

———. "The Modern Scholarly Wisdom Tradition and the Threat of Pan-Sapientialism: A Case Report." In *Was There a Wisdom Tradition? New Prospects in Israelite Wisdom Studies*, ed. Mark Sneed, 11–38. AIL. Atlanta: SBL, 2015.

———. "The Nineteenth-Century Beginnings of 'Wisdom Literature,' and Its Twenty-First-century End?" In *Perspectives on Israelite Wisdom: Proceedings of the Oxford Old Testament Seminar*, ed. John Jarick, 83–108. LHBOTS 618. London: Bloomsbury T&T Clark, 2015.

———. "'Wisdom' as Mask and Mirror: Response to Russell L. Meek." Paper presented at the annual meeting of the Society of Biblical Literature, Baltimore, MD, 22 November 2013.

Lakoff, George, and Mark Johnson. *Metaphors We Live By.* Chicago: University of Chicago Press, 2003.

Lambert, W. G. *Babylonian Wisdom Literature.* Oxford: Clarendon, 1960.

———. "The Qualifications of Babylonian Diviners." In *Festschrift für Rykle Borger zu seinem 65. Geburtstag am 24. Mai 1994*, ed. S. Maul, 141–58. Groningen: Styx, 1998.

Landes, George M. "Jonah: A *MĀŠĀL?*" In *Israelite Wisdom: Theological and Literary Essays in Honor of Samuel Terrien*, ed. John G. Gammie, Walter Brueggemann, W. Lee Humphreys, and James M. Ward, 137–58. Missoula: Scholars Press, 1978.

LeCureux, J. T. *The Thematic Unity of the Book of the Twelve.* HBM 41. Sheffield: Sheffield Phoenix, 2012.

Leddy, Michael. "Limits of Allusion." *British Journal of Aesthetics* 32 (1992): 110–22.

Lee, Lydia. "'You Were the (Divine) Cherub': A Potential Challenge to YHWH's Sole Divinity in Ezekiel 28:14." *JSOT* 41 (2016): 99–116.

Lenzi, Alan. "The Curious Case of Failed Revelation in *Ludlul Bēl Nēmeqi*: A New Suggestion for the Poem's Scholarly Purpose." In *Mediating Between Heaven and Earth: Communicating with the Divine in the Ancient Near East*, ed. C. L. Crouch, Jonathan Stökl, and Anna Elise Zernecke, 26–66. LHBOTS 566. London: T&T Clark International, 2012.

Leonard, Jeffrey M. "Identifying Inner-Biblical Allusions: Psalm 78 as a Test Case." *JBL* 127 (2008): 241–65.

Lévêque, J. "L'interprétation des discours de YHWH (Job 38,1–42,6)." In *The Book of Job*, ed. W. A. M. Beuken, 203–22. BETL 114. Leuven: Leuven University Press, 1994.

Levin, Christoph. "Righteousness in the Joseph Story: Joseph Resists Seduction (Genesis 39)." In *The Pentateuch: International Perspectives on Current Research*, ed. Thomas B. Dozeman, Konrad Schmid, and Baruch J. Schwartz, 223–40. FAT 78. Tübingen: Mohr Siebeck, 2011.

Levin, Yigal. "Joseph, Judah and the 'Benjamin Conundrum.'" *ZAW* 116 (2004): 223–41.

Levinson, Bernard M. *A More Perfect Torah: At the Intersection of Philology and Hermeneutics in Deuteronomy and the Temple Scroll.* Critical Studies in the Hebrew Bible 1. Winona Lake: Eisenbrauns, 2013.

Lewis, Jack P. "A Prophet's Son (Amos 7:14) Reconsidered." *ResQ* 49, no. 4 (2007): 229–40.

Lindblom, Johannes. "Wisdom in the Old Testament Prophets." In *Wisdom in Israel and in the Ancient Near East*, ed. Martin Noth and D. Winton Thomas, 192–204. VTSup 3. Leiden: Brill, 1955.

Lloyd, Alan B. "Heka, Dreams, and Prophecy in Ancient Egyptian Stories." In *Through a Glass Darkly: Magic, Dreams & Prophecy in Ancient Egypt*, ed. Kasia Szpakowska, 71–94. Swansea: Classical Press of Wales, 2006.

Lohfink, Norbert. *Kohelet.* 2nd ed. Die Neue Echter Bibel. Stuttgart: Echter, 1980.

Longman, Tremper III. *Daniel.* NIVAC. Grand Rapids: Zondervan, 1999.

———. "Determining the Historical Context of Ecclesiastes." In *The Words of the Wise Are Like Goads: Engaging Qohelet in the 21st Century*, ed. Mark J. Boda, Tremper Longman III, and Cristian Rata, 89–102. Winona Lake: Eisenbrauns, 2013.

———. *The Fear of the Lord Is Wisdom: A Theological Introduction to Wisdom in Israel.* Grand Rapids: Baker, 2017.

———. *Fictional Akkadian Autobiography: A Generic and Comparative Study.* Winona Lake: Eisenbrauns, 1991.

———. "Form Criticism, Recent Developments in Genre Theory, and the Evangelical." *WTJ* 47 (1985): 46–67.

———. *Job.* BCOTWP. Grand Rapids: Baker Academic, 2012.

———. "Nahum." In *The Minor Prophets: An Exegetical and Expository Commentary*, ed. T. E. McComiskey, 2:765–829. Grand Rapids: Baker, 1993.

———. *Proverbs.* BCOTWP. Grand Rapids: Baker Academic, 2006.

Lyons, Michael A. "Marking Innerbiblical Allusion in the Book of Ezekiel." *Bib* 88 (2007): 245–50.

———. "Transformation of Law: Ezekiel's Use of the Holiness Code (Leviticus 17–26)." In *Transforming Visions: Transformations of Text, Tradition, and Theology in Ezekiel*, ed. William A. Tooman and Michael A. Lyons, 1–32. Princeton Theological Monographs 127. Eugene: Wipf & Stock, 2010.

Lyu, Sun Myung. *Righteousness in the Book of Proverbs*. FAT 2/55. Tübingen: Mohr Siebeck, 2012.

Macintosh, Andrew A. "Hosea and the Wisdom Tradition: Dependence and Independence." In *Wisdom in Ancient Israel: Essays in Honour of J. A. Emerton*, ed. John Day, Robert P. Gordon, and Hugh G. M. Williamson, 124–33. Cambridge: Cambridge University Press, 1995.

Mack-Fisher, Loren R. "A Survey and Reading Guide to the Didactic Literature of Ugarit: Prolegomenon to a Study on the Sage." In *The Sage in Israel and the Ancient Near East*, ed. John G. Gammie and Leo G. Perdue, 67–80. Winona Lake: Eisenbrauns, 1990.

Marzal, Angel. *Gleanings from the Wisdom of Mari*. StPohl 11. Rome: Pontifical Biblical Institute, 1976.

Mathews, Claire. *Defending Zion: Eden's Desolation and Jacob's Restoration (Isaiah 34–35) in Context*. BZAW 236. Berlin: de Gruyter, 1995.

Maul, Stefan M. "Divination Culture and the Handling of the Future." In *The Babylonian World*, ed. Gwendolyn Leick, 361–72. London: Routledge, 2007.

McConville, J. G. "Forgiveness as a Private and Public Act: A Reading of the Biblical Joseph Narrative." *CBQ* 75 (2013): 635–48.

McKane, William. *Jeremiah*. International Critical Commentary. 2 vols. Edinburgh: T. & T. Clark, 1986, 1996.

———. "Jeremiah and the Wise." In *Wisdom in Ancient Israel: Essays in Honour of J. A. Emerton*, ed. J. Day et al., 142–51. Cambridge: Cambridge University Press, 1995.

———. *Prophets and Wise Men*. London: SCM, 1965.

McLaughlin, J. L. "Is Amos (Still) Among the Wise?" *JBL* 133 (2014): 281–303.

Meek, Russell L. "Intertextuality, Inner-Biblical Exegesis, and Inner-Biblical Allusion: The Ethics of a Methodology." *Bib* 95 (2014): 280–91.

———. "The Meaning of הבל in Qohelet: An Intertextual Suggestion." In *The Words of the Wise Are Like Goads: Engaging Qohelet in the 21st Century*, ed. Mark J. Boda, Tremper Longman III, and Cristian G. Rata, 241–56. Winona Lake: Eisenbrauns, 2013.

———. "Prophet and Sage in Dialogue: History and Methodology." Paper presented at the annual meeting of the Society of Biblical Literature, Baltimore, MD, 22 November 2013.

Melton, Brittany. "Solomon, Wisdom, and Love: Intertextual Resonance Between Ecclesiastes and Song of Songs." In *Reading Ecclesiastes Intertextually*, ed. Katharine J. Dell and Will Kynes, 130–41. LHBOTS 587. London: Bloomsbury T&T Clark, 2014.

Mettinger, T. N. D. *The Eden Narrative: A Literary and Religio-historical Study of Genesis 2–3*. Winona Lake: Eisenbrauns, 2007.

Miles, John A. Jr. "Laughing at the Bible: Jonah as Parody." *JQR* 65 (1975): 168–81.

Millard, Alan R. "The Etymology of Eden." *VT* 34 (1984): 103–6.

Miller, D. "Wisdom in the Canon: Discerning the Early Intuition." In *Was There a Wisdom Tradition? New Prospects in Israelite Wisdom Studies*, ed. M. R. Sneed, 87–113. AIL 23. Atlanta: Society of Biblical Literature, 2015.

Miller, Geoffrey D. "Intertextuality in Old Testament Research." *CurBR* 9 (2010): 283–309.

Miller, Stephen R. *Daniel*. NAC 18. Nashville: Broadman & Holman, 1994.

Moore, Michael S. "Jeremiah's Progressive Paradox." *RB* 93, no. 3 (1986): 386–414.

———. Review of *Now My Eye Sees You: Unveiling an Apocalyptic Job* by Timothy J. Johnson. *Review of Biblical Literature* 06/2012. Online: http://prophetess.lstc. edu/~rklein/Doc13/michael.pdf (accessed 20 July 2017).

Morgan, Donald. *Wisdom in the Old Testament Traditions*. Atlanta: John Knox, 1981.

Morray-James, C. R. A. "The Opening of Heaven in the Book of Job." In *Revealed Wisdom: Studies in Apocalyptic in Honour of Christopher Rowland*, ed. J. Ashton, 10–36. Ancient Judaism and Early Christianity 88. Leiden: Brill, 2014.

Motyer, J. A. *The Prophecy of Isaiah: An Introduction and Commentary*. Downers Grove: InterVarsity, 1993.

Murphy, Roland E. "Assumptions and Problems in Old Testament Wisdom Research." *CBQ* 29 (1967): 407–18.

———. *Ecclesiastes*. WBC 23. Dallas: Word, 1992.

———. "The Fear of the Lord: The Fear to End All Fears." In *Overcoming Fear Between Jews and Christians*, ed. James H. Charlesworth et al., 172–80. New York: Crossroad, 1992.

———. *Proverbs*. WBC 22. Nashville: Thomas Nelson, 1998.

———. *Wisdom Literature*. FOTL 13. Grand Rapids: Eerdmans, 1981.

———. "Wisdom—Theses and Hypotheses." In *Israelite Wisdom: Theological and Literary Essays in Honor of Samuel Terrien*, ed. John G. Gammie, Walter A. Brueggemann, W. Lee Humphreys, and James M. Ward, 35–42. Missoula: Scholars Press, 1978.

Murray, Donald F. "The Rhetoric of Disputation: Reexamination of a Prophetic Genre." *JSOT* 38 (1987): 95–121.

Neujahr, Matthew. *Predicting the Past in the Ancient Near East: Mantic Historiography in Ancient Mesopotamia, Judah, and the Mediterranean World*. BJS 354. Providence: Brown University Press, 2012.

Newsom, Carol A. *The Book of Job: A Contest of Moral Imaginations*. Oxford: Oxford University Press, 2009.

———. "A Maker of Metaphors—Ezekiel's Oracles Against Tyre." *Int* 38, no 2 (1984): 151–64.

———. "Pairing Research Questions and Theories of Genre: A Case Study of the Hodayot." *DSD* 17 (2010): 241–59.

Nicholson, E. W. "The Limits of Theodicy as a Theme of the Book of Job." In *Wisdom in Ancient Israel: Essays in Honour of J. A. Emerton*, ed. J. Day, R. P. Gordon and H. G. M. Williamson, 71–82. Cambridge: Cambridge University Press, 1995.

Nickelsburg, George W. E. "Wisdom and Apocalypticism in Early Judaism: Some Points for Discussion." In *Conflicted Boundaries in Wisdom and Apocalypticism*, ed. B. G. Wright and L. Wills, 715–32. SBLSymS. Atlanta: SBL, 2005.

Nissinen, Martti, "Neither Prophecies Nor Apocalypses: The Akkadian Literary Predictive Texts." In *Knowing the End from the Beginning: The Prophetic, the Apocalyptic, and Their Relationship*, ed. Lester L. Grabbe and Robert D. Haak, 134–48. JSPSup 46. London: T&T Clark International, 2003.

———. "Prophecy and Omen Divination: Two Sides of the Same Coin." In *Divination and Interpretation of Signs in the Ancient World*, ed. Amar Annus, 341–51. OIS 6. Chicago: Oriental Institute of the University of Chicago, 2010.

―――. "What Is Prophecy? An Ancient Near Eastern Perspective." In *Inspired Speech: Prophecy in the Ancient Near East (Essays in Honour of Herbert B. Huffmon)*, ed. John Kaltner and Louis Stulman, 17–37. JSOTSup 378. London: T&T Clark International, 2004.

Nissinen, Martti, C. L. Seow, and Robert K. Ritner. *Prophets and Prophecy in the Ancient Near East*, ed. Theodore J. Lewis. WAW 12. Atlanta: Society of Biblical Literature, 2003.

Noble, Paul R. "Esau, Tamar, and Joseph: Criteria for Identifying Inner-Biblical Allusions." *VT* 52 (2002): 219–52.

O'Dell, Margaret. *Ezekiel*. Smyth & Helwys Bible Commentary. Macon: Smyth & Helwys, 2005.

O'Dowd, R. "Poetic Allusions in Agur's Oracle in Proverbs 30:1–9." In *Inner-Biblical Allusion in the Poetry of Psalms and Wisdom*. Edited by Mark J. Boda, Beth Tanner, and Kevin Chau. London: Bloomsbury T&T Clark, forthcoming.

Oates, J. "The Fall of Assyria." In *CAH* III:2, ed. J. Boardman et al., 162–93. Cambridge: Cambridge University Press, 1991.

Oppenheim, A. L. *The Interpretation of Dreams in the Ancient Near East*. Philadelphia: American Philosophical Society, 1956.

Osborne, William R. *Trees and Kings: A Comparative Analysis of Tree Imagery in Israel's Prophetic Tradition and the Ancient Near East*. BBRSup 18. University Park, PA: Eisenbrauns, 2017.

Oswalt, John. *The Book of Isaiah, Chapters 1–39*. NICOT. Grand Rapids: Eerdmans, 1986.

Overholt, Thomas W. *Cultural Anthropology and the Old Testament*. Guides to Biblical Scholarship. Minneapolis: Fortress, 1996.

―――. *The Threat of Falsehood: A Study in the Theology of the Book of Jeremiah*. SBT 2/16. Naperville: Allenson, 1970.

Overland, Paul. "Structure in the *Wisdom of Amenemope* and Proverbs." In *"Go to the Land I Will Show You": Studies in Honor of Dwight W. Young*, ed. Joseph E Colleson and Victor H. Matthews, 271–91. Winona Lake: Eisenbrauns, 1996.

Park, C.-W. "Central Contents of Job 38–42 Reconsidered in Relation to the Call Narrative (Isaiah 6)." *Korean Journal of Old Testament Studies* 20, no. 2 (2014): 94–126.

Parpola, Simo. *Assyrian Prophecies*. SAA 9. Helsinki: University of Helsinki Press, 1997.

―――. *Letters from Assyrian and Babylonian Scholars*. SAA 10. Helsinki: University of Helsinki Press, 1993.

Patmore, Hector M. *Adam, Satan, and the King of Tyre: The Interpretation of Ezekiel 28:11–19 in Late Antiquity*. Jewish and Christian Perspective Series 20. Leiden: Brill, 2012.

―――. "Did the Masoretes Get It Wrong? The Vocalization and Accentuation of Ezekiel XXVIII 12–19." *VT* 58 (2008): 245–57.

Perdue, Leo G. "Wisdom and Apocalyptic: The Case of Qohelet." In *Wisdom and Apocalypticism in the Dead Sea Scrolls and in the Biblical Tradition*, ed. F. García Martínez, 231–58. BETL 168. Leuven: Leuven University Press, 2003.

―――. *Wisdom and Creation: The Theology of the Wisdom Literature*. Nashville: Abingdon, 1994.

―――. "Wisdom in the Book of Job." In *In Search of Wisdom: Essays in Memory of John G. Gammie*, ed. L. Perdue, B. B. Scott and W. J. Wiseman, 73–98. Louisville: Westminster John Knox, 1993.

———. *Wisdom in Revolt: Metaphorical Theology in the Book of Job.* London: Sheffield Academic Press, 1991.

———. *Wisdom Literature: A Theological History.* Louisville: Westminster John Knox, 2007.

———. "Wisdom Theology and Social History in Proverbs 1–9." In *Wisdom, You Are My Sister: Studies in Honor of Roland E. Murphy, O. Carm., on the Occasion of His Eightieth Birthday,* ed. Michael L. Barré, 78–101. CBQMS 29. Washington, DC: Catholic Biblical Association of America, 1997.

Perlitt, L. *Die Propheten Nahum, Habakkuk, Zephanja.* ATD 25/1. Göttingen: Vandenhoeck & Ruprecht, 2004.

Perri, Carmela. "On Alluding," *Poetics* 7 (1978): 289–307.

Petersen, David L. "Eschatology (Old Testament)." *ABD* 2:575–79.

———. "Rethinking the Nature of Prophetic Literature." In *Prophecy and Prophets: The Diversity of Contemporary Issues in Scholarship,* ed. Yehoshua Gitay, 23–40. SemeiaSt 33. Atlanta: Scholars Press, 1997.

Pfeiffer, Henrik. "Der Baume in der Mitte des Gartens: Zum überlieferungsgeschtichtlichen Ursprung der Paradieserzählung (Gen 2,4–3,24), Teil II: Prägende Tradition und theologische Akzente." *ZAW* 113 (2001): 2–16.

Pfeiffer, R. H. "The Priority of Job Over Is. 40–55." *JBL* 46 (1927): 202–6.

Phinney, D. N. "Call/Commission Narratives." In *Dictionary of the Old Testament: Prophets,* ed. Mark J. Boda and J. Gordon McConville, 65–71. Downers Grove: InterVarsity, 2012.

Pietersma, Albert, and Ben Wright, eds. *A New Translation of the Septuagint.* New York: Oxford University Press, 2007.

Polk, Timothy. *The Prophetic Persona: Jeremiah and the Language of Self.* JSOTSup 32. Sheffield: JSOT Press, 1984.

Pongratz-Leisten, Beate. *Herrschaftswissen in Mesopotamien: Formen der Kommunikation zwischen Gott und König im 2. und 1. Jahrtausend v. Chr.* SAAS 10. Helsinki: University of Helsinki Press, 1999.

Pope, M. H. *Job.* AB 15. New York: Doubleday, 1973.

Porter, Stanley E. "Allusions and Echoes." In *As It Is Written: Studying Paul's Use of Scripture,* ed. S. E. Porter and C. D. Stanley, 29–40. SBLSymS 50. Atlanta: Society of Biblical Literature, 2008.

Postell, A. "Wineskin or Windbag? Elihu and the Problem of Justice in the Book of Job." *Ramify* 2 (2011): 38–53.

Prinsloo, G. T. M. "Life for the Righteous, Doom for the Wicked: Reading Habakkuk from a Wisdom Perspective." *Skrif en kerk* 21 (2000): 621–40.

———. "Two Poems in a Sea of Prose: The Content and Context of Daniel 2.20–23 and 6.27–28." *JSOT* 59 (1993): 93–108.

Rad, Gerhard von. "The Joseph Narrative and Ancient Wisdom." In *The Problem of the Hexateuch and Other Essays.* Translated by E. W. Trueman Dicken, 292–300. London: SCM, 1984.

———. *Old Testament Theology.* Translated by D. M. G. Stalker. 2 vols. New York: Harper & Row.

———. *Wisdom in Israel.* Translated by J. D. Martin. Nashville: Abingdon, 1972.

Rainey, Anson F., and R. Steven Notley. *The Sacred Bridge: Carta's Atlas of the Biblical World.* 2nd ed. Jerusalem: Carta, 2006.

Reichenbach, Gregor. "Zeit und Gericht' (Koh 8,5f): Anmerkungen zu Kohelets prophetischen Erbe." In *Mensch und König: Studien zur Anthropologie des Alten Testaments*, ed. Angelika Berlejung and Raik Heckl, 191–201. Herders Biblische Studien. Freiburg im Breisgau: Herder, 2008.

Richelle, Matthieu. "Le portrait changeant du roi de Tyr (Ezéchiel 28, 11–18) dans les traditions textuelles anciennes." In *Phéniciens d'Orient et d'Occident: Mélanges J. Elayi*, ed. A. Lemaire, 113–25. Cahiers de l'Institut du Proche-Orient Ancien du Collège de France 2. Paris: Maisonneuve, 2014.

Rindge, Matthew S. "Jewish Identity under Foreign Rule: Daniel 2 as a Reconfiguration of Genesis 41." *JBL* 129 (2010): 85–104.

Ritner, Robert K. *The Mechanics of Ancient Egyptian Magical Practice*. SAOC 54. Chicago: The Oriental Institute, 1993.

Robert, A. "Les Attaches Littéraires Bibliques de Prov. I–IX." *RB* 43 (1934): 42–68; 172–204; 374–84; *RB* 44 (1935): 344–65; 502–25.

Roberts, Adam. *Fredric Jameson*. Routledge Critical Thinkers: Essential Guides for Literary Studies. London: Routledge, 2000.

Roberts, J. J. M. *Nahum, Habakkuk, and Zephaniah: A Commentary*. OTL. Louisville: Westminster John Knox, 1991.

Rochberg, Francesca. *The Heavenly Writing: Divination, Horoscopy, and Astronomy in Mesopotamian Culture*. Cambridge: Cambridge University Press, 2004.

Rollston, Christopher A. *Writing and Literacy in the World of Ancient Israel: Epigraphic Evidence from the Iron Age*. Archaeology and Biblical Studies 11. Atlanta: SBL, 2010.

Römer, T. *La sagessse dans l'Ancien Testament*. Cahiers Bibliques 3. Aubonne: Moulin, 1991.

Rowland, Christopher. *The Open Heaven: A Study of Apocalyptic in Judaism and Early Christianity*. New York: Crossroad, 1982.

Ruffle, John. "The Teaching of Amenemope and Its Connection with the Book of Proverbs." *TynBul* 29 (1977): 29–68.

Samet, Nili. "The Gilgamesh Epic and the Book of Qohelet: A New Look." *Bib* 96 (2015): 375–90.

Sanders, J. *Adaptation and Appropriation*. The New Critical Idiom. London: Routledge, 2006.

Sandoval, Timothy J. *The Discourse of Wealth and Poverty in the Book of Proverbs*. BibInt 77. Leiden: Brill, 2006.

Sasson, Jack M. "Water beneath Straw: Adventures of a Prophetic Phrase in the Mari Archives." In *Solving Riddles and Untying Knots: Biblical, Epigraphic, and Semitic Studies in Honor of Jonas C. Greenfield*, ed. Ziony Zevit, Seymour Gitin, and Michael Sokoloff, 599–608. Winona Lake: Eisenbrauns, 1995.

Savran, G. "Theophany as Type Scene." *Prooftexts* 23, no. 2 (2003): 119–49.

Schellenberg, Annette. "A 'Lying Pen of the Scribes' (Jer 8:8)? Orality and Writing in the Formation of the Prophetic Books." In *The Interface of Orality and Writing: Speaking, Seeing, Writing in the Shaping of New Genres*, ed. Annette Weissenrieder and Robert B. Coote, 285–309. Biblical Performance Criticism 11. Tübingen: Mohr Siebeck. 2010.

———. "'Wisdom Cries Out in the Street' (Prov 1:20) On the Role of Revelation in Wisdom Literature and the Relatedness and Differences Between Sapiential and Prophetic Epistemologies." In *Scribes as Sages and Prophets*, ed. Jutta Krispenz. Berlin: de Gruyter, forthcoming.

Schmid, H. H. "Creation, Righteousness, and Salvation: 'Creation Theology' as the Broad Horizon of Biblical Theology." In *Creation in the Old Testament*, ed. B. W. Anderson, 102–17. Issues in Religion and Theology 6. Philadelphia: Fortress, 1984.

Schmid, Konrad. "Josephs zweiter Traum: Beobachtungen zu seiner literarischen Funktion und sachlichen Bedeutung in der Josephsgeschichte (Gen 37–50)." *ZAW* 128 (2016): 374–88.

Schmid, Konrad, and Christoph Riedweg, eds. *Beyond Eden: The Biblical Story of Paradise (Gen 2–3) and Its Reception History*. FAT 2/34. Tübingen: Mohr Siebeck, 2008.

Schmidt, Brian B., ed. *Contextualizng Israel's Sacred Writings: Ancient Literacy, Orality, and Literary Production*. AIL 22. Atlanta: SBL, 2015.

Schneider, Thomas. "Knowledge and Knowledgeable Persons in Ancient Egypt: Queries and Arguments About an Unsettled Issue." In *Scribes, Sages, and Seers: The Sage in the Eastern Mediterranean World*, ed. Leo G. Perdue, 35–46. FRLANT 219. Göttingen: Vandenhoeck & Ruprecht, 2008.

Schniedewind, William M. *How the Bible Became a Book: The Textualization of Ancient Israel*. Cambridge: Cambridge University Press, 2010.

Schultz, Richard L. "'Fear God and Keep His Commandments' (Eccl 12:13): An Examination of Some Intertextual Relationships Between Deuteronomy and Ecclesiastes." In *For Our Good Always: Studies on the Message and Influence of Deuteronomy in Honor of Daniel I. Block*, ed. Jason S. DeRouchie, Jason Gile, and Kenneth J. Turner, 327–43. Winona Lake: Eisenbrauns, 2013.

———. "Qohelet and Isaiah in Dialogue." In *Reading Ecclesiastes Intertextually*, ed. Katherine Dell and Will Kynes, 57–70. LHBOTS 574. New York: Bloomsbury T&T Clark, 2014.

———. *The Search for Quotation: Verbal Parallels in the Prophets*. JSOTSup 180. Sheffield: Sheffield Academic, 1999.

Schwáb, Zóltan. "Is Fear of the Lord the Source of Wisdom or Vice Versa?" *VT* (2013): 652–62.

Seow, C. L. *Ecclesiastes*. AB 18C. New York: Doubleday, 1997.

———. "Hosea 14:10 and the Foolish People Motif." *CBQ* 44 (1982): 212–24.

———. *Job 1–21: Interpretation and Commentary*. Grand Rapids: Eerdmans, 2013.

———. "Qohelet's Eschatological Poem." *JBL* 118 (1997): 209–34.

Sewall, Richard. *The Vision of Tragedy*. Enlarged ed. New Haven: Yale University Press, 1980.

Seybold, K. *Profane Prophetie: Studien zum Buch Nahum*. Stuttgarter Bibestudien 135. Stuttgart: Katholisches Bibelwerk, 1989.

Shields, M. A. "Malevolent or Mysterious? God's Character in the Prologue of Job." *TynBul* 61 (2010): 255–70.

———. "Prophecy and Wisdom." In *Dictionary of the Old Testament: Prophets*, ed. Mark J. Boda and J. Gordon McConville, 642–50. Downers Grove: InterVarsity, 2012.

———. "Was Elihu Right?" *JETS* 3, no. 2 (2014): 155–70.

Shupak, Nili. "The Egyptian 'Prophecy'—a Reconsideration." In *Von Reichlich Aegyptischem Verstande: Festschrift für Waltraud Guglielmi zum 65. Geburtstag*, ed. Hans-W. Fischer-Elfert and Karol Zibelius-Chen, 133–44. Wiesbaden: Harrassowitz, 2006.

———. "Egyptian 'Prophecy' and Biblical Prophecy: Did the Phenomenon of Prophecy, in the Biblical Sense, Exist in Ancient Egypt?" *JEOL* 31 (1989–1990): 5–40.

Skehan, Patrick W. "A Single Editor for the Whole Book of Proverbs." *CBQ* 9 (1947): 190–98.

Smick, E. B. "Job." In *The Expositor's Bible Commentary*, ed. F. E. Gæbelein, 4:841–1060. Grand Rapids: Zondervan, 1988.

Sneed, Mark. "'Grasping After the Wind': The Elusive Attempt to Define and Delimit Wisdom." In *Was There a Wisdom Tradition? New Prospects in Israelite Wisdom Studies*, ed. Mark Sneed, 39–68. AIL 23. Atlanta: SBL, 2015.

———. "Inspired Sages: *Massa'* and the Confluence of Wisdom and Prophecy." In *Schreiber als Weisheitslehrer und Propheten: Prophetische une weisheitliche Traditionen in dem Wiesheitsschriften une im Zwölfprophetenbuch.* BZAW 496. Berlin: de Gruyter, forthcoming.

———. "Is the 'Wisdom Tradition' a Tradition?" *CBQ* 73 (2011): 50–71.

———. *The Social World of the Sages: An Introduction to Israelite and Jewish Wisdom Literature.* Minneapolis: Augsburg Fortress, 2015.

———. *Was There a Wisdom Tradition? New Prospects in Israelite Wisdom Studies.* AIL 23. Atlanta: SBL, 2015.

Soggins, J. A. "Amos and Wisdom." In *Wisdom in Ancient Israel: Essays in Honour of J. A. Emerton*, ed. John Day, Robert P. Gordon, and H. G. M. Williamson, 119–23. Cambridge: Cambridge University Press, 1995.

Sommer, Benjamin D. "Allusions and Illusions: The Unity of the Book of Isaiah in Light of Deutero-Isaiah's Use of Prophetic Tradition." In *New Visions of Isaiah*, ed. Roy Melugin and Marvin Sweeney, 156–86. JSOTSup 214. Sheffield: Sheffield Academic, 1996.

———. "Dating Pentateuchal Texts and the Perils of Pseudo-Historicism." In *The Pentateuch: International Perspectives on Current Research*, ed. T. B. Dozeman, K. Schmid and B. W. Schwartz, 85–108. FAT 78. Tübingen: Mohr Siebeck, 2011.

Spieckermann, Hermann. "Eden, Garden of." *Encyclopedia of the Bible and Its Reception*, ed. Christine Helmer et al., 7:362–64. 15 vols. Berlin: de Gruyter, 2009–.

Spies, Dawn Lyn. "The Fear of the Lord in Numbers 13–14." *Lutheran Forum* 44 (2010): 10–12.

Stead, R. *The Intertextuality of Zechariah 1–8.* LHBOTS 506. New York: T&T Clark International, 2009.

Steinmann, Andrew E. *Daniel.* Concordia Commentary. St. Louis: Concordia, 2008.

———. *The Oracles of God: The Old Testament Canon.* St. Louis: Concordia, 1999.

———. "Proverbs 1–9 as a Solomonic Composition." *JETS* 43 (2000): 659–74.

Sternberg, Meir. "Proteus in Quotation-Land: Mimesis and the Forms of Reported Discourse." *Poetics Today* 3 (1982): 108.

Stökl, Jonathan. *Prophecy in the Ancient Near East: A Philological and Sociological Comparison.* CHANE 56. Leiden: Brill, 2012.

———. "'A Youth without Blemish, Handsome, Proficient in all Wisdom, Knowledgeable and Intelligent': Ezekiel's Access to Babylonian Culture." In *Exile and Return: The Babylonian Context*, ed. Jonathan Stökl and Caroline Waaerzeggers, 223–52. BZAW 478. Berlin: de Gruyter, 2015.

Stone, Michael. "List of Revealed Things in the Apocalyptic Literature." In *Magnalia Dei: The Mighty Acts of God*, ed. F. M. Cross, W. Lemke, and P. Miller, 414–52. Garden City: Doubleday, 1976.

Stordalen, T. *Echoes of Eden: Gen 2–3 and Symbolism of the Eden Garden in Biblical Hebrew Literature.* CBET 25. Leuven: Peeters, 2000.

Strong, John T. "Ezekiel's Oracles Against the Nations within the Context of His Message." PhD diss., Union Theological Seminary, 1993.

———. "In Defense of the Great King: Ezekiel's Oracles Against Tyre." In *Concerning the Nations: Essays on the Oracles Against the Nations in Isaiah, Jeremiah, and Ezekiel*, ed. E. K. Holt, H. C. P. Kim, and A. Mein, 179–94. LHBOTS 612. London: Bloomsbury T&T Clark, 2015.

Sweeney, Marvin A. "Myth and History in Ezekiel's Oracle Concerning Tyre (Ezekiel 26–28)." In *Myth and Scripture: Contemporary Perspectives on Religion, Language, and Imagination*, ed. Dexter Callender, Jr., 129–47. Resources for Biblical Study 78. Atlanta: SBL, 2014.

Sweet, Ronald F. G. "The Sage in Akkadian Literature: A Philological Study." In *The Sage in Israel and the Ancient Near East*, ed. J. G. Gammie and L. G. Perdue, 45–65. Winona Lake: Eisenbrauns, 1990.

Talstra, Eep. "Second Isaiah and Qohelet: Could One Get Them on Speaking Terms?" In *New Things: Eschatology in Old Testament Prophecy. FS for Henk Leene*, ed. P. Postma et al., 225–36. ACEBT Supplement Series 3. Maastricht: Uitgeverij Shaker, 2002.

Tan, Nancy Nam Hoon. *The "Foreignness" of the Foreign Woman in Proverbs 1–9: A Study of the Origin and Development of a Biblical Motif*. BZAW 381. Berlin: de Gruyter, 2008.

Terrien, Samuel. "Amos and Wisdom." In *Israel's Prophetic Heritage: Essays in Honor of James Muilenburg*, ed. Bernard W. Anderson and Walter J. Harrelson, 108–15. London: Harper, 1962. Reprinted in *Studies in Ancient Israelite Wisdom*, ed. James J. Crenshaw, 448–55. LBS. New York: Ktav, 1976.

———. "Quelques Remarques sur les Affinités de Job avec le Deutéro-Ésaïe." In *Volume du congrès: Genève 1965*, ed. P. A. H. de Boer, 295–310. VTSup 15. Leiden: Brill, 1966.

Timmer, Daniel. "God's Speeches, Job's Responses, and the Problem of Coherence in the Book of Job: Sapiential Pedagogy Revisited." *CBQ* 71 (2009): 286–305.

———. *The Non-Israelite Nations in the Book of the Twelve: Thematic Coherence and the Diachronic–Synchronic Relationship in the Minor Prophets*. BibInt 135. Leiden: Brill, 2015.

Tov, Emanuel. "Different Editions of the Song of Hannah and of Its Narrative Framework." In *Tehillah le-Moshe: Biblical and Judaic Studies in Honor of Moshe Greenberg*, ed. M. Cogan et al., 149–70. Winona Lake: Eisenbrauns, 1977.

Tuttle, G. A. "Wisdom and Habakkuk." *Studia Biblica et Theologica* 3 (1973): 3–14.

Urbanz, W. "Weisheit und Prophetie." Paper presented at the annual meeting of the Arbeitsgemeinschaft der Assistentinnen und Assistenten an bibelwissenschaftlichen Instituten in Österreich, Salzburg, 2013.

Van de Mieroop, Marc. *Philosophy Before the Greeks: The Pursuit of Truth in Ancient Babylonia*. Princeton: Princeton University Press; Oxford: Oxford University Press, 2016.

Van der Toorn, Karel. *Scribal Culture and the Making of the Hebrew Bible*. Cambridge, MA: Harvard University Press, 2007.

———. "Why Wisdom Became a Secret: On Wisdom as a Written Genre." In *Wisdom Literature in Mesopotamia and Israel*, ed. Richard J. Clifford, 21–32. SymS 36. Leiden: Brill, 2007.

Van Dijk, H. J. *Ezekiel's Prophecy on Tyre (Ez. 26:1–28:19): A New Approach.* BibOr 20. Rome: Pontifical Biblical Institute, 1968.

Van Leeuwen, R. C. *Context and Meaning in Proverbs 25–27.* SBLDS 96. Atlanta: Scholars Press, 1998.

———. "The Sage in the Prophetic Literature." In *The Sage in Israel and the Ancient Near East*, ed. John G. Gammie and Leo. G. Perdue, 295–306. Winona Lake: Eisenbrauns, 1990.

———. "Scribal Wisdom and Theodicy in the Book of the Twelve." In *In Search of Wisdom*, ed. L. Perdue, B. B. Scott, and W. J. Wiseman, 31–49. Louisville: Westminster John Knox, 1993.

———. "Wealth and Poverty: System and Contradiction in Proverbs." *HS* 33 (1992): 25–36.

———. "Wisdom Literature." In *Dictionary for Theological Interpretation of Scripture*, ed. K. J. Vanhoozer, 847–50. London: SPCK; Grand Rapids: Baker Academic, 2005.

Veldhuis, Niek. "Sumerian Proverbs in their Curricular Context." *JAOS* 120 (2000): 383–99.

Vermeylen, Jacques. "Le Proto-Isaïe et La Sagesse d'Israël." In *La Sagesse de l'Ancien Testament*, ed. M. Gilbert, 39–58. BETL 51. Leuven: Leuven University Press, 1990.

Vervenne, M. "Genesis 1,1–2,4: The Compositional Texture of the Priestly Overture to the Pentateuch." In *Studies in the Book of Genesis*, ed. A. Wénin 35–79. BETL 155. Leuven: Peeters, 2001.

Viljoen, Anneke, and P. M. Venter. "An Exploration of the Symbolic World of Proverbs 10:1–15:33 with Specific Reference to 'the Fear of the Lord.'" *HTS* 69 (2013): 1–6.

Wahl, Harald-Martin. "Noah, Daniel und Hiob in Ezechiel XIV 12–20 (21–3): Anmerkungen zum Traditionsgeschichtlichen Hintergrund." *VT* 42 (1992): 542–53.

Wallace, Howard N. *The Eden Narrative.* HSM 32. Atlanta: Scholars, 1985.

Waltke, Bruce. "The Fear of the Lord." *Journal of the Christian Brethren Research Fellowship* (1992): 12–16.

———. *Proverbs 1–15.* NICOT. Grand Rapids: Eerdmans, 2004.

———. "Righteousness in Proverbs." *WTJ* 70 (2008): 225–37.

Waltke, Bruce, and M. O'Connor. *An Introduction to Biblical Hebrew Syntax.* Winona Lake: Eisenbrauns, 1990.

Wanke, Gunther. "Weisheit im Jeremiabuch." In *Weisheit ausserhalb der kanonischen Weisheitschriften*, ed. B. Janowski, 87–106. Veröffentlichungen der Weisheitschaftlichen Gesellschaft für Theologie. Gutersloh: Chr. Kaiser, 1996.

Ward, James. "The Servant's Knowledge in Isaiah 40–55." In *Israelite Wisdom*, ed. John Gammie, 121–36. Missoula: Scholars Press, 1978.

Washington, Harold C. *Wealth and Poverty in the Instruction of Amenemope and the Hebrew Proverbs.* SBLDS 142. Atlanta: Scholars, 1994.

Watson, Duane F. "The Second Letter of Peter: Introduction, Commentary, and Reflections." In *New Interpreter's Bible*, ed. Leander Keck, 12:323–61. Nashville: Abingdon, 2001.

Webb, Robert. "Apocalyptic: Observations on a Slippery Term." *JNES* 49 (1990): 115–26.

Weeks, Stuart. *Instruction and Imagery in Proverbs 1–9.* Oxford: Oxford University Press, 2007.

———. *An Introduction to the Study of Wisdom Literature.* New York: T&T Clark International, 2010.

———. "Is 'Wisdom Literature' a Useful Category?" In *Tracing Sapiential Traditions in Ancient Judaism*, ed. Hindy Najman and Jean-Sébastien Rey, 3–23. JSJSup 174. Leiden: Brill, 2016.

———. "The Limits of Form Criticism in the Study of Literature, with Reflections on Psalm 34." In *Biblical Interpretation and Method: Essays in Honour of John Barton*, ed. Katharine J. Dell and Paul M. Joyce, 15–25. Oxford: Oxford University Press, 2013.

———. "Predictive and Prophetic Literature: Can Neferti Help Us Read the Bible?" In *Prophecy and the Prophets in Ancient Israel: Proceedings of the Oxford Old Testament Seminar*, ed. John Day, 25–46. LHBOTS 531. London: T&T Clark International, 2010.

———. "Whose Words? Qoheleth, Hosea and Attribution in Biblical Literature." In *New Heaven and New Earth: Prophecy and the Millennium. Essays in Honour of Anthony Gelston*, ed. P. J. Harland and C. T. R. Hayward, 151–70. VTSup 77. Leiden: Brill, 1999.

———. "Wisdom, Form and Genre." In *Was There a Wisdom Tradition? New Prospects in Israelite Wisdom Studies*, ed. Mark R. Sneed, 161–77. AIL 23. Atlanta: SBL, 2015.

Weippert, Manfred. "Aspekte Israelitischer Prophetie im Lichte Verwandter Erscheinungen des Alten Orients." In *Ad Bene et Fideliter Seminandum: Festgabe für Karlheinz Deller zum 21. Februar 1987*, ed. Gerlinde Mauer and Ursula Magen, 287–319. AOAT 220. Kevelaer: Butzon & Bercker, 1988.

West, Caroline. "Pornography and Censorship." In *The Stanford Encyclopedia of Philosophy*, ed. Edward N. Zalta. Stanford: Metaphysics Research Lab, Stanford University, 2013. Online: http://plato.stanford.edu/archives/fall2013/entries/pornography-censorship (accessed 8 December 2015).

Westermann, Claus. *The Basic Forms of Prophetic Speech*. Translated by Hugh Clayton White. Louisville: Westminster John Knox, 1991.

———. *The Structure of the Book of Job: A Form-Critical Analysis*. Translated by Charles Meunchow. Philadelphia: Fortress, 1981.

Whedbee, William J. *Isaiah and Wisdom*. Nashville: Abingdon, 1971.

Whybray, R. N. *The Book of Proverbs: A Survey of Modern Study*. History of Biblical Interpretation 1. Leiden: Brill, 1995.

———. *The Composition of the Book of Proverbs*. JSOTSup 168. Sheffield: Sheffield Academic, 1994.

———. *The Intellectual Tradition in the Old Testament*. BZAW 135. Berlin: de Gruyter, 1974.

———. "Poverty, Wealth, and Point of View in Proverbs." *ExpTim* 100 (1989): 332–36.

———. "Prophecy and Wisdom." In *Israel's Prophetic Tradition: Essays in Honour of Peter R. Ackroyd*, ed. Richard Coggins, Anthony Phillips, and Michael Knibb, 181–99. Cambridge: Cambridge University Press, 1982.

———. "Slippery Words. IV. Wisdom." In *Wisdom: The Collected Articles of Norman Whybray*, ed. Katherine J. Dell and Margaret Barker, 6–9. SOTSMS 4. Hants: Ashgate, 2005.

Widder, Wendy L. "The Court Stories of Joseph (Gen 41) and Daniel (Dan 2) in Canonical Context: A Theological Paradigm for God's Word Among the Nations." *OTE* 27 (2014): 1112–28.

Wilcox, M. "Text Form." In *It is Written: Scripture Citing Scripture*, ed. D. A. Carson and H. G. M. Williamson, 193–204. Cambridge: Cambridge University Press, 1988.

Wildberger, Hans. *Isaiah 28–39*. Translated by Thomas Trapp. Continental Commentary; Minneapolis: Fortress, 2002.

———. *Jahwewort und prophetische Rede bei Jeremia*. Zürich: Zwingli-Verlag, 1942.

Williams, James G. "The Prophetic 'Father': A Brief Explanation of the Term 'Sons of the Prophets.'" *JBL* 98 (1979): 344–48.

Williamson, H. G. M. "A Christian View of Wealth and Possessions: An Old Testament Perspective." *Ex Auditu* 27 (2011): 1–19.

———. "Isaiah and the wise." In *Wisdom in Israel: Essays in Honour of J. A. Emerton*, ed. J. Day, R. P. Gordon and H. G. M. Williamson, 133–41. Cambridge: Cambridge University Press, 1995.

Willis, John T. "National 'Beauty' and Yahweh's 'Glory' as a Dialectical Key to Ezekielien Theology." *HBT* 34 (2012): 1–18.

Wilson, Ian Douglas. "Tyre, a Ship: The Metaphorical World of Ezekiel 27 in Ancient Judah." *ZAW* 125 (2013): 249–62.

Wilson, Lindsay. "Wisdom in Isaiah." In *Interpreting Isaiah: Issues and Approaches*, ed. David Firth and H. G. M. Williamson, 145–67. Downers Grove: IVP Academic, 2009.

Wilson, R. R. "The Death of the King of Tyre: The Editorial History of Ezekiel 28." In *Love and Death in the Ancient Near East: Essays in Honor of Marvin H. Pope*, ed. J. H. Marks and R. M. Good, 211–18. Guilford: Four Quarters, 1987.

Wittenberg, G. H. "The Situational Context of Statements Concerning Poverty and Wealth in the Book of Proverbs." *Scriptura* 21 (1987): 1–23.

Wöhrle, J. *Der Abschluss des Zwölfprophetenbuches: Buchübergreifende Redaktion-prozesse in den späten Sammlungen.* BZAW 389. Berlin: de Gruyter, 2008.

Wolfers, D. *Deep Things Out of Darkness: The Book of Job, Essays and a New English Translation.* Grand Rapids: Eerdmans, 1995.

Wright, Benjamin G. "Joining the Club: A Suggestion About Genre in Early Jewish Texts." *DSD* 17 (2010): 289–314.

Yoder, Christine Roy. "'Forming 'Fearers of Yahweh': Repetition and Contradiction as Pedagogy in Proverbs." In *Seeking out the Wisdom of the Ancients: Essays Offered to Honor Michael V. Fox on the Occasion of His Sixty-Fifth Birthday*, ed. Ronald L. Troxel et al., 167–83. Winona Lake: Eisenbrauns, 2005.

Yona, Shamir. "The Influence of Legal Style on the Style of Aphorism: The Origin of the Retribution Formula and the Clause *Lō' Yinnāqeh* 'He Will Not Go Unpunished' in the Book of Proverbs." In *Birkat Shalom.* Vol. 1, *Studies in the Bible, Ancient Near Eastern Literature, and Postbiblical Judaism Presented to Shalom M. Paul on the Occasion of His Seventieth Birthday*, ed. Chaim Cohen et al., 413–23. Winona Lake: Eisenbrauns, 2008.

Zevit, Ziony. *What Really Happened in the Garden of Eden?* New Haven: Yale University Press, 2013.

Zimmerli, Walther. *Ezekiel 1: A Commentary on the Book of the Prophet Ezekiel, Chapters 1–24.* Translated by Ronald E. Clements. Hermeneia. Minneapolis: Fortress, 1979.

———. *Ezekiel 2: A Commentary on the Book of the Prophet Ezekiel Chapters 25–48.* Translated by James D. Martin. Hermeneia. Philadelphia: Fortress, 1983.

———. "The Place and Limit of Wisdom in the Framework of the Old Testament Theology." *SJT* 17 (1964): 146–58.

INDEX OF REFERENCES

Hosea			*Nahum*			*Malachi*	
2:1	81		1:2–8	159, 160		2:11	178
2:2	179		1:2	162		2:14–16	178
2:8–13	179		1:3	133		2:14–15	179
2:19	101		1:5	160		2:15	178
2:20	101		1:9–11	160		2:17–3:6	163
2:21 MT	101		1:12	159		2:17	192
2:22 MT	101		1:13–15	160		3:1–5	213
4–14	8		1:15	159, 161		3:14	192
5:1–15	179		2:2	160			
6:7	179		3:14–16	160		NEW TESTAMENT	
11:1	81		3:19	160		*Matthew*	
13:13	147					5:17	125
14:9 MT	147		*Habakkuk*			6:11	134
14:10	8, 147		1–2	156		7:12	125
			1	158		11:13	125
Joel			1:2–4	156, 157		19:24	134
2:2	206		1:2	157		22:24	125
2:10	206		1:5–11	157		24:29	206
2:13	133		1:9	157		24:36	231
3:2 ET	210		1:12–2:1	156			
3:4	206		1:13	157		*Mark*	
4:2	210, 213		2	158		7:9–13	98
4:15	206		2:2–20	157		10:25	134
			2:18	87		13:24	206
Amos			3	156–59		13:32	231
5:8	206		3:1–15	157			
5:16	100		3:3–11	157		*Luke*	
8:9	206		3:13–14	157		11:3	134
			3:13	157		16:16	125
Obadiah						16:29	125
8	105, 147,		*Zephaniah*			16:31	125
	170, 264		1:15	206		18:25	134
11	174		1:18	134		23:45	206
			3:3–4	17		24:27	125
Jonah			3:6–8	213			
1:1–2	190					*John*	
1:1	191		*Haggai*			1:45	125
3:1	191		1:3	191			
4:2	133					*Acts*	
			Zechariah			2:20	206
Micah			1:1	191		13:15	125
2:3	203		7:11–14	254		24:14	125
3:6	206		9:2	147		26:22	125
4:12	81					28:23	125
6:9	85, 147						

Index of Authors

Fowler, A. 25, 30, 125, 219
Fox, M. V. 42, 56, 64, 71, 77, 82, 86, 131, 170, 175, 176, 205, 207, 208, 212
Frankel, D. 154
Fredericks, D. C. 207
Frow, J. 30, 31
Fyall, R. S. 155

Gadamer, H.-G. 171, 172
Gammie, J. G. 162
Geller, S. 225
Gerstenberger, E. 75, 79, 80
Geyer, J. B. 113
Gilbert, M. 99
Glassner, J.-J. 66
Goff, M. 22, 24, 26, 216, 218
Goldingay, J. 91, 170
Gordis, R. 41, 193, 196, 240
Gordon, R. P. 64, 109
Gowan, D. E. 10, 156
Grabbe, L. L. 10
Grayson, A. K. 61
Green, J. N. 33
Green, W. S. 253
Greenberg, M. 118, 119
Grossman, Y. 127
Guinan, A. K. 55, 56, 64, 67
Gunkel, H. 33, 34, 219, 236, 239
Gupta, N. K. 209

Habel, N. 155
Hagedorn, A. 160
Hallo, W. W. 61, 120
Halton, C. 59
Hamilton, M. 109, 111, 122
Hamori, A. J. 56
Hanson, P. 216, 232
Harding, J. E. 192
Harman, L. F. 142
Hartin, P. 228
Hartley, J. E. 186, 188, 193, 196, 213, 232, 253
Hatton, P. T. H. 143
Hayes, K. 76, 80, 86, 93
Hays, C. B. 4
Hays, R. B. 14, 107
Heim, K. M. 33
Hermisson, H.-J. 10, 76, 80, 82, 86, 97
Hilber, J. W. 58, 62
Hirsch, E. D. 220, 228

Holladay, W. L. 103
Holmgren, F. C. 145
Howe, B. 114
Huffmon, H. B. 38
Hunter, A. 25
Hurowitz, V. A. 69

Illman, K.-J. 153
Irwin, W. 48

Jacobs, M. R. 126
Janzen, J. G. 89
Jaroš, K. 120
Jensen, J. 10, 76, 78
Jindo, J. Y. 114
Johnson, E. 215
Johnson, M. 114
Johnson, T. 215, 220, 224, 228
Jones, D. R. 97
Jones, S. 225, 228
Joyce, P. 109, 118

Kaiser, W. C., Jr. 132
Kent, T. 125
Kessler, R. 152
Koch, K. 143
Koole, J. 90–92
Kovacs, B. 43
Köveces, Z. 114
Kratz, R. G. 177
Krüger, T. 155, 202, 206, 207, 209
Kubina, V. 154
Kutsch, E. 101
Kynes, W. 20, 23, 26, 28, 124, 149, 151, 152, 193–96, 236, 259

Lakoff, G. 114
Lambert, W. G. 57, 59–61, 65, 67–69
Landes, G. M. 7
Lange, A. 71
Lauha, A. 201
LeCureux, J. T. 153
Leddy, M. 48
Lee, L. 119, 120
Lenzi, A. 60
Leonard, J. M. 14, 15
Lévêque, J. 154
Levin, C. 127
Levin, Y. 126, 127
Levinson, B. M. 49

CPSIA information can be obtained
at www.ICGtesting.com
Printed in the USA
LVHW081107110620
657867LV00013B/457